Mother of Mercy, Bane of the Jews

Mother of Mercy, Bane of the Jews

DEVOTION TO THE VIRGIN MARY IN ANGLO-NORMAN ENGLAND

Kati Ihnat

PRINCETON UNIVERSITY PRESS

PRINCETON AND OXFORD

Library of Congress Cataloging-in-Publication Data

Names: Ihnat, Kati, 1981– author.
Title: Mother of Mercy, Bane of the Jews : devotion to the Virgin Mary in
Anglo-Norman England / Kati Ihnat.
Description: Princeton, NJ : Princeton University Press, 2016. | Includes
bibliographical references and index.
Identifiers: LCCN 2016033116 | ISBN 9780691169538 (hardcover)
Subjects: LCSH: Mary, Blessed Virgin, Saint—Devotion to—England—
History. | England—Church history—1066–1485. | Judaism—
Controversial literature.
Classification: LCC BT652.E54 I36 2016 | DDC 232.910942/09021—dc23 LC
record available at https://lccn.loc.gov/2016033116

British Library Cataloging-in-Publication Data is available

To my teachers

Contents

IIIIIIIIIIIIIIIIIIIIII

Illustrations

||||||||||||||||||||||||||

Acknowledgments

IIIIIIIIIIIIIIIIIIIIIIIIIIIIIIIIIIIIIIIIIIIIIII

OVER THE YEARS IT HAS TAKEN TO WRITE, this book has accrued many debts. First and foremost, it owes everything to the teachers who have inspired and supported me from the very beginning. Without the emphasis they placed on fostering creativity above all—something I fear is sadly being lost in education—this book would probably not exist, and it is in recognition of their contribution and effort that this book is dedicated to them.

Teachers come in many forms, but perhaps most central to the undertaking of this work has been Miri Rubin, my PhD supervisor, but so much more besides and since: mentor, example, cheerleader. Anyone who meets Miri is struck by her energy and devotion to her students and the profession of historian. I have benefited enormously from a number of additional scholars. To mention just those who read parts of this book in various incarnations and gave me invaluable advice, my sincere thanks go to Anthony Bale, Susan Boynton, Giles Constable, Eyal Poleg, Laura Slater, Rodney Thomson, and Ian Wei. The anonymous readers for Princeton University Press have allowed me to improve the book immeasurably, and I am also grateful to Fred Appel and Juliana Fidler for helping with every little thing.

Several fellowships have allowed me to refine and rework my doctoral research into the form it now takes. I have to thank Laura Cleaver of the Anglo-Norman Books project at Trinity College Dublin, where I spent a wonderful few months with the manuscripts in the library's Long Room. I also would like to express my gratitude to the staff and colleagues at the University of Pennsylvania's Herbert D. Katz Center for Advanced Judaic Studies, a haven for research and collegial exchange. Currently at the University of Bristol and working on another facet of Marian devotion, this time in medieval Iberia, I have my colleagues to thank, and especially Emma Hornby for her kindness and understanding. Without being exhaustive, colleagues who have helped me along the way, not just by reading, but also by engaging in discussions and offering support, have included (but are in no way limited to) Elisheva Baumgarten, Christopher Brooke, Peter Denley, Margot Fassler, Roy Flechner, Ora Limor, Sara Lipton, Brian Patrick McGuire, Katelyn Mesler, Carolyn Muessig, Nils Holger Petersen, Nicholas Vincent, and Simon Yarrow. The staff of the British Library, Bibliothèque nationale de France (Paris), Royal Library (Copenhagen), Cambridge University Library, Bodleian Library (Oxford), Parker Library (Cambridge), Wren Library (Cambridge), Balliol College Library (Oxford), and Worcester Cathedral Library were especially helpful, and the librarians at the Chicago University Library were extremely kind in providing me with a digital copy of Chicago UL MS 147. Funding from the Social Sciences and Humanities Research Council of Canada, Westfield Trust, and Royal Historical Society (through the Institute of Historical Research) made the initial stages of this study possible. I must also express deep gratitude to the generosity of Michael Winterbottom, who together with Rodney Thomson allowed me to see an early draft of their important translation and edition of William of Malmesbury's miracles, which now exists in a wonderful published version.

There is no separating the professional from the personal in the pursuit of something so absorbing, so I must above all recognize the friendship and love of those who helped me in so many different ways. Friends too numerous to mention, in Canada, the United Kingdom, Belgium, Ireland, and the United States, and my family in Spain, have been anchoring points in my nomadic years. The two most important teachers in my life, my parents, Miron and Charo, and my aunt Natalie have given me a home—in all senses of the word—to come back to. My sister, Lisa, and sisters in spirit, Elianna Fetterolf and Olaia Zarketa, have given nothing but love. And finally, I thank Philipp Steinkrueger for keeping me real, which is possibly the most important thing anyone can do.

Mother of Mercy, Bane of the Jews

Introduction

||||||||||||||||||||||||||||||||||||||||||

THE LATE ELEVENTH AND TWELFTH CENTURIES saw the rise of the age of Mary. It was during this period that scholars have consistently pointed to the emergence of the Virgin Mary as a figure central to medieval religious culture in western Europe. These centuries saw theological, artistic, literary, and musical manifestations of Mary's growing importance as saintly intercessor, heavenly patron, and queen. It was here that Mary rapidly became a dominant figure sculpted in wood and painted on the page. New theological ideas about Mary blossomed, treating her as second only to God, special and distinct from all other human beings. Mary began to appear increasingly as merciful mother in stories of miracles, which described how her mercy won the day over the forces of evil. Churches were dedicated to her, relics of her hair and gown were circulated, and pilgrimages were made to visit the objects and the institutions that housed them. But above all, Mary became the subject of devotion performed in the liturgy. In the chants, readings, prayers, and sermons of the Divine Office and mass, Mary was increasingly commemorated as the universal Christian mother. The liturgical calendar came to mark more moments of her life with special feast days, just as she was accorded an ever more prominent place in the weekly and daily cycles of liturgical prayer and praise. This period saw Mary become the most celebrated figure in the Christian rite, outside of Christ himself, remembered in frequent and regular rituals developed to honor her role as mother of God and protector of Christians. Never, perhaps, since the early centuries of Christianity in the East was Mary such a source of devotional energy and innovation.

As much as Mary was cast as the mother of mercy for her devoted followers, she was also given another, more sinister side. To those who turned their backs on her, she could exercise a cruel vengeance. Again and again in religious sources, from stories to chants to sermons, those who most opposed her were Jews.[1] Jews featured as Mary's prototypical enemies, doubting her virginity, and challenging her status as saint and mother of God. This was nothing new. Throughout Christian history, discussions about Mary had addressed the Jews. Christian theologians consistently cited the Jewish refusal of the virgin birth and the Incarnation in bitter invectives that condemned the Jewish position as they sought to defend Mary as *Theotokos*, mother of the human and divine Christ.[2] Christians sought proof of their belief in the prophecies of the Hebrew Bible, pointing out to the Jews that Christ's birth of a virgin was to be found there in plain sight. Christian theological apologetics pitted their allegorical reading of the scriptures against the Jewish interpretation, which held that God could never have taken human form and been born of a woman, as this would have been too great a debasement for an ineffable deity.[3] Additionally, sermons, hymns, and stories were composed to establish that Mary was in fact worthy of veneration for her instrumental role in the history of salvation, for how could Christ have redeemed humanity had he not taken on the flesh of the Virgin then to be crucified and resurrected? The battle around Mary even brought in the Jews when various Christian groups were actually the target, which was often the case. So-called heretics—Arians, Nestorians, and iconoclasts—became tarred with the Jewish brush, accused of siding with the Jews in their contempt for the Theotokos.[4] This imagined antagonism—between Mary and the Jews—traveled wherever Mary was especially venerated, as the sources designed in the fraught early centuries of Christianity were reused in other contexts. The sermons were incorporated into the liturgy for Marian feasts, treatises recycled for their relevance to Christological and Mariological questions, and accounts of miracles repeated in works of history. The Jews became part of the Marian story, and the conflicts of the past were remembered in the intervening centuries.

This book is about the sources developed to perform and justify devotion to Mary, many of which called on the figure of the Jew to illustrate proper Christian approaches to her. The Marian movement was not the same in all places, however. Even with a cult as widespread and seemingly universal as that of the Virgin mother of God, it is possible and even necessary to locate trends in particular places. Anglo-Norman England is one such place. The monasteries of England in the century following the Norman Conquest of 1066 created some of the most original displays of Marian devotion—ones that had a considerable legacy throughout the rest of the Middle Ages and beyond. This is not to say that none of the same or similar manifestations can be seen in other areas, or that other places lacked originality when it came to venerating Mary. There were plenty of local virgins throughout the European continent, some with highly developed cults as well as their own special forms of literature, music, and artwork. Margot Fassler has highlighted one such cult at Chartres Cathedral that underwent considerable expansion starting in the early eleventh century.[5] Mary also became a standard-bearer for Christian orthodoxy in Iberia, as illustrated by Amy Remensnyder, particularly beginning in the late twelfth and thirteenth centuries.[6] Other scholars, especially Rachel Fulton and Miri Rubin, have brought together many diverse works by theologians, artists, and composers from across western Europe to reveal a general shift in devotion to Mary over this period, explaining it as part of the wider changes in devotional culture that encouraged greater identification with Christ and Mary.[7] But some of the most groundbreaking and influential expressions of devotion to Mary can be located in late eleventh- and early twelfth-century England. Here we find the first ever articulation of the doctrine of the Immaculate Conception, the celebration of the feast of Mary's Conception, the first commemoration of Anne, Mary's mother, the earliest evidence of the daily Little Office performed in Mary's honor, and the origins of the Marian miracle collections, which went on to become one of the most popular devotional literary genres. It is only by considering these elements together in their context that we can begin to understand how and why Mary was the center of so much activity.

This study seeks to trace the development of the Marian cult over this crucial period in England, between 1066 and 1154, uncovering the connections between the different sources to reveal a general underlying desire and considerable effort toward increasing devotion to Mary. As a result, it will inevitably draw comparisons with Mary Clayton's instrumental study of Mary in Anglo-Saxon England.[8] I owe a great debt to her thorough and painstaking research, but I do not have the same aim of producing an exhaustive catalog of every source connected to the Virgin, specifically because sheer numbers would make this an unmanageable task. What I seek to do is to place religious practice, especially through the liturgy, at the heart of the story, and illustrate how liturgical innovation sparked creativity in other spheres: artistic, theological, and literary. A caveat is required here, however, because for a book so interested in the liturgy, it will seem unnervingly silent to many. As a historian who acknowledges how important music is to understanding the history of the liturgy, I am currently working in collaboration with musicologists.[9] The music associated with the texts discussed in this book would no doubt help to shed considerable light on their meaning. In anticipation of such additional insight, the chapters here focus on the connection between the different manifestations of Marian devotion: how liturgy shaped theology, and how theology justified liturgy; how literature was inspired by liturgical practice and went on to inspire people to perform the liturgy in particular ways; and how the performance of veneration to Mary as mother of mercy was reinforced through various means in different media. This is a cultural study with an eye toward exploring how these seemingly diverse expressions of devotion to Mary—liturgical, theological, and literary—were actually profoundly intertwined, each influencing the other, and all produced in a common monastic milieu.

The monastic setting is key. In addition to localizing the cultural products associated with Marian devotion and considering the echoes between them, this book helps to overturn a misconception about the rise of Mary's cult.[10] In the late eleventh and early twelfth centuries, it was not strictly speaking a popular cult. It was not a question of catering to a lay population eager for a kindlier, more merciful mother figure to counterbalance the fear elicited by Christ in judgment. Rather, as James Clarke has suggested, "the monks of this period were not in thrall to but in advance of the preoccupations of their secular counterparts," and Nigel Morgan went on to show that this statement aptly describes the cult of Mary.[11] Those who were spearheading the growth of Marian devotion in this period were monks, specifically the Benedictine monks of England's large and ancient monasteries.[12] Monastic houses had a long history of importance and influence over religious culture in the kingdom, especially after the late tenth century, when monastic reformers sought to reform the clergy, and replaced numerous communities of canons with monks vowed to chastity, poverty, and obedience. Many bishops came from a monastic background and ran their cathedrals like monasteries; Christ Church, Worcester, Winchester, and Exeter thus joined the many important monasteries, like Glastonbury, Malmesbury, Evesham, and Peterborough, among others.[13] Consequently, English Benedictines held an unusually prominent role, and contrary to the cathedral schools on the Continent, Benedictine monks became the main purveyors and preservers of religious cultural materials throughout which their ethos permeated.[14] They also exercised an important function in the provision of pastoral care, particularly in the cathedrals, which served as religious centers in the towns.[15] It may not be too much of an exaggeration to repeat David Knowles's words that "[monasteries] were the cultural heart of England."[16]

The Benedictine identity of these monks is significant. We are used to thinking of the Cistercians, that order universally dedicated to Mary, as the most ardent defenders and supporters of their patron, with Bernard of Clairvaux a forerunner of Marian devotion such that he was attributed one of the most famous Marian miracles: a stream of milk direct from her breast.[17] But Bernard was fairly conservative on the issue of Mary compared to the English monks we will encounter in this book. Nor was Cistercian commemoration of Mary especially extreme or inventive, and drew largely from the precedent set by the abbey of Molesmes from which the first monks left for Cîteaux.[18] As Chrysogonus Waddel has explained, the earliest Marian material in the Cistercian liturgy was actually pruned under the reforming impulse of the abbot Stephen Harding in the early twelfth century.[19] Therefore, well before the Cistercians established themselves as the Marian order par excellence, the Benedictines in England had already made considerable headway in promoting Marian veneration and proved far more creative in their liturgical commemoration. In fact, their Benedictine affiliation per se allowed greater room for liturgical novelty. Not restricted by the specific requirements of a shared practice imposed by a motherhouse, the Benedictines were at liberty to adopt more feasts and religious practices as well as honor the saints with greater freedom, with practices that varied from house to house.[20] As a result, their forms of devotional expression were manifold and elaborate, not least when it came to Mary.

In order to highlight the full diversity of sources produced to venerate Mary, and the ways in which they were connected, the first three chapters will explore each source type in turn. Chapter 1 will examine the liturgy and prayer, laying out the most important innovations in the liturgical celebration of Mary, both communal and private. Chapter 2 will deal with the theological expressions that used new scholarly methods to help justify liturgical practices, focusing especially on the doctrines of the Immaculate Conception and bodily Assumption. Chapter 3 will turn to the collections of miracle stories, which featured particular religious practices in an attempt to illustrate just how to receive Mary's mercy and narrated the rewards for the proper expressions of devotion. These were the primary but linked forms in which devotion to Mary was developed and fostered in Anglo-Norman England. Some of these sources have been the subject of previous study. For the liturgical material, the crucial work undertaken by Sally Roper, Richard Pfaff, and especially Nigel Morgan has been formative, as have individual studies by Antonia Gransden and T. A. Heslop, providing me with a wealth of examples from which to build a picture of practice in this period.[21] In terms of prayer and theology, Fulton's foundational study *From Judgment to Passion* takes in numerous theologians, with more pointed studies by Marielle Lamy on the doctrine of the Immaculate Conception and Henry Mayr-Harting on the bodily Assumption.[22] The Latin miracle stories have been less covered, despite Richard Southern's seminal article that located their origins in England; even his student Benedicta Ward only briefly touched on them in her *Miracles and the Medieval Mind*, and many studies concentrate only on their later vernacular versions.[23] Despite many excellent studies of isolated sources, my goal is to understand them in function of each other. Only by considering these diverse sources together can we see them as part of an elaborate matrix of performative action—rituals of devotion that best express how Mary was understood and approached.

In the move to create elaborate and innovative modes of venerating Mary in Anglo-Norman England, the Jews once more made an appearance. Mary's saintly identity was shaped as two sides of one coin: she was the all-merciful mother, listening to the pleas of her followers in prayer and praise in the liturgy; she was also the resistant opponent of the Jews, withstanding their attacks and proving them wrong in their rejection of her role in human redemption. Benedictine monks in England incorporated the sources of the past into their own works to enhance Mary's role, pitting her against the Jews in sermons, liturgy, and miracle stories. Throughout the chapters of this book, therefore, the introduction of Jews into diverse sources designed for the exaltation of Mary will be highlighted as a key way in which monks developed her cult. In many cases, they drew from previous examples, but made them relevant and new as the sources were updated and changed. This is perhaps nowhere more obvious than in the miracle stories that contain enough material to this effect to receive their own study in chapter 4. Many of the tales that appear in the new collections of Marian miracles produced in English monasteries were ancient—some originated in the first centuries of Christianity. But in rewriting them, English monks fashioned them anew, heightening the Jews' hostility just as they enhanced Mary's mercy and power.[24] The image given of the Jews in these stories became one of considerable evil; they were depicted as murderers, blasphemers, necromancers, cheats, and liars. Such antagonists were contrasted with the understanding of Mary as heavenly queen, merciful and generous, and a staunch protector of her followers. To cite Rubin, who has also noted the prevalence of Jews in medieval Marian sources, "If Mary defended the faith and protected each monk against sin, then she was also the bulwark against heretics and Jews."[25]

Imagined as violently anti-Christian, the Jews in materials created for the cult of Mary did not just serve to highlight Mary's mercy and love for her devotees. The figure of the Jew also provided Christians with a model *not* to follow in terms of performing devotion to Mary: whenever a Jew was shown to desecrate an image instead of venerate it, blaspheme against Christ and his mother instead of singing their praises, and choose to ally himself with the devil instead of praying to Mary, Christians were taught how important it was to do exactly the opposite. The Jews thus served to dramatize the contrast between proper versus improper behavior. The idea of the Jew as a theoretical construct, the so-called 'hermeneutic Jew' who helped to define Christianity by supplying a contrary belief against which to argue, has been well discussed in the scholarship.[26] Here, quite apart from defining what it meant to believe like a Christian, Jews in the Marian sources helped to exemplify what it meant to act like one.

✳✳✳

Why devotion to Mary developed in these particular ways specifically around the turn of the twelfth century is a complex question, and one that will be touched on throughout this work but deserves summarizing here. To begin with, Mary had been a potent symbol of monastic values since early in the medieval period. From the time of the early ascetic writers—Augustine, Ambrose, and Jerome—Mary was presented as an example of virginity, especially for women.[27] Mary was the mother of virgins; she had made the pursuit of virginity not only legitimate but also desirable, for she had been chosen and blessed by God with the conception and birth of the Messiah all the while maintaining her purity intact. Virginity was nevertheless a virtue for men, too, and while they had Christ to look to, Mary provided an entirely human precedent. Bede had centuries before cast Mary as an appropriate example for monks, the *ancilla Domini* who bent her will to God in an example of monastic obedience.[28] As a result, Mary's virginity appealed to the monks who sought to reform the clergy along monastic lines in late tenth-century England. Helen Scheck has argued that "the Virgin Mary is probably the most influential hagiographical model adopted for reform objectives in Anglo-Saxon England. It is certainly no accident that the Benedictine reform movement coincides with the blossoming cult of the Virgin Mary in Anglo-Saxon England."[29] Mary's potential for offering a template to those devoted to a life of chastity was recognized not just in England but by monastic reformers elsewhere as well, particularly by the Cluniacs Odo (d. 942) and Odilo (d. 1049) of Cluny and William of Volpiano (d. 1031), and the Italian Peter Damian (d. 1072), all of whose devotion to Mary has been noted.[30] But despite Mary's significance for reform movements elsewhere in Europe, Clayton has argued that Anglo-Saxon religious culture gave Mary an especially prominent place. In art, liturgy, poetry, and sermons, Anglo-Saxon monks demonstrated a will to make her a patron most fitting of their profession.[31]

The Norman Conquest of 1066 marked a turning point. While debate continues about the consequences of Duke William's invasion of England, it can hardly be disputed that change was in the air.[32] New ecclesiastical leaders were brought in from abroad, and placed in charge of churches and monasteries, until by 1095, there was no bishop of Anglo-Saxon origin left. Indigenous traditions such as the monk-bishop slowly diminished, although others, like the monastic cathedral, clearly appealed to the newcomers and drew new members in their thousands.[33] Frank Barlow has summarized the paradox: "The initial effect of the Norman conquest was greatly to disturb the monasteries. New direction, new constitutions, reorganization, and rebuilding at their worst upset monastic life, [and] at their best gave renewed purpose and interest."[34] Some of the growing numbers of monks and nuns may have been attracted to the profession by the active new church leaders, such as Lanfranc (d. 1089) and Anselm (d. 1109), the influential abbots of Bec in Normandy before becoming successive archbishops of Canterbury.[35] This was a golden age of history writing undertaken primarily by monks.[36] Many volumes of local hagiography and miracles of the Anglo-Saxon saints were recorded, and liturgies were composed to go along with them.[37] Far from dismissing local saints, as has been argued, ecclesiastical leaders saw the usefulness in having powerful saintly allies, both as symbols of their houses' prestige and miraculous avengers of injustices done to the community.[38] Despite such a flurry of activity, the monastic reaction to the Norman Conquest was complex, and not all monks felt entirely favorable toward the changes they saw.[39] But what cannot be disputed is that the Norman Conquest marked the beginning of a period of cultural flourishing in the monasteries of England.[40]

Apart from the national narratives that tend to enter into any discussion of England in the late eleventh century, we can view the changes that affected religious culture in this period as the result of wider currents.[41] Crucially, the Norman Conquest coincided with the religious reform movement since associated with Pope Gregory VII. As Giles Constable has described, in the period of religious reformation of the eleventh and twelfth centuries, the general aim was to monasticize the clergy by imposing the monastic way of life on all clerics, and thereby elevate monasticism to the highest form of Christian existence.[42] The abbot of Westminster, Gilbert Crispin (d. 1117), expressed this explicitly when he wrote that "no one can finally be saved unless he follows the life of a monk as much as he can."[43] The monk-archbishops Lanfranc and Anselm were steeped in the reforming ethos.[44] Anselm especially sought to disentangle the English church from the involvement of secular authority and took a tough stance on simony.[45] Clerical celibacy was equally on the table, as council after council met and legislated on the subject, in what appears to have been a more pressing issue in England than elsewhere in Europe.[46] Monastic involvement in the priesthood, particularly through pastoral care, became the subject of considerable debate in this period, with monks such as Anselm and his student Honorius Augustodunensis (d. ca. 1154) composing heartfelt apologia for the right of monks to exercise priestly duties, particularly preaching, leading up to official discussion of the matter at the First Lateran Council in 1123.[47] Liturgical reform was an extension of these efforts, with a tendency to reduce the liturgy but also to stress its more sincere performance.[48] An underlying general desire for monastic values to become universal serves as a backdrop for much of the material examined in this book.

The cult of the Virgin Mary has not been incorporated into this story of conquest and reform, despite the important place of Mary in Anglo-Saxon culture. In many ways, the growth of Mary's cult mirrors that of other saints' cults in England. Because so many of the houses reformed in the late tenth century had Mary as their patron saint, and others saw her as a crucial auxiliary saint, it was only natural that many of these institutions produced for Mary the same kinds of materials—miracles and liturgies—they did for other saints. The fact that the same individual, the precentor or cantor, was increasingly taking responsibility for both the library and liturgy of an institution meant that hagiography, history, and liturgy were all the more intimately connected, as different forms of expressing allegiance to a saint and commemorating their significance for the community.[49] We can see conflicting forces at work here, too, though. Some of the unique and especially elaborate practices for celebrating Mary in the Anglo-Saxon tradition were challenged or simply disappeared. There were virulent debates about the cancellation of the feast of Mary's Conception, and the daily Little Office seems likewise to have disappeared after the Norman Conquest. At the same time, new feasts appeared, such as that of Mary's mother, Anne. Theological treatises claimed glorious things for Mary: that she had been conceived without original sin; that she had risen to heaven in body and soul at her death. Biblical commentaries read Mary into books that had never traditionally been applied to her, such as the Song of Songs, and this creative reading made its way into aural and visual media, sermons, illuminations, and wall paintings. Like other saints, Mary became the subject of volumes of miracle stories that featured her intercessory actions on earth for a host of different beneficiaries. Whatever resistance there may have been to the veneration of Mary in the period immediately following the Norman Conquest quickly dissolved, as this became one of the periods of most marked development for the Marian cult in its history.

There was a key difference between Mary and the other saints, however; it lay in her status as universal saint. No one monastery or church could claim her uniquely for their own, because she was the patron of many. Nor were there relics that became the special focus of a Marian cult in England the way they were in some continental churches, such as Chartres. Of course, if one followed the doctrine of Mary's bodily Assumption, she left no bodily remains at all, but even secondary relics—of hair, milk, and clothing—do not seem to have attracted special attention in England in this period. Although ownership of items connected to the Virgin are listed in earlier relic inventories that include pieces of clothing, strands of hair, and even remnants of her milk, no accounts of miracles performed by these items exist, suggesting that they were ubiquitous and not recognized as particularly worthy sites of pilgrimage.[50] Nor do carved statues, such as those in France, seem to have gained traction as significant cult sites.[51] As far as is possible to ascertain, the first properly Marian shrine appeared in the mid-twelfth century, when a reconstruction of Mary's house in Nazareth was first founded at Walsingham as an Augustinian priory, circa 1153.[52] Because it marks the start of a new phase in the development of the Marian cult, and coincides with the beginning of the Angevin realm, the establishment of the shrine at Walsingham thus serves as a convenient end point to the period discussed in this book and so will fall outside its scope. In the century that this book covers, devotion to Mary does not appear to have been connected to particular relic sites, and her role as universal queen of Christendom was one of the major distinguishing features of the Marian cult as developed in Anglo-Norman England.

Mary's universality made her especially useful in this new age of monastic reform. While Lanfranc seems to have viewed Christ as the primary unifying figure, other individuals in Anglo-Norman England saw in Mary an opportunity to bind Christians together, particularly under the banner of monastic ideals.[53] As we have seen, Mary had been a potent symbol of monastic reform in the past. With the general inward turn toward penitence that was a feature of the twelfth-century religious reform movement, her role as intercessor with Christ as judge came to appear all the more essential.[54] The effusive prayers composed in her honor are a testament to the faith placed in her powers of mediation for the sinful, who were more aware of their own sin and feared for the harshness of Christ's judgment.[55] These sources also encouraged empathy with Mary in her suffering and love for Christ as a means for monks and nuns to identify with Mary and her son, as illustrated by Fulton.[56] Mary was not just a figure of succor, however, for she was presented as an example to follow in the campaign for clerical celibacy.[57] She took on this role in ascetic works and sermons, where she acts as a role model for men and women in their pursuit of the religious life, as well as in miracle stories, where she comes to the rescue of monks and nuns struggling with their vows. Wider interests in chastity as a necessary quality for religious professionals—be they secular or regular—is certainly reflected in the contemporary interest in virgin saints such as Edmund and Edward, not to mention the many Anglo-Saxon female saints.[58] We can therefore see devotion to Mary as the queen of virgins in the context of a more general trend that involved glorifying the monastic life of chastity and virginity.

A word must be said here about gender. There has been a tendency to consider Mary as the natural model for women and hence a saint who mattered most to the female population of medieval Europe. In Anglo-Norman England, this is reflected in the fact that all female monastic houses were dedicated to the Virgin, generally in addition to another local saint. Educational literature written for women, such as *De arma castitatis* by Osbert of Clare (d. ca. 1158) for Adelidis (d. ca. 1166), abbess of Barking Abbey, presented Mary as a good example and motivational prompt for fighting the sin of lust in the female pursuit of absolute physical purity.[59] Prayers and hymns to Mary and her mother, Anne, are found in the female voice, and collections of prayers were composed for high-profile women including Matilda of Tuscany (d. 1115) and Adeliza (d. ca. 1113), the daughter of William the Conqueror.[60] Images of Mary in books created for women's houses contain images of female penitents praying to Mary, such as the large-scale illumination of Mary in the Shaftesbury Psalter, which shows a woman kneeling at her feet.[61] In the St. Albans Psalter, commissioned for the mystic Christina of Markyate, Mary plays a key role in the prefatory cycles of images and the calendar.[62] Scholars have argued that Mary's protagonism in these manuscripts catered to their female owners. The lack of surviving manuscripts from female religious houses of the period nonetheless makes it difficult to conclude generally about the prevalence of Mary in female religious culture.[63] From what we do have in liturgical, artistic, and most important, pedagogical terms, however, Mary does seem to have been recognized as a significant saint among nuns.

Still, limiting Mary to the female sphere would do injustice to her prominence in works written by monks for other monks. The vast majority of the sources cited in this book were produced by men, and there is little evidence that they were intended specifically for female audiences; for this reason, I refer throughout to the contribution mostly of *monks* to the cult of Mary in Anglo-Norman England, since the evidence for female authorship, even of the manuscripts found at female institutions, is as yet unclear.[64] This is not to say that the liturgical practices, prayers, images, devotional literature, and theological texts explored here were inaccessible or foreign to women. On the contrary, similar trends seem to have affected men and women equally. Women celebrated the same feast days as men, embraced the same daily and weekly liturgies, prayed similarly, and perhaps read the same literature to fire up their commitment to the religious life.[65] In the same way, men seem to have been as taken with images of Mary as were women; they imagined her as a useful model for men pursuing a life of virginity, and described her appearing as often, if not more so, to men than to women in the miracle stories that depicted Mary's intervention in the world. Women may not have been considered equal to the men writing the texts; William of Malmesbury (d. ca. 1143) pointedly placed his stories about women toward the end of his hierarchically arranged miracle collection, after those featuring popes, bishops, monks, priests, and laymen. Still, women and men largely shared the same culture in which Mary was to be praised as a saint beloved by both sexes. In response to an old argument by Marina Warner, this book shows that Mary was not explicitly designed by men to impose impossible ideals of purity on women but rather as a universal mother figure cherished by her children, female and male alike.[66] If ever there was a need for an integrated history that treated male and female spheres as part of the same wider culture, devotion to Mary in Anglo-Norman monasteries certainly seems to call for it.

Having established the social context in which devotion to Mary grew so markedly, we must address the contemporary forces that may have created additional interest in the Jews as a counterweight to Mary as merciful queen. England saw fundamental changes in relations between Christians and Jews, not the least of which was the first immigration of Jews to the island after 1066. There was no known Jewish settlement in England prior to the conquest, and the first mention of Jews settling in the kingdom attributes their arrival to William the Conqueror, thought to have brought "his" Norman Jews over with him.[67] These early immigrants constituted a small community, restricted almost entirely to London at first. But the violent persecution of Jews in Normandy following the call to the First Crusade by Urban II in 1095 may have encouraged growing numbers to emigrate and establish themselves in the major market towns of the kingdom.[68] In the century that followed the conquest, the evidence for Jewish life and activity is still limited, with only glimpses caught in the chancery records and histories. From what these reveal, Jews were important contributors to royal coffers in the form of taxes and fines, were lending money to both individuals and religious institutions, and were under the sole protection of the king, who provided the muscle to enforce the collection of debts.[69] Granted privileges on account of the king's direct overlordship, some Jews became heavily involved in the financial sector, more so, it seems, than on the other side of the English Channel.[70] Such heavy reliance on royal authority and favor meant their position could either be advantageous or precarious, depending on the circumstances, as later centuries would attest.[71] For some monastic authors, this particular configuration seems to have been regarded with skepticism and unease, although Jews do not enter into histories with nearly as much frequency or derision as they do later on in the twelfth and thirteenth centuries.[72] Concern about the arrival of Jews to England is sporadic and muted in the Anglo-Norman period, but it is there among the criticisms of the new regime.

Given the context of recent immigration, we might think that English monks were inspired to incorporate Jews into their sources about Mary not just because they were concerned about the new social reality but also specifically because they came into contact with Jewish skepticism of Mary. After all, there was a Jewish literary tradition—referred to collectively as the Toledot Yeshu—that described Mary as an adulterous woman and Jesus as a bastard born of menstruation. Peter Schäfer has explored this tradition and highlighted its popularity as a counternarrative to the Christian Gospels.[73] In the thirteenth century, the traces of the Toledot tradition found in the Talmud may have created such horror among the Christian authorities in Paris that they placed the book on trial and had it condemned as the vilest blasphemy.[74] It is possible, though, that more than a century before these events took place, Christians had already come to know Jewish opinions of Mary. During the persecution of Norman and Rhenish Jews following the call to the First Crusades in 1095, the victims are said to have cursed Mary in terms reminiscent of the Toledot legends when confronted by would-be crusaders. Chronicles and liturgical poetry (piyyutim) that memorialize these reactions mention verbal attacks on Jesus as the "son of a menstruating woman," "son of lechery," and "son of whoredom," "conceived by a menstruating and wanton woman," all implicit blasphemies against Mary.[75] A polemical dialogue written by Odo, bishop of Tournai has Odo's potentially real-life interlocutor, Leo, express profound disgust at the idea that God was born of a woman.[76] Contrary to what Israel Yuval has argued about Christian exposure to Jewish invective, whatever knowledge there was of the satiric tradition or the curses against Mary, we find no explicit comments made about them in the contemporary sources in England.[77] We must be wary of concluding that Christians came to know of the Jews' rejection of Mary directly from Jews themselves, although the heightened interest in formulating arguments against Jews among twelfth-century monastic writers allows us to assume basic familiarity with the Jewish position.[78]

Can we assume, therefore, that the Jews found in the sources that are discussed in this book are meant as a reflection of those who had so recently arrived on English shores? During the Anglo-Saxon period, as Andrew Scheil has contended, Jews could only be "imaginative, textual constructs, manifest only in the distorted shadow cast by the Christian tradition," just as they would be again after their expulsion from the kingdom in 1290, as explored by Anthony Bale.[79] During the period in between, we might wonder whether interaction with Jews changed the perception of the monks recording stories, histories, and sermons. But looking for the "real Jews" behind their fictional counterparts is a trap, for the sources examined in this book are not historical records but instead tools for religious practice. Liturgy, sermons, and miracle stories sought to transmit a devotional message rather than an accurate record of Jewish presence and activity in Anglo-Norman England. In fact, they often cast Jews in the biblical past or eschatological future, alluding to Jewish cruelty to Christ and Synagoga's conversion at the end of time in order to highlight Mary's eternal struggle to bring Jews on side. Those who produced these sources were perhaps not totally immune to their environments, and introduced subtle—and not so subtle—commentaries into their works about the evils of Jewish-Christian coexistence, including accusations of magic, corruption, and greed, all reflective of contemporary social concerns, as we will see. Yet this appeal to lived experience would only have served to increase the sense of Mary's victory over the forces of evil by bringing it into the present. If these sources depicted Jews in particular ways, it was to reinforce shared Christian values, particularly monastic ones.[80] Dominique Iogna-Prat has remarked on this same dynamic at twelfth-century Cluny, where an attempt to establish the abbey's role as a microcosm of universal Christendom led to its condemnation of outside groups such as Jews and Muslims.[81] In a similar way among English Benedictines, the figure of the Jew helped monks to establish Mary as a figurehead for the way of life they sought to promote—one aligned with their own ideals for a Christian society.

We should remember that these sources did not ultimately stay within the confines of the monastic world. Because of the inherent communicability of liturgy, homilies, and miracles to wide audiences, some of them engineered specifically for transmission to the general lay public, there remained a strong possibility that their message about Jewish evil and Mary's virtue could be received in largely unintended ways. Suddenly a message about the danger of Jews meant to highlight Mary's triumph over her doubters could result in a warning about Jewish-Christian interaction more generally. This in turn might lead those experiencing these practices, clerical and lay, to associate theoretical violence against Mary with real violence against Mary's followers. Enough repetition of a particular image of a Jew as the avaricious enemy of Mary in a sermon heard every year on the feast of the Assumption or every Saturday as part of the Marian commemorative office or every day in a Marian votive office could lead people to form a vision of the Jews in their midst based on the message they were hearing; it was not a necessary but certainly a possible conse-quence.[82] After all, as one scholar recently summarized it, "an increasing num-ber of scholars now subscribe to the notion that public behaviour [i.e. ritual practice] exteriorized certain ideas on how society should be organized and that, through the 'performance' of encoded gestures and rituals, these ideas could become part of a social *habitus*."[83] Sermons have started to receive atten-tion as vehicles for images of Jews that had the potential to inform opinions about Jews living in Christian society, although largely in the context of mendi-cant preaching.[84] Much of the scholarship on the development of medieval Christian ideas about Jews in the twelfth century has focused on theological ideas formulated in explicitly polemical treatises and dialogues, without fully clarifying how and if such ideas came to inform social behaviour.[85] Emphasis on these theological works also fails to account in meaningful ways for the emergence of accusations of violent behaviour in Jews: ritual murder, blood libel, host desecration. Miri Rubin has shed considerable light on the host des-ecration charge by placing it in the context of rising Eucharistic devotion, par-ticularly with the establishment of the Corpus Christi feast in the thirteenth century.[86] This study seeks to examine another devotional dimension, one that emerged over a century earlier, by exploring how Marian liturgy, theology and legend entwined to produce potentially powerful new understandings of Jews in Christian society.

Despite the instinct to treat liturgical sources as inherently communicable and therefore natural conduits for ideas and images between clerical and lay spheres, any attempt to establish with any certainty their effects on twelfth cen-tury society is bound to be fraught. The problem of language (the main one of liturgical communication being Latin), the diversity of congregations, and the multiplicity of potential meanings of these practices, would have deeply af-fected any experience of the texts discussed here, even assuming they were per-formed as written in manuscripts.[87] What relation these textual traces have to actual performance is often impossible to establish, particularly given the scar-city of additional sources to confirm how they were used or interpreted at spe-cific institutions.[88] We therefore have to be wary about concluding anything about the direct social impact of the texts I explore in this book, and I do not venture to do so, except for some brief suggestions in the conclusion. These dif-ficulties do not reduce the value of the sources, however. There was an intention in writing them down, a desire to record a script that tells us a great deal about the aims and assumptions of those doing the recording; liturgical rites are "valuable for understanding the initiatives of particular individuals, for re-gional traditions, for institutional history, for ideas and ideals and—some-times—for practice."[89] It is also important to remember that the liturgy was in-tended to be participatory, to bring together the Christian community in the celebration and affirmation of their shared beliefs and "to establish a connection between the faithful and their biblical models."[90] We cannot know how these events were carried out or experienced, perhaps, but we can assume that the liturgy was designed as an expression of Christian identity, and in this way, sought to communicate a clear message about belonging—and did so also by excluding.

If anything, then, this book concludes by opening up bigger questions, about the importance of performative sources in the transmission and experience of religious culture, for understanding both how Mary was conceived as a universal saint and how ideas about Jews were communicated in medieval Christian culture. Current trends in liturgical history have moved well past representations of the liturgy as an unchanging monolith, and as such, uninteresting to the study of religious change or the transmission of ideas.[91] Liturgical historians are reminding us increasingly that liturgy was constantly evolving, differed from place to place, and reflected the carefully constructed identities of the institutions for which they were produced and at which they were to be performed.[92] The rich variety of materials produced to celebrate Mary in English Benedictine culture thus provides fertile ground for understanding the development of the Marian cult, and what message monks wanted to transmit about her, in relation to themselves, their values, their institutions, and Christian identity more widely. The general message that emerges is one of Mary's preeminence as mediator between Christ and as example for Christian living. The Jews were equally part of this construction, highlighting her glory with their vices, and bringing the Christian community together under her protection at their expense. This study illustrates how understanding the ways in which Mary became the foremost saint and primary intercessor, and Jews were envisaged increasingly as her enemies, can best be grasped through the study of diverse sources and their relation to each other—liturgical, homiletic, and literary—as all part of a complex web of devotion with Mary at its center and in which the Jews unwittingly became caught.

CHAPTER 1

||||||||||||||||||||

Praising Mary

LITURGY AND PRAYER

FOR MONKS IN THE ELEVENTH AND TWELFTH CENTURIES, devotion to Mary was expressed above all in the sung and intoned texts of the Divine Office and mass. Liturgy and prayer were defining features of monastic religious life and culture. Monks and nuns devoted themselves to the daily performance of the *opus dei*; it shaped their lives and permeated every aspect of it.[1] As Susan Boynton has written, "Like the monastic garment, the liturgy was a habit that could not be shed, a fundamental and underlying condition of life in a religious community."[2] The Divine Office was their primary task and responsibility as stipulated in the Benedictine rule, and earned them a livelihood from donations by penitents eager to have the monks' prayers. This practice was both praise and prayer—exalting God and the saints while also asking for mercy—expressed most especially in the psalmody.[3] The daily recitation of the Psalms, the basis of the monastic life, was nevertheless couched in a rich tapestry of additional sung and spoken texts, prayers, and readings, all accompanied by prescribed actions in deliberate, elaborate stagings. The cult of saints, both major and minor ones, local and universal, was enacted through the liturgical celebration of their feast days, with the chants, processions, and ritual actions this entailed. Sermons explained the biblical texts used for a given day, providing deeper understandings of scripture and extrapolating essential moral lessons.[4] Private prayer and contemplation supplemented public praise as monks expressed their individual commitment to their chosen way of life.[5] Liturgy and prayer were the primary manifestations of the monastic identity, and through the liturgy's complex and variable structures, which evolved over time and place, monks communicated their ideals, values, and most dearly held beliefs.[6] It is in liturgy and prayer, then, that we find the most significant expression of the cult of the Virgin Mary in Anglo-Norman English monastic culture.

The monks of Anglo-Norman England developed the communal liturgy and individual prayer in unusual and significant ways. The process by which this occurred was complex, with religious and political change as well as challenge eliciting creative responses. Hints that church leaders attempted to curb the more extravagant practices of Marian veneration after the Norman Conquest are nonetheless countered by an unprecedented richness of liturgical and devotional materials composed in Mary's honor. Anglo-Saxon feasts such as the Conception and Presentation were revived in the midst of heated debate, extensive communal practices like the Office of Mary reappeared, and new celebrations were created such as the feast of Mary's mother, Anne. It was in this context that the archbishop of Canterbury, Anselm, wrote his effusive prayers to Mary, responding to the requests of his fellow monks. These prayers further inspired others to write lengthy meditational texts that ascribed Mary a more central place in the story of Christian salvation than ever before. Praise was heaped on Mary in order to appeal to her as a powerful and merciful mediator with her Son, and seek protection for entire communities and salvation for individual souls. At the same time, the rejection by Jews of Mary's essential role in the economy of salvation found its way into liturgical sources to remind performers and audiences alike of the proper way to approach the queen of heaven: with belief and reverence rather than doubt. The promotion of Mary as a saintly model drew inspiration not only from the English heritage but also from Norman, Italian, and even Iberian traditions; this was not a question of uniquely English patrimony but rather of a culture open to outside influence, absorbing elements from without to enhance what was already in place. Nigel Morgan made a seminal survey of the English materials that showed how the major developments in Marian devotion in the twelfth century were monastic as opposed to secular in origin.[7] Taking his work as a useful starting point, this first chapter will focus on the diverse monastic means of addressing Mary in prayer and song, revealing the active contribution made by monks in the Anglo-Norman sphere to devotion to Mary as mother of mercy.

LITURGY: FEASTS

By the time the Normans arrived in 1066, devotion to the Virgin Mary had already "reached cult proportions" in England, according to Sally Roper.[8] Marian devotion was an important feature of monastic culture in the Anglo-Saxon period, in many ways ahead of continental developments. Mary Clayton's extensive study of the cult of Mary in Anglo-Saxon England has illustrated the considerable innovation and originality with which it developed, particularly as a result of the monastic reforms undertaken in the late tenth century, radiated out of Winchester Cathedral.[9] The surviving evidence from Anglo-Saxon sermons, narratives, and liturgical poetry, in both Latin and the vernacular, as well as prayer, art, and song, paint a picture of Mary as an especially significant saint among the growing numbers of religious institutions that boasted her patronage. Numerous churches, cathedrals, and monasteries were founded in Mary's name in this period, and several changed allegiance to adopt her saintly patronage; double dedications, to Mary and another saint, were also popular.[10] The overwhelming evidence of foundations and refoundations points to dedication to Mary as "a hallmark of the reform, an outward sign of a truly monastic, celibate community."[11]

This trend was then echoed in the liturgy. Mary was honored with daily antiphons and a weekly mass on Saturdays that developed into a daily celebration of the Hours of Mary in the eleventh century. In addition to the four traditional feasts of the Purification, Annunciation, Assumption, and Nativity, celebrated in the Roman calendar since the seventh century, several unusual feast days were adopted in England, including the Byzantine feasts of Mary's Conception on December 8 and Presentation in the Temple on November 21.[12] The eighth- and ninth-century Books of Nunnaminster and Cerne attest to a rich tradition of private prayer to Mary fostered in Anglo-Saxon England. Such practices helped to establish a powerful link between monks and nuns in Anglo-Saxon England with their saintly patron and figurehead, memorializing their bond with her and calling on her intercessory powers to protect them, both individually and collectively.

With the coming of the Normans in 1066, patterns of Marian devotion seem to have shifted. Although scholars have long been revising the previously held assumption that the post–Conquest period was one of deep religious rupture, it can hardly be denied that the incoming clerical leaders had an interest in liturgical reform.[13] There is considerable evidence that Archbishop Lanfranc, who was brought in from Bec to lead the English church, imposed changes to the liturgy, although perhaps not as sweeping as was once thought.[14] At the Council of Winchester in 1072, Lanfranc is said to have "instituted many things to be observed in the practice of the Christian religion," which included many small alterations, such as revising the church dedication rite and changing the date of certain feasts, like that of St. Bartholomew, to the Norman use.[15] The *Vita Lanfranci*, his Bec-written biography, praises him for taking action, such that "the people, when their empty and barbarous rites had been forbidden, were led toward the right pattern of believing and living."[16] The disappearance of uniquely Anglo-Saxon feasts in the post–Norman Conquest period, such as the Conception of John the Baptist and the Ordination of St. Gregory, suggest attempts to bring the liturgy into line with what Lanfranc had known on the Continent.[17] There is some suggestion that Lanfranc's impulse toward reform led him to minimize the importance of the saints in order to promote a universal devotion to Christ, who was to be the powerful unifying figure under which all Christians could unite in the new, reformed church.[18] That reforms such as these could be taken badly by local monks is suggested by the clashes at St.

Augustine's Canterbury thanks to Lanfranc's interventions.[19] At other houses, there are records that the saints were the object of special scrutiny—at Evesham, for example, where the abbot Walter of Cerisy (formerly chaplain to Lanfranc) allegedly put the Anglo-Saxon relics to a trial by fire.[20] Nowhere did conflicts over religious heritage and practice come to a bloodier end than at Glastonbury, where the monks staged a rebellion against the changes to liturgical practice imposed by the abbot Thurstan, and ended up facing the royal troops.[21]

Reform did not always end in violence and destruction, however, and most ecclesiastical leaders realized the importance of preserving local traditions. Supporting the saints could be a smart political decision, particularly in the context of disputes between rival religious houses. In a seminal article that reversed ideas about Norman hostility to English saints, Susan Ridyard maintained that "those churchmen were characterised not by scepticism towards the English saints, by contempt of them or by hostility to them, but rather by a business-like readiness to make the heroes of the past serve the politics of the present."[22] Most scholars now agree, although many have pointed out that newcomers did not always immediately embrace local traditions, and that locals were not always content to see any alteration, no matter how small.[23] This constitutes a key caveat when thinking about how church reforms were experienced, particularly with respect to the liturgy. What may seem to us a minor change could have appeared a major devaluation of a given saint or liturgical tradition, as Jay Rubenstein has pointed out.[24]

Attitudes toward Mary in this period reflect this same complexity. On the one hand, there is evidence of widespread acceptance and enthusiasm for the cult of Mary in post–Conquest England. In the period from 1066–100, 30 institutions adopted Mary as their patron, with a further 96 between 1101 and 1150, compared to 7 and 14, respectively, for the next most popular saint, Peter. In total, 235 churches were dedicated to the Virgin between 1066 and 1216, almost ten times the number of dedications to Peter.[25] With respect to liturgical celebration, there seems to have been no question of the significance of the main Marian feast days. Lanfranc's *Constitutions*, the monastic rule he commissioned for Christ Church, includes the feast of the Assumption, for example, as one of the principal feasts of the liturgical year.[26] At the same time, we have hints of change. As Helen Gittos has shown, the Anglo-Saxon rite for the Purification (Candlemas) at Canterbury was considerably altered under Lanfranc, notably omitting the procession through the town and participation of the laity.[27] She points out that this may have been done to privilege the monastic community within the cathedral, so it may not have been read as a "demotion" of the feast. Later on, in the early twelfth century, the monks of Christ Church Canterbury went on to request the celebration of the octave of Mary's

Nativity, suggesting that liturgical commemoration of her feasts was even enhanced.[28]

Despite this, some of the more unusual Marian features of the liturgy proved controversial. This is especially the case with the feast of Mary's Conception. Edmund Bishop was the first to note that the feast "suffered a brief eclipse" after the conquest.[29] While Richard Pfaff has generally argued that there was no deliberate purge of the liturgical calendar post-1066, he has nevertheless observed that the Conception and Presentation feasts disappeared from the liturgical record by the end of the eleventh century.[30] The Conception feast may have survived at the institutions headed by the last Anglo-Saxon bishops, Leofric (1016–72) at Exeter and Wulfstan (ca. 1008–95) at Worcester.[31] At Christ Church, however, there is no indication of either feast in the earliest post–Conquest manuscripts.[32] No entries for the feasts are found in the calendar attached to an early twelfth-century psalter from St. Augustine's either, nor in two twelfth-century psalters from Winchester.[33] The Samson Pontifical, originally an early eleventh-century manuscript produced at Winchester and supplemented at Worcester under Bishop Samson (1095–112), also omits both feasts.[34] Despite an admittedly patchy record that makes it risky to draw conclusions, it is remarkable that there is so little evidence for the continued celebration of the feasts of the Conception and Presentation in the period directly following the conquest.[35]

A treatise dedicated entirely to the question of the Conception feast written by Eadmer of Canterbury (d. ca. 1130), a monk at Christ Church Canterbury, provides an illuminating glimpse into what may have happened to this unique Anglo-Saxon custom. Born in approximately 1060 to an Anglo-Saxon family, Eadmer entered the monastic community of Christ Church at a young age and spent most of his life at the cathedral priory. He eventually returned to Christ Church after a series of professional problems that saw him reject the archbishopric of St. Andrews because it would not subject itself to the primacy of Canterbury.[36] As a further expression of his loyalty to Christ Church, and perhaps because he became the precentor, and was responsible for the liturgy and library, he showed considerable attachment to the liturgical traditions of the cathedral including celebration of its most minor saints.[37] Jay Rubenstein has explained Eadmer's fervor in defending Christ Church's customs as stemming from an emotional investment in the institution's history and heritage.[38] The *Tractatus de conceptione beatae Mariae*, whose contents will be discussed in greater detail in the next chapter, reveals that the feast of the Conception was one of these real concerns for him:

> I wish to consider the celebration that falls today, which concerns the conception
> of the blessed mother of God, Mary, celebrated once more as a feast day in many
> places. For it was celebrated more frequently in ancient times, especially by those

in whom pure simplicity and a humbler devotion to God flourished. Where greater learning and great powers of inquiry filled the minds of certain men and puffed them up, having spurned the simplicity of poor men, they removed the celebration from among them, as if it lacked all reason (*ratione*). . . . Their decision was made very forcefully because those who made it excelled in both their secular and ecclesiastical authority and in the abundance of their wealth. . . . [T]hey did not fear to abolish the feast, namely that of the conception of the most sacred lady herself, on account of their authority, by which they boasted that they could prevail.[39]

Some have interpreted the conflict referred to here as between learned theologians and a lay population eager to maintain the celebration of the Conception feast. Yet it likely reflects Eadmer's desire to make what was an internal ecclesiastical matter seem more general.[40] It would have been in Eadmer's interest to imagine widespread popular support for the Conception feast, with their affection for the feast an expression of simple but sincere devotion to Mary that would further contrast with the feast's opponents as arrogant intellectuals. In talking about these intellectuals, Eadmer may well have meant Lanfranc and his contemporaries. Eadmer thought Lanfranc initially skeptical of certain Anglo-Saxon traditions, famously complaining that Lanfranc, "as an Englishman, was still somewhat green, and some of the customs which he found in England had not yet found acceptance with him."[41] Although there is no surviving opinion from Lanfranc on the question of the Conception feast, his *Constitutions* do not include it or the Presentation feasts, from which Christopher Brooke assumed they were among the minor festivals that Lanfranc purposefully removed.[42]

The fact that the Anglo-Saxon Marian feasts were not just unique to England but were also based on noncanonical sources would no doubt have made them seem all the more problematic for a reformer like Lanfranc. Both the Conception and Presentation feasts commemorated events in Mary's life mentioned only in apocryphal materials: the second-century *Protevangelium Jacobi*, fifth-century *Gospel of Pseudo-Matthew*, and early eleventh-century *Liber de nativitate Mariae*.[43] These texts describe how Mary's virtuous parents, Joachim and Anne, had their offering at the Temple refused on account of their childlessness. While Joachim went out into the wilderness to fast as penance, Anne prayed fervently that if she were granted a child, she would consecrate it to the Temple. An angel then visited Anne, telling her that she would yet be a mother, despite her advanced age. The same annunciation was made to Joachim, who returned home to be reunited with his wife, resulting ultimately in Mary's birth. Whether the child's conception occurred via sexual union or angelic annunciation depends on the version of the narrative. The event is mentioned in a blessing for the feast found in a Christ Church manuscript, circa 1030:

Blessing for the day of the Conception of Holy Mary:

> He who inspires the heavenly graces and redeems earthly minds, and who proclaimed by the angelic annunciation that the blessed mother of God was to be conceived (*beatam Dei genetricem angelico concipiendam preconavit oraculo*), may he deign to enrich you with the abundance of her blessings and with the flowers of her virtues. Amen.[44]

Although the feast was celebrated and the apocryphal narratives copied with considerable interest in Anglo-Saxon England, they did not meet with universal approval, as the skepticisim of the Old English homilist Aelfric attests (ca. 955–1010).[45] It would hardly be surprising, then, if Lanfranc, who is said to have been "keen to emend all the books of the Old as well as the New Testament, together with the writings of the holy Fathers, to accord with orthodox faith," had doubts about the legitimacy of the feast that went beyond just its Anglo-Saxon character.[46]

Whatever the status of the Apocrypha and their expression in the liturgy, there is evidence of renewed interest in both by the early twelfth century. Latin versions of the *Protevangelium Jacobi* and *Gospel of Pseudo-Matthew* survive from Glastonbury, Malmesbury, and Worcester, from the late eleventh and mid-twelfth centuries.[47] The abbot of Bury St. Edmunds, Baldwin, who came to England from Saint-Denis before the Norman Conquest, may have brought with him another version of the *Protevangelium Jacobi*.[48] Copies of the Nativity Apocrypha survive in Old English in three homiliaries from the late eleventh and early twelfth centuries, two of which were copied at Worcester.[49] George Younge has recently underlined the Marian content of a compilation of Old English homiletic and educational materials, likely made for the monks at Christ Church in the early twelfth century, including extracts from the Apocrypha.[50] Monastic fascination with Mary's life even extended to her mother, Anne. An abbreviated version of an apocryphal legend excerpted from Haymo of Auxerre's ninth-century *Sacred History* that describes Anne's life and three marriages, the *Trinubium Annae*, was copied at Bury St. Edmunds in the early twelfth century.[51] The fact that apocryphal materials pertaining to Mary continued to be copied into the twelfth century, in both Latin and Old English, implies that their significance to Anglo-Norman monks outweighed whatever doubts arose around the trustworthiness of such texts.

The interest that monks in Anglo-Norman England showed in the Apocrypha was echoed by the progressive revival of the feast of the Conception. Even if it had once been only a relatively minor celebration, by the 1120s, this feast was deemed important enough for a number of contemporary historical sources to record its readoption. Eadmer himself wrote in his treatise (ca. 1125) that it "has been restored as a feast day in many places."[52] In some cases, all memory of a previous celebration seems to have been erased. The *History of St*

Peter's, Gloucester, records that between 1113 and 1131, "at this same time, the celebration of the Conception of holy mother Mary began to be celebrated for the first time in England."[53] This entry is related to one that appears in the Worcester annals, which states the same thing for 1125.[54] The Winchcombe annals record the feast's adoption there in 1126: "In that same year, we first began to celebrate the feast of the Conception of holy Mary."[55] Some scholars have interpreted these entries to indicate that the Conception feast was a Norman importation.[56] We nevertheless have to remember the eleventh-century evidence for the feast in England, the lack of equivalent evidence for its presence in Normandy, and the comments made by Eadmer about the feast's loss and subsequent revival in England, not as a result of Norman influence, but in spite of it.

The liturgical evidence lends support to the idea that there was renewed interest in the Conception feast in the early twelfth century. Prayers, legendaries, and calendars in manuscripts from the first half of the twelfth century suggest the feast's celebration at Sherborne, St. Augustine's Canterbury, and Ely.[57] Despite its absence from the eleventh-century post–Norman Conquest sources, at least three Christ Church calendars from the twelfth and thirteenth centuries contain entries for the feast, two of which show that the Conception was celebrated *in cappis altis*, meaning it was conferred the highest-possible liturgical status.[58] At St. Albans, the Norman-appointed abbot Geoffrey Gorron (d. 1146) upgraded the feast to the status *in cappis*, as testified by a number of calendars from his abbacy, including the St. Albans Psalter.[59] By the thirteenth century, the feast was celebrated at Abingdon, Chester Abbey, Ely, Evesham, St. Peter's Abbey Gloucester, and Westminster.[60] The Conception feast's readoption may have additionally paved the way for the revival of the feast of Mary's Presentation in the Temple, which reappears in calendars after 1100.[61]

The case of Bury St. Edmunds deserves special mention. The liturgical and historical sources indicate that the feast of the Conception was adopted between 1121 and 1148 during the abbacy of Anselm (d. 1148), nephew of Anselm of Canterbury and a native of Lombardy.[62] Like Eadmer, the younger Anselm was an important figure in the development of the Marian cult in England and will feature repeatedly throughout this book. Anselm had been a monk at the abbey of St. Michael of Chiusa, in northern Italy, and abbot of St. Sabas in Rome, before traveling to England to become abbot of Bury St. Edmunds, which had a double dedication to Edmund and Mary. Anselm seems to have harbored special personal devotion to the Virgin, and may even have thought himself the recipient of a miracle of Mary's doing, as we will see in a later chapter.[63] He was additionally responsible for the completion of a church in Mary's honor during his abbacy at Bury.[64] The Bury Cartulary records that "this Anselm instituted two feasts at our house, namely the Conception of Holy Mary, which was already celebrated in many churches thanks to him, and the com-

memoration of her instituted by Hildefonsus during Advent."[65] The feast attributed here to the Visigothic bishop of Toledo, ldefonsus (d. 667), was a feast of
the Annunciation that had been celebrated on December 18 only on the Iberian
Peninsula as part of the Old Hispanic rite, which remained in place there until
the end of the eleventh century.[66] The feast had an extended office, which was
made even longer by the use of Ildefonsus's treatise *On the Perpetual Virginity
of Mary* as readings for the morning office. A copy of this treatise is listed
among the late twelfth-century holdings of the Bury library, and could reflect
Anselm's interest in the feast and materials related to it.[67] We additionally find a
record of the feast in an East Anglian calendar from an unknown house copied
in the twelfth century that may reflect Anselm's influence.[68] These are nevertheless the only references to the feast in England until the late Middle Ages, and
its appearance outside Spain is itself extremely unusual. Still, both it and the
feast of the Conception were considered important enough at Bury that pittances of twenty shillings—the same amount reserved for the feast of St. Edmund, and double that for other feast days—are stipulated in Anselm's ordi-
nance; pittances would have provided the monks with extra dishes at meals,
ensuring that the feasts would be regarded fondly.[69] The presence of these unusual feasts at Bury points to the abbot's special interest in Mary. More prag-
matically, he may also have recognized that they could play a crucial role in
promoting Bury's Marian heritage and enhance the profile of the abbey, as proposed by Antonia Gransden.[70]

Abbot Anselm's personal involvement in fostering the Conception feast is
further laid out in a letter addressed to him in early 1129 by Osbert, the prior
of Westminster intermittently until his death in circa 1160.[71] The chronology
of Osbert's life and career is unclear, but what we do know comes from a surviving collection of his letters.[72] These letters show that he was a well-connected
monk with many high-profile friends, including prominent abbots and ab-
besses, and great hopes for a sucessful ecclesiastical career. Yet Osbert failed in
his candidacy for the abbacy at Westminster in the 1120s to the Norman almo-
ner appointed by the king, after which he was exiled from the abbey several
times during the course of his career.[73] Although Osbert did finally return to
Westminster as prior in 1134, his story is one of frustrated ambitions despite
continuous efforts to promote the abbey, even if it required charter forgery and
attempts to have Edward the Confessor canonized as Westminster's own royal
saint.[74] His desire to preserve and promote Anglo-Saxon saints and traditions
may have included the feast of the Conception of Mary, to which his letters
show he was particularly committed.[75]

In his letter to Anselm from 1129, Osbert provided considerable detail about
the controversies that surrounded the celebration of the Conception feast. One
event he recounted involved a heated disagreement that broke out among the
monks of Westminster as they prepared to celebrate the feast of the Conception

of Mary the previous December. Some of the monks went off in protest to find support for their refusal to celebrate the feast, returning with two bishops, Roger of Salisbury and Bernard of St. David's.[76] The bishops demanded a halt to the celebration, saying that the feast had not only been abolished but also forbidden at a previous council.[77] Unfortunately, there is no indication as to which council they meant, nor any record of such a cancellation.[78] Whether or not the bishops were justified in their claim, Osbert wrote in no uncertain terms about their animosity toward the monks who refused to abort the proceedings:

> We, however, persisting joyfully in the services of the day that we had begun, carried out the glorious festival with a solemn celebration. Then my rivals and those who bite like dogs in envy at other's good fortune, who are always striving to advance their own follies for approval, and endeavoring to bring into disrepute the words and deeds of the religious, as the apostle says, "not knowing neither the things they say nor whereof they affirm" (1 Tim. 1:7), they vomited up the poison of their iniquity, and shooting at me the arrows of their pestilent tongues, declared that a festival could not be continued whose origins lacked the authority of the Roman church.[79]

In response to these accusations, Osbert sought precedent for the feast in the Roman tradition from Anselm. "Since you know the customs of the Roman church, by use and experience of them, we beg that you reveal to us whether there is anything in them worthy of authority that could or will be found about this conception of the mother of God, which ought to be celebrated," he asked the abbot.[80] Here, Osbert was referring to the fact that the Conception feast was celebrated at the abbey of St. Sabas in Rome, where Anselm had been abbot before arriving at Bury; the abbey had been founded by monks from St. Sabas in Jerusalem and had maintained Eastern traditions.[81] Anselm must have held great store by the traditions of his former house since he is known to have initiated the celebration of the feast of St. Sabas at Bury together with the feast of the Conception.[82] But Osbert credited him with wanting to revive the Conception feast on a general level, not just at Bury,

> because the intensity of your zeal feverishly inflames many people throughout the world to the love of the blessed and glorious mother of God, Mary, who conceived and gave birth to Christ our lord, the creator of heaven and earth, in her chaste womb of perpetual virginity, and it is by your persistence that the feast of her Conception is celebrated in many places.[83]

Osbert's appeal for Anselm's help may well have secured him the official sanction he sought for the feast's acceptance. An interpolation made in the Gloucester version of the chronicle of John of Worcester relates that in 1129, "a council was held in London in the presence of King Henry where the feast of the Conception of the holy mother of God, Mary, was approved by apostolic authority."[84] The annals of Tewkesbury confirm this.[85] The event to which both annals refer is a council held in London over which King Henry I presided together with a papal legate, and at which the principal issue under discussion was clerical celibacy.[86] Anselm of Bury likely took advantage of his closeness to Henry I in having the feast approved at the council, no doubt with the support of other important ecclesiastical leaders; Osbert had explicitly asked Anselm in his letter to enlist Gilbert, bishop of London (d. 1134), and Hugh, abbot of Reading (d. 1164), in the cause.[87] The second of these was Osbert's friend as the former prior of Lewes, where Osbert had spent years in exile.[88] Osbert claimed in his letter that Hugh had already instituted the Conception feast at the royal abbey of Reading, founded in 1121, on orders from King Henry himself.[89] While Henry's involvement cannot be verified, Hugh's own interest in the feast is made apparent by the fact that he later established it at Rouen, where he became archbishop in 1130.[90] From there, it spread throughout Normandy and northern France.[91] The highly unusual English practice was thus introduced to the Continent, where it stirred up further controversy, as we will see in a later chapter.

For indications of how the feast was actually celebrated, the sources are far less generous. There are only a handful of manuscripts containing the Conception office from the twelfth century that have been surveyed by Solange Corbin, from Lyon, Moissac, Saint-Airy, and Verdun, and the most complete from the abbey of Saint-Martin-des-Champs.[92] The fact that no complete offices from England survive from this period should not discourage us, however. Hugh of Amiens, the abbot of Reading, provides an intriguing link between England and the Saint-Martin office, which is found in a twelfth-century *libellus* inserted into an eleventh-century sermon collection.[93] Like Reading, Saint-Martin had been reformed under Cluniac influence in 1079.[94] Hugh maintained ties with this Parisian house, since his cousin, Matthew of Albano (d. 1134), was prior there before becoming papal legate in 1126.[95] We know that Hugh composed a Marian poem that he sent to a fellow monk and friend at Saint-Martin named William.[96] Could the manuscript with the Conception office have been sent to Saint-Martin by Hugh, a known supporter of the feast? The office is attached to a collection of Marian miracle stories, including a foundation story for the feast of the Conception set in England; as we will see, these collections originated in English monasteries. Further connections to England include the prayer that appears before the Invitatory Antiphon for matins and again as Chapter for Terce, which is shared with the eleventh-century Leofric and Winchester Missals.[97] This prayer is additionally found in a thirteenth-century office in a breviary/missal from Ely.[98] Although many other texts in the Saint-Martin and Ely offices are different, there are enough shared elements to suggest that they may have been based on a common exemplar. It is certainly tempting to see this office as a copy of an English exemplar and then disseminated by an enthusiastic advocate of the feast.

The textual content of the liturgy for the Conception feast is itself a testament of the ways in which it sought to enhance Mary's profile. First of all, the chants are all proper for the feast.[99] Even the hymn for vespers, *Plaude caterva lux*, is unique and not found in the *Analecta Hymnica*.[100] The sequence sung at the mass, *Concinat orbis orians*, is also proper.[101] This indicates that the sung elements were designed specifically for the feast and were not borrowed from other Marian feasts. At first glance, the readings for matins, many of which are shared between the Saint-Martin and Ely offices, seem to be derived from the feast of Mary's Nativity. They are taken from two separate texts: a sermon for the feast of Mary's Nativity attributed to Bernier of Homblières, used for lessons one to eight, in which every mention of Mary's nativity is replaced with her conception, and extracts from Paschasius Radbertus's *Commentary on the Gospel of Matthew* for lessons nine to twelve.[102] The sermon appears earliest in an eleventh-century manuscript from Fécamp, from where it may then have made its way to England, as it is found in a late eleventh-century collection of Marian sermons from Exeter and Leicester as well as twelfth-century manuscripts from Rochester and St. Mary's York.[103] The combination of these two texts establishes Mary's place in a broad conception of time. Lessons one to eight, based on the sermon, begin with Creation and go through biblical history, pointing out the signs and portents for Mary's arrival and her virgin motherhood. The next four lessons, based on the commentary, extend into gospel territory, establishing Mary's genealogy from Paschasius's commentary on the first book of Matthew.[104] Each chant picks up on the theme of the reading and extrapolates with passages from the Hebrew Bible that were read in a Mariological light: the burning bush, the rod of Aaron, the root of Jesse, the cloud of Daniel, and above all Mary's reversal of Eve. Such an accumulation of prophecies, laid out in chronological order, reinterpreted biblical history in a Marian light and placed her at its center.

If many of the above biblical and homiletic texts are standard Marian tropes used in the liturgies for other Marian feast days, the Conception feast was shaped by a unique underlying idea. In both the Saint-Martin and Ely offices, the epistle of the mass that provides the scriptural basis for the entire office is Proverbs 8:22–31: "The Lord brought me forth as the first of his works, before his first deeds. I was formed long ages ago, at the very beginning, before the earth was made. When there were no depths, I was already conceived (*concepta eram*)." The voice that speaks here is that of God's Wisdom. The use of the Proverbs text thus likens Mary to Holy Wisdom as conceived before all things, and the analogy is reinforced with references to Ecclesiastes, which is likewise voiced by Wisdom.[105] The text from Proverbs was used for the chapter of vespers as well, thus setting the tone for the entire day. It echoes a phrase from the fourth lesson of matins: "The very holy body of the Mother of God was predestined from before time for the generating of God's son, and was blessed by the

fathers named here, even though she was born near to the end of the world."[106]
The theme throughout the Conception office is one of prophecy and genealogy,
similar to the feast of the Nativity, but distinct in its emphasis on Mary's origin
and lineage as "conceived" from the beginning of time. As a result, Mary is
placed outside history, with her conception an integral part of God's plan from
the moment of creation. Strikingly, there is no reference to the apocryphal narratives here, apart from a reference in the chapter for terce to the angelic annunciation that accompanied Mary's conception.[107] Rather, it is both the extra-
temporal and biblical roots of Mary's origins that are emphasized: she was
conceived before time but also in time, of Davidic stock. In the office designed
for the feast day, Mary's conception took on eternal proportions.

The importance attributed to Mary by the celebration of her Conception was
expressed in an even more innovative and unusual celebration that originated
in twelfth-century England. The feast of St. Anne, the mother of the Virgin, is
typically considered to be a late medieval innovation, although it may have
been celebrated in the East as early as the sixth century, and there are isolated
and fragmentary liturgical materials from the ninth and eleventh centuries.[108]
The presence of the apocryphal *Trinubium* legend at Bury St. Edmunds, mentioned above, which recounts Anne's own life, attests to awareness in England
of Anne's role as Mary's mother by the end of the eleventh century. In the
twelfth century, however, this interest came to be expressed liturgically. A letter
dated circa 1137 from Osbert to Simon, bishop of Worcester Cathedral, was
written in response to Simon's request for liturgical materials with which to
celebrate the feast of Anne. The fact that the feast was being celebrated with an
extra monastic meal and an octave suggests just how important it already
was.[109] The texts that Osbert produced for it include a sermon, two rhyming
texts, probably hymns for lauds and vespers, and two long prayers, all of which
follow the letter in the manuscript.[110] Osbert wrote these without a direct model
and declares them to be *nova et inusitata*. He nevertheless relied heavily on the
liturgies for other Marian feast days, most notably for the feast of the Conception.[111] In fact, the biblical imagery applied to Anne in the texts that Osbert
composed closely echoes the sermon for the feast of the Conception he composed for Warin the year after.[112] The celebration of the feast of Anne was clearly
connected to the feast of the Conception, both inspired by and perhaps even
thought capable of supporting it; if Mary's mother were a figure worthy of veneration, there would have been no obstacle to celebrating her conception of
Mary. Creating a cult of Anne would have turned the moment of conception
from an act of sin—according to the feast's critics—into a divine act God bestowed on Anne as a saint in her own right.[113]

Osbert's texts for the feast of the Conception and feast of Anne, which
framed Mary's mother as a virtuous and holy person, played into wider issues
of monastic reform, particularly regarding the question of virginity with spe-

cial concern for religious women.[114] As Barbara Newman, Vera Morton, and Jocelyn Wogan-Browne have illustrated, Osbert was one of a group of monks writing advice for nuns, encouraging them to follow a chaste lifestyle that turned their inherently female weakness into *virile* strength.[115] In several letters to female correspondents, including his niece Cecilia, a nun called Ida, and the abbess of Barking abbey, Adelidis, Osbert provided advice and support with a marked emphasis on virginity as the highest virtue.[116] He presented many of the same biblical images in these letters as appear in the liturgy for the Conception and Anne feasts, suggesting that he saw both Mary and Anne as potential role models for nuns.[117] His letter to Adelidis, dated circa 1154, contains a treatise he called "*De armatura castitatis*," in which he listed a number of examples of holy virgins for nuns to follow, including the biblical figure Judith, Cecilia, and the Anglo-Saxon saint Aethelberga. Mary is the prototype, however, listed at the beginning of his treatise as the first virgin who set the mark for all others:

> For virginity, taking its heavenly origin among those above, has obtained the chief place among the first and most excellent citizens of the heavenly city, and has descended in perfect form in the coming of God to man, and of man in the Virgin mother, queen of purity. For she is the mistress of virtues, the jewel of all good works, for in her child-bearing God has become expressly united with man, and without the virtue of virginity his worthy and unstained mother would neither have conceived nor given birth. Other women give birth without the blessing of viginity; from corruptible flesh they give birth to mortal flesh; they give birth, I say to what they conceive; sin from sin, and not seldom do they bring forth a happy issue at great cost to their own life. But indeed virgins are in no way put in danger in childbirth of that kind when they bear spiritual offspring to God; when the creator of virginity, the virgin bridegroom, is he who begets and bears the virgin heart and as a father makes the flesh fruitful with that grace and heavenly seed. These women are imitators of her who, unstained in flesh, bore the Son of God, the son who has consecrated you for himself as bride and virgin.[118]

Osbert went on to give examples of early Christian virgins who were able to remain so because Mary reversed the curse placed on all those who did not bear offspring in Israel; "under grace, she was blessed, the mother who bore Emmanuel for the king and the daughters of Judah for the Lord."[119] In further developing the benefits of marriage to Christ over marriage to mortal men, Osbert made use of the Song of Songs, with all its nuptial imagery, to describe the ideal relationship of the nun with Christ; the text had recently received a uniquely Marian reading by another monk in England, Honorius, as we will see.[120] The fact that Anne appears third among virgins in the litany found in the Shaftesbury Psalter from circa 1130–40 points to just how early Anne was held up as an important saint for religious women in England.[121]

As much as Mary and her mother served as useful illustrations for nuns, the feast of Anne was not envisioned strictly as a celebration for women and was clearly popular at the male monastic cathedral of Worcester. Anne was placed first among the virgins in a twelfth-century litany added to Wulfstan's Portiforium, the eleventh-century prayer book that belonged to the last Anglo-Saxon bishop of Worcester.[122] A unique sequence was added in the twelfth century to the end of the Caligula Troper, an eleventh-century collection of neumed tropes, likely produced at Worcester.[123] The sequence, accompanied by Anglo-Norman neumes, shares considerable biblical echoes with the texts Osbert composed, and may have been inspired by them.[124] The feast clearly was not just celebrated at Worcester, though. Osbert writes in a later letter to Warin, the dean of Worcester, that "the treatise I wrote concerning Anne, having done so in order to please the faithful, has already spread to many churches for the feast's solemn veneration."[125] This chimes with the manuscript evidence. Anne features in a late twelfth-century litany from Winchester, two thirteenth-century litanies from Evesham, and thirteenth-century litanies from Bury St. Edmunds, Christ Church Canterbury, Shrewsbury, and Reading, in addition to the women's houses of Wilton and Carrow; apart from the first example, she appears either first or second in all of these.[126] For evidence in calendars of the feast's celebration, we have to wait until the thirteenth century, when it begins to appear in manuscripts from Winchester and Evesham; there is also a surviving mass text from thirteenth-century St. Augustine's.[127] The feast of Anne provides a noteworthy instance of how the already-pioneering liturgical practice of celebrating Mary's Conception went one step further: through the adoption of a new feast for a new saint linked to the Virgin, and one that was designed to appeal to male and female monastics alike.[128]

Such liturgical innovation was reflected in the distinct and unusually prominent role Anne was given in visual sources in this period. At least one of these had older roots, since we find images in the eleventh-century section of the Caligula Troper that depict Mary's parents and early life in unusual ways. Embedded within the tropes for the feast of the Assumption are unprecedented depictions of Joachim and Anne; while there are earlier Byzantine models for the image of Joachim tending his flock, a second image of Joachim and Anne holding the baby Mary has no known prototype.[129] The Winchester Psalter adds further original scenes to the early life cycle of Mary. The first, full-page, tripartite image has recently been reinterpreted to exclude the possibility that it represents Joachim receiving the annunciation about Mary's birth, as some scholars had thought, although its model was certainly the Caligula Troper.[130] The second image in the Winchester manuscript, appearing some folios later, is nevertheless unmistakable in its depiction of scenes from the early life of Mary (figure 1).

Figure 1. Winchester Psalter, in BL Cotton Nero C. iv, f. 8r, circa 1150. © The British Library Board, British Library Cotton MS Nero C. iv, f. 8.

The top third of the image shows Anne receiving an angelic message of Mary's birth, and next to this, meeting Joachim at the Golden Gate.[131] In the middle register of this same folio, Anne lies in childbirth. In the lowest section, Anne presents the baby Mary at the Temple, followed by Joachim and a woman, each bearing doves. The images are strongly reminiscent of those that depict the equivalent moments in Christ's life (the Annunciation, Visitation, Nativity, and Presentation) in the same manuscript and others. Yet they are the first representations in English art of Mary's own life cycle.[132] By providing Mary with a parallel sequence to Christ's, they offered a visual dimension to the liturgical innovations that had given new importance to the events of Mary's life.

LITURGY: OFFICES

Devotion to Mary was manifested in the liturgy not just by the addition of feast days but also by an increase in more regular practices, which included masses and offices that both replaced and supplemented the regular hours of the day. The daily Little Office was a votive office celebrated in Mary's honor in addition to the canonical hours of a given day, whereas the weekly Saturday office was a commemorative office that replaced each of the hours, making every Saturday a celebration of Mary. These practices became the most notable expressions of Marian devotion, bringing Mary into the daily and weekly celebration of the liturgy. Such frequent repetition would have made the Marian offices and masses some of the best-known parts of the liturgy. Contrary to the general reform ideal of pruning the liturgy, as carried out most notably by the Cistercians, the addition of elaborate Marian commemoration—public as well as private—extended it considerably. Such practices are therefore a testament to how central she was becoming in medieval religious culture.

Many of the regular Marian practices originated or were inspired by monastic reform movements of the early Middle Ages. Weekly masses entered the liturgical landscape in the Carolingian era. Alcuin of York promoted and perhaps even composed a Marian mass for Saturdays as part of a series of masses for each day of the week perhaps from an Eastern example.[133] By the late tenth century, the weekly Marian mass had expanded into a weekly three-lesson office recited every Saturday at German monasteries of the Görze reform movement and was adopted at Monte Cassino by the early eleventh century.[134] Cluny seems to have adopted a daily votive office for Mary, or Little Office sung in addition to the canonical office, by the late eleventh century.[135] It seems however, that the Marian office was restricted to the infirmary chapel, which was dedicated to Mary, according to the customary of Bernard (ca. 1074) and statues of the abbot Peter the Venerable (d. 1156).[136] The late eleventh-century reformer Peter Damian promoted a daily Marian office, claiming he celebrated a commemorative office on Saturdays because "whosoever strives to recite these hours daily in her honour will have the mother of the Judge as his helper and advocate in his day of need."[137] In a letter dated 1066, Peter described how the monks of St. Vincent, in the northeastern Italian region of Marche, had been celebrating the daily Little Office for three years by that point, until it was canceled because it was deemed excessive.[138] Jean Leclercq identified a number of other eleventh- and twelfth-century examples of these offices, the majority of which appear to be Benedictine in origin.[139]

The spread of the practice of singing the Hours of Mary may have received a significant boost from Pope Urban II, the reform pope who issued the call to the First Crusade. Later records by the chronicler Geoffrey of Vigeois (d. 1184) and Vincent of Beauvais (d. ca. 1264) of the Council of Clermont-Ferrand in 1095, where Urban gave his sermon urging the armies of Europe to free Jerusalem, describe that Urban at the same time decreed that a daily Little Office and full commemorative office on Saturdays should be celebrated in every church.[140] Some churches already had the practice, Geoffrey explained, and celebrated it with a nine-lesson matins, except on important feast days and vigils.[141] From these references it is difficult to know whether the decree was indeed made.[142] Still, other evidence of the growing popularity and importance of celebrating Mary with both votive and commemorative offices toward the turn of the twelfth century complements this record.

Once again, England seems to have been ahead of the times with respect to the performance of regular Marian offices. The *Regularis Concordia*, the monastic customary produced as a result of the Anglo-Saxon monastic reforms of the late tenth century, includes distinctive practices such as Alcuin's Saturday Marian mass and daily antiphons to be sung for the Virgin.[143] Expanding on these practices, E. S. Dewick was convinced from his survey of manuscripts that the earliest surviving examples of the daily votive Marian office were English in origin, and other sources support an early adoption of the practice in England, as surveyed by both Clayton and Sally Roper.[144] These scholars indicate that Bishop Aethelwold (d. 984) was responsible for the introduction at Winchester of a short daily office, modeled on vespers, in Mary's honor, at least according to his twelfth-century biography (*horas regulares et peculiares sibi ad singulare servitium instituit . . . ad laudem Dei genitricis*).[145] Just such an office is found in the Aelfwine Prayerbook (ca. 1023–35).[146] This daily office then grew to comprise a complete parallel cursus in the mid- to late eleventh century, the date of two Anglo-Saxon offices found in a psalter and a miscellany. Dewick considered these the earliest examples of such offices to survive anywhere in Europe.[147] The offices correspond to each of the canonical hours, from matins to compline, and include a lengthy litany.[148] Not only do they have unique features that differentiate them from offices that appeared later on the Continent, but there is some indication that they were intended for communal recitation by the entire monastic community in the choir rather than for personal devotional practice.[149] In addition, Roper notes that the Marian office found in the late eleventh-century Portiforium of Wulstan of Worcester, which seems to have been said in addition to the normal office for the day, is probably the earliest-surviving example of its kind specifically for Saturdays.[150] Moreover, Wulfstan's *Vita*, written by William of Malmesbury, describes the bishop frequently saying the Hours of the Virgin, sometimes taking a reluctant monk as companion in his all-night vigils.[151] The evidence for both kinds of offices—daily and weekly offices—points to an unusually early and especially full celebration of Mary in eleventh-century England.

After the Norman Conquest, there is some suggestion that the communal practice of singing the Hours of Mary disappeared. Edmund Bishop argued explicitly that the Marian office "was abolished by the newcomers, the men of model observance, as mere Englishry," and this seems to be confirmed by Roper's assessment of the sources.[152] The office may have encountered the same opposition as the Conception feast for its elevation of Mary to such special status, although there is no testimony on the question equivalent to Eadmer's treatise or Osbert's letters. Lanfranc's monastic customary, the *Constitutions*, makes no mention of the practice, even though it does maintain votive practices for All Saints and the dead.[153] Lanfranc also changed the location of the Marian altar in his reconstruction of Christ Church cathedral after the fire of 1067, from the raised west end oratory it shared with the archbishop's seat, to the north side of the nave beside the choir.[154] Although he had a Lady Chapel installed, this was a secondary altar, and suggests use for private votive offices and masses, not communal ones.[155] None of the post–Norman Conquest liturgical manuscripts from Christ Church contain the Marian office, private or communal.[156]

As with the Conception feast, there are signs that votive and commemorative masses along with offices of Mary were revived in the early twelfth century. Morgan cites several examples of such practices—communal and private, daily and weekly—established in this period, which Roper has surveyed, providing helpful lists in extensive appendixes.[157] Once, again, we see various forms of practice being adopted. First, there is the daily Marian mass, which was adopted on a communal level for the first time at Rochester between 1134 and 1154, according to Gerald of Wales, and at Bury St. Edmunds and Tewkesbury.[158] The Saturday mass was increased to a full Saturday commemoration in the earliest-surviving English breviary, from Winchcombe, circa 1125–50, which contains a fragmentary Saturday office with a twelve-lesson matins office.[159] At St. Albans, the Saturday commemoration was held in such high esteem by circa

1140–50 that it was celebrated in albs with provisions for wine or mead.[160] The *Gesta Abbatum* has a record that the abbot Radulf (1146–51) added a procession to the altar of the Virgin as part of the celebration.[161] By 1200, the St. Albans monks were saying the weekly office from memory, without candles.[162] The same record indicates that the office was still not celebrated everywhere, or at least not in albs, which is indicative of its importance at St. Albans.[163]

The twelfth century saw the introduction of daily votive offices for Mary more generally in England, although their length varied greatly. Normally, the Little Office had a single nocturn with three lessons for matins.[164] A three-lesson office is found in the same St. Albans breviary that contains the full twelve-lesson Saturday commemorative office.[165] Longer daily offices with a full twelve-lesson matins are found in a psalter from Mulcheney, and one that may have become the personal property of Matilda of Balleuil, abbess of Wherwell, each of which contain the hours from matins to compline.[166] The supporter of the Conception feast, Abbot Anselm, is also said to have established the Little Office at Bury St. Edmunds, in addition to a daily Marian mass. The Bury Customary describes how the office was to be celebrated on ferial days communally, with modifications when the day on which it fell was significant enough to be celebrated in copes—that is, only the most important feast days.[167] The manuscript also contains a full commemorative office at the end, together with one for Edmund, the abbey's other patron saint.[168] Roper concluded from her survey of the sources that "communal daily recitation of all or part of this office [of Mary] seems to have been commonplace in English Benedictine houses by c. 1250."[169]

To illustrate what votive practice in Benedictine houses looked like, it is worth briefly presenting the structure of matins with a few examples of chants and readings from the Little Office performed at Muchelney abbey, a small Anglo-Saxon foundation in the vicinity of Glastonbury.[170] The office comes at the end of a psalter and follows a fairly standard format found in other similar offices, such as the mid-twelfth-century office associated with Matilda of Balleuil, although there is enough variety among surviving examples to suggest that there was no one uniform use of texts in the Little Office.[171] After the usual prefatory material that precedes all monastic matins, we find the hymn *Quem terra pontus aethera*, written by the sixth-century Latin poet Venantius Fortunatus (d. ca. 600). The hymn introduces the idea that the almighty Lord and God rested in the womb of the Virgin, and then addresses Mary as the blessed mother whose womb was the ark that contained the great Creator.[172] "And in this way, the dwelling place of all us happy ones is in you, Holy mother of God," reads the antiphon that follows (*Sicut laetantium omnium*), shifting the idea from Mary physically housing Christ to Mary spiritually protecting her followers. The lessons and their corresponding responsories then run as follows:

Table 1. BL Add. MS 21927

Lectio prima

Sancta Maria virgo virginum mater et filia regis regum omnium tuum nobis impende solatium ut celestis regni per te habere mereamur premium.

    Tu autem miserere nobis.

First lesson

Holy Virgin Mary, mother of virgins and daughter of the king of all kings, bestow your consolation on us that through you we might deserve to have the reward of the heavenly kingdom.

    Have mercy on us.

Responsorium

Sancta et inmaculata virginitas quibus te laudibus referam nescio quia quem celi capere non poterant tuo gremio contulisti.

Responsory

Holy and immaculate virginity, I do not know with what praise to shower you, because you bore in your womb he whom the heavens could not contain.

Versus

Benedicta tu in mulieribus et benedictus fructus ventris tui. [Quia quem celi.]

Verse

Blessed are you among women and blessed is the fruit of your womb. [Repetition of "because you bore in your womb he whom the heavens could not contain" from the responsory.]

Lectio secunda

Sancta Maria piarum piissima intercede pro nobis sanctarum sanctissima per te virgo nostra sumat precamina qui pro nobis natus regnat super ethera ut sua caritate nostra deleantur peccata. Tu autem.

Second lesson

Holy Mary, most pious of the pious, intercede on our behalf, most saintly of the saints, that through you, our virgin, he might take up our prayers, your son who reigns for us over the heavens and may our sins be absolved by his love.

    Have mercy on us.

Responsorium

Beata es Maria quae dominum portasti creatorem mundi genuisti qui te fecit et in eternum permanes virgo.

Responsory

Blessed are you Mary, who carried the Lord and gave birth to the creator of the world (who made you) and remain forever a virgin.

Versus

Ave Maria gratia plena dominus tecum. Genuisti.

Verse

Hail Mary, full of grace, the Lord be with you. [Repetition from "gave birth."]

Lectio tertia

Sancta dei genitrix quae digne meruisti concipere quem totus orbis nequivit comprehendere tuo pio interventu culpas nostras ablue ut perhennis sedem gloriae per te redempti valeamus scandere ubi regnas cum filio sine tempore. Tu.

Third lesson

Holy mother of God, you who rightfully deserved to conceive what the entire world could not understand, absolve our sins by your pious intercession that we, once redeemed, might be worthy of the seat of glory forever more and ascend to where you reign with your son for eternity.

    Have mercy on us.

Table 1. BL Add. MS 21927

Responsorium	Responsory
Felix namque es sacra virgo Maria et omni laude dignissima quia ex te ortus est sol iustitiae Christus Deus noster.	For happy are you, holy virgin Mary, and most worthy of all praise because from you was born the sun of justice, Christ, our God.
Versus Ora pro populo interveni pro clero intercede pro devoto femineo sexu sentiant omnes tuum iuvamen qui cumque celebrant tuam commemorationem. [Quia ex] Gloria.	*Verse* Pray for your people, intervene on behalf of clerics, intercede on behalf of devoted women, may all receive your aid, those who celebrate your commemoration. [Repetition from "because from you."] *Doxology* Glory be to God.

The accumulation of imagery in this section of the office, although not particularly radical in its theological content, nevertheless presents a powerful picture of Mary's importance as greatest of virgins and merciful mother; she is called on repeatedly to bestow her mercy on the penitent. Thinking that this office would have been performed every day, except during certain especially solemn times of the year, gives us a sense of just how central Mary would have been in the devotional world of the monks and nuns performing it—a centrality expressed in every chant and reading of the office.[173]

The practice of performing offices in Mary's honor so frequently would have created a distinct and special relationship between Mary and her earthly followers. First, by praising Mary every day in such heightened terms, it created and reinforced the sense that Mary stood above all other saints, even if she was not the patron of a particular institution. But the liturgy was not just about praising; the expectation was that the individuals who sang Mary's praise would be rewarded in turn. Calling on her in the second person, as so many of the chants and readings in both commemorative and votive offices do, Mary was brought into the present, and invited to come forth among the choirs of monks and nuns performing the liturgy, with the specific purpose of bestowing her mercy on them. As can be seen from the above examples, many of the lessons of matins for both commemorative and votive offices were in fact prayers, asking for Mary's personal intercession on behalf of her penitent supplicants. Liturgy *was* prayer, with the hope that Mary would return the favor, as this prayer from a twelfth-century Westminster office makes plain: "O blessed virgin Mary, most worthy of all praise, queen of heaven, ruler of angels, intercessor for sinners . . . we entrust ourselves to your intercession, Lady, and also to your advocacy, imploring that, while we celebrate your divine service on earth, you, glorious lady, with assiduous prayer design to help us in heaven."[174] Prayers could also be particularly affective in nature. "We beseech you with tearful sighs, that you might bend your ear to the moan of our sadness," reads part of the first lesson of matins in the St. Albans commemorative office.[175] Hope was not lost as long as appeal was made to Mary, for "there is nothing so depraved in us that you cannot eradicate by praying, if you should so wish," as reads the second lesson in the same office.[176] The performance of commemorative and votive offices for Mary thus created a reciprocal relationship between the community and Mary through the expression of the penitents' hope to receive Mary's intercession, sung and intoned in the liturgy.

This desire to obtain Mary's intercession on behalf of the community singing her praises could become especially pressing under specific historical circumstances, as we find in one key manuscript. One of the two earliest-surviving Marian offices was added to a psalter associated with the female religious house connected to Winchester, Nunnaminster. It attests to a particular motivation for performing the communal office, which is explained only by the immediate context in which it was written.[177] A prayer precedes the eleventh-century office, asking for Mary's support:

> To our anguish, holy Mary and perpetual virgin, the possession of your holy church, which contributed to the nourishment of your servants, was snatched by the hand of our enemy. Please ensure, lady, that the enemy who did not fear to take over your possession does not rejoice. Repay him according to his acts of malice because he troubled our hearts, which are set in our faith in you, and set no store in reverence to your house. Promise that all of those who supported him will feel the strength of your vengeance, and because they insulted you with abuse, let them understand what torment is. We pray also to you, St. Machutus, confessor, and you, venerable virgin St. Eadburga, that you might commend our tribulation to God, and punish the depraved counsels of our enemies with their own perpetual damnation, and obtain his eternal mercy for us.[178]

Dewick has explained that this prayer refers to the fact that the manor of Itchen Abbas was stripped from Nunnaminster by Hugh Fitz Baldric, a Norman noble.[179] Mary is asked to punish him for having plundered the house, beseeched as a vengeful saint as well as merciful protector of the abbey.[180] The prayer may have been intended to precede the performance of the Little Office that follows it in the manuscript, the whole of which would then have been performed as a plea for Mary to defend the convent's property and recover what was lost. This use of the Hours of Mary for the pragmatic purpose of guaranteeing the protection of a community is not unprecedented. It is attested in Damian's letters the century before; he chastised his fellow monks for failing to keep up the Little Office, which in his view explained the succession of plagues, attacks, and natural disasters the abbey had suffered.[181] At Nunnaminster too, an institution dedicated to the Virgin, Mary was clearly seen not just as a symbolic figurehead but also as a real protector, who could act in the world when called on via the liturgy to help preserve her devotees in troubled times. In addition to praising Mary in ever more elaborate forms, the liturgy was a way to affirm her patronage, and as Parkes has described with respect to Edmund at Bury, "Patronage was a personal relationship to be nourished continually through prayer."[182] Through the adoption of liturgical appeals to Mary for safety and support, monastic institutions helped consolidate her role as an especially valued saintly intercessor for both devoted individuals and entire communities.

PRAYER

The liturgical celebration of Mary as a saint worthy of appeal for help, both spiritual and material, became supplemented in the twelfth century by new forms of prayer.[183] As is made evident in the Nunnaminster manuscript, liturgical practices like the Little Office were intimately connected with prayer. There was in fact no clear distinction between private and communal forms of prayer in the monastic context, as many of the prayers embedded in Marian offices attest.[184] Still, collections of prayers were produced in growing numbers in the eleventh and twelfth centuries.[185] Many such collections surveyed by Boynton may have served to occupy the monks as they sat in the church between matins and lauds, placing them in a liturgical context, though not officially as part of the liturgy.[186] Since these manuscripts also tend to contain commemorative and votive offices, it is difficult to tell what was intended for public performance and what was reserved for private contemplation. This is not to say that there was no provision for private prayer. Lanfranc's *Constitutions* stipulates that should a monk wish to pray on his own, he could do so at side altars or in other parts of the church.[187] The inward turn of twelfth-century religious life meant that prayer became a key means by which monks and nuns, as much alone as together, could approach the saints—and especially Mary—by appealing for aid, succor, and salvation.[188]

Prayer to Mary was evolving in the late eleventh century, as explored especially by Rachel Fulton.[189] It was in this period that the most famous of Marian invocations, the "Hail Mary" (*Ave Maria*), came into its own as a prayer independent of the liturgical context. The formula dates back to the seventh century, when it became the offertory for the mass of Ember Wednesday and feast of the Annunciation; the text continued to be used in liturgical contexts throughout the Middle Ages, particularly as antiphons.[190] Use of the text independently as a prayer only really emerged in the late eleventh century, however, and it was not until the thirteenth century that it became mandatory for all Christians to know it.[191]

Morgan has pointed to the rich tradition of Marian prayer that emerged in Anglo-Norman England as a part of this wider trend. The *Ave* prayer was already being reinterpreted in innovative ways in the twelfth century, such as in a prayer to the Virgin found at the end of a psalter associated with the female house of Shaftesbury, circa 1125.[192] It consists of twenty-six verses of praise beginning with the word *Ave* in a litany of praise for Mary. The prayer runs through Christ's life, highlighting Mary's role in it, and praising her for having been chosen by God to bear Christ, giving birth and tending to him as a baby, listening to him preach, witnessing him die and resurrect, and generally being the lady of angels, queen of heaven, haven of the sinful, and the eternal immaculate Virgin. The simple but rich text of the Shaftesbury prayer is shared with and even expanded on in two other manuscripts of English origin, from Winchcombe and Winchester, pointing to its popularity among monks as well as nuns.[193] It is also strikingly similar in form to the hymn *Ave mater advocati*, made popular because of its attribution to Anselm, though the actual author is still unknown.[194] The hymn is long, with three parts containing fifty verses each, every verse beginning with the word *Ave* and an address to Mary, invoking her as *advocatrix* and *reparatrix*, terms whose significance will be made clear in the next chapter.[195] Other innovations include the first-known use of famous prayers such as *O beata et intemerata* and *Intemerata Virgo Maria*.[196] Many new such prayers to Mary are found in psalters produced in twelfth-century England.

Perhaps the best-known Marian prayers produced in this period were by Anselm, the second post–Norman Conquest archbishop of Canterbury (1093–1109). While still abbot of Bec, Anselm wrote a series of nineteen prayers, three among them dedicated to the Virgin. These texts are seen by some scholars as having heralded a new era in devotional writing as well as being a watershed in approaches to Mary. Richard Southern certainly thought Anselm a seminal influence on Marian devotion in twelfth-century religious culture, claiming that his prayers and meditations represented an "Anselmian Revolution" in affective piety with special relevance for evolving attitudes toward Mary.[197] Fulton has since made a similar case, expanding considerably on Southern's observation and discussing Anselm's prayers from the perspective of lived experience.[198]

In some ways, Anselm's revolution was built on quite-old foundations.[199] His approach clearly inherited from the emotional style of Anglo-Saxon prayers, with their stress on the contrast between the self-abasing sinner and exalted Virgin.[200] Northern French and specifically Norman sources were formative, too, including the affective works of John of Fécamp (d. 1078), Fulbert of Chartres (d. 1028), and Maurilius, archbishop of Rouen (d. 1067).[201] Maurilius in particular had exercised personal influence on Anselm, encouraging him to take up the monastic habit at Bec. He had also written a popular and effusive prayer to the Virgin by adapting one of the famous Carolingian prayers, *Singularis meriti*. Maurilius lengthened it considerably and infused it with more plaintive language:

> What am I doing, repeating my obscenities to unpolluted ears? I shudder, my lady, I shudder and, my conscience betraying me, blush to stand dejectedly before you, naked. To whom should I, who lie dying, offer my wound? Whom will I go to, to whom will I bemoan my pain? And when and from where can I hope for the gifts of wholeness, if that singular resting place of eternal piety is closed to me? Therefore hear me, lady, hear my prayers, hear and listen to the citizen, lost from a share in your inheritance, returning, after a long exile, after foul wantonness, after many sufferings, to the breast of your consolation.[202]

Maurilius's prayer appealed to monastic sensibilities in England, where his plea to the "uncorrupted mother of mercy" is found in at least eleven late eleventh- and twelfth-century psalters, including the Shaftesbury Psalter, in which it directly follows the *Ave* prayer mentioned above.[203] There was clearly an interest in this form of penitential prayer on both sides of the English Channel in the late eleventh century from which Anselm could draw.[204]

There are further indications beyond his possible use of external sources that Anselm's prayers were part of a wider movement in private monastic prayer in the Anglo-Norman realm that came to involve Mary. While some of his other prayers were written for Adelaide, daughter of William the Conqueror (ca. 1072), and a full collection was sent to Matilda, Countess of Tuscany (ca. 1104), the impetus for his three prayers to Mary (1072–77) came at the repeated insistence of a monk of Bec. In his introductory letter to the dedicatee of the Marian prayers, Gundulf, the former sacrist of Bec and eventual bishop of Rochester, Anselm reveals that he had been asked "not once but many times" to compose "a great prayer to St Mary." Apparently not Gundulf but another monk had made the request, though Anselm concedes that "what he [the other monk], being present, asked outwardly (*exterius*), you, being absent, persuaded me inwardly (*interius*)."[205] The monk was apparently dissatisfied with Anselm's preliminary efforts, and for this reason, Anselm felt compelled to write two further prayers: "I wrote the first prayer as was asked of me, but knowing that I had not satisfied the asker, I was invited to write another. With this one I similarly failed to satisfy, but I pulled off the third one, which is finally all right."[206] In the now-standard English translation of Anselm's *Meditations* by Benedicta Ward, Anselm's belaboring is attributed to his own perfectionism, perhaps under the assumption that the petitioner was invented as a trope of humility.[207] The Latin here nevertheless points a finger at another monk who first asked for the text and urged Anselm to improve on his initial attempt. While such remarks in prefaces are common in twelfth-century works, as Gransden has argued, they should not necessarily be dismissed from the outset as mere topoi.[208]

Without needing to take the words of his introductory letter at face value, I think we have to acknowledge this important aspect of Anselm's contribution to twelfth-century Marian devotion.[209] We need to consider the possibility that Anselm's work was a response to an existing form of prayer rather than a case of invention ex nihilo. This would not have been altogether unexpected since Bec was dedicated to Mary—one of a small number of Norman houses that boasted the Virgin's patronage—and Anselm fully recognized Mary's significance to Bec's institutional identity.[210] As he wrote to one of the Bec novices, "I beseech almighty God, who has cut you off from love of worldly vanity, and his most holy mother, who received you into her protection when you fled to her, to guard you against all confusion at the outset of your newly begun life."[211] Anselm's prayers therefore should not be taken just as an indicator of his own, personal devotion to the Virgin.[212] Sarah McNamer argued the same with respect to the devotional works of John of Fécamp.[213] In Anselm's case, the horizon of expectation was such that his contemporaries may not have considered his prayers to be quite so radical—in fact, not radical enough. The process by which Anselm arrived at his Marian prayers could imply a culture that sought out the forms of piety thought by scholars to have been invented by Anselm.

Despite the fact that he may just have been fulfilling a need expressed by his monks, Anselm did take prayer to the Virgin in new directions.[214] His writing process suggests this, since these are among his most heavily edited works, bearing the marks of numerous emendations and additions, particularly the third prayer.[215] There is a distinct progression in the prayers, from more conventional to more radical in their claims about Mary's role in the history of salvation. The rubrics of Anselm's prayers indicate they were envisioned in their final version as one meditative work that sought to inspire the highest love for the Virgin, although Anselm specifies that due to their considerable length, the penitent should be able to jump in wherever he wishes.[216] But if read through, there is a clear trajectory, which as described by Marilyn McCord Adams,

> exercises to train *the emotions*, according to a dialectical pattern reaching back through Benedict to Cassian to Origen: first the reader is stirred out of inertia into self-knowledge, which produces sorrow for sin, dread of its consequences, and anxiety over distance from God; these last in turn produce humility and issue in prayers for help, which resolve into a compunction of desire which energizes the soul's renewed search for God.[217]

The first prayer, titled "Prayer to Holy Mary When the Mind Is Burdened by Heaviness" (*Oratio ad Sanctam Mariam cum mens gravatur torpore*), centers on the ignominy of the sinner hoping for Mary's intervention.[218] In this it echoes the long tradition of pious supplication in much of the Anglo-Saxon and Carolingian material already in general circulation, and particularly the prayer of Maurilius.[219] The next prayer, to be said "when the mind is anxious with fear" (*cum mens est sollicita timore*), presents the penitent in great fear on Judgment Day, calling on Mary as *mundi reconciliatrix* (reconciler of the world) to intercede with Christ as *mundi judex* (judge of the world). But rather than maintain a clear separation between the merciful mother and her harsh son, Anselm's prayer addresses the two in tandem: "when I have sinned against the son, I have alienated the mother," laments the penitent, but equally finds hope that "good Lord and good Lady, dear son and dear mother, by this truth which is the only hope of sinners, that you will be her son and you will be his mother to save this sinner."[220] Later he implores, "God, who was made the son of a woman out of mercy; woman, who was made mother of God out of mercy; have mercy on this wretch, you forgiving, you interceding."[221] Blurring the lines between the two by constantly addressing one in the function of the other, Anselm links mother and son inextricably in the penitent's plea for salvation, while considering each a source of succor and support: "So the accused flees from the just God to the good mother of the merciful God; the accused finds refuge from the mother he has offended in the good son of the kind mother."[222] "It was this effort that set Anselm's prayers in a class of their own, it being the goal to establish no less than the salvific reciprocity of Christ and Mary, their mutual interdependence as Son and Mother in the work of salvation," Fulton writes on the subject of Anselm's second prayer.[223]

After prayer number one shows the penitent debased before Mary, and prayer number two pleads with her and her son on Judgment Day, the third prayer "to Mary in seeking her and Christ's love" (*pro impetrando eius et Christi amore*) completes the cycle by allowing the penitent some hope in the love and mercy of Christ's mother. Here Mary is addressed alone, placed at the center of the penitent's attention, because as the prayer says, "I am sure that since through the Son I could receive grace, I can receive it again through the merits of the mother."[224] Mary's ability to provide this makes her worthy of infinite praise, which is what the rest of the prayer offers. Anselm's final version of the prayer gave her a more exalted position than ever before:

> Nothing equals Mary, nothing but God is greater than Mary. God gave his own Son, who alone from his heart was born equal to him, loved as he loves himself, to Mary, and of Mary was then born a Son not another but the same one, that naturally one might be the Son of God and of Mary. All nature is created by God, and God is born of Mary. God created all things, and Mary gave birth to God. God who made all things made himself of Mary, and thus he refashioned everything he had made. He who was able to make all things out of nothing refused to remake it by force, but first became the Son of Mary. So God is the Father of all created things, and Mary is the mother of all re-created things. God is the Father of all that is established, and Mary is the mother of all that is reestablished. For God gave birth to him by whom all things were made, and Mary brought forth

him by whom all are saved. God brought forth him without whom nothing is, Mary bore him without whom nothing is good.[225]

Mary is in a position of almost total supremacy, here placed just below God. As Fulton puts it, in giving the Virgin such centrality in the work of salvation, Anselm made "Mary . . . the way through whom all creation came back to life: as Mother of the God-man, she is the Re-creator of God's creation."[226] It is crucial to remember that Anselm himself thought this third prayer best captured what he had wanted to say about Mary.[227] It brings the penitent from cowering fear in prayers one and two, to the incitement of love for the Virgin, the ultimate goal of meditating with Anselm's texts. Although Fulton has portrayed Anselm's contribution to Marian devotion as one in which we see the "translation of the queenly Intercessor into the grieving Mother," it instead seems that this queenly—if also human—intercessor is most dominant in the three prayers to the Virgin.[228] Mary does not weep at the foot of the cross in the Marian prayers as she does in one of Anselm's prayers to Christ but rather stands triumphant at her son's side, worthy of the penitent's veneration and love by virtue of her almost-complete identification with Christ.[229] In Anselm's new language for addressing Mary, she was the ultimate *mediatrix* with Christ because she was so close to him by virtue of their shared flesh. While giving Mary unprecedented status, the prayers also bring her into the most intimate relationship with her all too human supplicants: "*Mater dei est mater nostra*" (The mother of God is our mother). The characteristics that were increasingly being attributed to Christ—humility and humanity—were equally to be found in Mary, if not more so, and Anselm's prayers went a long way in pushing forward the potential for closeness between the universal mother and her children. It was the paradox of her humble humanity and exalted status that made her the perfect saint to whom to appeal for aid and forgiveness.

The reception history of Anselm's prayers points to a receptive audience that recognized Anselm's unique style of approaching Mary. It was no doubt in part thanks to Gundulf, who had already followed Lanfranc across the English Channel when the prayers were composed, that they began to circulate in considerable numbers in monasteries in England as well as Normandy.[230] Anselm's prayers were initially integrated into the prayer tradition, copied without specific attribution in collections of prayers that followed the style of the anonymous Anglo-Saxon and Carolingian prayer books. They were also at times appended to psalters, as had commonly been the case.[231] Anselm's name was firmly attached, however, to later collections of prayers. Some of these prayers were his own, whereas others were mistakenly attributed to him, including that of Maurilius and a series of prayers by Ralph, abbot of Battle Abbey. This consciousness about the authorship of devotional texts for private prayer was new; no prayers had previously circulated under the name of a known author.[232] The spur to compose prayers in Mary's honor may have come from a preexisting practice of appealing to the Virgin in contrite and emotional forms in the Anglo-Norman monastic milieu, but the shape that Anselm's prayers took from early on in their history reveals his unique contribution to making Mary an instrumental figure of intercession.

One of the eager recipients for Anselm's Marian prayers was Eadmer, his onetime secretary and companion. Eadmer was not just wholeheartedly devoted to his mentor but also to the Virgin Mary. In laying out a Marian theology, Eadmer went further than Anselm had ever dared go in exalting her above other human beings. This is especially evident in his treatise on the Conception, which will be discussed in greater detail in a following chapter. About a decade before he composed *De conceptione*, though, he had written an extensive devotional treatise in praise of Mary with a similar tone to Anselm's prayers. This text, *De excellentia Virginis Mariae*, was written, in Southern's view, circa 1115.[233] Despite the fact that it has received little scholarly attention, it represents one of the clearest examples of the early twelfth-century monastic interest in the cult of the Virgin, along with the innovative directions it took and heights to which Mary was elevated as a result.[234]

De excellentia is a meditative text designed for contemplation of various important moments in the Virgin's life. It covers her birth and childhood, the Annunciation, the Crucifixion, and Ascension of Christ, through to her own Dormition and Assumption. The central sections concern her relationship with Christ, dealing with her love for her son, as she suffered alongside him during the Passion, and her joy at both his resurrection and ascension. Eadmer described the love God had for Mary that made him choose her as his dwelling place, and the love she showed him in turn by vowing her virginity to him. He also compared the magnitude of their love for each other to that which comes naturally between a mother and her only offspring, expressed in the sweet care Mary took in holding the child Jesus and comforting him as he cried on her knee.[235] With such great love, how much greater, then, was her suffering at his death? While the rest of the apostles disappeared, apart from John, Mary stood staunchly by her son as he died, with "[her] soul pierced by the sword of pain," as prophesied to her by Simeon (Luke 1:35). Here Eadmer echoed Anselm's prayer to Christ on the cross, in which Anselm invited the penitent to look on the Crucifixion scene through Mary's eyes: "My most merciful Lady, what can I say about the fountains that flowed from your most pure eyes when you saw your only Son before you, bound beaten and hurt?"[236] But for Eadmer, after the horror, Mary rejoiced more than any other at seeing her son not just resurrected but also made Lord of all creation. Eadmer encouraged the penitent to meditate on her love, thereby bringing them to think about Mary's joy. "Therefore, if it is so useful to bring to mind the name of the mother of God, it should be no surprise if frequent meditation on her great love bears the fruit of great salvation, and if the magnitude of her joy is remembered again and again with sweet zeal, it brings about complete happiness," he urged.[237] From fear and pain to love: the penitent followed the same course as Mary herself through the events of her life, and the same course as Anselm set out in his meditations, thereby drawing the penitent into Mary's life, and Mary into the penitent's.[238]

De excellentia does not limit itself, however, to retelling biblical events but instead dedicates considerable space to praising the Virgin in effusive terms. Some of Eadmer's praise echoes Anselm's, such as when describing Mary as "surpassing every height that can be said or thought, after God."[239] This is the main thrust of his treatise: that Mary was greater than any other human being. Three chapters of Eadmer's treatise are dedicated to her supremacy: "That Mary surpasses all creatures," "How greatly the blessed Virgin Mary outshines human nature," and "How much she surpasses ever creature, even above every human." In these passages, Mary's flesh is described as exalted by the fact that God chose it for his plan of Redemption; without her, humanity would have remained in its fallen state. Mary thus effected the turnaround of humanity's fate that had been suffered since Adam and Eve's disobedience. In language drawn from Anselm's prayers, Eadmer explained that "Just as God is the father and lord of all things, in his power to prepare all things, so is the blessed Mary the mother and lady of things, through her merits repairing all things; for the Lord is God of all things, unique in his nature to create by his own command; and Mary is the lady of all things, unique in her innate dignity to restore through that grace which she merited."[240] He asked, rhetorically, how anyone could not stand dumbfounded and utterly incapable of understanding the marvel that Mary brought about in the virgin birth.[241]

At a loss for words, Eadmer concluded with the only possible course of action: a prayer to the Virgin.[242] Reminding Mary that Christ was born from her to save and not damn humanity, the penitent begs her to help the lowly creatures who venerate her, reproaching her that any neglect on her part would make her seem complacent in her exalted position and uninterested in sharing it with those who love her.[243] Eadmer's meditative treatise thus ends on a plaintive note, urging Mary to remember the penitent from the heights of her lofty position. Having spent the entire text praising Mary such that she comes across as more superhuman than even Anselm made her out to be, Eadmer pressed her to turn her superhuman compassion to the penitent. He went so far as to present Mary as a more effective and worthy recipient of prayer than even Christ himself: "Salvation comes about at times more quickly with the remembrance of her name than the invocation of her only son's, the lord Jesus. . . . At the invocation of his mother's name, even if the merits of the person who invokes it are not worthy, the merits *of the mother* [i.e., Mary] nevertheless intercede so that he is heard."[244] This is Anselm's prayer taken a step further, and as we will see in the next chapter, it would not be the only time Eadmer would push his ideas about Mary to the extreme. Eadmer's *De excellentia* might not have the elegance of Anselm's prayers, but the power he ascribed her intercessrion is indicative of the kind of extreme devotional fervor Anselm helped foster.

The prominence that prayers and meditative works like Eadmer's gave to Mary came to be reflected in many of the visual depictions of her produced in Anglo-Norman England. This is especially true for image cycles normally found appended to psalters. Only in the twelfth century did Mary become the focus of such cycles, which Holger A. Klein has attributed to the growing popularity of prayer to Mary.[245] In the Shaftesbury Psalter, Mary has a central place in the depiction of the Gospel accounts; she is front and center in the depiction of the Ascension and Pentecost, and in the latter image, she sits crowned, staring triumphantly out from the page at the observer.[246] This is the same stance she holds in the image of the *Sedes Sapientiae* (Throne of Wisdom), which faces the *Ave* prayer—a position that emphasizes her power as queen of heaven (figure 2). The same prominence is given to her in almost-contemporary images found in the St. Albans and Winchester psalters, with similar sets of images that also feature her at the Passion.[247] The Winchester manuscript additionally includes the innovative iconography drawn from Mary's life story, mentioned above. The "Byzantine Diptych" in the same manuscript shows Mary's Dormition and her reign in heaven (figure 3).[248] Produced between 1129 and 1140, the diptych's Byzantine character does not necessarily mean it directly reproduced a Byzantine icon, and it has been attributed to an English artist trained in the Byzantine style.[249] The second of the two full-page illustrations of the diptych depicts Mary enthroned and flanked by angels, facing front, her hands outstretched and palyms forward. This stance has been read as a representation of her intercession; such a position is often found in images connected to the Last Judgment, portraying Mary's mediation on the penitent's behalf and the need for prayer in order to secure it.[250] New trends in illumination in psalters thus connect to innovations in prayer, as Mary's power to intercede with penitents was given visual form.

Interestingly, a growing number of monastic seals came to feature an image of Mary enthroned much like the illumination at the end of the Shaftesbury Psalter.[251] Mary appears in the guise of *Sedes Sapientiae* on the earliest-known monastic seals, one from St. Mary's York, and another belonging to Worcester Cathedral, circa 1140; she sits crowned, holding Jesus in her lap and a flowering rod in her hand.[252] These seals also strongly resemble those of Great Malvern priory, a dependency of Worcester, Abingdon, Pershore, and Kelso abbeys, and Lincoln Cathedral, all from the first half of the twelfth century, as well as Reading.[253] As objects that publicly expressed the corporate identity of monastic houses, seals were particularly meaningful.[254] The patronage of Mary at all the institutions mentioned above explains her placement on their seals, asserting

Figure 2. Shaftesbury Psalter, in BL Lansdowne MS 383, f. 165v, 1125/1150. © The British Library Board, British Library Lansdowne MS 383, f. 165v.

Figure 3. Winchester Psalter, in BL Cotton Nero C. iv, f. 30r, circa 1150. © The British Library Board, British Library Cotton MS Nero C. iv, f. 30.

the houses' affiliation to the Virgin and emphasizing her role as protector. The specific image of Mary enthroned could also refer back to the prayers, liturgies, and images that portrayed her as the most powerful of patrons, second only to God. This would have been especially significant in the turbulent times after the conquest, giving force to the land claims of monastic houses through appeal to so powerful a saint. The presence of Mary on a seal would have acted to confirm her approval and backing for the right of the institution in question to the lands detailed in the document being sealed, ensuring the intercession of Mary for the concerns of the house in question, much like the Nunnaminster prayer preceding the Little Office. But as Brigitte Bedos-Rezak points out, seals did not necessarily serve solely to validate documents (or at all, she argues).[255] Seals were part of a wider semiotic trend that saw signs becoming increasingly reified, objects that captured the "real presence" of the individual being represented in "a more general and unprecedented shift toward mediation, representation and the formulation of personal identity in the medieval West."[256] While institutional seals sought to make real the presence of that institution wherever the document was, Mary's likeness on them made her just as present. Monastic seals are therefore perhaps the most explicit expression of belief in Mary's powers of intercession.

JEWS IN THE LITURGY

Like material representations of the chants, readings, and prayers of the liturgy, seals bearing Mary's image functioned as confirmation that Mary was worthy of being commemorated just as they expressed the need to approach her with reverence in the hopes of receiving her patronage. But as the monastic authors and composers illustrated and enacted the veneration owed to Mary as queen of heaven, they also made use of another strategy in order to promote devotion to Mary: highlighting the evil that came of *not* venerating her. In the interest of teaching the appropriate ways to think about and address Mary, these sources additionally provided counterexamples, purposely articulating what it might be to have an improper attitude toward Mary—in order to condemn it. By this I mean that the liturgy explicitly attacked doubt about Mary's virgin motherhood as a means to encourage faith. This role of expressing doubt with respect to Mary was often assigned to Jews.

Jews held a special place in the history of Marian devotion. They had been envisioned as doubters of the virgin birth and Incarnation from early Christian times and were therefore seen as Mary's natural enemy. Mary was a line drawn in the sand between Jews and Christians from the first centuries CE, since the idea of a Messiah who is God in human form and was born of a woman firmly divided the communities. As a result, early Christian sermons and treatises, such as Origen's *Contra Celsus*, took issue with the Jews' refusal to accept Mary's place in the history of Salvation: bringing about the Redemption of humanity by giving birth to a Messiah who was both man and God. By the fifth century, when the cult of Mary expanded in the Byzantine Empire, Jews found themselves the targets of sermons for rejecting what her Christian supporters saw to be Mary's crucial role as Theotokos, mother of both God and man. Byzantine homilists, such as Proclus of Constantinople, Hesychius of Jerusalem, and Abraham of Ephesus, and later Andrew of Crete, Germannos of Constantinople, John of Damascus, and John of Euboea, argued in favor of a Christological reading of the Hebrew scriptures against the Jews' resistance to the idea that Mary's virgin motherhood of God had been prophesied in their own texts. [257] Sometimes the Jews were taken as foils for other Christian groups, such as Nestorians, Arians, and Manicheans.[258] Tarring so-called heretical groups with the brush of Judaism became a well-established tactic for condemning unorthodox positions and amplifying the charge of heresy. This meant that any individual or group that questioned whether Mary had been a perpetual virgin or given birth to God could find themselves subject to accusations of Judaizing. As a consequence, Jews became immortalized as the stereotypical opponents of Marian doctrine, with their disbelief in her virginal conception and birth of Christ referred to in Christian apologetics as a defining feature of their error.

Since many of the Christian polemics on the subject of the virgin birth took the form of homilies, this polemical element easily found its way into the liturgy. We see this particularly in the season of Advent. A notable example is the sermon addressed against the Jews, Arians, and Pagans, *Contra Judaeos, Arianos et Paganos*, by the fifth-century bishop of Carthage Quodvultdeus.[259] In the course of adaptation for liturgical use, the sections of the treatise addressed to the Arians and Pagans were excised, and the anti-Jewish polemic that remained was divided up into sections for readings for the office of matins. The same principle applied to the equally polemical sermon *Legimus Sanctum Moysen*, also an early Christian composition written against the Jews that was used for readings during Advent. [260] The liturgy of Advent was an especially good fit for these sermons, seeing as the scriptural prophecies about the coming of the Messiah dominated the chants and readings of the season, especially Isaiah.[261] But while Christ's birth was at the center of the celebration of Advent, Mary also played a key role in this commemoration. Prophecies about Mary's virgin motherhood permeated the period, culminating in the last Wednesday in Advent, Ember Wednesday, when the moment of the Annunciation was commemorated in the Roman tradition.[262] The juxtaposition of praise for Mary and attack on the Jews was felt throughout the season, in both sung and read texts, creating an accumulation of imagery that exalted Mary's position as mother of God while debasing the Jews for their unbelief.

A twelfth-century votive office associated with Westminster presents an illustration of the ways in which Jewish refusal to accept the Christian position on Mary was incorporated into the extensive Marian liturgies that were increasingly being adopted in twelfth-century England.[263] Although the nine-lesson office follows a secular cursus, and is found in a psalter that has recently been described as a gift to the young king Henry II for his coronation, it has striking similarities to Benedictine votive offices, which tend to follow a secular cursus in any case.[264] The last nocturn of matins in this office interweaves polemical material in meaningful ways. The seventh lesson comprises a reading of the Gospel for the day, as was standard, in this case starting at Luke 11:27: the narrative of Jesus's encounter with the woman who says to him, "Blessed is the womb that carried you and the breasts that gave you suck." The lesson then continues with Bede's gloss on this passage from his *Commentary on Luke*: "This woman is shown to have great devotion and faith, who recognised in her all-encompassing sincerity that the scribes and Pharisees were tempting the Lord and at the same time blaspheming against his Incarnation. She confessed with such confidence the calumny of these leaders in the present that she might condemn the perfidy of future heretics."[265] The woman's praise of Mary is therefore taken as an expression of faith that Christ was in fact the incarnate God born of a human woman. Bede opposes this faith not just to the "calumnies" of the biblical high priests but also those of heretics, who centuries later likewise questioned the doctrine. The responsory that follows the lesson, which was commonly sung during the Christmas season, *Te laudant angeli*, then reconfirms Mary's praiseworthiness for conceiving the Lord in her womb, having done so not through sexual intercourse but instead through her ear (*per aurem*)—that is to say, at the moment of the Annunciation through the workings of the Holy Spirit.[266]

The next lesson continues on with Bede's commentary, expanding on the previous lesson by explaining the wider implications of his gloss on Luke: "For just as the Jews, blaspheming against the works of the Holy Spirit, then denied that the son was true and consubstantial with God the Father, so did the heretics, denying that Mary, the perpetual virgin, had bestowed her flesh by the powerful workings of the Holy Spirit, to the son, the only born son of God in the flesh, from her human members, say that the son of man ought not to have been made true and cosubstantial with the mother."[267] This is followed by the responsory *Gaude Maria virgo*, which takes explicit issue with refusal of the virgin birth: "Rejoice Mary, virgin, you alone opposed all heresies, you who believed the words of the Archangel Gabriel. Then the virgin gave birth to man and God and remained a virgin after the birth."[268] The corresponding verse answers: "We know that Gabriel announced by divine act to you, and we believe that your womb was impregnated by the Holy Spirit; may the unhappy Jew blush, who says that Christ was born from the seed of Joseph."[269] The responsory originated in the ninth century, and is first attested in England in the eleventh-century Winchester Troper.[270] It was also incorporated as the antiphon for vespers in both the Anglo-Saxon offices of Mary discussed above.[271] On the Continent, however, only in the late eleventh century do two Marian offices of unknown provenance include it as a responsory and antiphon.[272] Michel Huglo has argued that the abbot Baldwin introduced the responsory at Bury St. Edmunds, although the fact that it is included in Anglo-Saxon offices indicates it was already known in England.[273]

In the Westminster office, the *Gaude Maria virgo* responsory exercised a specific function in combination with the lesson that precedes it. It reinforced the sense that the high priests of the Gospel narrative represent the historical Jews and heretics who continue to doubt the virgin birth. The responsory also emphasized Mary's own acceptance of her miraculous conception of Christ, which is presented as a paradigm for Christian belief; Mary's acceptance of the angel's message about Christ's advent effectively makes her the first Christian. We are therefore meant to understand that the woman in Luke 11:27 is a figure for Mary, both of whom proclaimed their faith in Christ. At the same time, the responsory condemns the Jews—and not the heretics, who are absent from the verse text—for their lack of faith. Together, the components of the eighth lesson give additional layers of meaning to Luke's Gospel, contrasting the unbelievers with the woman of the Gospel narrative and Mary herself, and by extension, with the choir of monks or nuns performing the office.

After exposing the Jews' and heretics' lack of faith in the eighth lesson, the ninth and final lesson of the office concludes by underscoring the need for belief in the virgin birth as a necessary means to secure Mary's aid. Continuing with Bede's commentary, it states that those who think Jesus was born from Mary under the law—that is, by natural means—should be ignored.[274] It goes on to explain in the first-person plural that "we" should all take the example of the woman in the Gospel, for she is a type of the church. We should therefore repeat her words of belief, for only then will Christ answer us in the same way as he did to her: "Yea rather, blessed are they who hear the word of God and keep it" (Luke 11:28). The responsory that follows repeats the idea of potential rewards in store for those who believe in the virgin birth: "Sweetest virgin of Christ, and worker of powers (*virtutum operatrix*), bear the burden for the wretched and, lady, come in aid of those who call out to you."[275] This is answered by the verse "because we are oppressed by the weight of our sins and there is no one to help us."[276] The final lesson thus concludes the interpretation of the Gospel by providing a tropological gloss that moves from condemning unbelievers to recognizing that only by proclaiming faith can there be any hope for personal salvation.

The nocturn as a whole, the most important in the entire matins office, is in this way a lesson in Christian devotion.[277] What emerges from the juxtaposition of chants and lessons is the need to declare faith in Mary's virgin motherhood of God as a prerequisite for seeking her intercession. Because the liturgy was itself a collective statement of belief in word and song, its performance would have achieved both these things, affirming faith while asking for assistance. The Jews and heretics, on the other hand, do neither, and as such, will gain no reward, as the liturgy makes clear. By contrasting the proper approach to faith exemplified by the woman in Luke (who is herself a figure for Mary) with the attitude of the Jews, the liturgy underlined the risks of not approaching Mary by the right means. Reference to the disbelief of heretics and Jews therefore exercised an important function in the liturgy. Although the texts selected for the office were intended to urge Christians to place their faith in Mary and openly proclaim their allegiance to her, the finger-pointing at Jews for their doubt would nevertheless have instilled a sense of Jewish error with every repetition of the office. We have to remember that the office was performed daily and would have been one of the most familiar elements of the liturgy. The message that its regular repetition would have ingrained is not only that of the Christian's duty to proclaim faith in Mary but also that of the Jew's tendency to reject her.

A similar theme of Jewish unbelief is found in the text of a sequence in a mid-twelfth-century troper from St. Albans.[278] It was later attributed to Bernard of Clairvaux, but is found as early as the eleventh century in a liturgical play from Freising, in southern Germany.[279] Although normally part of the liturgy for the Christmas season in later manuscripts, including the Sarum missal, in the St. Albans manuscript it appears under the rubric *De Sancta Maria*, indicating its intended use for a Marian mass, perhaps the daily or weekly votive masses sung in her honor:

> Let the faithful choir joyfully rejoice, Hallelujah! Alleluia!
> The womb of the undefiled one hath brought forth the King of kings: a
>   thing of wonder.
> The angel of counsel is born of the Virgin, the sun of the star,
> The sun that knows no setting, the star that is ever shining, ever bright.
> As the star its ray, in like manner the Virgin brings forth her son.
> Neither the star by its ray, nor the mother by her son becomes defiled.
> The lofty cedar of Lebanon is conformed to the hyssop in our valley.
> The Word, the being of the most high, has deigned to become incarnate,
>   having assumed flesh.
> Isaiah foretold it, the Synagogue remembers it, yet never does she cease to
>   be blind.

If not her own prophets, let her at least believe the Gentiles; in the Sibylline
 verses these things are predicted.
O unhappy one, hasten; at least believe the ancient things.
O wretched race, why will you be condemned?
Behold the child of whom the scripture teaches: the mother hath brought
 him forth.
Hallelujah![280]

After Mary has been praised as the star to Christ's sun, the final verses of this
sequence address the Jews directly, accusing them of refusing to believe what
even their own prophecies announce: the advent of Christ through Mary. The
Jews are blamed for ignoring not only their own prophets, namely Isaiah, but
also the pagan Sybil, both of whom make an appearance in the *Contra Judaeos*
homily by Quodvultdeus. The sequence would have provided an echo of the
homily read out in the matins office during Advent, and was no doubt composed with it in mind: polemic made song. But divorced from the Advent season as it is in the St. Albans Troper, and reserved for a Marian celebration, the
focus would have shifted specifically onto the Jews' rejection of Mary's virginity.
As a result, the position of the Jews on the subject of the virgin birth would have
highlighted their antagonism toward Mary specifically.

Just as the unbelief of Jews became a feature of the liturgy in the general
Marian commemorative offices in the early twelfth century, so too was it incorporated into the liturgies for some of the new feasts that appeared at this time.
Although no liturgical materials survive from its celebration in England, the
Ildefonsine office of Mary adopted at Bury St. Edmunds under Anselm is full of
polemical imagery.[281] The readings of the feast in the Old Hispanic tradition
were made up of a polemical treatise that Ildefonsus had composed to commemorate the establishment of the December 18 feast in Iberia.[282] Although
there are short sections addressed to two heretics—Helvidius and Jovinian—on
the subject of Mary's virginity in- and postpartum, the treatise is aimed almost
entirely at the Jews in defense of the virgin birth and Incarnation.[283] Many of
the same proof texts used by Ildefonsus to demonstrate to the Jews that Mary is
referred to in their own prophecies are also present in the chants of the liturgy.
In addition to the polemical readings in the office liturgy, the mass included a
sermon directed at the Jews, with the incipit *Exhortatur nos*. It was initially attributed to Ildefonsus, although as is now known, it was constructed from a
patchwork of other sermons, including the *Contra Iudeos* of Quodvultdeus and
Legimus Sanctum Moysen, reiterating the attack on the Jews for their lack of
belief in the virgin birth.[284] Together, the chants, readings, and sermon of this
feast day transmitted a clear message about the Christian understanding about
Mary in opposition to Jews. If Anselm reproduced the Marian office as it sur-

vives in the early Iberian manuscript tradition, his community at Bury would have been starkly reminded with every celebration of the Jewish rejection of Mary's virgin motherhood of God.

In creating materials for the feast of Mary's mother, Anne, Osbert also made reference to Jewish unbelief. Osbert described Anne in his sermon as the turning point between Judaism and Christianity, since she "is like the hinge of Law and grace, through whom the dignity of human nature is seen to flourish again in Christ."[285] His praise of Anne also involves defending Mary's purity and virgin motherhood. In the first of the two hymns he composed (*O praeclara mater matris*), this defense is articulated against the unbelieving Jews:

> Oh mother of the mother of God, remember me when you are with him,
> Cleanse the filth of my sins, by which I am weighed down.
> And may she to whom you gave birth, the chaste mother and chamber of Christ,
> Purge me of all filth together with your holy prayer,
> Happy ark of the Testament, in whom Judea does not believe.[286]

Here, by taking the Jewish people as a whole—Judea—Osbert underscored the fact that Jews do not accept that the ark of the covenant (Exod. 25:10–22) is in fact a figure for Mary. Jewish unbelief is mentioned later in the same hymn, although this time striking a more sinister note:

> So may you [Anne] become the consoler of many wretches
> Console me as I cry and comfort me as I repent
> And bring me back to the path of life and let me see the Messiah.
> The accused Hebrew people know not that he has come but
> Assert and affirm that he is yet to, thus remaining as perfidious as they were.[287]

In this hymn, Osbert condemned the "Hebrew people" for their refusal to acknowledge that the Messiah had in fact come, accusing them of perfidy. Osbert thus presented the continuing unbelief of the Jews as a real and present problem; Jews refused Christ not just in a biblical past but in Osbert's own day as well. The appearance of statements about the incredulity of Jews in new liturgical sources reflects just how integral polemicizing against the Jews was becoming to reflection on Mary and her extended family. Recently composed texts connected to her cult were incorporating polemical references, both old and new, bringing engagement with Jews into praise of Mary. In this way, the memory of Jewish doubt and opposition to the virgin birth became a feature of Marian commemoration, reminding performers and listeners of Jewish unbelief, as they articulated their own faith in Mary through the annual, weekly, and daily practices performed in her honor.

CONCLUSION

Embedded within the commemorative practices honoring Mary, the unbelief of Jews was designed to highlight the folly of refusing the virgin birth and Mary's redemptive role in the history of salvation. Not only that, it reaffirmed by negative example the increasingly elaborate practices of praising and praying to the Virgin as a necessary means to obtain Mary's all-important intercession. The long history of juxtaposing Jewish rejection with Christian belief in the virgin birth presented monks in Anglo-Norman England with an effective justification for further praising her in the liturgy as the most powerful saintly intercessor. Highlighting doubt and refusal as the approach of a condemned and wayward people, they showed Mary's followers the humble veneration and admiration of which she was worthy. This veneration was to be carried out by means of the tools devised in unprecedented numbers and innovative forms: liturgies and prayers along with the visual images inspired by them. At the same time as monks praised her in the offices for Marian feasts and more regular practices, they prayed to her as a powerful intercessor on behalf of individual pentients and whole communities. If the liturgy was the expression of the *fides ecclesiae*, affirming the faith in every chant and reading, it helped to define the boundaries of this *ecclesia* with reference to the Jews.[288] Devotion to Mary was in the process of becoming a marker of this true faith and real piety—a shared experience in medieval Christian culture fashioned in the monastic image. Raising the specter of Jewish unbelief only served to enhance this message of Christian unity in praising Mary.

Monastic communities in twelfth-century England, with influence from their Norman counterparts, were instrumental in providing the materials, unique forms of liturgy, and prayers that made praise of Mary possible. The cult of Mary had historic roots in England, and this in part explains the efforts to revive and develop it following the Norman Conquest. Drawing from a rich Anglo-Saxon tradition, monks were inspired to revive old practices as they created new ones. New feast days were added, such as the feast of Anne and the Visigothic feast of the Annunciation, as others were renewed, such as that of the Conception. Lengthy liturgical practices, such as the various offices of Mary, were also revived and spread throughout the monasteries of the kingdom. Prayer to the Virgin was made more effusive, ascribing her an ever-greater status as cosavior with Christ. Art, too, came to reflect the changing face of Mary, as she was increasingly depicted as a central figure of the biblical and apocryphal narratives. In all media, Mary's role was consistently enhanced, and she was looked on as the main intermediary with Christ. Monks in England seem to have recognized the usefulness of having a queen as mother, and it was this aspect of Mary's identity that they brought to the fore in their veneration of her—the rich cycles of liturgical practice that dominated the Benedictine life. We should remember, too, that monasteries played a central role in providing pastoral care for the lay population, and thus would have transmitted much of the material discussed in this chapter—not least the Westminster Little Office— to a much wider audience.[289] The consequences of this is considerable, for monks helped to transform the Virgin Mary into more than a local patron saint, more than a monastic symbol and role model, but rather a universal Christian queen, the very embodiment of the church triumphant.

CHAPTER 2

||||||||||||||||||||||

Understanding Mary

THEOLOGICAL TREATISES

AT THE SAME TIME AS MARY WAS HONORED in Anglo-Norman England with increasingly elaborate liturgical practices, theology took on an important role in providing justification for devotion. It was not enough merely to claim in liturgy and prayer that Mary was worthy of the highest praise; the monks involved in developing her cult wanted to prove beyond reasonable doubt that this was true. There emerged in this period a series of strikingly bold treatises that set out elaborate arguments to demonstrate that Mary was distinct and far superior to all other human beings. In producing these works, their monastic authors participated in a growing trend in Anglo-Norman monastic circles of approaching questions of the faith in new ways. Anselm of Canterbury has generally been credited with starting a movement of treating matters of faith as rational problems: *fidens quaerens intellectum* (faith seeking understanding).[1] No longer was the text of the Bible itself deemed sufficient for proving the idea of a god-man born of a human mother. Anselm and his intellectual heirs presented arguments that did not rely on the ultimately subjective nature of biblical interpretation, looking instead to establish it from first principles.[2] The rational basis Anselm elaborated for the doctrine of the Incarnation unavoidably had to engage with the problem of Christ's human parent. In setting out how God uniquely took human form in Mary's body, Anselm ultimately made her an indispensable feature of Christian salvation history. Anselm's discussion of Mary's virgin motherhood thus gave her an unprecedented status made all the more compelling by virtue of his claims to rational certainty, such that he thought he could convince even non-Christians.

If Anselm's treatment of the virgin birth within his scheme for the Incarnation already attributed a crucial role to Mary, some of his disciples nevertheless pushed the boundaries set by their teacher far beyond what he was prepared to argue. They pursued his method of discourse into uncharted territory, claiming that Mary was of necessity supremely unique and pure in ways Anselm explicitly opposed. Their incentive to do so was not just theological but also liturgical, as they sought to justify the expressions of devotion explored in the previous chapter. Eadmer, for example, took inspiration from Anselm's writings on the Incarnation in asserting for the first time in Christian history that Mary was free from original sin. Driven to do so by his desire to have the feast of Mary's Conception reinstated after its cancellation, Eadmer effectively articulated for the first time the much-contested doctrine of the Immaculate Conception. Perhaps inspired in part by the debates about Mary's sinlessness at her conception, William of Malmesbury and Honorius Augustodunensis took part in an older but no less heated debate about the end of Mary's life. Employing Anselm's rational method, they maintained that her body was too glorious to have been left on earth and thus that it ascended to heaven, where she now resides—body and soul—at her son's right hand. Importantly, Honorius incorporated the figure of the Jew into his discussion of Mary's Assumption in the *Sigillum de Beata Maria*, his innovative commentary on the liturgy for the feast of the Assumption. Glossing the Song of Songs for the first time as a dialogue between Christ and Mary, Honorius reserved a key role for the wayward Synagoga, who would come to see the error of her ways and be converted on recognizing Mary's greatness. These theological explorations are witnesses to the considerable originality of monks in the Anglo-Norman sphere not just in venerating Mary in innovative ways but also in contending that such veneration was justified given her unique and supreme role, thereby putting theology to the service of the liturgy.

INCARNATION

The impulse in twelfth-century theology to reconsider Mary's place in Christian history drew considerably from renewed interest in the problem of the Incarnation. Anselm of Canterbury was a major player in this theological development. Inspired by a general revival in dialectic as well as discussions at Bec with his students, Anselm helped develop a novel methodology for dealing with questions of faith by approaching them as problems of logic.[3] Eschewing biblical exegesis as a source of authority, Anselm went back to first principles in order to look at questions such as the existence of God, free will, original sin, and the Incarnation.[4] He did so on the premise that since God is the ultimate rational being, creation must be subject to rational investigation. Anselm is perhaps best known for his ontological argument for the existence of God, by which he claimed to have proven beyond doubt that God as "that than which nothing greater can be thought" must exist.[5] He subjected the Incarnation to the same scrutiny, developing a complex rationale for the necessary redemption of humanity through an individual who was both fully God and fully man. The question of how and why it was that God chose to take human form involved

Mary in important ways. Although Anselm's intention was never to discuss the Incarnation solely for its relevance to Mary, in exploring the need for God to have been born of a human mother, Anselm had to address Mary's place in the scheme of Christian salvation. With its novel methodology, Anselm's reflection on the Incarnation fundamentally shaped the understanding of Mary.

The principal texts in which Anselm developed his ideas about the Incarnation and virgin birth were the *Cur Deus Homo*, composed circa 1093, and its close follow-up, *De virginali conceptu et originali peccato*.[6] The *Cur Deus Homo*, although written as a dialogue with his disciple Boso from Bec, was probably also inspired by conversations Anselm had with Gilbert Crispin, the abbot of Westminster Abbey, who had formerly been a monk at Bec.[7] *De virginali conceptu* was written afterward to address questions that remained from the *Cur Deus Homo*, specifically on the issue of Christ's generation. In both works, Anselm sought to establish the theological necessity of God becoming man. In the first book of Anselm's *Cur Deus Homo*, he explained that since the fall of Adam and Eve, humanity had been corrupted, leaving a great debt that all of humankind owed to God. Anselm argued that while God wished for humanity to be redeemed, he could not simply erase the stain on humanity since this would have done him a dishonor, and as such, been contrary to his infinitely just nature. Book two then explores the nature of God's chosen redeemer. Only a human being who shared Adam's lineage and was taken from the sinful mass that constitutes all of humanity would be capable of repaying the debt and thus make up for humanity's fallen state. But this had to be a special human being to cancel humanity's debt to God—one "who would make payment to God greater than everything that exists apart from God."[8] Anselm concluded that because there is nothing in existence greater than God, it follows that the redeemer must be both fully human and fully God.[9]

Having established that only a God-man could save humanity, Anselm went on to explore the human nature of this individual. This God-man could have been created in one of four ways: from a man and woman together, as is the usual method; from neither a man nor woman, like Adam; from a man without a woman, like Eve; or from a woman without a man. Anselm decided that the last of these cases was the correct one, as having a woman bring about salvation would be a fitting reversal of Eve's responsibility for Adam's downfall.[10] Anselm asked his interlocutor in the dialogue whether it would not also have been appropriate for this woman "who is to be the cause of all good" to have been a virgin, just like the woman "who has been the cause of all the evil besetting the human race."[11] The fact that Christ must have been born of a virgin was therefore established by virtue of the neat symmetry it produced between the fall and salvation of humanity, with a virgin woman bringing about both one and the other. Anselm's reasoning is based on what is appropriate to God's nature because of its absolute purity and goodness, for God's actions are nothing if not elegant in their rationality: it is fitting that a virgin woman should have borne the redeemer in order to reverse the sin of the first woman.

Anselm's second work on the Incarnation, *De virginali conceptu et originali peccato*, expands on the question of the God-man's nature that lies at the heart of his *Cur Deus Homo*. The man who would reconcile humanity to God by buying back its sins must have been himself sinless, for he is also God. Anselm's partner in the dialogue, Boso, expresses disatisfaction with Anselm's initial answer to his question about the way in which the redeemer could have escaped the original sin present in the human nature he inherited; his concern suggests a marked interest in the theology of original sin shared also by other contemporary scholars such as Odo of Tournai (d. 1113).[12] Anselm gave a rather vague answer in the *Cur Deus Homo*: "Who may presume even to think that a human intellect might be capable of fathoming how it is that such an act has been performed, so wisely and so wonderfully?"[13] Although he did go on to give a preliminary answer based on predestination, he must have realized it was insufficient and addressed the problem more fully in *De virginali conceptu*.[14] This time, Anselm tackled the question from the perspective of original sin itself.[15] He explained that original sin is so called because it originated with the first parents. Because they were the only human beings in existence when they sinned and therefore encompassed all of humanity, they therefore tainted all of humanity with their sin. Anselm did not mean, however, that a fetus at the moment of conception is tainted with original sin, for sin only exists in the rational will, which descends with the soul into the body only once it has been formed in the womb. Rather, original sin implies that every human being is born with the capacity to sin, and in fact, will sin of necessity.

Christ was the exception to the rule of universal original sin. As the redeemer of humanity and also fully God, Christ's human nature could not have been subject to original sin. It would have been "grossly unfitting," in Anselm's words, for "it will be plain to the rational mind that he [God] could not make a man, created likewise through his own will and power, subject to any evil."[16] The way in which this was made possible was that unlike every other human being, Christ was not produced through the union of a man and woman but instead from an act of God's will on Mary's body. Christ was therefore not engendered via the same reproductive nature that was corrupted by the will of Adam and Eve. Original sin was transmitted through the will in sexual reproduction, thereby affecting all of humanity. But in Christ's conception, there was no carnal intercourse, no concupiscence, only the Holy Spirit acting on Mary's virginal body, and hence no original sin.[17] Anselm elaborated on this process in a passage taken down by his students:

> The conception of the Virgin Mary . . . can be thought of in terms of this similitude. If someone asks how the virgin gave birth, how the virgin conceived, and

how she remained a virgin *post partum*, answer by asking 'how is a crystal filled with the brightness of the sun without cracking." . . . Far be it from God who is the maker of all things, not to be able to do by himself in the virgin what he brings about so often by his command through something he created in a thing of creation. So to those who ask about the intactness of the virgin giving birth and the whole of the crystal filled with brightness and radiating it, one and the same reply must be given, namely that it is as God has wished it.[18]

This is not to say that Christ's mother had to be sinless herself. God could have chosen any sinful woman for the task. Yet he selected Mary on account of her virtuous nature and lack of personal sin, because, again, this was most fitting:

Although it is true that the Son of God was born of a spotless Virgin, this was not out of necessity . . . but because it was fitting that the conception of this man [the Son of God] should be of a pure mother. Indeed it was fitting that that Virgin should shine with a purity which was only exceeded by God's own, because it was to her that God the Father disposed to give his only Son, whom he loved in his heart as equal to himself, begotten equal to himself, so that in nature he should be at the same time the son of God and of the Virgin; the Son himself substantially chose her for himself to be his mother, and from her the Holy Spirit willed and was to effect the conception and birth of the Son from whom the Spirit should proceed.[19]

If the argument makes God's actions seem contingent and arbitrary, it nevertheless establishes that Mary was not just pure but truly surpassed all others in her purity, too. Her selection for the task of bearing Christ, then, seems to have been in recognition of her own unique virtue. God thus further purified Mary's body of all remaining sin, including original sin, at the moment of the Annunciation.[20] This allowed Christ to be formed of flesh untainted by original sin from the point of his conception, which coincided with the Annunciation. Anselm made this explicit in the *Cur Deus Homo*: "The Virgin from whom that man was taken of whom we are speaking, was amongst those who were purified from their sins through him before his birth, and he was taken out of her in purity."[21] If Mary's original purity does not seem to have been strictly necessary, her importance in Anselm's theological works echoes his earlier prayers, in which the degree of her purity places her second only to God. It must be acknowledged that Anselm did not devote extensive space to Mary in his work on the Incarnation, as one recent scholar has argued.[22] But because he seems to have considered the appropriateness of God's actions a measure of their rationality and truth, Anselm's claims for Mary being the most fitting of vehicles through which God brought about salvation could be understood as particularly strong support for her unique place in the Christian scheme of history.

CONCEPTION

Anselm's study of the Incarnation and virgin birth exercised a critical influence on his contemporaries, who almost immediately took his method and used it to defend far more elaborate claims for Mary than he himself did. The most striking example of this is Eadmer's *De conceptione sanctae Mariae*, a treatise composed circa 1125, a decade after his *De excellentia*.[23] It is a remarkable and unduly neglected work of early twelfth-century theology as well as an important historical witness to the debates about liturgical practice in Anglo-Norman England, as we have seen.[24] The previous chapter mentioned Eadmer's treatise as one of the principal testimonies for the controversy that surrounded the feast of Mary's Conception on December 8. In it, he provided invaluable information that the feast's uniqueness to England cast doubt on its continued celebration in the period following the Norman Conquest, and that its progressive revival in the early decades of the twelfth century encountered resistance and even open opposition. In order to tackle opposition to the feast, Eadmer used Anselm's methodology to such an extent that his work was confused with Anselm's for centuries, although it was correctly attributed in 1904 with the discovery of an autograph manuscript.[25] Still, Eadmer explicitly and knowingly contradicted Anselm in reflecting on Mary's special conception as honored by the feast. Just how special Eadmer thought it was makes this treatise entirely unprecedented— a testament to how far some monks were willing to go in seeking to honor Mary to the highest-possible degree.

Eadmer's main challenge in writing *De conceptione* was to account for why the feast of the Conception ought to be revived a liturgical celebration. Eadmer explained the need to address the feast's opponents because he thought it necessary "to consider with my own faculties and pious meditation what they [the feast's detractors] think about particular points, and to what extent is proven by their authority that which ought to be attributed to it [the Conception] and thus ought to be followed with greater certainty by those like me [other monks]."[26] He then mentioned some of the arguments that were put forward against the feast's celebration:

> So that no memory of the conception of the Virgin mother should be made in the church of her Son, those men indeed declare that it does not seem reasonable to them with the argument that by her Nativity, which is celebrated everywhere as a feast day, the origin of her conception is remembered enough; for they say that she would not have been born if she had not been conceived, and when she came forth into the light out of her mother's dark womb, it was clear that she took shape in human form, conceived in her mother's womb. Since the particular composition of her body and its delivery into this world are venerated by all, it is redun-

dant to worship what was up until that point unformed matter, which not un-commonly dies or is destroyed before it is transformed fully into human form.[27]

Two points emerge here, both hinging on the fact that there was already an accepted and widespread feast celebrating Mary's Nativity (on September 8). The first is that it was considered superfluous to honor the moment of conception given that there was already a commemoration of her birth, with the latter necessarily implying the former. Second, it is not just superfluous but mis-guided too, based on a principle from biology. Since a fetus is only unformed matter until it is infused with a soul, to honor the moment of conception would amount to celebrating the creation of shapeless, soulless flesh. This statement seems to reflect the current thinking on the formation of the soul and its en-trance into the body, which was thought to occur sometime after conception; this was the theory put forward by Anselm.[28] As a result, it apparently seemed much more sensible to Eadmer's adversaries to venerate Mary's birth only and see the event as encompassing her conception as well.

In response to such arguments, Eadmer could theoretically have answered the opponents of the feast by appealing to the apocryphal traditions that as-cribed Mary a special conception, announced by an angel to her parents, Anne and Joachim. He had nonetheless already expressed skepticism about the trust-worthiness of these accounts in his treatise *De excellentia virginis Mariae*, in a section on Mary's origins:

> For the church of God does not hold that this text, which refers to Mary's origin as having been announced by an angel, is of firm authority. Although the blessed Jerome wrote it, along with some other scriptural material that he had read in his youth, and confessed he did not know who the author was, he nevertheless said that he had not agreed to write what he wrote in order to introduce into the churches any certainty regarding the things described, but simply to gratify a few friends who made the request. Hence, as I have said, the church refused to accept that work as authoritative, thinking it indecent to say anything about the blessed mother of God that could be only be said in praise of her with some doubt.[29]

This extract indicates that Eadmer must have had access to a version of the *Liber de nativitatis Mariae* attributed in a series of spurious prefatory letters to Jerome, although there is no known copy of this precise version from Anglo-Norman England.[30] Examples of other Nativity Apocrypha, though, survive from Worcester, Glastonbury, and Bury St. Edmunds.[31] Eadmer emphasized the fact that Jerome never intended for the apocryphal text to be included among the canonical Gospels since its authorship was unknown, thereby giving voice to his own misgivings about the reliability of the literary traditions that described Mary's conception. Eadmer does not seem to have changed his opin-ion about the Apocrypha by the time he composed *De conceptione*, in which he conceded that "whether she who was soon to be born was so announced by an angel or a prochecy (*oraculo aut angelo nuntiata sit*), or however you might think . . . is not contained in the holy scripture nor is it found in the canonical writings."[32] It is striking that this phrase contains echoes of the blessing found in the eleventh-century Christ Church benedictional for the Conception feast (*angelo concipiendam preconavit oraculo*), referred to in the previous chapter— a benediction that Eadmer would have heard as a child and with which he would have been familiar as precentor at Christ Church.[33] Given this, it is safe to assume that Eadmer would not have felt the case for the Conception feast could be made on the basis of the Apocrypha, and this was likely one of the criticisms to which he felt he had to respond.

Eadmer's attempt to answer the feast's detractors and establish a watertight case for its revival set aside the apocryphal legends, and turned instead to cur-rent trends in theological argument obviously inherited from Anselm. In so doing, Eadmer set out a radical new understanding of Mary's purity with the aim of demonstrating that Mary was so glorious from the moment of her con-ception that it would be a dishonor not to commemorate this event. Contrary to Anselm's clearly articulated strategy of arguing solely from first principles, Eadmer opened his *De conceptione* with references to biblical prophecy. The prophetic texts, many of which were used for the liturgies of Marian feast days, foretold that Mary was destined for greatness from the beginning of time, Ead-mer contended. Isaiah, for example, announced that the root of Jesse (Isa. 11:3) would produce a stem, Mary, from which would emerge the flower, Jesus. How could the stalk that would ultimately nourish the body of the Redeemer have been tainted?[34] Biblical precedents were also established when John the Baptist and Jeremiah were blessed in the womb, as the scriptures recount; Mary could not have been any less so.[35] Mary was the foundation and temple, which the Holy Spirit itself inhabited.[36] This made Mary's conception an unusual affair, given that she had been chosen by God not only to house him but also to confer her own flesh to him. As Eadmer mused, "On this account, I do not think that it would go against the faith for the simple sons of the church to think the ori-gins of such a conception so sublime, divine, and ineffable that the human mind would not be able to reach an understanding of it."[37]

Despite his claims for its unknowable nature, Eadmer went on to demon-strate that he had clear ideas about Mary's conception in *De conceptione*. He certainly acknowledged that his view was distinct from anyone else's prior to him:

> If anyone shall say that she was not altogether free from original sin (since it is very true that she was conceived through the union of a man and a woman under the law), if that is the catholic opinion, I do not wish by any means to dissent from the truth of the catholic and universal church; nevertheless when I consider, so

far as I can with a certain cloudiness of mind, the magnificence of the workings of divine power, I seem to see that if there was anything of original sin in the procreation of the mother of God and my own Lord, it belonged to the parents and not to the progeny.[38]

Eadmer realized that he was on shaky doctrinal ground in making this radical claim. Up until this point he had been discussing a splendid, if incomprehensible, conception. Here, Eadmer took it a step further in asserting that Mary was actually free from original sin at the moment of her conception. *De conceptione* therefore contains the first-ever explicit articulation of the doctrine of the Immaculate Conception of Mary—one that proclaimed her to be untainted not just by personal but also original sin.[39] To illustrate what he meant, Eadmer presented his famous example from the natural world: if God had been able to make the chestnut, which comes out shiny and smooth from a rough and prickly exterior without being blemished, what would have prevented him from having Mary emerge, untouched by sin (including Adam's) from the sinful body of her mother?[40] Eadmer then asked how it was that God had saved the good angels from sinning while others had fallen, yet we are to believe that he had not been able to make his own mother spotless.[41] Mary is queen of heaven and earth, above the angels, and her near equality with Christ makes it far more suitable that God would have made her completely sinless. Since God was capable of this, he must have made it happen; he wanted Mary to become his sinless mother, and because he wanted it to be so, so it was done.[42] The church may not have accepted this, but Eadmer's argument derives from the fittingness of it: it was most proper for Christ to have a mother who was cleansed of all sin, and hence Mary must have been conceived without original sin.[43]

As comes across clearly, Eadmer's proof for Mary's Immaculate Conception draws heavily on the work of his mentor, Anselm.[44] Eadmer even reproduced Anselm's argument for the Incarnation in a long section of his *De conceptione*.[45] Eadmer recognized that Anselm's theory of the God-man's sinlessness relied on the fact that Christ had not been born by natural processes but rather by divine intervention from a virgin, thereby disrupting the pattern of natural law to which humanity is subject. As Anselm had admitted, anyone born in this way would be free from original sin.[46] Eadmer took eager advantage of this fact. He appropriated Anselm's arguments for a sinless Christ and transposed them back a generation.[47] In so doing, Eadmer reasoned:

> But when I reflect on the eminence of God's grace in you [Mary], just as I consider you to be not among all created things but immeasurably above them, except for your son, so too do I think that you were not subject to natural law in your conception as others are but were completely freed by the power and operation of the divine from the addition of any sin, in a way that is both singular and impenetrable to the human mind.[48]

It is difficult to know what Eadmer imagined by "not subject to natural law," particularly given the doubts he expressed about the apocryphal narratives; in some versions, the angelic annunciation is treated as the moment of Mary's conception, with no further involvement of Joachim. Eadmer seems to have remained deliberately vague on this count, merely reiterating Anselm's arguments about Christ's conception and applying them to Mary.

Despite what would become Eadmer's conviction, Anselm did not consider it as anything but a hypothetical possibility that someone other than Christ could escape original sin.[49] For his theory of redemption to function, all of humanity has to be corrupted by original sin, and Christ must be the only human being not to have had any trace of it; the distinction is rooted in Christ's divinity, and the need for a perfect man and perfect God to redeem an inherently corrupt humanity.[50] As such, Mary could not have been exempt from the sin that afflicted the rest of the human race and was cleansed only through her faith in the Incarnation, as illustrated earlier.[51] Although it is Boso who articulates this in the *Cur Deus Homo*, Anselm does not himself deny it:

> For, granted that the actual conception of this man [i.e., Christ] was untainted and devoid of the sin of carnal pleasure, the Virgin from whom he was taken was "conceived amid iniquities" and her mother conceived her "in sin" (cf. Psalms 51:6/50:7); and she was born with original sin, since she sinned in Adam, "in whom all have sinned" (cf. Rom. 15:12).[52]

From this it is apparent that Anselm never upheld the doctrine of Mary's Immaculate Conception.[53] Had he held any store in the Apocrypha, Anselm's explanation of Mary's conception would no doubt have been similar to the one he gave to explain other miraculous births, such as that of John the Baptist. In these cases, God miraculously put right a human nature that was physically marred in order for aged or barren people to give birth naturally.[54] There is nothing in such a restoration of fertility that eliminates original sin, and I suspect this is as far as Anselm would have gone in acknowledging that Mary's conception was in any way special.

Eadmer must have been aware of what Anselm would have thought of his arguments. In fact, he shows explicit knowledge of Anselm's theory of Mary's sinlessness through faith when he writes,

> If it is the orthodox position, then I do not deny it if someone asserts that the mother of God was tainted with original sin up until the annunciation of Christ, and believe that she was cleansed by her faith in the angel, in accordance with what is said "by faith does he cleanse their hearts" (Acts 15:9). Nevertheless, a higher consideration tears my mind from this. For as I have said, considering that the mother of God is above all things apart from God, I protest that this radiant woman must be more sublime in the grace of God than the apostles or anything

else that is said to have been created outside of God and his Son. Therefore, if I suggest that the beginning of her creation was in some respects different from that of Adam's offspring, I beg that no one turn his face mockingly, and no one, I say, who is moved toward the mother of God by a feeling of pure devotion and piety, which God gives, should be temtpted to subvert [what I have said], led by some animosity in his reasoning, unless there is for certain something that is inherently contrary to the Christian faith.[55]

Eadmer clearly realized how far he was going in his defense of the unorthodox, so much so that this passage is absent from all but the first copy of *De conceptione*.[56] Eadmer just could not fathom how Mary, superior as she was to other human beings, could have been subject to the same sinful state as them. He acknowledged the fact that his theory makes Mary's origins seem greater than those of Christ himself: "If there is anything that exceeds [the conception of Christ] and surpasses the human intellect, we ought to think that this refers to the conception of the blessed Mary, for it seems by reasonable argument that greater glory and more perfect dignity shone divinely forth from it than from that of Christ our Lord."[57] Eadmer did not mean here that Mary really surpassed Christ in the glory of her conception. He explained that it might seem this way only because Christ's conception was announced by an angel and was made manifest by his taking on of human flesh for all of humanity to witness.[58] By comparison, Mary's conception is still shrouded in mystery, inaccessible to lowly human minds, although necessity dictates that it was at the very least as sinless as her son's. For Eadmer, Mary's selection as mother of God placed her in an utterly unique position above all of humanity, and this distinction must have been present from her beginning.

For all that his assertions were inspired by the wider interest in the problem of original sin expressed in the works of Anselm, we must remember that Eadmer's innovative and controversial thinking emerged as a response to the attacks made against the celebration of the Conception feast. It explains his polemical intent in defending both liturgy and doctrine, for he concluded, "Let he who wants, consider this; let he who wants prove with his own arguments; let he who wants to oppose what I have said, do so. . . . I will not silence what I have written."[59] His defensive attitude betrays knowledge of how groundbreaking yet precarious his case was. Unable to draw support for the feast from the apocryphal writings or Anselm, Eadmer still drew considerable inspiration from his teacher in creating a theological case for the necessity of observing the feast day on the basis that Mary's conception was without parallel. This would only be possible if it differed from all other human conceptions in lacking the contagion of original sin. In developing his arguments following an Anselmian model, Eadmer appealed to reason rather than tradition or precedent for the need to celebrate Mary's conception. He seemed to think that by proving beyond doubt that the event had been utterly special and unique, no one could refuse to commemorate it liturgically. Liturgy spurred on theology, as Eadmer's desire to see the Conception feast reinstated compelled him to produce one of the most daring and original claims about Mary in Christian history.

Eadmer's *De conceptione* was indeed recognized by his monastic contemporaries for its potential to support their own campaigns to revive the feast of Mary's Conception. Osbert's letters, mentioned in the previous chapter, provide a revealing glimpse of how the heated debate concerning the celebration of the feast in the late 1120s came to incorporate Eadmer's revolutionary ideas about the Virgin. As noted earlier, the letter Osbert sent to Anselm in 1128 or 1129 was prompted by an altercation that took place at Westminster in December 1127/28, in which two bishops halted the celebration of the Conception feast as it was under way.[60] Having asked for Anselm's assistance in supplying the "Roman precedent" sought by the feast's opponents, Osbert then set out his own defense for the feast in the same letter, inspired by the work of Eadmer. First Osbert cited the examples of John the Baptist and Jeremiah, both of whom are credited in scripture with having been sanctified in the womb; as the future mother of God, Mary must have been blessed with an even greater honor. Additionally, God must have cleansed his future dwelling place and tabernacle, thus removing all impurity from the body of the woman who was to bear the source of human redemption. God ultimately was able to create the first woman from the rib of Adam, and so it could not have been impossible for him to lift Mary unstained by sin out of the sinful mass (*ex massa praevaricationis*).[61] Taking the formulation almost verbatim from Eadmer's treatise, Osbert reiterated the doctrine of Mary's Immaculate Conception, if with somewhat more hesitation: "We do not believe it to be impossible that . . . God sanctified the blessed Virgin Mary without the contagion of sin at her conception."[62] Osbert's rhetoric, though, is even more virulent than Eadmer's concerning the obstructions he met in trying to revive the feast:

> And because the schisms of those who would create controversy, and the scandals of those who would stir them up, as well as the heresies of those who would go on uselessly, are to be opposed in the house of the Lord by catholic truth and the ecclesiastical defense of the faithful, I lend my pen to the cause so that when you speak with such devout and literate people about this calumny of the envious and the glorious conception of the mother of God, either in writing or by word of mouth, those who are not ignorant of the subtle arguments found in holy scripture might not fear to defend alongside you the cause of the blessed Virgin Mary against the enemies of faith.[63]

If Osbert did not address any letters to Eadmer himself, this is probably because Eadmer was no longer alive; Southern has suggested that Eadmer probably died before 1128, not long after writing his *De conceptione* treatise.[64] Yet Osbert was familiar with Eadmer's work, proving that *De conceptione* was circulating among supporters of the Conception feast and may have had some role in the ultimate success of the case for the feast in 1129.[65]

We might expect the debate to have gone quiet once the feast had received official sanction. But questions about the way in which Mary was conceived only seem to have intensified in the 1130s. Perhaps this was because not even supporters of the feast universally accepted the doctrine of the Immaculate Conception. Hugh of Amiens, the abbot who instated the feast at Reading, wrote explicitly that Mary was sinless only from the moment of the Annunciation onward, reiterating Anselm's position.[66] Even Osbert, after his vociferous approval of the feast and obvious interest in Eadmer's arguments, suddenly became cautious in discussing the subject of Mary's Conception in a letter written in 1138 to Warin, prior of Worcester, a decade after his letter to Anselm.[67] The letter accompanied a sermon for the Conception feast that Warin had requested of him. Despite the fact that the feast was celebrated openly, Osbert complained in the letter that he did "not dare to say what I believe in my heart about this holy generation lest someone begrudging me should cynically begin to gnaw away at me with his teeth, and attack the integrity of my faith, ripping it apart with perverse detractions."[68] He merely hoped that "infidels and heretics" would desist from talking about the feast as if it were pointless and commemorated a sinful act as opposed to the beginnings of redemption.[69] He finally expressed a desire

> that the universal church share in my belief, by which the catholic and orthodox faith might protect me and claim me in defense of itself. I believe in my heart, however, and confess with my voice that God chose for himself a virgin mother before time, in whose virgin womb he made a dwelling place from which the most pious redeemer of mortal humanity would emerge.[70]

This was a step back from arguing that Mary lacked original sin; Osbert only declared that she was chosen from the beginning of time. Osbert's perceived inability to claim anything more than this about Mary's conception probably explains why his sermon contains no mention of the doctrine of the Immaculate Conception. It is built entirely on biblical prophecy, and especially the standard allegories that are applicable to Mary: the burning bush (Exod. 3:2), the flowering rod of Aaron (Num. 17:8), Balaam's prophecy (Num. 22:25–35), the eastern gates of Jerusalem (Ezek. 44:1), and the cloud that carried the lord into Egypt (Isa. 19:1). These commonplaces generally have more to do with the Virgin birth than with the conception of Mary, but Osbert referred to them as evidence that Mary's greatness was foretold in Old Testament prophecy, primarily justified by Proverbs 8:22–31, which was the scriptural foundation as the feast's Epistle.[71] He also proclaimed that her birth was announced to her mother, Anne, by an angel, but only so as to make Mary's selection by God from the beginning of time into an allegory, again referring to the text of Proverbs.[72] Osbert did include terms familiar from his letter of 1128/29, stating that Mary had been formed like clay from the sinful mass of humanity (*ex massa praevaricationis*), yet this time without referring to her own lack of sin.[73] The sermon's principal message is that God began to build his earthly home that has no beginnings, only eternal foundations, and that the sun of justice in its wisdom chose Mary before time itself (*ante tempora saecularia*).[74]

The kind of opposition that Osbert and other supporters of the feast continued to encounter in the 1130s came to be exemplified by the stance of Bernard of Clairvaux. In 1139 or 1140, the charismatic Cistercian abbot launched an attack on the canons of Lyon for celebrating the Conception feast.[75] Why the cathedral canons were commemorating the Conception is unknown, but an incomplete office with neumes typical of Lyon has been dated to the early twelfth century; perhaps the canons were made aware of it by English monks, since Anselm of Canterbury was close friends with the archbishop of Lyon, Hugh, and stayed with him frequently during his periods of exile together with Eadmer.[76] Bernard launched an attack on the feast on three grounds: it was unknown in the wider church, it had no basis in reason, and there was no precedent for it in ancient tradition.[77] In a manner reminiscent of the feast's opponents in England, Bernard could not fathom why the celebration of Mary's conception was necessary: "The Virgin has many true titles of honor, many real marks of dignity, and does not need any that are false."[78] He goes so far as to admit that Mary was purified of sin before she was born, which justifies the feast of her Nativity, but she did not lack sin at the moment of her conception. Her parents had conceived her in carnal sin, and given this, she could not be exempt from the sin of the first parents.[79] To the claim that the Conception feast celebrated the beginnings of salvation, Bernard answered that one could conceivably say the same thing for the births and conceptions of all Mary's ancestors, in an infinite regress. In a reproach that resonates with the opening lines of Eadmer's treatise, Bernard wrote that he had tolerated the error so far because it emanated from love for Mary in the hearts of the simple. But though he was himself a devotee of the Virgin, his devotion did not extend to supporting her Immaculate Conception, nor to celebrating the Conception feast. His opposition ensured the debate continued well into the later Middle Ages, for although he and the Cistercians became famous for their dedication to Mary as their saintly patron, commemorating her conception was a step too far.[80]

ASSUMPTION

Questions about Mary's conception and birth may have reignited interest in another thorny question related to Mary's sanctity and purity, this time concerning the end of her life. Her death or Dormition presented a difficult dilemma: did she ascend to heaven in body *and* soul? The issue was largely resolved by the visions of the Rhineland mystic Elizabeth of Schönau, whose account of having witnessed Mary's body ascend to heaven, recorded by her brother Eckhard circa 1165, gave the doctrine considerable authority.[81] But before this time, the question captured the attention of several monks in the same circles as those interested in the matter of the Conception. This led Henry Mayr-Harting to wonder whether the doctrine of Mary's Assumption emerged in England as a direct response to the controversy over her conception, given that "it was not only that the Son of God shared her flesh, but also that she was neither conceived in concupiscence, nor in principle was able to feel concupiscence, which made it right that her flesh should not see corruption."[82]

Despite drawing a comparison between the two debates, Mayr-Harting distinguished between the purely theological impetus for the Assumption debate and the liturgically motivated reasoning behind reflection on the Conception.[83] Yet ongoing discussion concerning the liturgy for the feast of the Assumption, as we will see, suggests that here too there was a prevailing desire to understand what precisely the liturgical celebration was marking. Granted, the feast of Mary's Assumption had been part of the liturgical calendar for centuries, and there was no question of its legitimacy.[84] But like the Conception, the feast had problematic roots—namely, it too was based on apocryphal accounts. In the description of Mary's death or Dormition, the *Transitus beatae semper virginis Mariae* by Pseudo-Melito, Peter is said to ask Christ, who had come to collect his mother, to "raise up the body of your mother and take her with you rejoicing in heaven."[85] Although immensely popular, the *Transitus* never gained canonical status, making generations of medieval theologians hesitant to claim Mary underwent anything more than a "spiritual" assumption to heaven, particularly in the texts of the liturgy.[86] As we will see, the liturgical texts used for the Assumption feast left the nature of her assumption profoundly ambiguous.[87] As a result, theologians in early twelfth-century England did not just grapple with Mary's Assumption as a theological problem but also as a liturgical one.

One sustained attempt to reason out the nature of Mary's Assumption comes in the form of a short treatise that acts as prologue to a collection of Marian miracles composed between 1136 and 1137 by William, a monk and prolific historian of Malmesbury abbey. The miracles will be discussed in the following chapter, but the prologue deserves exploration in its own right for its engagement with the Assumption debate. The text is purely theological in nature, arguing from first principles in a way that resonates with Anselm's method of examining theological questions, much like Eadmer's *De conceptione*.[88] Because William certainly knew Eadmer, and was familiar with his work, we might suppose that William sought to imitate Eadmer's defense of Mary's conception. He nevertheless turned his theological skills to establishing proof of Mary's unique status in another way, this time ascribing her a death like no other human being. Significantly, like Eadmer, William was a precentor, meaning he was responsible for Malmesbury's liturgical practice in addition to the library.[89] That William was interested in the liturgy is made evident by the fact that he wrote his own version of Amalarius of Metz's liturgical commentary *De ecclesiasticis officiis*.[90] It may have been William's need to understand what precisely the Assumption feast was commemorating that led him to approach the question of its nature in quite the way he did.

Before embarking on the subject of the Assumption, William's treatise progresses through various stages of argument. He first set out to demonstrate just how virtuous the Virgin was in every respect. As befits a prologue to a volume of miracles, the first section explains that Mary's continuing desire to aid her devotees comes from her life of virtue: "What a store of virtues *once* flowed into her, with what readiness she *now* aids mortals in their need; with what grace of gifts she was *then* lofty and wonderful, with what compassion she is *now* powerfully unique and uniquely sweet."[91] William went on to attribute the four cardinal virtues to her—justice, wisdom, courage, and temperance—which Mary embodies to the highest degree. William was borrowing here from Fulbert's sermon for the Nativity, *Approbatae consuetudinis*, which also attributes to Mary the fourfold scheme of virtues laid out in Cicero's *De Inventione*.[92] On this basis, William presented Mary as a clear example for right living: "It was therefore a mark of Justice that she did good, of Prudence that she understood how to do it, of Courage that she persevered, of Temperance that though placed on such a height she had the humility to take care not to fall."[93] Mary's embodiment of every virtue supplied a framework for understanding why she performed the miracles that William related in the second part of his work; as we will see, the miracles provided examples for the theory set out in this first, theoretical section. But it was also the initial step in establishing just how unique and special Mary was.

William's exposition of Mary's virtue allowed him to state that only Mary could have helped accomplish God's plan for salvation:

> Hence, it seems to me that those who say that God could have saved man either through another virgin or by other means than through a virgin are very far from the truth. As for those who think that God could have been embodied in some other virgin, I make a summary reply: On the contrary, he could not have because he did not wish to, and vice versa: He did not wish to because he could not. . . . It is obvious that God, the author of reason, wishes to do nothing, and what is more can do nothing, that is contrary to reason. But who could fail to see that God would have been recoiling from reason if, when he saw that absolutely all women were inferior in sanctity to the blessed Mary, he had spurned her and chosen

some other to be his mother? Now I imagine that anyone who takes note of what has come earlier understands that she was superior in sanctity to all women. For other women merited *parts* of graces, but she is greeted by the angel as "full of grace."[94]

Here, William was clearly reacting to Anselm's *Cur Deus Homo*.[95] As we have seen, Anselm argued that Mary was not chosen for her role as mother of God out of necessity but merely because it was fitting, although Anselm's distinction between these characteristics is not always apparent.[96] Yet for William, it was inconceivable that God should have brought about human redemption via another method than through Mary *herself*, and to do so, he used Anselm's formula about God's rational nature against him. For William, claiming Mary's virgin motherhood had not been necessary seemed to question God's plan:

> What is more, to say that God should or could have repaired the sin of Adam otherwise than by a virgin birth is the same as to say that he should have done better or that he could have done equally well in another way. But if he should have done better or could have done equally well in another way, yet did not do so, he either did not wish to or did not know how to.[97]

If God is pure reason, then the virgin birth through Mary, by virtue of its having facilitated redemption through Christ, was not just aesthetically appropriate but rationally imperative as well. God acted in this way, and it is therefore impossible to conceive that he could have acted otherwise. William, like Eadmer before him, was not satisfied with the role Anselm reserved for Mary in the scheme of salvation and pushed his claims about her further than Anselm had ever been willing to concede.

Establishing Mary's uniqueness in her all-encompassing virtue was merely the first step in William's reasoning. He went on to claim that Mary's complete purity merited her not just election by God as mother for his Son but also the highest degree of love between Father and daughter, mother and Son. In this, William was indebted to Eadmer's *De excellentia*, whose emphasis on this love is discussed in the previous chapter. Further traces of Eadmer's work are evident in William's account of Mary's joys and sufferings in tandem with Christ's, whereby their closeness was reinforced. The work of Anselm lies behind William's formulation that "just as God is Father and Creator of everything, so this virgin is mother and re-creator (*recreatrix*) of everything, because just as nothing exists except what God made, so nothing is re-created except what the son of Holy Mary redeems."[98] Like Anselm's third prayer to the Virgin from which William plainly drew here, William's treatise reasons that this lofty status puts the Virgin in an ideal position to hear the appeals of earthly sinners, as Mary bends the ear of her only-born son on behalf of her adopted children. Mary is not just the "*recreatrix*" of humanity as a whole, by giving birth to the Redeemer, but also the means of redemption for each individual soul, since "it is impossible for a man to be damned if he turns to her and is looked on by her." William thus followed in the tradition of maintaining that Mary was a unique co-redeemer with Christ. "There is no doubt that the merits of the blessed Mary were in God's eyes uniquely distinguished: no single saint, or even all of them together, can be thought equal to her alone," he wrote.[99]

Exploring Mary's role as most beloved creature of God and foremost intercessor brought William to the vexed question of her Assumption. The dignity God visited on her body by being born from her made the issue of her death problematic: Was her pure and holy body really left to decompose on earth? The question appears to have concerned the monks at Malmesbury. But in seeking to address their concerns, William was confronted by a lack of authoritative sources:

> A further inference may be made as to the loftiness of this virgin: a matter not of affirmation but of argumentation. I speak without prejudice either to the caution of the ancients, who made no definite statement about her Assumption or ascension, or to any more probable opinion that may have occurred to moderns. For some—and I am of their company—are not a little worried as to why our writers have either deliberately passed the matter over or hesitatingly kept silence, failing to assert roundly that the Lady, the Mother of the Lord, has already risen, and ascended to heaven with her virgin body.[100]

As this passage makes clear, there was still considerable confusion surrounding the question of Mary's Assumption, despite the long history of the problem, to which William points by mentioning the "cautious statements of the ancients." These may have included a number of Carolingian scholars, who expressed considerable doubt with respect to the Assumption Apocrypha.[101] The most important of these, Paschasius Radbertus (785–865), had urged caution with respect to the Apocrypha in a letter of advice to the nuns under his care on the texts to use for the Assumption liturgy and advised the Song of Songs instead.[102] Fulton has pointed out that Paschasius recommended the text on the basis that it could be read as a narrative of Mary's relationship with Christ, and ultimately her own life and death.[103] The letter in which Paschasius laid out his ideas, referred to as the *Cogitis me*, became incorporated into the Assumption liturgy as office readings throughout western Europe. Despite Paschasius's convictions about the reliability of the Song of Songs in relation to Mary's life and death, the text's ambiguous phrase "*Who is she who rises up from the desert?*" found repeatedly throughout the liturgy for the feast day did not resolve the confusion about the precise nature of Mary's ascension. Paschasius's contemporaries, such as Ambrose Autpertus (d. 784) and later Usuardus (d. ca. 875), noted the troubling absence of Mary's relics on earth, though without coming to any conclusions.[104] The same is true for Adamnán, abbot of Iona, in his account of the holy sites of Byzantium and the Holy Land; he noted her body's absence from its tomb in Josaphat, but refused to decide whether she had ascended bodily to heaven.[105] In eleventh-century England, the homilist Aelfric removed some of Paschasius's doubts and digressions from the *Cogitis me*, when reworking it into a sermon for the Assumption, but gave no more credence to the apocryphal materials on Mary's death than he did to those about her birth.[106] An acrostic poem in an Abingdon manuscript circa 1000 chooses to focus on Mary's reign in heaven over the angelic armies following her Assumption, without pronouncing on the issue explicitly.[107]

To these "ancients," William added "contemporary men" he claimed also expressed hesitation on the issue of Mary's Assumption. William may have been thinking here, among others, of Ralph d'Escures (d. 1122), who was the abbot of Saint-Martin-de-Séez in Normandy until he became Anselm's successor as archbishop of Canterbury in 1114. Ralph had made the opaque statement in a sermon for the Assumption feast that "she is exalted above the choirs of angels, and her greatest desire is fulfilled in good things; she sees God, face to face, as she is, and rejoices with her Son forever."[108] Even Eadmer, despite his fervent belief in Mary's sinlessness at the moment of her conception, left it unclear whether he thought her ascension to heaven had been corporeal, instead preferring to describe the rejoicing in heaven on her arrival as she was welcomed to reign by Christ's side.[109]

Such confusion is even reflected in the liturgical sources for the feast of the Assumption as it was celebrated during William's time. The standard collect for the mass, which we find in a number of missals from St. Augustine's Canterbury, Exeter, St. Albans, and Worcester, seems to leave room for interpretation: "The feast to be venerated by us on this day confers eternal aid in which the holy mother of God suffered temporal death, but she could not however be weighed down by death, she who gave birth to your son, Lord, incarnate from her own body."[110] This ambiguous phrasing seems to suggest that Mary did experience some kind of bodily assumption to heaven, although it remains unclear whether the phrase "she could not . . . be weighed down by death" ought to be understood materially or spiritually. The offertory prayer of the same mass does not clarify the question: "Although she left the world, *according to the condition of the flesh*, let us know that she prays for us in the heavenly glory by your side."[111] Echoing this text, the entry for the Assumption in the martyrology of Usuardus, which exists in an early twelfth-century copy from St. Augustine's Canterbury, makes clear that the offertory prayer refers only to her physical death:

> Even if [Mary's] most holy body is not found on earth, still the holy mother church, in no doubt that [Mary] died in accordance with the condition of flesh, celebrates [Mary's] blessed memory on this feast day. As to where that most ven-

erable temple of the Holy Spirit has been hidden away by divine decree and will, is a matter on which the sober devotion of the church has preferred to know nothing rather than to profess some frivolous and apocryphal tenet.[112]

This text, which would likely have been read out in the chapterhouse or at mealtimes, thus explicitly cautions against believing that Mary rose bodily.[113] Although the feast would appear to celebrate a bodily Assumption, and the absence of Mary's body on earth would seem to indicate that it rose, the martyrology issued a sharp warning about trusting this unconfirmed conclusion. As such, the liturgy for the feast reflected the prevailing hesitation on the issue, and warned those who celebrated it against asking too many questions about what was being celebrated.

In spite of the ambiguity surrounding the Assumption of the Virgin in both the liturgical and theological traditions, there was a growing sense in the eleventh and twelfth centuries that Mary's body could not have been subject to the putrefaction undergone by normal human bodies. In addition to scholars such as Fulbert of Chartres, Peter Damian, and Peter Abelard, Herbert of Losinga, the first bishop of Norwich (from 1091 to 1119), wrote in a sermon for the Assumption that "the most blessed Virgin Mary, made immortal both in body and soul, sits at the right hand of God with her Son, our Lord Jesus Christ, being the mother of penitents and the most effectual intercessor for our sins with her most gracious Son."[114] The anonymous *De Assumptione Beatae Mariae Virginis Liber Uno* was another likely source for William of Malmesbury. It is grouped together with works attributed to Augustine in the *Patrologia Latina*, although he was certainly not the author. But there is little concrete evidence to indicate where or when it was originally produced. It has been variously associated with Alcuin of York, Hrabanus Maurus, and Cosmas Vestitor, all ninth-century scholars, although the earliest-existing copy is found in an early eleventh-century manuscript from the abbey of Saint-Martial in Limoges.[115] The text was of interest in England, and William may have consulted one of two manuscripts: an early twelfth-century copy now attributed to Rochester and a twelfth-century copy from Worcester.[116] The work has several Anselmian formulations, which has confused some scholars into thinking that someone associated with Anselm produced it.[117] The fact that it has received little scholarly attention means a brief exposition of its contents will be useful for understanding William's use of it in his own treatise.

Although the question of authorship of *De Assumptione* remains unresolved, there is little doubt that its message was deemed controversial at the time of writing. The text's hesitant introduction and guarded language throughout points to the fact it was going against the grain in arguing for the bodily Assumption. Despite the fact that things not found in scripture must be treated with caution, "there are certain things," the text contends, "that although they are completely absent from commemoration, nevertheless are believed on the basis of true reason."[118] The text then launches into an argument explaining that while Mary is thought to have died naturally, Jesus also suffered death before his resurrection; in sharing his flesh, there is every possibility that Mary experienced the same fate. Mary certainly deserved to avoid the indignity of being consumed by worms, as Christ himself had. Just as Christ reversed the nature of Adam, so too did Mary with respect to Eve, and thus escaped both sexual intercourse and pain in labor. If God had also been able to preserve Mary's virginity throughout her life, why would he not have done her the honor of saving her flesh from rotting? Having established that God is capable of all things, the author then explained why Christ would have wanted to raise Mary's body to heaven. In chapter 5, he asserted that Christ came to fulfill the law, so would not have ignored the commandment to honor his mother. Since it is a much greater honor for the body to reside in heaven than on earth, because bodily death means disintegration into abject dust, Mary could not have been allowed to suffer such a fate. Indeed, Christ promised those who ministered to him that they would follow him everywhere, but who ministered to him more throughout his life than his own mother? The author ended as he began, with a plea for understanding:

> If anyone should choose to resist these things, but does not want to say that Christ is not capable of them, let him put forward why it is not fitting that Christ should have wanted them, and because of this, that they did not happen. And if he should show that he truly knows the will of God on these matters, then I will begin to believe him, concerning which things I did not otherwise presume to know. . . . If the things I have written are really true, I thank you, Christ, because I was not able to think anything about your virgin mother apart from how pious and worthy is the sight of her. If I have said what I ought to, please approve of me, Christ, I pray, you and yours; if I have nevertheless said what I ought not to, would you and yours overlook it?[119]

The text's obscure identity does not allow us to conclude who the author was, but the tone is strikingly similar to that of Eadmer and Anselm in their own writings on the Incarnation and virgin birth. This in turn clearly proved inspirational for William.

William's approach to the question of Mary's Assumption was to present a logical rationale "for this [the bodily Assumption] can, it seems, be proved by probable and perhaps true arguments."[120] First William argued from the perspective of Mary's purity. The long exposition at the beginning of his prologue established that Mary surpassed the saints because she encompassed all the virtues to their ultimate degree.[121] If Mary had been perfect in every respect, he then claimed, she must have been shown every possible honor, including full resurrection, since such a perfect being could not have been left to wither on earth. In fact, her body was more pure than the soul of the most just man, and if the souls of the saints rise to heaven, then her body must have risen too. Second, he argued from the principle of Christ's love for her, like the author of *De Assumptione*. Mary's greatest joy would have been to stand next to her son in heaven, not just in soul, but also in the body that had housed and nurtured him. In addition to his own overwhelming love for Mary, Christ had instituted the law "honor thy parents." It is therefore impossible that he ignored his own mother and kept her from fulfilling her utmost wish to join him. Finally, William returned to the notion of physical evidence, repeating the argument of Paul the Deacon (d. 870) in his Assumption homily.[122] Mary's body must either be in heaven or on earth. If it is on earth, it is unlikely to be under the sea, so it must be somewhere on land. Christ would never have allowed such a holy body to remain hidden without it performing miracles of any kind, so Mary's body must be found in heaven. Although William claimed at the end that he had done nothing but summarize the arguments of his predecessors, his succinct and carefully plotted line of reasoning brought these together with a new clarity.

William's interest in the doctrine of Mary's bodily Assumption must have been widely shared, or at least enough that it came to be reflected in a number of unusual images that appeared in English manuscripts at approximately the same time as his treatise. These are among some of the earliest images to suggest a bodily Assumption—a shift from earlier traditions of depicting the Virgin's Dormition.[123] The so-called Byzantine diptych in the Winchester Psalter is one of the most unusual depictions of Mary's Assumption from twelfth-century England.[124] The first of two full-page images shows the *Koimesis*—that is, the Dormition of the Virgin, with Christ grasping Mary's tiny swaddled soul to take it up to heaven (figure 4). Scholars have additionally argued that the empty tomb depicted beside the Virgin's bed is a reference to Mary's bodily Assumption.[125] A similar image, though without the empty tomb, is found in the Queen Melisende Psalter, which was also produced from Byzantine models and may have had a Winchester connection.[126] A later cycle of images based on the *Transitus* narrative in the Hunterian Psalter (ca. 1170) went on to depict the bodily Assumption quite literally, with the final image showing Christ pointing to an empty tomb from which a shrouded body is lifted by angels (figure 5).[127] The assurance with which this particular artist illustrated the doctrine of Mary's bodily Assumption in a completely unparalleled way, unique in Christian art, could reflect its newfound acceptance following the visions of Elizabeth of Schönau, although the unusual iconography may have benefited from the English context in which it was produced.[128]

Although William's arguments in favor of the bodily Assumption must be viewed against the backdrop of the prevailing obscurity surrounding the Assumption and the feast that celebrated it, he never explicitly referred to a litur-

Figure 4. Winchester Psalter, in BL Cotton Nero C. iv, ff. 29r, circa 1150. © The British Library Board, British Library Cotton MS Nero C. iv, f. 29v.

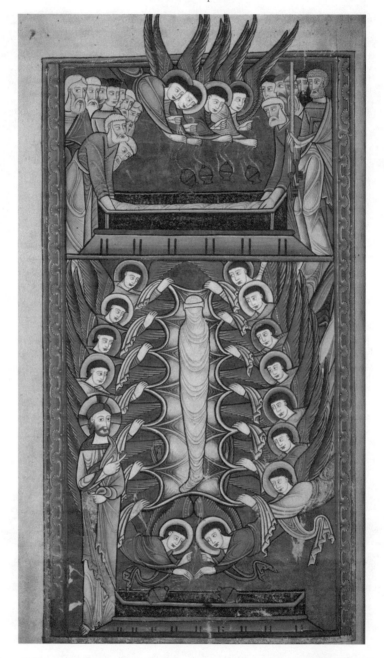

Figure 5. Hunterian Psalter, in Glasgow University Special Collection MS Hunter U.3.2 (229), f. 19v, circa 1170. By permission of the University of Glasgow Library, Special Collections.

gical celebration as the source of his treatise. Honorius Augustodunensis, another Benedictine monk and disciple of Anselm, nevertheless responded to the Assumption liturgy directly in his writings on the question.[129] Honorius is known to have spent part of his early career in England, most likely after having arrived as a wandering scholar. He is thought to have become a Benedictine at Worcester Cathedral, where Valerie Flint has contended he was in residence around 1100 after having also spent time at Christ Church Canterbury.[130] It was while at Christ Church that he would have come into contact with Anselm and his intellectual circle, and also encountered ideas of monastic reform that inspired a number of his works. Honorius took his cues from Anselm in campaigning for the reform of the priesthood, such as in his *Offendiculum* against married and simoniac priests—a work more scathing even than its model, Anselm's *De Presbyteris Concubinariis seu Offendiculum Sacerdotum.*[131]

While at Worcester, Honorius wrote two major works that combined his interest in monastic reform with Marian devotion. The first, the *Speculum Ecclesiae*, is a series of sermons for the liturgical year, including one for each of the Marian feast days celebrated there at the time: Assumption, Nativity, Purification, and Annunciation.[132] Although addressed to the monks of Christ Church, the collection seems to have been intended for a wider audience that likely included laypeople present for the monks' preaching at the cathedral on important feast days.[133] Together with the *Elucidarius, Gemma animae*, and *Sacramentarium*, the *Speculum Ecclesiae* demonstrates Honorius's desire to make provisions for clerical education.[134] This impulse was also behind the most important work in which Honorius discussed the Virgin, his *Sigillum de Beata Maria*. The work is an unprecedented examination of the liturgical texts used for the office of the Assumption, many of which were drawn from the Song of Songs. The treatise thus comprises a line-by-line commentary of the Song of Songs—the first to systematically read Mary into the text.[135] Honorius additionally cast Mary as an example for monks in the spirit of the ecclesiastical reforms of which he was an active proponent. As such, the *Sigillum* is a clear example of the English Benedictine interest in Mary, and the original responses that such interest prompted.

At least at the very outset of his text, Honorius staged the *Sigillum* as a discussion between a group of disciples and their master on the question of the liturgy used for the feast of the Assumption.[136] Honorius reports that some monks inquired about the reasons behind the texts used in the Assumption liturgy, since "they do not seem to pertain to [Mary] at all (*cum nihil penitus ad eam pertinere videantur*)."[137] The Song of Songs, the biblical book that dominated the chants of the Assumption office, had generally been read in the exegetical tradition as an allegory for the loving relationship between Christ and the church, or Christ and the soul.[138] This made its use for the Assumption feast perplexing, which Honorius then sought to address. Despite the possibility that

Honorius's appeal to the request of the monks was a rhetorical device that merely served to justify his innovative approach to the question, it could also point once again to a more general curiosity about particular features of Marian devotion, as argued by Valerie Flint.[139] Honorius's work certainly struck a chord with monastic audiences in England, as suggested by the earliest-surviving manuscripts of the *Sigillum* from the diocese of Worcester, including one copy from Evesham and another from Malmesbury.[140]

Like Eadmer, Honorius's purpose in composing the *Sigillum* had more to do with liturgy than theology. Faced with the problem that the texts used in the liturgy for the Assumption were not explicitly connected to Mary, Honorius created a new exegesis that placed Mary at its center. His efforts were not entirely unprecedented. Ambrose of Milan had used verses of the Song of Songs to describe Mary as the ideal virgin and an example to virgins everywhere, in his numerous ascetic works of advice for women, most recently explored by Karl Shuve.[141] So too had Aldhelm, the eighth-century bishop of Sherborne, who in a work of advice to the nuns of Barking Abbey, *De virginitate*, echoed Ambrose in presenting Mary as a role model, describing her with a series of images from the Song of Songs: "Blessed Mary, perpetual virgin, *enclosed garden, sealed fountain* (Song of Songs 4:12), etc."[142] But no theologian had incorporated this Marian sense into a commentary of the entire Song of Songs until Honorius. Acknowledging the exegetical tradition of reading the Song of Songs as an exchange between Christ and the church, Honorius set up a parallel between Mary and the church:

> The glorious Virgin Mary represents that type of the church, which exists as virgin and mother, for she is proclaimed as mother because she, fertile through the Holy Spirit, daily brings forth children through baptism. But she is said to be a virgin because, serving inviolate the purity of faith, she is not corrupted by vicious heresy. Thus Mary was mother in giving birth to Christ, and remaining closed even after giving birth, she was a virgin. Therefore all that is written of the church is suitably ascribed to her as well.[143]

Honorius then applied this likeness, line by line, to the entire text. The association between the church and Mary may not have been new, but Honorius's understanding that the Song of Songs could be applied to Mary as a main player certainly was.

While more exegetical than theological in nature, Honorius's treatise reveals direct influence from Anselm's thinking with reference to Mary—something pointed out by Flint and Southern.[144] In addition to taking on the device of staging his text as a dialogue between a master and disciple—at least initially; the pretense is hardly sustained—the content of Honorius's work shows obvious familiarity with Anselm's theological treatment of the Incarnation. Echoing the language used by Anselm, Honorius described how Mary was chosen as mother for the sun of justice, who flowed through her like light through a window—an image reminiscent of Anselm's analogy that Mary is like crystal, undefiled by the sun's rays.[145] She rose like the dawn, emerging from the *peccatrice massa*, wrote Honorius, using a term familiar from the *Cur Deus Homo*.[146] Honorius also reiterated Anselm's fourfold scheme of human generation, including the singular creation of Christ from woman alone, "a privilege that [God] kept for himself."[147] Honorius's syllogistic explanation for the virgin birth is also redolent with Anselmian reasoning: God is capable of doing anything he wishes and he wanted to be born of a virgin; therefore a Virgin gave birth to both God and man.[148] This was fitting "because just as death entered through a virgin woman, so life had to enter through a virgin woman."[149] Like Eadmer and William, Honorius thought Anselm's arguments effective in establishing Mary's worthiness as virgin mother of God.

As theologians had done since Origen, Honorius ascribed the Song of Songs text to various voices, with each verse attributed to different characters in an extended drama.[150] Yet Honorius radically altered the text's meaning by including Mary as one of the protagonists. In so doing, Honorius presented the Canticle as a loving dialogue between Christ and his mother, which Fulton has helpfully described as a drama in two acts.[151] The first act depicts Mary's life on earth, her son's death, and her sadness at his ascension until the moment he summoned her, allowing her to be assumed into heaven. This event is described by a key passage (Song of Songs 3:6): "*Then follows the praise of the angels when they hasten to meet her as she seeks the kingdom of heaven: Who*—that is, how glorious—*is she that goes up* to the palaces of heaven, *by the desert*—that is, deserting the dangerous world?"[152] The second act of the drama depicts Mary presiding over the court of heaven as queen of all the saints, encouraging those on earth to pray to her for intercession. It ends with the church yet to be converted (*Ecclesia convertendae*—that is, the Jews) turning to Mary and converting to the true faith. This important section, concerned with conversion and the supersession of the new law over the old through Mary's actions, will be discussed below. In the main, Honorius's reading of the Song of Songs crafted a narrative about the love between Mary and Jesus, and the triumph of her Assumption to heaven.

Although Honorius's aim was not to develop theological arguments for Mary's Assumption as William did, he did address the issue in his *Sigillum*. In glossing the central phrase of the Song of Songs text, *quae est ista quae ascendit per desertum*, Honorius wrote that this "seem[s] to be the church's words on the Assumption of the body of Mary."[153] If the word "seems" (*videtur*) suggests residual hesitation, Honorius included more explicit statements in his gloss of Song of Songs 3:7–8 ("Behold threescore valiant ones of the most valiant of Israel, surrounded the bed of Solomon, all holding swords and most expert in war: every man's sword on his thigh, because of fears in the night"). The couch of Solomon surrounded by sixty guards is the body of the Virgin, which rose to heaven encircled by many thousands of angels, armed with swords to protect her from demons and other aerial powers that might have threatened her.[154] This interpretation may have derived from the *Transitus*, in which Mary begs the angel who announces her impending death to protect her from Satan on her heavenly voyage.[155] At the end of the commentary, Honorius repeated the same image to explain why there was a procession on the feast day: one reason was because her body was processed through the streets of Jerusalem by the apostles, as was known from the Apocrypha; "secondly, because her most blessed spirit was borne into heaven by angels, in procession with the Son of God. Her body was revived afterward, and is believed to have been gathered up into the glory of heaven."[156] The idea of a two-part ascension is also derived from the Apocrypha, in which several days elapse between Mary's death and the assumption of her body.[157] Honorius therefore clearly envisioned Mary's Assumption to heaven in body as well as soul as a fundamental element of what the feast celebrated. The key point of his liturgical explanation was to illustrate that in bringing his mother to his side—through her assumption to heaven—Christ founded a new feast day worthy of the greatest celebration.

The fact that Mary merited the singular privilege of a bodily Assumption comes across as a direct consequence of her supreme physical purity and moral virtue in the works by Honorius and William. While she was elevated as a result of a superiority that fundamentally distinguished her from all other women, Honorius also saw her as setting an excellent example to her Christian followers. Like Osbert, who later in the 1130s portrayed Mary as a role model for all virgins and especially nuns, Honorius saw Mary as the first virgin to reverse the biblical curse on infertility by making virginity the highest virtue. His sermon for the feast of the Nativity in the *Speculum Ecclesiae* collection describes Mary's childhood, in which she alone expressed a desire to remain a virgin while all the other girls serving in the Temple were married off. "This first among women vowed her virginity to God and therefore she alone among women deserved the fertility of the greatest offspring, as a virgin," explained Honorius.[158] Virginity is thus put forward as Mary's choice, and one that reflects her inner purity. In this way, Mary is held up as an example to monks and nuns in the *Sigillum*: "The Virgin, mother of God, was the cypress tree on Mt. Sion, to wit, the true watchtower—that is to say, the church—whose mind, once it has dried up to vices and desires, never grows back to the joys of the world; therefore she is held up in preaching as a model before those who are to be mortified for Christ's sake."[159] Mary herself is said to urge her followers:

> if you wish my prayers not to be in vain, in these things you should imitate me. *I have put off my garment*—that is, I have rejected worldly things. . . . *I have washed my feet*—that is, I have walled off my affection. . . . *[M]y hands dropped with*

myrrh—that is, my exercises of carnal mortification abounded. *And my fingers were full of the choicest myrrh*—that is, my pursuits of various austerities were approved.[160]

In emphasizing Mary's agency in choosing to preserve her virginity, Honorius cast her as a proto-nun that chimed with contemporary monastic reform ideals.[161]

For all its relevance particularly to religious professionals, Honorius's understanding of Mary as a role model was ultimately much broader in scope. In glossing the Gospel text for the mass (Luke 10:38–41), Honorius's analysis in the *Sigillum* and sermon for the Assumption feast drew heavily from a sermon for the Assumption by Ralph d'Escures (d. 1122), Anselm's successor as archbishop of Canterbury.[162] In interpreting the account of Jesus's visit to the house of the sisters Martha and Mary, Honorius, like Ralph, read the "town" (*castellum*) into which Jesus entered (Luke 10:38) as Mary's womb, who preserved both her virtue and virginity intact while allowing Christ in.[163] As Giles Constable has explored, the two sisters were thought to represent the active and contemplative lives, both of which Honorius and Ralph attributed to the Virgin.[164] The metaphor is also echoed in Honorius's gloss of the Song of Songs: "*Your breasts are more beautiful than wine*: The breasts of the Virgin were examples in active and contemplative life, with which, as if with milk, she nourished the little ones in faith."[165] Mary thus served as a model for both the regular and secular clergy, as reiterated in Honorius's sermon for the feast of the Assumption.[166]

The interpretation of the Epistle of the mass (Ecclus. 24:11–23) in the *Sigillum* took up the same theme. It too draws from a sermon for the Assumption erroneously attributed in the manuscript record to Anselm.[167] In this case, however, Honorius diverged from his source in applying the Ecclesiasticus text entirely to the Virgin and her Assumption. The passage with critical relevance to the feast day is glossed as follows: "*And in the holy city likewise I rested*. The holy city is the supernal homeland . . . in which the perpetual virgin now rests with saints and angels, but crowned with glory and honor, she shone above all the rest."[168] Echoing the interpretation of Mary as paradigm for both active and contemplative lifestyles, the heavenly queen is depicted as shining forth among the married peoples of the world, but also acting as an example to cloistered men and women: "For all those who renounce the world and have recourse to Christ, this Virgin Mary . . . crucified her body to the enticements of the world, and afflicted herself through fasting and vigils."[169] She has a central place in the church representing both groups, which Honorius made clear in no uncertain terms: "Sion is called the watchtower and it is the church, in which the mother of God is established as a column by writing and preaching; and on her praiseworthy life the whole church is supported."[170] In this unprecedented interpretation, Mary is described as the central pillar of the church, that which supports its entire structure. The anonymous sermon that served as Honorius's source refers only to the church, not to Mary. Honorius thus shifted preexisting exegetical frameworks to accommodate a more Marian reading of the texts used for the feast of the Assumption, with the result that Mary was now understood to serve as the very foundation of the church, an illustration of virtue and right living to all its members. This would only have helped to justify celebrating her with all the elaborate liturgical practices developed in this period: a model Christian to be commemorated for her unique role in underpinning the church itself.

There has been a recent suggestion that Honorius's innovative gloss on the Song of Songs, with Mary as heavenly queen and column of the church, was given a striking visual component in England when visual images of Mary in precisely this guise began to proliferate in the twelfth century. The Winchester Bible (1160/75) is a good example. In the first initial of the book, the "O" of "Osculetur" (Song of Songs 1:1), the Queen of Sheba is shown next to Solomon, the legendary author of the text.[171] Since Solomon was traditionally a figure for Christ, the queen could have been interpreted as the church and bride of the Son. Yet she looks remarkably like contemporary images of Mary, adorned with a typically English crown, and holding a lily and flowering orb.[172] Morgan pointed out several additional examples of this kind of iconography, but did not note the possible relation of these images to Honorius's *Sigillum*, which established an explicit link between the church, bride, and Mary in the context of the Song of Songs.[173] Diane Reilly and Jean-Claude Schmitt have discussed other similar images related to the Song of Songs, generally remarking on their relation to Song of Songs commentaries by Bernard of Clairvaux and Rupert of Deutz, although as far as we can tell, Honorius's was first.[174]

This imagery could be linked to another iconographic innovation that appeared in early twelfth-century England and was likely inspired by Honorius's reading of the Canticle in a Marian light. The "Coronation of the Virgin" depicts an episode in which Mary is in heaven and sits by Christ's side while he places a crown on her head. Until recently, the earliest example of this iconographic scene was assumed to have been a capital at the abbey of Reading, founded by Henry I in 1121 and dedicated to Mary (figure 6).[175] T. A. Heslop, though, has argued that there was an even earlier instance of this type of image in a series of paintings from circa 1100 that once adorned the ceiling of Worcester chapterhouse.[176] Now lost, the images are preserved in a manuscript dated circa 1260, together with the verses that accompanied each painted roundel.[177] The artistic program of the chapterhouse seems to have been planned as an allegorical representation of Mary, with a particular focus on her Assumption that bears a striking resemblance to Honorius's *Sigillum*.[178] The image of Christ crowning his mother on her arrival is shared with Honorius's reading of the

Figure 6. Capital, Reading Abbey, circa 1120. Reading Museum, Coronation of the Virgin Capital. © Reading Museum (Reading Borough Council). All rights reserved.

biblical text, especially the line "Come, you will be crowned" (Song of Songs 4:8). The roundel (figure 7) additionally shows the coronation as taking place on a cart, around which are placed the four symbols of the evangelists.[179] This was precisely Honorius's understanding of the enigmatic quadriga of Aminadab in Song of Songs 6:11. From this Heslop concluded that Honorius's presence at Worcester and the interest shown in his *Sigillum* there were formative for the pictorial cycle in the Worcester chapterhouse.[180] Some additional suggestion of Honorius's influence can be detected in the images in the church at Regensburg, where he spent some thirty years after leaving England.[181] Art and commentary thus echoed each other, giving visual dimension to the exegetical understanding of Mary as the bride and queen of the Song of Songs, assumed to heaven in body and soul.

CONVERSION

Honorius's innovative and influential reading of the Marian liturgy of the Assumption portrayed Mary's triumph as so great that it would even turn unbe-

Figure 7. Eton College MS 177, f. 7r, early thirteenth century. Reproduced by permission of the Provost and Fellows of Eton College.

lievers to her cause. In so doing, like the liturgy explored in the previous chapter, his work incorporated a polemical dimension that resonated with important theological trends. The discussions that Anselm sparked with his incarnational works were obviously internal Christian controversies; Anselm and his heirs were interested in answering questions posed by Christians for the benefit of Christians. But Anselm was so convinced of his reasons for the need of an incarnate God that he claimed they might convince anyone with the faculty of reason, "not only Jews, but even pagans."[182] Anselm put this device to use, writing the *Cur Deus Homo* as a dialogue between himself and his disciple, Boso, but attributing arguments to Boso that a non-Christian might put forward. Anselm neatly summarized this opposing position in writing, "Unbelievers, deriding us for our simplicity, object that we are inflicting injury and insult on God when we assert that he descended into a woman's womb; was born of a woman," which he then countered in the rest of the treatise.[183]

Whether or not Anselm was referring here to the Jewish standpoint, several of Anselm's students took the idea of discussing with unbelievers literally.[184] Arguing mainly for the Incarnation and virgin birth in a style reminiscent of Anselm, a growing number of theologians began to explore questions of Christian doctrine in the form of a dialogue between a Jewish and Christian interlocutor, although whether they are based on real conversations has been the source of some debate.[185] These works, by Odo of Tournai, Guibert of Nogent (d. 1124), Pseudo-William of Champeaux, and Peter Alfonsi (d. ca. 1110), in addition to Gilbert, are generally discussed as marking a new phase in Christian thinking about Jews, one that saw a turn to reason in arguing for Christian doctrine that left Jews looking decidedly "unreasonable" and at worst, borderline inhuman.[186] There has been a great deal of research done on the renewed popularity of this genre.[187] It is worth noting that two of the earliest polemicists in the movement, Gilbert and Alfonsi, were resident in England at one time.[188] Gilbert was formerly a monk of Bec before becoming the abbot of Westminster, where he allegedly met the Jewish businessman who inspired his work of polemic, the *Disputatio*.[189] The Aragonese convert from Judaism and author of the *Dialogue against the Jews*, Alfonsi is thought to have been the personal physician of Henry I.[190] Through the *Dialogue*, a self-justifying conversation between his former Jewish and present Christian selves, Peter introduced the Talmud to Christian scholars in northwestern Europe, but also articulated several arguments for the Incarnation that echo Anselm's writings.[191] The works of Gilbert and Alfonsi were the most popular polemics produced in the twelfth century, with the largest number of surviving manuscripts, including many English manuscripts almost exclusively from Benedictine houses, which suggests a marked interest in the genre among English monks.[192] While polemical writing was popular in other regions, including Lotharingia and northern France, it is interesting to note that it was largely a monastic pursuit in this early period, with a particular presence in English monasteries.[193] This is especially notewor-thy given the convergence of interest in polemic with growing devotion to Mary.

The importance of Mary in twelfth-century polemics is nowhere more evi-dent than in the works of Odo and Guibert, who while not based in England, deserve a brief mention due to their clear Anselmian inheritance. Both made the virgin birth the main subject of their polemical works, ultimately highlight-ing the fundamental gap between Christians and Jews on the subject of Mary.[194] Odo had his Jewish character Leo exclaim: "We laugh at you and judge you in-sane, for you say that God was enclosed in the obscene prison of the disgusting belly of his mother for nine months, only to come out in the tenth month from her shameful exit (*pudendo exitu*), which cannot be looked on without hor-ror."[195] The appropriate Christian response to this, according to Odo, was to argue that bodies are fundamentally clean, and it is only souls that can be sul-lied by sin; Mary, who lacked all sin, was therefore a perfectly fitting vessel for even the Almighty.[196] Following a similar and equally ascerbic argument against the virgin birth by his Jewish interlocutor, Guibert made the same argument about the inherent goodness of the human body, while also providing examples from nature of other nonsexual forms of reproduction: cats born of catnip, goats of plants, and vultures and bees reproducing without coition.[197] Although these treatises are not directly related to the debates on Mary's Immaculate Conception and Assumption produced in England, they nevertheless reflect a shared interest in Mary's paradigmatic virtue and purity as well as a similar way of arguing for it. Anselm's new approach to exploring the Incarnation and vir-gin birth thus incited theologians to place Jews squarely in the conversation on Mary's role in the scheme of Christian salvation.

Returning to the English context, this convergence of polemic and Marian devotion is perhaps most clear in the works of Honorius.[198] As we have seen, Honorius ascribed the diverses voices in the Song of Songs to Mary and Christ, but also to additional characters: the Church and the Synagogue, or "converting Church." Although referred to predominantly as the "penitent church that is to be converted from the Jews," there is little doubt that by this term Honorius meant the Synagogue. Neither of these allegorical figures was new; they were standard players in earlier interpretations of the text going back to Origen.[199] But Honorius's gloss changed the general message of the dialogue between the characters, placing Mary at the center of an unfolding drama of conversion. After describing her rise to heaven, the "narrative" related in the Song of Songs, as Honorius interpreted it, follows the realization by unbelievers of the glory of Christ and especially of his mother, such that they become the converting Church. Hope for the conversion of the Jews is therefore a theme that runs throughout the text, as Honorius imagined a time near the end of days when the Jews would come to understand the folly of their past unbelief and specifically their unbelief concerning Mary.[200] The first words uttered by the converting Church or Synagogue in the *Sigillum* express the pain she feels at having erred so long in denying the Virgin:

> *I knew not*, o glorious Virgin, that *you* were full of grace and that a fount of grace flowed out of you. *My soul troubled me*—that is, the zeal for the law that I had within my soul prevented me from knowing—and this comes to pass *for the chariots of Aminadab*—that is, for the gospels of Christ—so that having been repelled by me, they should rather be propelled through the regions of the world.[201]

Here, the former Synagogue admits the emptiness of the law by which she has abided, and comes to recognize the Gospels and with them the message of Mary's virgin motherhood. The Sunamite, that mysterious figure riding in on the four-wheeled cart of Aminadab in Song of Songs 6:11, is glossed as a figure of the Synagogue, who was "so long captive to the devil" in her unbelief and is called to return to the faith.[202] As suggested by her triumphant entrance, borne by the word of God contained in the Gospels, her conversion will be complete, and "in the Church that is converted from the Jews, nothing will be seen if not the companies of those praising God, and the camps of those fighting against vice."[203] Having turned to Christ, the converting Church begins to praise the Virgin, addressing her as the "prince's daughter," from the line of David, thereby acknowledging the Virgin's royal Jewish heritage.[204] Accepting the things prophesied of Mary, the Synagogue becomes one of the faithful peoples nourished by the Virgin's breasts, "those of the circumcised and those with foreskin" who have already sucked from her milk of humility and chastity—that is, Christian converts from paganism and Judaism.[205] Honorius depicts belief in Mary's virgin motherhood as a key element in the Synagogue's conversion, for acknowledgment of her glorious virginal body is what brings it about.

Mary is not just a passive catalyst in the Synagogue's transformation, the object of a changing belief. She is herself depicted as actively bringing the Christian message to unbelievers, and her proselytizing efforts are first and foremost directed toward the Jews. "In the following words, the Virgin recalls those things she has done for the Church that will be converted from the Jews," announced Honorius:

> I have poured out prayers *to my beloved* for you, *and his turning to me*—that is, through me he wanted to turn to you in mercy. And thus I said: *Come my beloved*, to the Synagogue, out of mercy, since you fled from it on account of its fault of perfidy. *Let us go forth* by faith *into the field*—namely, into the whole world; *let us abide* by works *in the villages*—that is, among all peoples. *Let us get up early to the vineyards*—that is, to the synagogues of the Jews—which is to say, let us bring it about as soon as possible that the final moment shine in their hearts. *Let us see if the vineyards flourish*—that is, let us make them see in their minds how the

church has flourished in faith. *If the flowers be ready to bring forth fruits*—that is, let us see how they have become known through good works—and *if the pomegranates flourish*—that is, let us see how they have become *breasts*—that is, they will imitate my example unto your honor.[206]

The Gentiles have already been converted, and now it is time for the Jews to follow suit and recognize that Christ fulfilled the old law. Although the Jews sucked at the breasts of the Synagogue—that is, from the old law—and still stand outside the faith, Mary has great hopes that they will worship Christ and love him, such that "*no man will despise me*—namely, there will be no one of the Jews who will not believe that I remained a Virgin. *I will take hold of you*—that is, I will prove that you [Christ] took flesh of me without the seed of man."[207] Once they have accepted the virgin birth, and Christ has entered the body of the Synagogue, the Jews will have a new understanding of the law, and will turn away from temporal things and toward spiritual ones. As a result, Christ warns the converted Church not to think anything untoward about his mother, repeating his threat three times "so that they may learn how much veneration is owing to God's mother."[208] Mary presents herself as an example to the Jews, stating that her breasts will be a wall against sin, such that she will teach them to be impregnable to vice by her example.[209] Only through Mary, the embodiment of virtue, will the Jews find an example to follow and thus be brought to faith in Christ.[210] In this way, the liturgy of the Assumption could be understood on an eschatological scale, commemorating not just Mary's ascension to heaven but also her ultimate triumph, reigning over all peoples as their universal queen.

Honorius's vision of Mary's eschatological role may have inspired another first in Western art: the iconography of Synagoga's unveiling. In the same set of wall paintings that once adorned the ceiling of the Worcester chapterhouse, mentioned earlier, there was an image of the Synagogue, figuratively represented as a young woman, with a veil being pulled from her eyes (figure 8). The roundel, which was found in the bay adjacent to that of Mary's coronation, was encircled by the verse: "Hitherto concealed in the clouded configurations of the Law, o Synagoga, with the advent of Faith, see the reality. Let Synagoga be made new in the refashioned cloak of the Law, let grace adorn her in the garment of the faith."[211] This, according to T. A. Heslop, relates directly to the gloss of the verse *Quae est ista qui ascendit?* (Song of Songs 8:5), which is attributed in the *Sigillum* to *Ecclesia convertenda.*[212] The juxtaposition of the image of Synagoga's unveiling with that of Mary's coronation in the next bay over points to a relation between the two images. To the paintings' observers, it would have looked as if Synagoga sees the light and converts to Christ by witnessing Mary become queen of heaven, in direct relation to Honorius's gloss.

Figure 8. Eton College MS 177, f. 7v, early thirteenth century. Reproduced by permission of the Provost and Fellows of Eton College.

In a related roundel adjacent to the scene of the coronation, "Judaea" and "Idumea"—the Jews and the nation of Edom (figurative here for pagans)—are shown as two women, each holding an arm of the cross, with the verse: "Here Judaea binds herself to Christ, as likewise does Idumea. Thus can one flock be made for the Lord out of two."[213] Although Heslop argues that this in fact refers to the union of Anglo-Saxon and Norman peoples in the marriage of Henry I to Matilda of Scotland, the more immediate reading has to do with the conversion of peoples referred to in Honorius's *Sigillum*. The idea is that Synagoga will be converted, and all peoples will become one in Christ.[214] The Worcester chapterhouse's artistic program thus visually reproduced the *Sigillum*'s insistance on Mary, crowned as queen of heaven, in bringing about the future conversion of the Jews.[215] We should remember that the chapterhouse was where the monks gathered every day for their general chapter meeting and *collatio*, before compline, where readings not just of the Rule but also other instructive texts were read out—including miracles of the Virgin, many of which featured the conversion of Jews, as we will see.[216] Liturgical readings would have echoed the images over the heads of the monks, as they contemplated their patron's power even over nonbelievers.

For Anglo-Norman art more widely, Honorius's exegetical interpretation of the Song of Songs proved formative. The Lambeth Bible, produced circa 1140, possibly in Canterbury by Master Hugo, contains two images that are linked to the Worcester roundels.[217] The "O" initial that begins the book of the prophet Habakkuk shows a Crucifixion scene in which the crowned Ecclesia and Synagoga, both holding banners, although Synagoga's is broken in half, flank Christ.[218] While losing her crown, Synagoga still has her veil pulled up off her face by a hand coming from the left. Similar imagery is reproduced again in the Lambeth Bible's "Jesse Tree" image. Derived from the Isaiah 11:1–2 text— "There shall come forth a shoot from the root of Jesse, and a flower shall grow out of his roots"—the iconography glossed the prophetic text as a reference to Mary's royal genealogy, showing her in a long line of kings that ended in Christ, the flower.[219] Although Arthur Watson's survey of the earliest instances of the Jesse Tree highlights the French examples, C. M. Kauffmann argues that examples such as that found in the Shaftesbury Psalter are among the earliest, with the Winchester and Eadwine psalters produced not long after.[220]

The artist of the Lambeth Bible gave his depiction of the Jesse Tree additional unique features (figure 9). In this magnificent image, highlighted in gold, Mary takes up the entire page, standing tall in a blue gown and red mantle, her head uncovered, joining the sleeping Jesse at her feet to Christ at her head. In the six roundels adjacent to her and in the corners, we find four kings and prophets, four additional prophets, four virtues (Mercy, Truth, Justice, and Peace from Psalm 84, which was often interpreted as an allegory for the Incarnation, and is also depicted in the Worcester roundels), and the contrasting

Figure 9. Lambeth Bible, in Lambeth Palace Library MS 3, f. 198, Canterbury, 1140–50. © Lambeth Palace Library, London, UK/Bridgeman Images.

figures of Ecclesia and Synagoga. The presence of the last two figures is highly unusual for Jesse Tree images and is shared with only two other Bibles, both produced later in the twelfth century.[221] Kauffmann has called the image of Synagoga's unveiling an innovation of the Lambeth Bible's artist, but it would have been preceded by the Worcester wall paintings and could have been influenced by its iconography.[222] Sara Lipton has insightfully pointed out that the kinds of exegetical and theological innovations discussed above can help to explain the interest of monks in creating these allegorical representations of the polemical encounter, but do not provide an all-encompassing account why these images emerged at this time.[223] I would argue that central to understanding this particular image is its appearance in a Marian context. Mary's depiction as the very stalk of Isaiah's prophecy, stretching the full length between Jesse and Jesus on the vertical axis, means she stands between the Church and Synagogue on the horizontal axis in the Jesse Tree images. The visual representation of Mary's genealogy portrays her explicitly as an interface between old and new laws, echoing the placement of the Jesse Tree images themselves. These are often found between scenes from the Old and New Testaments, such as in the Winchester and Eadwine psalters. In the case of the Shaftesbury Psalter, the Jesse Tree image joins the New Testament cycle of illuminations to the psalter itself.[224] Just like the Jesse Tree, Mary was depicted as a bridge between Christians and Jews in more ways than one: as the Jewish mother of Davidic ancestry who brought forth Christ, and as the means by which the Synagogue can turn to Christ and thus join the Church.

CONCLUSION

The marvelous results brought about by actively contemplating and reasoning about Mary emerges in stark relief in art and theology, as twelfth-century writers and artists ascribed Mary a more significant status than ever before. The radical theological treatises composed by Eadmer, William, and Honorius emphasized her utter uniqueness through unprecedented claims: she was conceived without original sin, ascended bodily to heaven, and was capable of converting unbelievers to the Christian faith. Using the most up-to-date methods developed by Anselm, these writers reasoned with absolute certainty that Mary was greater than even their teacher could claim. Anselm's focus on the Incarnation certainly provided the raw materials for discussing Mary in similar terms to the God-man, particularly given the shared nature of their flesh.[225] His students pushed this idea to its natural limit, contending that Mary's body was indeed as pure as that of her son, which merited her the greatest of privileges, such as an Immaculate Conception and bodily Assumption. By ascribing Mary such purity, from its origins to its end, monks in Anglo-Norman England transformed the understanding of her human nature. Mary may have shared the humanity of her devoted followers, for which reason she deigned to help them in their suffering. Yet she was entirely unlike them in her proximity to Christ, and this attributed her an unparalleled status among the saints that would only have enhanced the sense of her power as intercessor.

The doctrines of the Immaculate Conception and bodily Assumption, although they participated in the new climate of theological debate stimulated by Anselm, were intimately related to the devotional world of the monks who wrote about them in Anglo-Norman England. The Conception feast was subject to far more doubt than the well-established feast of the Assumption, yet the precise nature of the event that the Assumption feast commemorated still required explanation. In both cases, it was deemed necessary to provide theological reasons for each celebration. And in both cases, the reason given was that Mary deserved the highest degree of veneration based on the unparalleled nature of her immaculate body. As a result, both conversations reflected interest in understanding not just points of doctrine but also liturgical practices; we should not forget that both Eadmer and William were precentors, and William even wrote his own liturgical commentary.[226] Liturgy and theology intertwined, as monks in Anglo-Norman England grappled with the question of celebrating Mary, and ultimately extended the boundaries of what could be celebrated about her. They even came to see her as the crucial figure able to bring unbelievers—and especially the Jews—to accept Christianity, because all that was needed was to convince these doubters of the inherent rationality of the virgin birth. Taking up the theme of the popular polemical dialogues, the Jews—and their collective representative, the Synagogue—were thus made important figures of doubt and recalcitrance, but also of belief and conversion. The certainty with which Anglo-Norman monks expressed their vision of Mary's nature and role in the scheme of Christian salvation is striking. To them, Mary was indisputably the queen of heaven, supreme in her place as foreordained mother of God, as should be obvious to anyone capable of reasoning. Not only had monks in England demonstrated this by praying and singing; they had proven its "truth."

CHAPTER 3

||||||||||||||||||||||

Hagiographies of Mary

MIRACLE COLLECTIONS

As THEOLOGICAL TREATISES AIMED TO PROVE through reasoned argument that Mary was worthy of devotion, a new form of literature emerged in twelfth-century England that sought to do the same thing, but this time by way of example. It was in English monasteries in the early twelfth century, that collections of Marian miracle stories first appeared, the most explicit reflection in narrative form of Mary's power to intercede on behalf of her followers. Such tales depicted the imagined rewards of entreating Mary to act on their behalf. They described how Mary had bestowed her mercy on those who appealed to her in the past and offered the promise that she might do so again in the future. Appearing to people in visions, Mary healed bodies and saved souls, turned men and women away from lives of sin, and snatched souls from the very literal grip of the devil. She preserved cities from attack, protected her devotees by punishing their enemies, and constantly encouraged her followers to lead a religious life. Mary's beneficiaries came from all walks of life, from the monks and nuns who vowed their lives to her, to popes, bishops, laymen, and women. These tales were the ultimate proof that she was able to bend Christ's ear, and more important, that she wished to. The equation was simple: call on Mary as the mother of mercy, and her mercy would be forthcoming.

Much has been made of Marian miracles as evidence for Mary's growing prominence as saintly intercessor, particularly in the context of penitential culture.[1] With the inward turn characteristic of monastic reform culture, individual sin took on greater proportions and the need to have a sympathetic advocate in heaven came to look especially crucial; miracle stories were the proof that Mary would help.[2] The thaumaturgic power of Marian shrines for pilgrims seeking cures and the role of miracles in advertising these sites has also been much studied.[3] Less has been done, however, to understand just *how* people thought they could get Mary's sympathy. The performance of devotional acts has been a neglected aspect of the miracle tales, despite the wealth of information they contain about contemporary religious practices.

In order to understand the part miracle collections played in the development of the Marian cult, this chapter will examine afresh their inception and early development within wider literary and devotional patterns. As part of a trend in hagiographic writing, the Marian miracles reflect attempts to develop the kinds of literature for Mary produced for many Anglo-Saxon saints in England during this period. In the Marian miracles, though, the same processes of veneration do not quite apply. Here, we do not find emphasis on pilgrimage to specific sites where relics were housed. Although Marian relics do feature, there is no one shrine that is privileged above others, and stories about the performance of the liturgy outweigh those about particular pilgrimage sites. Why monks in England chose to record these miracles therefore remains a mystery in the face of general trends of miracle collecting as an aspect of promoting relics and saints—both to promote pilgrimage and increase the profile of the saints' home institution. Still, looking at the practices described in the Marian miracle stories provides considerable insight into why these stories were recorded and compiled. Although some stories were old, many of them appear for the first time in the collections and feature many of the practices being adopted in England around this time, as described in chapter 1. This chapter will place the stories' themes in relation to those practices, highlighting correspondences and seeking to understand the appearance of the collections within the context of the religious culture explored in this book so far.

Examination of the manuscripts in which the miracles were copied sheds additional light onto how the message of Mary's mercy was transmitted. The collection of miracles into volumes made them readily available for use in the liturgy, as readings and in sermons, and they were grouped together with other liturgical materials. In this way, miracles became a part of the practices they described and promoted. Before turning in the next chapter to the ways in which miracles came to feature Jews in order to further underscore proper approaches to Mary, this chapter will consider how her devotees were encouraged to perform particular acts through these lively narratives. Just as theological treatises set out what should be believed about Mary in order to explain and justify liturgical celebration, miracle stories emerged as templates for religious practice, telling readers and hearers what to do in order to benefit from Mary's boundless mercy.

ORIGINS

Marian miracles were not themselves a novelty when they were first collected together in self-standing volumes in the early twelfth century. As single narrative units, they date back to the earliest interest in Mary, and especially the fifth and sixth centuries. Legends about her miraculous body in the Apocrypha supplemented the sparse comments made about her in the Gospels just as they engaged with debates circulating about the characteristics of the Theotokos, particularly in early Christian Byzantium.[4] Accounts of her "posthumous" actions also appeared around the same time—tales about the miracles Mary performed on earth and in heaven. These went on to be integrated into sermons, legendaries, chronicles, and theological treatises. Marian miracles became widespread, but were always tucked away inside larger works, such as *De gloria martyrum* of Gregory of Tours (538–593), *De carne et sanguinis* of Paschasius, and the *Chronicon* of Sigebert of Gembloux (d. 1112), among others.[5]

The early twelfth century saw the emergence of two distinct forms of the Marian miracle collection. The first was largely witnessed in northern France. The earliest example is a short series of miracles attributed to the Marian relics of the Cathedral of Notre Dame of Laon, which were taken on several fundraising tours in 1112–13. Soon after the return of the Laon canons, Guibert, a monk at the nearby abbey of Nogent, wrote an account of the miracles the relics were meant to have performed along the way, presumably based on notes recorded during the trip by the canons themselves.[6] A more complete redaction of the same set of accounts was made in the 1140s by the canon Hermann of Tournai.[7] This coincided with the appearance of a number of similar collections, predominantly tied to French churches dedicated to the Virgin—Coutances, Soissons, Saint-Pierre-sur-Dives, Rocamadour, Chartres, and Dormans—promoting them as sites of pilgrimage based around relics or images of Mary.[8] As such, these collections followed what has come to be identified as the traditional pattern of miracle recording: authorizing and advertising particular shrines.[9]

Contrary to the regional interests at heart in the French collections, quite a different focus is discernible in the miracle collections that emerged simultaneously, if not earlier, in England.[10] This may have been due to the absence of such relic cults in England, at least until the shrine at Walsingham was built in the 1150s.[11] It is important to recognize that at least one of the French collections (Laon) predates the English equivalents, and may have provided an additional prompt to compilers in England. The canons of Laon had after all made one of their relic tours in England, with several miracles said to have happened on English soil.[12] But the focus of the English collections was completely different. Whereas the French collections were associated with specific institutions, the miracles in the so-called universal collections were drawn from a variety of sources, performed by Mary not at any one site but everywhere and anywhere—from northern Italy, to Constantinople, to England. The earliest examples of these volumes appeared in the early twelfth century. Although Adolfo Mussafia had made initial suggestions of their English origins in the late nineteenth century, Southern was the first scholar to identify English authors.[13] One compiler was Dominic, prior of Evesham from circa 1125 to at least 1130, a collector of

legends and saints' lives connected with his abbey as well as author of a chronicle that mentions he was responsible for putting together a volume of Marian
stories.[14] The series of fourteen stories to which he refers in this account, complete with a prologue, is found in a number of manuscripts, although other
stories have generally been added.[15]

Southern tracked down a second collection that was circulating in various
versions in the twelfth century and also found an author: Anselm, abbot of
Bury St. Edmunds. His attribution was based on a number of stories that show
connections with the circle of Anselm of Canterbury, Anselm of Bury's uncle.[16]
A number of stories appear in a slightly different form in the *Dicta Anselmi*, a
collection of Anselm of Canterbury's sayings written by his scribe Alexander—
a copy of which was sent to Anselm of Bury.[17] One particular story among the
Marian miracles supposedly features the nephew himself accidentally spilling
communion wine on the altar cloth at the abbey of St. Michael of Chiusa, where
he had previously been a monk.[18] Southern pointed to Anselm's involvement in
reinstating the feast of the Conception at Bury as further support of his devotion to Mary, to which we can add his responsibility for the adoption of the
communal Little Office and Old Hispanic feast of the Virgin at the abbey, both
of which feature in miracle stories in the collection. Although there is no direct
evidence that links Anselm to this particular collection, his patronage in 1124–
25 of a hagiographic life of Bury's other saint, Edmund, complete with a series
of the saint's miracles, adds weight to the idea that he at least commissioned, if
not himself wrote, the Marian volume.[19] Southern described the collection as
containing thirty-five stories, which were separated into two books (referred to
in the scholarship as HM and TS after the story titles that bookend each one:
(H)Ildefonsus-Murieldis and Toledo-Saturday) when they were combined in
larger collections together with the first four stories of Dominic's series (the
"Elements" series). Variety in the style and form of the stories in the second
book of seventeen stories (TS) suggests that these were not part of Anselm's
original collection but rather were added incrementally in the decades that followed the volume's composition.[20] The fact that Anselm was likely only responsible for the first book of eighteen stories, while the second accrued over time,
makes the traditional discussion of the two series as HM and TS inappropriate,
since TS was never really a collection and rarely appears in series; as such, these
designators will not be used here.[21] I will refer to Anselm's collection instead of
HM, and will indicate the stories that were added later as opposed to referring
to TS.[22]

In exploring the English origins of the Marian miracles, Southern also
briefly discussed a third distinct collection, composed before 1140 in England.[23]
This collection was compiled by William of Malmesbury, and in a recent edition and translation of the work by Michael Winterbottom and Rodney Thomson, its date of composition has been placed between 1136 and 1137.[24] The

volume complemented William's work on the lives of local saints, such as Wulfstan, Dunstan, Patrick, Benignus, and Indract as well as Malmesbury's founder, Aldhelm, whose life and acts take up a significant portion of William's ecclesiastical history, the *Gesta Pontificum Anglorum*.[25] William had access to copies of both Dominic's and Anselm's Marian collections; he is known to have visited Bury St. Edmunds and may also have encountered Anselm's collection at Christ Church Canterbury, where it was copied in the twelfth century and augmented with additional stories.[26] Never satisfied to simply copy his sources, William completely rearranged the stories according to the rank of their protagonists: from popes down to women and Jews. Despite his new ordering system, William's Marian miracles were less popular than the preceding volumes, and his collection was more frequently mined for individual stories than copied as a whole, and these were often simplified. The collection was substantially longer than the other two, numbering fifty-three miracles in total.[27]

The fact that the three authors identified by Southern were important hagiographers of local saints, combined with the fact that Mary was patron of Bury St. Edmunds, Evesham, and Malmesbury, provides a relatively straightforward explanation for their interest in collecting the miracles of the Virgin. This was what Rachel Koopmans assumed when she briefly mentioned the Marian miracles as part of a wider post–Conquest movement in miracle collecting.[28] A considerable number of new hagiographies were written especially for the Anglo-Saxon saints in the century after the Norman Conquest in English Benedictine monasteries, and accounts of their posthumous miracles circulated both separately and attached to the saintly biographies. Koopmans explains that the fashion for recording miracles was another reflection of the transition from an oral to an increasingly literate culture.[29] Miracle collections were generated to preserve oral tradition, and the upheavals of the Norman Conquest presented a unique impetus for setting the Anglo-Saxon past in writing: "What they [miracle collectors] were seeking to defend themselves against with these texts, it appears, was the weight of time and the fragility of human memory."[30] Another notable example is the *Dicta Anselmi*. The volume includes many miracle stories heard and told by Anselm and his friends—some of which are also found in the Marian miracle collections.[31] Although stories continued to evolve in the telling and retelling, recording them in writing gave them not only a higher chance of longevity but also conveyed to them a degree of authority.

The lives and miracles of the saints were central to the historical memory of the particular institutions with which they were associated. Native English clerics and Norman newcomers alike recognized the importance of preserving a record of the miracles produced by relics to confer status to their respective churches as well as to act as reminders of their religious heritage. Miracle stories additionally bestowed legitimacy on claims of saintly patronage, illustrating the saint's "desire" to be buried at a particular location and their support for the establishment.[32] Stories of saintly apparitions and healing miracles performed by relics were thus crucial to securing a church's prestige and helping to garner income from pilgrimage. As Paul A. Hayward, Simon Yarrow, and Jay Rubenstein have shown, relics were at the heart of negotiations about institutional identity in the post–Conquest period—a time of shifting power structures.[33] As the rights and privileges of institutions became subject to dispute under the conquerors, establishments sought to fix their history in writing in order to guard against the alienation of lands and challenge to local traditions. The saints were viewed as useful allies in this. The miracles of St. Edmund (patron of Bury), for example, which were recorded during Anselm's time as abbot, depict the saint punishing those who challenged the monastery's claims to property; the saint's support was considered essential to the institution's protection.[34] Miracle collecting played an instrumental role in responding to the complex post–Conquest situation in which religious foundations sought to establish written proof of an institution's illustrious history based on the ongoing patronage of the saints.

Given what we know about the cults of other saints in this period and the evidence for religious practice discussed in previous chapters, it becomes apparent that the Marian miracle collections were the product of a monastic culture in which two impulses intersected: the development of a prominent Marian cult met a hagiographic trend that saw miracle accounts become an increasingly significant means of preserving a memory of the saints. The prologue that preceded Anselm's series, which was the most commonly copied prologue attached to the Marian collections, certainly suggests a similar reason for collecting Mary's miracles as for those of other saints:

> Since the miracles of the saints, by way of which the divine mercy acts through the saints, are often recited in praise of God's omnipotence, the deeds of the holy mother of God, Mary, should be proclaimed most of all, as they are sweeter than any honey. Therefore, let us endeavor to recite them, God willing, in order to bolster the minds of the faithful in their love for her and move the hearts of the unlearned with those things that we have heard faithfully told.[35]

This clearly places the Marian miracles in a wider context of storytelling about the saints.

In his prologue, Dominic of Evesham also describes the challenge of the task he had undertaken:

> Although certain [miracles] had been set down by the pen of our forefathers, because they were dispersed throughout various books such that they could be found only with great difficulty or not at all by those who sought them, I have tried to collect the dispersed stories so they can more easily be discovered when redacted in one volume.[36]

This passage points to the diverse sources in which Marian miracles had been found up until this time, and Dominic's desire to bring them together for ease of reference. It also suggests that while many existing hagiographies were rewritten in this period, there was no equivalent source for the Marian miracles, which certain monastic writers felt needed to be addressed. This may not have been a fanciful claim. The collections of Dominic and Anselm have only one story in common, and this story is different enough in each version as to indicate a shared oral rather than a written source. It is possible, then, that neither had access to the other's collection when compiling their own.

Although the same impulse to record the marvelous deeds of their local saints no doubt lay behind the Marian miracle collections, the Anglo-Norman authors recognized that the Virgin occupied a unique status. Mary was not just any saint but rather the queen of heaven praised so highly in the prayers, liturgies, and theological treatises of the period. Dominic's prologue accordingly heaps praise on Mary, presenting the virgin birth as the greatest miracle of all time.[37] If she surpasses the other saints in all things, he asked, would it not do her a great injustice to keep silent about her powers, demonstrated as they are to faithful Christians?[38] "For truly," Dominic wrote,

> although it is in no way necessary to do so, nevertheless it is worth examining new things much more carefully alongside old ones, so that in the same way the body does with different kinds of food, so too should the soul cling with greater appetite to diverse miracles and virtues; when the soul is cautiously open to all living things, we know that no good can harm the one just as, on the other hand, no evil can serve the other. This is the material cause, on which account, although the work had long lain at the feet of others, nevertheless we had been obliged to complete it to satisfy the brothers and their many friends who were asking and comply with their wishes, we who had been taught to have more faith in the wisdom of God than in any spark of secular science. The final cause then follows, by which it is understood that the greatest hope we can seek is that as much writers as readers and listeners be protected on the day of the terrible judgment from the wrath of the just judge through the merits of the most glorious mother of that same judge, she whose virtues we know are honored as much through writing as through reading and listening.[39]

What Dominic seems to be saying is that first, the soul is nourished by a great diversity of things, not just ancient and authoritative accounts, but also newer ones; these new accounts should therefore not be dismissed, despite their novelty. This could indicate some residual hesitation among Dominic's peers about the value of recent events for cultivating the faith, compared to ones that were anchored in tradition. Dominic's collection does in fact include anecdotes that are meant to have happened in his lifetime, alongside stories based in the far past. Second, he pointed to a prevailing appetite for miracle stories among his monastic brethren, despite whatever doubt there might have been about their value. While we might put this down once again to the trope of the eager petitioners, there may be some truth in Dominic's claim about a general desire to see these tales finally written down and collected together.[40]

Echoing both Dominic's and Anselm's words, William's prologue to his collection gives us a further glimpse into his reasons for recording Mary's miracles with additional echoes of the late eleventh-century reforming ethos. As we saw in the previous chapter, the text first proceeds through a lengthy exposition of Mary's virtues, with the aim of discussing the nature of her Assumption.[41] The length of William's prologue suggests that the text was conceived less as a mere introduction to the miracles than as a complete treatise in its own right. But for William, the two parts were intimately connected. In the short preface to the miracles, he explained that

> this [the prologue thus far], more or less, is what comes to mind of what our forebears said in praise of the blessed Mary. They poured it out in fuller words and sentences; I have made a digest. But if the saints will allow me to say it, much is still lacking from this important task. By chance or on purpose, they altogether suppressed what I think is an apter means of kindling love for this Lady in the souls of the simple: I mean examples of her pity and miracles, which are displayed to the world in no insignificant quantity. Reasonings may awaken the faith of the perfected, but it is the narration of miracles that awakens the hope and charity of the simple, as a sluggish fire revives when oil is thrown on it. Reasons teach that she *can* pity the pitiable, but it is examples of miracles that teach that she *wishes* to do what she is able to do.[42]

William here clarified the bipartite structure of his text: the miracles in part two were meant to do for the simpleminded what the theological treatise in part one aimed to do for those versed in theology. William's purpose was specifically to strengthen faith in Mary's mercy not just among clerics through theological reflection but also among the laity through hearing the miracles she has performed.[43] William's appeal to miracles for this purpose echoes Gregory the Great on the use of *exempla* in preaching ("more are usually pierced by examples than by words of reason").[44] As we will see in more detail below, William may have taken this advice to heart and compiled his collection for use in the liturgy. This passage of the prologue is therefore important for understanding his and the other Marian collections as participating in current monastic interests in pastoral care. William certainly recognized that miracle accounts could be an extremely effective means of fostering devotion among their hearers, as a witness to Mary's powers of intercession and illustration for the simple to follow in seeking them out.

Miracles reflected reform ideals in more ways than one. First of all, as William suggests, they provided examples of people addressing Mary as intercessor and thus encouraged the listener to act likewise. But Mary herself served as a crucial role model. As Sigbjørn Sønnesyn has recently written with respect to William's ethics, the Marian miracle collection is "a fundamentaly didactic work, and in its full version [prologue/treatise plus miracles] it contains most of the elements needed to constitute a treatise teaching ethics through the example of the Blessed Virgin."[45] She appears in miracle stories actively participating in the liturgy—namely, correcting liturgical practice and leading choirs of virgins. She was also an effective model for the life of chastity. As Katherine Allen Smith has discussed, stories of Mary becoming engaged or married to clerics and monks, on the one hand, and intervening to prevent nuns from giving in to their lust, on the other, communicated the significance of clerical celibacy in a period where the issue had come to the fore.[46] Mary's own commitment to virginity made her the ideal protector of virginal chastity in both men and women. The bodily emphasis of some of these stories would have served as a pertinent reminder for clerics of the importance of keeping their own bodies chaste.

As indicated by their prologues, the miracle collections of Anselm, Dominic, and William were an integral part of the rich and varied Marian cult developing in Anglo-Norman England. Just as Mary was increasingly praised in liturgy and prayer as a particularly effective saintly intercessor, with theological treatises buttressing these practices, miracles provided examples of her intercession. This leads me to repeat a key point mentioned earlier about the Marian miracle collections. Although the first collections can be tied to Marian institutions—Bury St. Edmunds, Evesham, and Malmesbury—she is never claimed in these volumes as the exclusive property of a single house. Neither in the prologues nor miracles themselves are specific shrines privileged, nor is her special favor shown toward one or another church. There are stories that involve Canterbury, Evesham, and Bury, but these appear in both Dominic's and William's collections. The rest of the stories are set in a variety of other locations around the world, with some concerning particular shrines or images, and others featuring nameless places where Mary comes to the aid of those who merely ask for it.[47] Some stories are adaptations of the hagiographies of other saints, with Mary replacing the saint as protagonist. An example is the story of the Pilgrim to Santiago, the original of which is found in the *Dicta Anselmi*, and which somewhat more fittingly features St. James.[48] But in the case of the Marian miracles, never is any one institution said to have a monopoly on Marian intervention. This makes the Marian miracle collections fundamentally different from the vast majority of others assembled for other saints in England as well as the various virgins of northern French houses.[49] The English Marian collections were truly universal. They presented the Virgin as a universal saint for anyone and everyone. As William writes, "I shall compose my unfolding narrative in such a way as to show that the blessed Virgin has poured out the bowels of her compassion on every rank, every condition of men, and on both sexes. And I shall adduce events differing in time, place, and type, like flowers woven into a garland for the queen of heaven."[50]

The universality of the Marian miracle collections is tied to an important feature of the stories themselves. Many of the tales—in fact the majority—involve liturgical practice: some form of devotional behavior that include prayers, masses, offices, and the celebration of feast days. In the group of eighteen stories attributed to Anselm of Bury, eleven involve identifiable liturgical practices. Six of Dominic's fourteen miracles have the protagonist rewarded for the same types of acts. William's extensive collection of fifty-one miracles has twenty-four that feature a particular Marian practice. The idea that emerges from these stories is that Mary looked kindly on the performance of the liturgy and prayer, and would reward such expressions accordingly. That Mary could be petitioned by anyone via these means, regardless of institutional affiliation, is reflected in the varied types of characters who feature in the stories, although many of these happen to be monks, nuns, and clerics.

The emphasis on liturgical practice can help to explain why they circulated almost immediately among an extensive network of monasteries, copied and recopied in growing numbers from their very inception, first in England and quickly on the other side of the English Channel. Any institution, even one that did not boast Mary's patronage, could be interested in owning a collection of her miracles, because they could all adopt the emerging religious practices: the celebration of feast days and the daily and weekly offices. Copies of miracle collections were made in the twelfth century at Christ Church, Ely, Glastonbury, and Cirencester, in addition to the French abbeys of Saint-Martin-des-Champs, Saint-Germain-des-Prés, Saint-Martin in Tournai, Saint-Victor, and Saint-Denis, many of which were not dedicated to Mary.[51] This in itself tells us about the common devotional culture shared by the houses that collected her miracles—one in which Mary's intercession was prized as especially effective in addition to and above that of the other saints. In this way, the redactors of the Marian miracles encouraged the widespread adoption of Marian practices with simple narratives of sin and redemption, piety and reward. Praise of Mary ought to be performed everywhere and by everyone, they seem to say, presenting the real rewards that Mary bestows on those who sing and pray to her.

It should be noted that the importance of liturgical practice in the Marian miracles has not escaped some of the few scholars who have examined the collections, such as Benedicta Ward.[52] In her look at the universal Marian miracles, Ward sketched out a number of the practices involved, describing the stories in which they featured. Yet she treated them as timeless, "universal devotions, untethered by place."[53] She was not entirely misguided in this; the actions portrayed for obtaining Mary's aid are often not localized in the tales, and could be performed anywhere. On consideration of the Anglo-Norman context, however, a conspicuous connection emerges between the liturgical actions depicted in the miracle accounts and those emerging in the twelfth-century monastic milieu, as discussed in the first chapter. Analysis of the stories reveals a variety of liturgical practices that include increasingly popular masses, antiphons, Marian offices, and "new" feast days, such as the Conception, all present in the surviving liturgical sources from the period. Miracle stories often prescribed in detail what action was necessary, with striking levels of precision, suggesting a desire to promote them and educate people about them.[54] It is therefore not enough to consider these stories as shaped solely by literary history. Taking the miracle collections as part of wider trends in the evolution of the cult of Mary, and considering each story in its historical and devotional context, will help to uncover how they were rooted in the religious culture of twelfth-century England. Miracles added yet another justification for expressing devotion to her, appealing not to reason but rather to the simple understanding of the wonderful consequences such acts could bring.

PRAYERS, CHANTS, AND OFFICES

Miracle accounts tend to be formulaic texts, and the so-called universal Marian miracles are no exception. In most stories concerning shrines and relic cults, a person falls ill or is subject to bad luck, travels to a holy site or makes a promise to do so, and is rewarded with the restoration of their health either at the end of the journey or in anticipation of it.[55] While this also applies in some of the Marian tales, they also frequently feature an individual who, although devoted to the Virgin, acts badly and so is faced with the prospect of suffering—either on earth or after death, as demons try to drag the unfortunate soul off to hell. Mary then plays the role of intercessor for the penitent soul, rewarding devotion in spite of whatever evil was committed.[56] Comfort is provided for the reader or listener, assuring them that Mary helps those in need, seemingly regardless of the severity of the crime. What is required is only the performance of the necessary devotions that guarantee Mary's sympathy, and herein lies the crux of each story. Clearly people had to *do something* in order to show their devotion. The performance of specific *ritual* actions was essential to securing Mary's assistance and lies at the heart of the universal miracle collections.

One particular expression of devotion that figures prominently in the miracle collections is the Hail Mary, the invocation based on the addresses to Mary by the Archangel Gabriel at the Annunciation (Luke 1:28) and Elizabeth at the Visitation (Luke 1:42). As we have seen, the Hail Mary prayer was a relatively recent devotional development in the twelfth century.[57] It is therefore interesting to see the prayer receive special endorsement in stories found in the twelfth-century collections. The tale of the Drowned Sacristan in Anselm's collection has the protagonist often saying *Ave Maria gratia plenum, Dominus tecum*; when he falls into the river on his way to visit his mistress, he is saved from drowning by Mary's intervention.[58] The Cleric of Chartres, the protagonist of a tale in the same collection, is buried outside of consecrated ground because of his sinful ways until Mary appears to his community to have him reburied because he had a habit of greeting her with the Hail Mary.[59] In another account, a peasant removes landmarks in order to expand his land bordering a monastery.[60] It is only his frequent recitation of the Hail Mary that saves him from demons eager to capitalize on his sin when he dies.

While these stories offer no hint of their origin, a story found in a number of manuscripts following Anselm's original group of miracles is directly tied to the Anglo-Norman context. It involves Eulalia, who was the abbess of Shaftesbury between 1074 and 1106 as well as a correspondent of archbishop Anselm.[61] The story describes how she was urged by Mary herself to say the Hail Mary more slowly and solemnly—a practice the abbess later imposed on her entire community.[62] After relating that she was rewarded for doing so, the narrator of Eulalia's story then addresses his brothers directly, encouraging them to follow suit: "And we, dearest brothers (who are not worthy to call ourselves her [Mary's] servants), if we aim to perform our service to her after this warning, according to her will, I believe that we brothers must do in eternal beatitude that which will be worthy of this holy woman."[63] It is worth remembering the *Ave* prayer in the Shaftesbury Psalter, which contains twenty-six verses all starting with the word "Ave."[64] Perhaps the story originated to explain the creation of such an elaborate version of the *Ave Maria* prayer for devotional use. But more general concern with the correct use of devotional and liturgical invocations, particularly the proper recitation of Psalms, was a feature of early twelfth-century monastic reform more generally.[65] Reference to a prominent individual would only have enhanced the miracle's didactic quality, encouraging the monks to do as Eulalia did and consider the merits of sincerely repeating this simple text. The number of English manuscripts into which the story of Eulalia was copied certainly points to interest in the adoption of such new forms of prayer.[66]

The proper singing of antiphons and responsories in Mary's honor similarly receives miraculous advertisement in a number of stories. In a story from the collection of William, a nun whose penance remained unfinished but who was saved by the Virgin nonetheless, not only repeated the Hail Mary, but also sang an antiphon: the *Gaude Dei genitrix*.[67] The daily singing of this same antiphon saves another cleric of Chartres; William commented in his case that its repetition was a way of remembering Mary's continual presence.[68] Both versions were likely inspired by the story of the Five Gaudes, found in Anselm's collection.[69] In this case, the antiphon sung by the clerical protagonist is written out in full:

Gaude Dei genitrix, virgo immaculata	Rejoice, mother of God, immaculate virgin
Gaude quae gaudium ab angelo suscepisti.	Rejoice that you received joy from the angel.
Gaude quae genuisti eterni luminis claritatem	Rejoice that you gave birth to the brightness of the eternal light
Gaude mater	Rejoice mother
Gaude sancta Dei genitrix virgo	Rejoice holy virgin mother of God
Tu sola mater innupta, te laudat omnis factura genitricem virgo	You alone are the mother unwedded, all creation praises you, virgin, as a mother
Tu sola mater innupta, te laudat omnis factura genitricem lucis,	You alone are virgin mother, all creation praises you, mother of light,
Sis pro nobis quasi perpetua interventrix.[70]	Be for us as intercessor forever.

The rest of the story, in which Mary appears to the cleric as he lies dying, is remarkably short when compared to the fact that the antiphon is spelled out in its complete form, just like in its probable source, Peter Damian's *De variis apparitionis et miraculis*.[71] Although the *Gaude dei genitrix* was composed as early as the late tenth century, it only became widespread toward the end of the eleventh century, when Damian was writing.[72] It was around this time that the antiphon was incorporated into liturgical practice in England. We see the text as the hymn for terce in one of the Anglo-Saxon offices of Mary at Christ Church, produced between 1032 and 1050, and later in a breviary from St. Albans.[73] The level of detail found in the story suggests that it remained relatively novel among those redactors who first copied it out and may have wished to familiarize listeners with the text as well as promote its adoption into practice.

Not to be confused with the *Gaude dei genitrix*, the responsory *Gaude Maria virgo* features in a miracle set in England, in both Dominic's and William's collections.[74] The story concerns a monk from Evesham or Eynsham who is confronted with evil spirits on his deathbed wishing to take away his soul to hell. He had often sung the responsory "Rejoice Mary, virgin, you alone opposed all heresies, you who believed the words of the Archangel Gabriel. Then the virgin gave birth to man and God, and remained a virgin after the birth."[75] This allowed Mary to claim his soul, taking on the active role presented in the chant text and fighting the demons with great success. William includes this same story in his *Gesta Pontificum*, where he attributes the event to 1124.[76] As we saw in a previous chapter, this responsory features in several Marian offices that were adopted in the eleventh and twelfth centuries in England, including the two earliest-known examples of the daily votive office.[77] The fact that it was introduced into daily and weekly use for Marian offices could explain the story's inclusion in the collections. There, placed in a familiar context, the story would have served to reinforce the idea of the chant's efficacy in ensuring salvation for those who performed it.

William's story about St. Dunstan (909–88), whose *Vita* he also wrote, similarly uses a relatable setting and noteworthy protagonist to advertise particular Marian chants.[78] To set the scene, William described Canterbury as a city "famous for the many saints whose ashes lie there," and the seat of the first archbishop, Augustine (d. 604/5), who was sent to England by Pope Gregory the Great.[79] Having first built the monastery of Peter and Paul, Augustine attached a chapel dedicated to the Virgin Mary, William explained. When Dunstan became archbishop in 959, he is said to have built an entire church in honor of Mary as well as for the apostle Andrew, to whom he was equally devoted. As a reward, he was witness to a miraculous vision of Mary and a choir of virgins singing the following hymn in the church:

Cantemus, Domino, sociae, cantemus honorem:	Let us sing to the lord, sisters, sing his praise:
Dulcis amor Christi personet ore pio.	Let sweet love of Christ resound from pious mouths.
Primus ad ima ruit, magna de luce superbus.	The first man in his pride rushed into the depths from the great light.
Sic homo, cum tumuit, primus ad ima ruit.	And so the man, when he swelled up (with pride), was first to fall into the depths.
Unius ad noxam cuncti periere minores:	His descendants perished for the offense of this one man:
Salvantur cuncti, unius ob meritum.	They are saved because of the merit of one individual.
Femina sola fuit, patuitque ianua laeto: Per quam vita redit, femina sola fuit.[80]	She was the only woman, and the door was happily open: through whom life returned, she was the only woman.

Dunstan is urged to participate, and sings the antiphon: *O rex gloriae, nate Maria virgine, salva genus Christianorum in hac terra peregrinantium.* The story must have been well known, for it is referred to in the reminiscences of Goscelin of Saint-Bertin about the translation of the relics of Augustine at St. Augustine's Canterbury. In pulling down the church of St. Mary, Goscelin had Abbot Scotland (1070–87) say, "That parent of the most High is known to have often been seen and the sweet choir of virgins heard with the ineffable sweetness of the celestial harmony," not least by Dunstan himself.[81] The miracle account found in the *Miracula* seems to be an amalgamation of two miracles in William's *Vita* of Dunstan: the first, in which Dunstan has a vision of his mother's heavenly wedding and is taught the hymn *O rex dominator gentium*, and the second in which he sees the choir of virgins singing but says nothing himself.[82] In combining the two accounts, William changed the antiphon Dunstan sang, adding the phrase *nate Maria virgine*, presumably in an effort to make the antiphon more clearly applicable to Mary. This miracle was thus the ultimate celebrity endorsement of a unique Marian chant. William's choice of Dunstan, famed as one of the leaders of the tenth-century monastic reform movement, presented the ideal example for twelfth-century monks to follow, with particular resonance in an English context.[83]

The choir of virgins with Mary as their leader appears again in another story of William's that features the Marian foundation and home institution of abbot Anselm: Bury St. Edmunds. In this case, the protagonist is a rustic who stumbles across a church from which he can hear "secret mumblings" (*arcani murmuris*), produced by a choir of virgins singing inside.[84] Peter Carter has noted that this tale, which appears for the first time in William's collection, could refer to a seventh-century Marian church that was torn down to make way for an extension to the abbey of Bury between 1102 and 1112—a process discussed in detail by Gransden.[85] Both this and the story of Dunstan share the idea that Mary honors new constructions dedicated to her by appearing in them to perform the liturgy herself. The idea of the heavenly choir gave additional meaning to the monks' performance of the liturgy as a representation on earth of what Mary herself performs in heaven as a kind of celestial precentor.

The ways in which miracle stories did not just promote but also taught liturgical texts is illustrated in a story found at the beginning of the Chicago UL 147 collection, where it was placed ahead of Anselm's series.[86] It depicts a monk diligently performing a service to Mary at compline when visited in a dream by the Virgin, who corrects his form of singing the office. In what ends up looking like an extract from a liturgical book, she specifies exactly the way in which the office should be sung:

In primis inquit ut mos est, V: *Converte nos deus salutaris noster* Debes incipere postea antiphonam: *Completi sunt dies Marie* [*ut pareret filium suum primogenitum*]. Ps. *Cum invocarem* (Ps. 4) et *In te domine* (Ps. 30). *Qui habitat* (Ps. 90), et *Ecce nunc* (Ps.	First it is said, as is the custom: [the versicle] *O, our salvific God, convert us.* After, you must begin the antiphon: *And the days of Mary are come* [*in order that she should give birth to her firstborn son*]. Psalm: *When I call* (Ps. 4). And: *In you, Lord* (Ps. 30). *Who dwells* (Ps. 90), and *Behold now* (Ps.

133). Capitulum, *Ecce virgo concipiet.* Responsorium, *Sancta Dei genitrix virgo semper Maria, intercede pro nobis ad dominum.* Hymnum, *Virgo singularis / vitam presta puram / sit laus Deo patri* [etc.].[87] Versus: *Ave Maria.* Antiphonam: *Ecce completa sunt omnia* [*quae dicta sunt per angelum de virgine Maria*]. Canticum: *Nunc dimittis* (Luke 2:29). Collectam: *Deus qui de beata Maria* [*Virginis utero Verbum tuum, Angelo nuntiante, carnem suscipere voluisti: praesta supplicibus tuis; ut, qui vere eam Genetricem Dei credimus, eius apud te intercessionibus adiuvemur. Per Christum Dominum nostrum*].[88]

(Ps. 133). The chapter: *Behold a virgin will conceive* (Isa. 7:14). Responsory: *Holy Mary, perpetual virgin mother of God, intercede for us with the Lord.* Hymn: *O unique virgin / bestow a pure life / Praise be to God the Father* [etc.]. Verse: *Hail Mary.* Antiphon: *Behold, all things are accomplished* [*which were said by the angel about the virgin Mary*]. Canticle: *Now do you dismiss* (Luke 2:29). Collect: *O God, you who desired that your Word should take up the flesh from the blessed Mary in the womb of the virgin, by the angelic annunciation; grant to your supplicants, that we, who believe her to be truly the Mother of God, may be helped by her intercession with you. Through Christ our Lord.*

These instructions match the Little Office in the Muchelney manuscript, described in an earlier chapter, almost exactly.[89] In a version of the same tale by Dominic, a dying man is told that although he was committed to Mary in life, he never sang compline in her honor. Embarrassed at his ignorance of the office, he asks Mary to tell him how it must be done, which she obliges with this information: "Between the first and last Psalm, you must insert—as is the custom—and say *In te Domine, speravi.* Use the chapter and collect, etc., from the feast of the Annunciation."[90] Dominic's instructions are in fact the same as the compline office provided above; the collect (*Deus qui de beata*) and chapter (*Ecce virgo concipiet*) were used for the Annunciation feast, as witnessed in a number of English manuscripts.[91] The difference between the two versions of this story is revealing, however. The lack of detail in Dominic's, compared to the other, could point to his familiarity with the practice. Alternatively, the redactor of the version in Chicago UL 147 may have wished to include more complete instructions with the purpose of educating his listeners. This is certainly indicated by the theme of the story, in which Mary appears to spell out exactly what the practice comprised. In this way, the redactor both justified the performance of the office, via Mary's sanction, and communicated its contents wherever the story was then circulated.

Marian masses also feature in miracle stories, in which they are treated as important liturgical observances worthy of reward. An English story rich in historical detail that became a popular feature of the Marian collections con-

cerns Leofric, a monk of Westminster Abbey, whom I have been unable to identify in any other source.[92] The account is attributed to Edricus, prior of Chertsey, and describes how Leofric wished to take over the abbacy of Chertsey
against the wishes of his own abbot at Westminster. The king nevertheless gave
him the post, but on realizing the displeasure of the abbot and monks of Westminster, exiled Leofric to the abbey of Dol in Brittany until his eventual return
to Chertsey as a monk. In the miracle story, the disgraced Leofric is ultimately
redeemed for his disobedience thanks to the one or two weekly masses he performed in honor of Mary.[93] Perhaps this mass was the same as that in the story
of the priest who knew only one mass and was therefore removed by his bishop.
The fact that the mass in this other story was the *Salve sancta parens* (so-called
for the introit chant) had won Mary's sympathy, and she intervened on his behalf so that he was reinstated in his post.[94] The same votive mass features in the
story of St. Bon, who received a vestment from Mary as reward for his performance of a mass in her honor.[95] In a late twelfth-century rhymed version of the
Bon story, the bishop of Norwich, Herbert of Losinga, is said to have seen and
touched the vestment.[96] The *Salve sancta parens* is a common votive Marian
mass found, for example, in a late eleventh- or early twelfth-century missal
from St. Augustine's, a twelfth-century sacramentary from St. Albans and at the
end of the Westminster Psalter that also contains the lengthy commemorative
Marian office.[97] We should remember that daily Marian masses such as these
were being introduced in England precisely around the time the collections
started circulating. Stories such as these would have further encouraged their
adoption.

The commemorative office that honored Mary on Saturdays receives remarkable attention in an account that points to the ways in which miracles
could seek to promote novel practices. Rather than a traditional story, it seems
to be a sermon, although it does include mention of several miracles.[98] Known
by its incipit, *Sollempnem memoriam*, the sermon begins by stating that "it is
proper for the sons of the church to celebrate the solemn commemoration of
Holy Mary, virgin mother of God, with a solemn office, since we naturally grant
this to many saints because they hold a special place on account of their closeness to us [i.e., patronage], lest anyone who celebrates them appear false in receiving the help of their patronage," and who is better to call on in times of
distress than the greatest of all the saints?[99] To illustrate Mary's intercessory
powers, the author referred to the legends of Theophilus, Mary of Egypt, and
the vision of Mary as *mater misericordiae* told by Odo of Cluny.[100] In recognition of Mary's efforts, he urged his brothers to commemorate Mary liturgically,
which can be done most fittingly on Saturday, as it is Mary's special day.[101]

> Strengthened by this hope, in many churches of the world (because they could
> not do so in all) they selected one day in the week in honor of so great a virgin

mother. Is it not fitting for Mary to have such a feast day as the seventh of the Sabbath, freed from all work of the other six days? Therefore on this day, many devotees burning with zeal in gratitude of Mary render solemn service to the gracious mother. But in order that a commemoration every hour not tire them, it is confirmed by the authority of a synod that such a mass be sung solemnly, not without the "*Gloria in excelsis deo*." And they prove this with reason, taking up the argument from the lesser to the greater. If king or emperor should arrive, they ask, what church is there that would not at once postpone its usual offices, adorning the front of the shrine with golden crowns and thuribles and other things arranged for procession? Therefore if the Paschal solemnities are renewed when earthly princes are present, it is most justified and pious that the Lady of the world, the glorious Mary, should be honored on her Saturday/Sabbath with a solemn office, in honor of the son who loves and honors his good mother. And so lest the foolish, confessing to one another that it is not true that we ought to rest on all feast days of Mary on Saturday because we do not see a precious sign of God at work, recount what God performs in the city of Constantinople, by which sign he defends the Sabbath of Mary.[102]

This is followed by an account of the miracle that allegedly took place every Saturday at the church of Blacherna in Constantinople, wherein the veil was miraculously lifted over an image of Mary for all of Saturday, as conclusive proof that the day ought to be dedicated to Mary's honor.[103]

Sollempnem memoriam is a remarkable apology for the practice of celebrating a full commemorative office for Mary on Saturdays.[104] Henri Barré thought the sermon had been composed in Cambrai during the episcopate of Lietbert (1051–76), who founded a church of the Holy Sepulchre in his city dedicated to Christ and the Virgin, after having attempted a pilgrimage to the Holy Land. It was in Constantinople that Lietbert apparently gained knowledge of the miraculous image at Blacherna, which then inspired the sermon. Barré's discovery of a late eleventh-century collection from Cambrai of readings for matins of the Saturday commemorative office together with this sermon and another for the same day lay behind his argument.[105] In his view, the sermon was written to justify the adoption of the Saturday commemoration in the wake of Pope Urban II's declaration at the Council of Clermont (1095) that a Saturday office should be celebrated in Mary's honor, as discussed in a previous chapter; this would explain the sermon's mention of a king "or emperor" in the sermon—namely, Henry IV.[106] If this identification is correct, the sermon certainly traveled quickly to England, since it appears in a late eleventh-century collection of Marian sermons from Exeter or Leicester, where it has been marked up in the margins for three or four lessons, presumably to be read out during matins of the Saturday office.[107] Further indicating a possible English connection is the fact that the sermon clearly extrapolated on a set of readings for matins found in the Cambrai manuscript. Clayton has argued that these readings were English in origin, since they appear in Wulfstan's Portiforium and several other English manuscripts.[108] Because she was not aware of any surviving English versions of the sermon itself, she conceded that the more detailed sermon was written in Cambrai to expand on the simpler English readings, as Barré had argued.[109] The presence of the sermon in the Exeter manuscript and miracle collections nonetheless points to a potential English precedent once again, although we cannot rule out the possibility of fertile exchange between Normandy and England at the turn of the twelfth century.

Regardless of the direction of influence, the inclusion of the Saturday sermon into the miracle collections would no doubt have helped with the spread of a relatively new commemorative practice. We have seen from the St. Albans chronicle that although it and other houses were celebrating the Saturday Marian commemoration with considerable pomp, this was by no means a universal practice, even by the turn of the thirteenth century.[110] The desire to spread the practice while it was still uncommon could explain why the whole sermon, and not just the miracle anecdotes at the end, appears in the twelfth-century collections. The combination of elements in this text—praise, miracle, and liturgical polemic—is certainly revealing of the ways in which miracle accounts could come to reflect contemporary developments in the celebration of Marian liturgies.

The extent to which Mary was seen to deserve full liturgical observance is apparent from the large number of miracle accounts that depict the Little Office. Dominic composed an extensive foundation story for the practice in which an unnamed pope (Urban II?) is chastised for his lax observance, and so instates the Little Office in addition to the Saturday commemoration: "He ordered that each and every an ordained cleric and monk should sing the hours of the Virgin Mary every day. He added that every week on every Saturday a commemoration of her most holy virginity and fertility should always be made at this institution, in the same way that every Sunday a commemoration is made of the resurrection of her son."[111] Another version of this story attributes the foundation of the Little Office rather to the act of an early pope, who after having snubbed St. Peter by allowing a candle in the Lateran church to burn out, is saved by Mary. She reconciles him to Peter, and in thanks, he instates the Little Office as well as the Saturday commemorative office.[112] In another story featuring the Little Office in Anselm's series, Jerome of Pavia is described as an upstanding cleric who "tried to please the holy mother of God, either by greeting her, singing her hours, or performing many forms of service in her honor."[113] This is also the case in the tale of the prior of St. Saviour, Pavia, in which an otherwise-immoral prior sings her praises at every office: *singulis horis laudes de eiusque canebat.*[114] A story that appears in verse in Chicago UL 147 has another monk singing praises to Mary after each of the canonical hours, and one in Lambeth Palace Library 214 sees a cleric saved for the same reason when he falls in a river while traveling to meet his mistress, in a version of the Drowned Sacristan.[115] In yet another tale a monk visiting an abbey in Cambrai witnesses the monks there celebrating the daily Marian office; this could be connected to the adoption of the Saturday office.[116]

The most famous of the Little Office stories is the Cleric of Pisa, which is found first of all starting in the collection attributed to Anselm.[117] A cleric devoted to the Virgin enough that he "daily sang the hours in her honor, which was done very rarely in that time," is married off by his family, but when he sneaks away from the wedding to perform the devotion one last time, Mary appears to him in a jealous rage; terrified, he runs away from his marriage bed to return to Mary's service.[118] The aside, in which the practice is said still to be unusual, is noteworthy. So too are the numerous Italian settings in stories featuring the Little Office, perhaps reflecting knowledge of the forms of Marian devotion that may have been established in part by the reformer Peter Damian in northern Italy. Peter included his own version of the story of the sinful cleric in his admonishments to fellow monks, urging them to follow this example and celebrate the Hours of Mary.[119] From the evidence of the miracle stories, for English monks as much as their Italian contemporaries, the daily Little Office was considered an effective means to compensate for sin and a marker of intense personal piety.

William featured the Little Office in a number of stories, some inspired by Anselm's, and some derived from other sources, thereby shedding additional light on its meaning for twelfth-century monks. In his version of the Cleric of Pisa, he reiterated the idea of a private devotional practice, remarking that the cleric "himself maintained the private hours, and the private offices."[120] In a similar story, the clerical protagonist of Love by Black Arts continues to perform the Little Office despite having made a pact with the devil in order to gain the affections of his beloved. He is cut short on his wedding day when Mary appears to him in a vision to remind him of his devotion to her and he breaks off the marriage.[121] Yet another story features a monk who ultimately receives Mary's milk and has the *Ave* written on his tongue for singing the Hours of Mary, frequently standing and more often kneeling in prayer—but never sitting or lying down, so as not to ruin the efficacy of his prayers through weakness.[122] In another story, a cleric of Chartres cathedral recites the Little Office secretly, and Mary subsequently defends him despite his avaricious tendencies.[123]

The stories about the Little Office may have had a special resonance in England, as suggested by a miracle that appears not in a collection but rather in the chronicle of John of Worcester. The account serves to show the Marian devotion of Prior Warin of Worcester, as he and Benedict, abbot of Tewkesbury (from 1124–37), are praised for their devotional practices:

This servant of God [Benedict] was completely devoted to the most blessed and glorious Mother of God. Chanting the hours every day, he would either celebrate on a festival or hear a mass in her honor. We know that the lord prior of Worcester [Warin] does likewise. Who has ever put his faith in Mary and been let down by her? No one, I say, no one. As the aforesaid abbot and chaplain of the most holy Mary was about to depart this world, her other chaplain was asleep at our township at Lindridge. Someone appeared to him in a dream, announcing good news, "Get up," this person said, "get up! The abbot of Tewkesbury and chaplain of St. Mary is about to depart this life. You are her chaplain, although not worthy of so great or such an honor." This happened three times. When he awakened, he told the story of the dream to a well-known monk who lay near to him. He demonstrated that this vision had been brought about through the power of God and that of His sweetest Mother.[124]

Warin may have been following the example of the now-deceased bishop of Worcester, Wulfstan, in singing the Hours of Mary together with Benedict.[125] William of Malmesbury explained elsewhere that Tewkesbury, in the diocese of Worcester, was so named because it was dedicated to the Theotokos, perhaps providing an additional reason for Benedict's devotion.[126] While it appears in a chronicle and not a miracle collection, this anecdote serves to illustrate that the daily votive office in Mary's honor was quickly becoming known for eliciting her miraculous intervention.

William reveals an important reason for his promotion of the Little Office in his adaptation of Odo of Cluny's story of Mary as *mater misericordiae* for his miracle collection. The story was included in John of Salerno's *Vita* of the great Cluniac abbot.[127] As the story goes, a renowned thief became a monk at Cluny, but after having spent a virtuous life at the abbey, he confessed while dying that he had in the meantime stolen one more thing: a rope to tie around his middle so as to restrict his appetite, and which had begun to cut into his flesh. At this point, he received a vision of Mary in recognition of his ascetic efforts, but also for reciting the Little Office. As a result of the miracle, as William related it, the Little Office spread throughout the communities reformed under the Cluniac banner:

This is why the monks of that place [Cluny] to this day venerate their common mistress with unparalleled honor. For example, in all their communities, which are spread widely over the Latin world, they are not content with each monk paying his respects to her in private but instead extol her in their assemblies with a public saying of the Hours. They have persuaded themselves that she appeared quite clearly in person to one of their number and taught him the compline that all who profess particular devotion to her now think should not be neglected. I do not say this to insult, rather to exult, for every occasion should be taken for a man to be attached more intimately to her service.[128]

Whatever William meant by the enigmatic last sentence of this passage—why should he have thought this a potential insult to the community?—he clearly considered the Cluniacs praiseworthy for their precocious devotion to Mary. Notwithstanding William's suggestion that the monks of Cluny were celebrating the Little Office communally in the choir, there is no evidence the practice was adopted before the mid-twelfth century, when it was still being celebrated in the infirmary chapel alone, as indicated in a previous chapter.[129] Cluny's prestige as a font of reformed monasticism would nevertheless have lent authority to William's description of the origins of the Little Office; more than a dozen Cluniac houses were founded in England by Henry I, with the abbey of Reading as his own mausoleum.[130] Tracing the roots of the practice to Cluny would have been a meaningful way to justify the incorporation of daily celebration of the Marian office into the liturgy of Benedictine houses more widely.

William's rhetorical strategy of citing the Cluniac example when speaking of the Little Office did more than just promote it as a generally desirable practice. Just as in the other stories that depict clerics performing the Hours of Mary, in the Cluny story, it starts out as something done in private. This is further reflected in the chronicle sources, where men such as Benedict, Wulfstan, and Warin are praised for privately performing the Hours of the Virgin. As noted in a previous chapter, the communal practice of saying the Little Office may have stopped in the post–Norman Conquest period, but it appeared once more in the early twelfth century at several institutions, including Bury St. Edmunds during Anselm's abbacy.[131] The miracles, then, could reflect this period of change in the status of the office as well as its gradual adoption at institutions where it had never been celebrated. Many of the stories capture its transition from private to public practice, and the miracle Mary performs in each account has a key role to play in persuading the entire community to adopt it. Given this context, William's description of the practice's origins at the renowned abbey of Cluny may have aimed specifically to endorse a shift from a private to communal recitation of the Hours. If such extensive Marian devotions were not just newly introduced but had also been downgraded or relegated to the private sphere, it would have been even more important to establish their legitimacy. Portraying the Little Office as a practice worthy of observance not just by devout individuals but by entire communities would certainly have helped in this aim.

FEAST DAYS

The idea that miracle stories could lend authority to disputed practices is given considerable weight by the appearance of foundation stories more elaborate than William's brief mention of the Little Office's Cluniac origins. One founda-

tion story that features in a large number of manuscripts is particularly revealing of the role stories could exercise in promoting practice specifically in an
Anglo-Norman context.[132] The tale relates how Aelfsige (or Elsinus), the abbot
of St. Augustine's Canterbury, was sent to negotiate with the king of Denmark
by William the Conqueror in order to avoid Danish attack on the newly conquered English territory.[133] On the way back from a successful mission, his ship
was rocked by storms. When the crew started to pray for relief, the ghostly figure of a bishop appeared to them and addressed Aelfsige with the following:

> "If you wish to escape from the danger of the sea, if you wish to return to your
> native country safely, promise me in the presence of God that you will solemnly
> celebrate and observe the feast day of the Conception of the mother of Christ."
> Then the abbot said: "How am I to do this or on what day?" The messenger said:
> "You will celebrate it on the eighth day of December and will preach wherever
> you can, that it may be celebrated by everybody." Aelfsige said: "And what sort of
> divine service do you command us to use on this feast?" He replied to him: "Let
> every service which is said at her Nativity be said also at her Conception. Thus,
> when her birthday is mentioned at her Nativity, let her conception be mentioned
> in this other celebration." After the abbot heard this, he reached the English shore
> with a favorable wind blowing. Soon he made known everything he had seen and
> heard to whomever he could, and he ordered in the church at Ramsey, over which
> he presided, that this feast be solemnly celebrated on December 8.[134]

The real-life Aelfsige was a monk at Winchester, Old Minister, before becoming abbot of St. Augustine's, Canterbury in 1061.[135] He traveled to Denmark probably less for diplomatic purposes than because he was exiled for the
close ties he had entertained with the disgraced Anglo-Saxon archbishop Stigand. Aelfsige returned in 1079 or 1080 to become abbot of Ramsey.[136] The
tense political situation is completely glossed over in the legend, however, and
some later versions even promote the Normans as worthy conquerors and Aelfsige as their valuable ally.[137] The liturgical detail is also skewed. As a former
monk of Winchester, Aelfsige would have been familiar with the Conception
feast celebrated there before 1066 and would not have needed the details of the
celebration spelled out for him.[138] As a result, Southern claimed the author was
simply confused or unaware of the historical details.[139] It is perhaps more likely
that he had a concrete purpose in twisting the facts.[140]

Scholars have generally made sense of the Aelfsige legend by inscribing it in
the debates surrounding the readoption of the Conception feast at the end of
the 1120s. Edmund Bishop, among other scholars, concluded on the basis of
this story that the Marian miracle collections as a whole were produced as part
of the dossier for the readoption of the feast, leading up to the Council of London in 1129 where it was officially approved; Anselm's involvement in supporting the feast and his role in putting together one of the first collections seemed

like undeniable proof of the connection.[141] According to this theory, the errone-
ous details of the story could be explained by a desire to authorize the feast's
origins. Aelfsige would have been an effective protagonist and defender of
Anglo-Saxon traditions since he represented the old ecclesiastical guard. In al-
leging Aelfsige was also a favorite of William I, the legend gave him royal sanction, thus appealing to the secular powers presiding over the decision at the
Council of London. If the anonymous ghostly bishop were additionally associated with St. Anselm, as Adrienne Williams Boyarin has argued, this would
only have made the case stronger.[142] Like Bishop before her, Boyarin concluded
that "the story could not at this time have been meant for any other purpose
than to persuade those in positions of ecclesiastical power that Mary's Conception should be celebrated."[143]

The neat lines of the argument nevertheless hide some unresolved complica-
tions. If the story and collections of which it was a part were first conceived as
support for the Conception feast, we might expect it to head the collections. But
actually, the earliest manuscripts containing Marian miracle collections omit
the Aelfsige legend entirely; it is not one the original eighteen stories normally
grouped together in manuscripts that Southern associated with Anselm of
Bury.[144] This suggests that an anonymous monastic scribe rather than Anselm
himself was responsible for adding it to a collection once these were in circulation.[145] It could have been a monk of Ramsey, a house with close ties to and a
strong interest in the culture of Bury St. Edmunds.[146] The addition of the Aelfsige legend may even have dated from after the feast's readoption, making sense
of the fact that neither Eadmer nor Osbert mention it anywhere in their works
devised precisely for justification of the feast.[147] A version of the legend appears
in Osbert's letter collection, but it is written in a different, probably later hand.[148]
Of course, it is possible that both Eadmer and Osbert chose not to rely on miraculous literature due to its flimsiness in argument, much like the apocryphal
material they also neglected; when chastising the canons at Lyon cathedral for
celebrating the Conception in the 1130s, Bernard of Clairvaux made an oblique
reference to the questionable miraculous evidence on which the feast's foundation rested.[149] The legend's lack of authority among those who opposed the feast
does not, however, preclude the possibility that it was added to miracle collections in order to further support the feast's official sanction after the fact and
help motivate its spread.

In addition to the Aelfsige legend, we find a number of other unusual feast
days that feature in the twelfth-century miracle collections. The Old Hispanic
feast of the Annunciation celebrated on December 18 is the subject of the first
story in the series attributed to Anselm, for example. Taken originally from the
Life of Ildefonsus written by his eighth-century successor, Cixila, and expanded
at Cluny in the eleventh century, the story concerns the foundation of the Hispanic Marian feast in the mid-seventh century:[150]

There once was in the city of Toledo, an archbishop named Ildefonsus, who was very pious and decorated with good works, among which was his great love for holy Mary, mother of God, and he revered her as much as he could with all his admiration. He composed in her honor a volume on her most sacred virginity, in an elegant style, which so pleased Holy Mary herself, that she appeared to him holding this book in her hands, and thanked him for such a work. Truly wishing to honor her even more, he established that a feast day be celebrated every year, an octave before Christmas, and so if the feast of the Annunciation should land around the time of Easter, it could fittingly be restored just before that same feast [Christmas] on the aforementioned day.[151]

Mary visits the bishop again at this point to thank him with a vestment that only he can wear; when his successor tries to put it on, he immediately dies. It may have been at Cluny that Anselm heard the story, when he visited with his uncle in the early twelfth century. Perhaps this is what inspired him to establish the same feast at Bury and additionally to include the story of its origins at the beginning of his miracle collection. From there, William of Malmesbury included a version of the story that is in fact closer to the original, with additional references to the council at which the new feast day was instated.[152]

Another story that promoted a new feast is William's tale of Bishop Guy of Lescar and St. Anne.[153] Imprisoned by the Saracens in the course of a military attack (ca. 1134) for his refusal to abjure his faith, Guy has a vision of the Virgin, who tells him to pray to her mother, Anne, in order to be freed: "If you begged me for love of St. Anne, my beloved mother, and by your deep-felt prayers won her as mediator for you with my only-begotten Son, you would walk free of your prison chains and swiftly win the grace of bodily freedom."[154] Guy does as Mary asks, and his ransom is paid the following day. The replacement of Mary with Anne in her traditional *mediatrix* role is particularly resonant in light of the recent innovation of the feast of St. Anne at Worcester in the 1130s.[155] William's links with Worcester and the prior Warin, for whom he wrote a life of bishop Wulfstan, would explain his interest in this miracle about Anne. So too would the close relation between the cult of Anne and Marian devotion at this early stage of its history.

The presence of stories about new and unfamiliar Marian feasts in the miracle collections does seem to suggest a desire to explain and justify novel practices being adopted in twelfth-century England. Yet we should not ignore that even universally accepted practices are given foundation stories in the collections. Dominic included a legend about the origins of the feast of the Nativity in which an extremely humble and virtuous man hears celestial singing (*caelestem harmoniam*) on the eve of Mary's Nativity. When an angel tells him what the music is celebrating, he promptly instates an official feast day.[156] Here Dominic is vague, giving us no information as to who the *solitarius* was, or where and when the events were meant to have taken place. William was more explicit in crediting Fulbert with spreading the feast:

> Fulbert was bishop in the same city. His assiduity and learning showed itself especially in his love of St. Mary. For example, not content with the traditional rites in honor of the ever virgin, he took particular pains by personal example to see that her Nativity should be celebrated throughout the Latin world. To cap her praises, he composed a sermon and responsories, which are so well known that they do not need to be recorded by me.[157]

The lack of specific detail about these sermons and responsories stands in stark contrast with some of the detail seen in other stories, suggesting a difference in levels of familiarity with the different practices. Fulbert's sermons for the Nativity and his responsory *Solem iustitiae regem* were certainly famous as standard elements of the liturgy for the feast. They were also thought to have merited him three drops of the Virgin's milk—a miracle conferred to few, as William wrote in his story.[158] An altogether different motivation led to the adoption of the feast of the Purification by the Emperor Justinian (527–65), as described in the final story of William's collection.[159] Led astray by his heretical wife, Emperor Justinian is said to have brought plagues and misery on his people. After having processed an image, presumably of the Virgin, around the city, all is restored, and in recognition, the emperor instated the feast of the Purification, which then spread to the rest of the world.[160] With these foundation stories, we see that the miracle collections included the promotion of well-established feast days alongside more novel ones.

Given the presence of stories about such a variety of feast days, old as well as new, we must rethink the idea that the miracle collections compiled in the early twelfth century were solely produced to support the Conception feast, as scholars have contended. Ultimately, the Aelfsige legend was just one of many similar miracles, and compilers were clearly interested in stories about a diverse set of Marian practices—from more obscure private devotions, to highly public and well-known feast days. Some of these may have been subject to liturgical reform immediately following the conquest and were in need of legitimacy, such as the Conception feast and Little Office. Others reflect the accumulation of increasingly elaborate practices, such as the antiphons and masses, feasts of Anne, and Old Hispanic December feast, practices that no doubt gained valuable advertising with the circulation of miracles associated with them. The evidence suggests that Anselm did not commission the first volume specifically with the Conception feast in mind. The aim of the early compilers seems to have been to promote the Marian cult more generally, in all its many liturgical expressions. Anonymous scribes recognized the wide scope of the collections, adding stories of their own about other Marian practices they wished to endorse. The miracle collections come across as a catchall for Marian liturgies of the moment, advancing new liturgical practices by giving them fixed foundations like those of much older ones.

This analysis of the Marian miracle collections points to their intimate connection with the development of the Marian cult in Anglo-Norman England. The context of blossoming devotion to the Virgin explains the appearance of the Marian miracle collections in this period and their focus on liturgical practices, which were being adopted at a growing number of institutions. As monks and nuns performed increasingly elaborate acts of devotion in Mary's honor, praising her for her powers of intercession, miracle stories provided that these were effective proof. The practices developed, revived, and embellished by monks in post–Conquest England even received sanction from the Virgin herself, who appears so often in them to perform and correct practice as well as reward it. Through additional endorsement by famous local figures such as Dunstan, Eulalia, Leofric, and Aelfsige, the veneration of Mary was encouraged with special relevance in an English context. Marian liturgies were also given Italian, Visigothic, and Cluniac roots to further establish their prestige through the precedent set by pious individuals and institutions the world over. But while the origins of the collections may have been tied to England and Anglo-Norman monastic culture in which they emerged, the genre was set to enjoy much wider appeal. Thanks to the diverse settings and universal practices, anyone could picture themselves performing the acts featured in the stories, and who would not want to call on Mary when the results were so spectacular? The miracle collections thus opened up these practices to widespread audiences, helping to spread the message of Mary's worthiness of veneration in prayer and song, and explaining just how this could be accomplished.

MIRACLES IN THE LITURGY

When discussing the power of miracle stories to communicate not only the idea of Mary's mercy but also how to be a beneficiary of it, we need to think carefully about how the stories themselves were communicated. Although scholars have acknowledged the incorporation of miracles into sermons, they have not necessarily connected the collection of miracles into volumes with the purpose of sermon writing.[161] Koopmans has explicitly argued that written miracle collections in this early period did not serve as compendia from which to draw in constructing a sermon, since so many stories were known already from oral reports and had also been used in sermons even before the appearance of the collections.[162] Tempering this assessment slightly, Marcus Bull introduced his edition of *The Miracles of Our Lady of Rocamadour* by pointing out that "while miracle collections could serve many useful functions such as providing material for readings and preaching, they were not in themselves fundamental elements of the liturgical or paraliturgical celebration of a cult."[163] The idea seems to be that individual stories could be used liturgically, but the volumes of miracles were created only to conserve the stories for posterity, not to take part in the ritual. For those few scholars who have addressed the question of use, therefore, Marian miracle collections preserved oral history in written form at most for private reading, but were not in themselves used in the performance of liturgical practice.[164]

A number of factors suggest the contrary: that miracle collections were used in religious practice. First, turning briefly again to Dominic's prologue to his collection, he claimed the purpose of his work was to instill hope for Mary's intercession "as much in writers, as readers and listeners," explaining that her "virtues we know must be venerated as much through writing, as through reading and listening." This provides us with invaluable information about the various ways in which the audience was meant to experience the text: in copying, silent and public reading, and hearing its oral delivery. More important still, Dominic clearly conceived of the tales as devotional tools in and of themselves; writing, reading, and listening were all means by which to express love for Mary, and thereby receive her love in return. Every experience of the text was to be edifying (supplying an example to follow) but also devotional in nature. Dominic tells us that miracle collecting was not merely a literary pursuit but conceived of as a religious act, too, with the telling of stories placed on par with the singing of chants and reciting of prayers.

At first the Marian collections seem to have taken the form of self-contained books that lack any explicit indication as to their use. Several early manuscripts have the miracle collections as their first item, with hand changes suggesting that other quires were added only when the codex was assembled at a later date. This is the case for Chicago UL MS 147, a French manuscript from the first half of the twelfth century; BL Egerton MS 2947, an English manuscript of indeterminate origin; and Copenhagen Thott MS 128, 2°, a thirteenth-century manuscript of unknown provenance.[165] The collection found in Oxford Bodl. Laud Miscellania MS 410, a twelfth-century collection of saints' lives of unknown origin, may have been similarly combined with other material, only later. The miracle collection is in a different hand from the saints' lives that precede it and starts a new quire; the presence of a missal fragment in between the saints' lives and miracle collection further indicates that the Marian volume was initially a separate one.[166] The difference in page size of a miracle collection and the texts that surround it in a manuscript made at the abbey of Saint-Denis in the twelfth century suggests that it was once self-standing as well.[167] Another twelfth-century manuscript from Dover priory in a Christ Church hand groups the miracle collection with saints' lives, including the English saints Edmund and Dunstan, although changes in hand suggest that it was copied separately from the other texts.[168] These early examples indicate that miracle collections were probably circulating as individual volumes. In addition to those mentioned, some of the works with which they were combined include other Marian miracle accounts from the northern French collections of Laon and Soissons, in ever-larger volumes of Marian miracles—such as found in the twelfth-century French manuscript BnF MS lat. 2873.

For manuscripts in which the miracles were part of a larger codex, there tends to be an obvious connection between the materials copied together: Mary. The term "Mariale" has been much used in the cataloging and description of manuscripts, with catalogers usually noting the grouping of texts with a Marian theme: sermons, hymns, commentaries, and miracle collections—including the "universal" collections and northern French volumes.[169] These manuscripts seem to imitate the *libelli* produced in increasing numbers starting in the eighth century that contain the lives of saints together with liturgical offices, masses, and prayers for the saint's corresponding feast day.[170] Several examples from Anglo-Norman England survive, including a life of Mildred by Goscelin of Saint-Bertin with accompanying lessons, responds, and antiphons, and the Pierpoint Morgan manuscript devoted to St. Edmund made at Bury St. Edmunds during the abbacy of Anselm.[171] Francis Wormald suggested that these volumes had a liturgical status in and of themselves, and were under the jurisdiction of the sacristan rather than the librarian as relics kept with gospel books and chalices.[172] As such, there is a crucial liturgical strand that connects many of the texts in the Mariales that needs to be emphasized.

In one of the Mariales's simplest forms, BL Cotton MS Cleo. C. x, produced at Glastonbury abbey in the twelfth century, a Marian miracle collection was copied together with the sermon for the Assumption by Ralph d'Escures, mentioned in a previous chapter.[173] The same sermon is found in BnF MS lat. 2873, which otherwise includes mainly miracle accounts, but also the visions of Elizabeth of Schönau concerning the bodily Assumption of the Virgin. This manuscript seems to be united by an interest not only in miraculous events but in the Assumption as well—a likely indicator that it was designed for this liturgical occasion.[174] Other sermons are found with a miracle collection in Oxford Balliol College MS 240, a manuscript produced in the diocese of Worcester in the twelfth century. The miracle collection does not continue on from the previous text, which is a collection of homilies for the liturgical year, but instead is followed in the same hand by an excerpt from Anselm's incarnational treatise, *De virginali conceptu et originali peccato*, and two sermons for the Nativity of Mary, the first of which is by Fulbert.[175] The excerpt from *De virginali conceptu* is chapter 7, on the sinlessness of the seed taken from the Virgin, which could suggest an interest in the question of Mary's Immaculate Conception. The miracle collection at the end of the twelfth-century Copenhagen Thott MS 26, 8°, follows the pseudo-Augustinian sermon on the bodily Assumption that in-

spired William's prologue, together with additional Marian stories from Gregory of Tours's *De gloria martyrum* (chapters 9–11), Paschasius's *Cogitis me* sermon, and a series of Marian Apocrypha: the *Gospel of Pseudo-Matthew* and
Transitus. BnF MS lat. 2672, a twelfth-century collection of Apocrypha, sermons, hymns, and visions of Mary, is a particularly intriguing compilation, into
which a nearly contemporary Marian miracle collection has been inserted. In
this manuscript, a version of the Theophilus legend by Paul the Deacon, is cut
off midway by a collection of miracles on a new quire added at f. 13, although
we cannot know when this occurred. It is clear that the miracles were inserted
with texts thought most appropriate, such as other Marian texts and most especially the Theophilus legend, which was often included in miracle collections.[176]
The concept of a codex devoted entirely to Mary had taken hold, and miracles
were obviously considered part of the canon of Marian materials, many of
which had a liturgical purpose, suggesting the miracles may have had as well.

More extensive compilations of Marian works contain various other types of
materials that limit somewhat the appropriateness of the term "Mariale." BL
Add. MS 35112 from the abbey of Saint-Martin of Tournai contains a wealth of
Marian material, such as poetry by Hildebert of Lavardin (d. 1133), hymns,
Hugh of St. Victor's (d. 1141) commentary on the Song of Songs, the *Gospel of
Pseudo-Matthew*, prayers to the Virgin, and sermons for Mary's Nativity, Annunciation, Purification, and for her Saturday commemoration.[177] This last
item is especially interesting because it is the Saturday sermon with the incipit
Solemnem memoriam, which is found in many collections as a miracle story, as
discussed above, and here may have been intended for the Saturday commemorative mass. In this case, the text is missing the final miracle about the image of
Mary in Constantinople. The omission is curious because so many of the other
elements in the manuscript deal with miraculous images: the Holy Face of
Lucca, images of Christ that bleed when desecrated by Jews (from Gregory's *De
gloria martyrum*), miraculous Eucharists, and a lengthy text attributed to Athanasius of Alexandria (ca. 293–373) about a miraculous image of Christ in Beirut.[178] The Pseudo-Athanasius text is also found in BnF MS lat. 2873, the only
non-Marian text in the manuscript, and in a volume from the abbey of Saint-
Victor in Paris, where it is combined not only with miracles but with the *Transitus* by Pseudo-Melito as well.[179] In a twelfth-century English manuscript of
unknown origin, a scribe appended three miracles to a preexisting collection
interspersed with hymns to Mary: a miraculous image of Christ follows a cleric
with its eyes, an image of Mary holding Jesus in her arms is stabbed by a Jew,
and a different version of the story in which a Marian image is used as surety for
a loan from the one that already appears in the collection.[180] Clearly the scribe
who added the stories at the end of the volume was particularly interested in
miraculous images, and it does not seem to have mattered much whether these

were Marian or not. The appearance of non-Marian miracles in volumes with a predominantly Marian theme indicates that image miracles tended to be considered together, for reasons that will be explored in the next chapter.

One especially illustrative manuscript indicates the extent to which miracle collections were not just loosely connected with but also directly related to Marian liturgical texts. BnF MS lat. 18168 is a compendium of Marian sermons, hymns, and miracles from the priory of Saint-Martin-des-Champs in Paris.[181] In the middle of a sermon for the Annunciation by Fulbert in the eleventh-century section, the text ends abruptly on the verso of f. 79, and a new quire in a twelfth-century hand has been inserted.[182] The inserted folios contain a miracle collection and full office for the feast of the Conception, both in the same hand. This office has been discussed in a previous chapter as an early example of the Conception office, suggesting an English model.[183] It is tempting to think that a little *libellus* containing the office together with one of the new miracle collections could have been sent to Saint-Martin by Hugh, the abbot of Reading, who both supported the reinstatement of the Conception feast in England and had important ties with this other Cluniac institution. The presence of a number of English miracles in the collection, including the legend of Aelfsige, further suggests that the point of origin of this particular pairing was England. While not entirely conclusive, it is certainly an intriguing thought that the miracle collection was included with the office with the intention of justifying the adoption of the Conception feast at Saint-Martin, providing the Aelfsige legend to authorize such a liturgical innovation.

Another French manuscript provides direct proof not only that miracles were linked to liturgical celebration but also that they became integral to it. A twelfth-century legendary from the abbey of Saint-Germain-des-Prés contains lives of the saints in the order of the liturgical year, from Stephen to Thomas, with an entry for the feast of the Conception.[184] The texts for the feast begin with the prologue of the miracle collection attributed to Anselm, *Ad omnipotentis dei laudem*, followed by twenty miracles. The final story, fittingly, is the one about Aelfsige. It is nevertheless unlike any other retelling of the legend of which I am aware, with a long narrative of King Harold's defeat at the hands of William and description of Aelfsige's diplomatic activities in Denmark.[185] The fact that the tale cuts off quite oddly at the point where the storm strikes the ship may be symptomatic of a scribe unfamiliar with and perhaps confused by the political analysis he was reading such that he missed the most important part of the story. Most interesting for our purposes, however, is the rubric that heads the miracle collection: "To be read on the day of the Conception of blessed Mary, at the collation, and at the main meal" (*In conceptione beate Marie lego ad collationem et ad prandium*).[186] This indicates a concrete purpose for the Elsinus legend as part of the liturgical commemoration it had originally been written to justify: it was to be read aloud during meals in the refectory and at the collatio, which was a short reading before compline. In a thirteenth-century Eynsham customary, the collatio reading was specifically dedicated to the Virgin.[187] Another example is found in a fourteenth-century legendary from southern France, where a group of miracles follow the *Gospel of Pseudo-Matthew* for the collatio of the feast of the Nativity.[188]

In her studies of monastic liturgical reading material, Teresa Webber has suggested that collections of Marian miracles would have been among the readings for Marian feast days, especially in the refectory.[189] Marian miracle collections appear in several of the lists of books dedicated to this purpose that she has examined, and they appear in numerous abbey book lists more generally, too.[190] There was considerable variety in the types of texts that could be used, and these often dovetailed with the readings for matins, meaning that they had a liturgical function in and of themselves, carrying the theme of the chants and lessons performed in church as part of the Divine Office into other areas of the monastery. Several eleventh- and twelfth-century English legendaries she has looked at include marginal markings indicating the start and end of numbered office lections.[191] She points to the eleventh-century Worcester Legendary as an example of this combination of miracles and Apocrypha, although it does not have explicit rubrics indicating reading for meals, as in the case of the Saint-Germain manuscript.[192] Because, as she argues, the responsibility for selecting these readings lay with the precentor, the fact that William of Malmesbury had this role could indicate that he intended his collection for just this sort of context.[193] Collecting miracles into volumes would have been an essential part of establishing their liturgical usefulness: gathering stories together so that they could be read in sequence in the refectory and chapterhouse.

A short collection of miracle stories would have been ideal for reading at mealtimes, providing a relatively lengthy text, but of varied and entertaining subject matter to keep listeners interested. Readings for the office itself, however, would have needed shorter pieces, and this is where we find individual miracles extracted and used particularly for the office of matins. The monastic night office of matins, when the monks gathered in the middle of the night for their most extensive period of singing and psalmody, included twelve sets of readings on a feast day. As Solange Corbin found in her extensive review of offices for the Conception feast, the story of Aelfsige became the main text used for matins readings relatively early on in the feast's liturgical history.[194] This is the case, for example, in the late thirteenth-century Hereford Breviary, in addition to an office for the feast in another thirteenth-century Hereford manuscript.[195] More miracles were eventually added to the Aelfsige legend to the point where by the fourteenth century, even the antiphons and responsories for the feast were based on miracle accounts. Corbin argued that this shift toward the incorporation of miracles into offices marked an attempt to appeal to wider audiences.[196] Strikingly, despite the fact that Anselm showed no sign of support for the feast, he is explicitly named in some of these office readings as the miracle story's author. This attribution provides additional proof of the authorizing power of miracle stories. The legend of Aelfsige, originally composed to support the liturgical celebration of Mary's Conception, thus came to justify each individual celebration of the feast by becoming an integral feature of the monastic office.

The incorporation of miracles into the chants and readings of matins would have had a profound effect on their status in monastic communities, as performative texts that embellished and supported the celebration of Mary's life cycle. The question that remains is the extent to which this exposure to miracles was limited to the monastery. The Marian sermons of Honorius illustrate another way in which individual Marian miracles were incorporated into the liturgy, and this time with important implications for the miracles' more general dissemination. As described in the previous chapter, the *Speculum Ecclesiae*, a collection of sermons for the entire year that he wrote for the monks of Christ Church Canterbury, contains four sermons for the main feasts of Mary: Purification, Annunciation, Assumption, and Nativity; the Conception feast is not among those included, perhaps because Honorius's sermons were composed circa 1100, before the feast was officially reinstated in England. Although the sermons predate the collection of Marian miracle stories, their use of miracles as edificatory examples represents a crucial way in which miracle stories were disseminated beyond the monastic context.

Honorius explicitly intended his sermons to be heard not just by the monks of Christ Church but also by lay audiences. He had a strong vision of monks exercising an important pastoral role, as attested in one of his later works, *That Monks Should Be Allowed to Preach*, written during his time in Regensburg, which suggests that he may have been inspired by what he saw monks doing in England and wished the model of the preaching monk to be adopted elsewhere.[197] This was certainly happening at Worcester, where Honorius composed the *Speculum Ecclesiae*, as Francesca Tinti has highlighted.[198] The monks of Christ Church would have exercised a similar function, since the cathedral would have attracted the town's population on significant feast days especially.[199] The fact that the *Speculum Ecclesiae* includes an *ad status* sermon provides evidence that it was meant to address lay audiences.[200] Referred to as the *sermo generalis*, it is divided into eight sections that correspond to different classes of society: priests, judges, the rich, the poor, soldiers, merchants, farmers, and married people. The *sermo generalis* was not the only one of his sermons to have a general audience, and Honorius attached instructions that all the sermons in the *Speculum Ecclesiae*, including those specific to each feast day, were to be translated into the vernacular line by line in the course of delivery: "With respect to all the sermons, you should first say the line in Latin, then explain in the local language."[201] His sermon for the Purification of Mary gives an idea of who he imagined might be present:

> Let young men and virgins, old men and young, praise the name of the Lord today because he comes to exalt the reign of his people. Let virgins exalt and prance about with devout praise for Christ, because the Virgin Mary gave forth the Savior to the world, who gave heavenly support to the virginal troops. Let widows rejoice and applaud Christ with a vow, whom the widow Anne today brought into the temple with Symeon, who welcomes the chaste into the temple of heaven. Let married women rejoice and sing praises to Christ with one voice, when the married Elisabeth prophesied, full of the Holy Spirit, at the entry of Christ's mother, that he will bind to himself in the heavenly bridal chamber those who live in legitimate union. Let pleasing infancy raise its voice resounding in praise to Christ, because he whom the heavens could not contain lay in a crib as a baby. The infant John saluted him in his mother's womb. Thousands of infants praised him in their death by Herod for his cause. Let flourishing childhood celebrate rejoicing in Christ, who as a boy stays sitting in the midst of learned men and provides a model of teaching to the boys. May the glowing age of youth applaud Christ, congratulating him, he who, once he had become a youth, illuminated the world with his miracles.[202]

The young and old, married and unmarried—all ages and social groups should be able to draw inspiration from his sermon, Honorius seems to say.

Seen in this context, the appearance of Marian miracle stories in Honorius's sermons illustrates one of the key ways in which monastic expressions of Marian devotion became meaningful beyond the monastery walls. "The sermon was the most widespread means of both enhancing the reputations of the saints, which was so important to the propagation of their cults, and communicating the theology of the miraculous to a wider public," wrote Michael Goodich.[203] Sermons were also fully integrated into liturgical commemoration: they were delivered during the mass (after the Gospel reading) and frequently commented on the Gospel text, expanding on its potential meaning.[204] Each of Honorius's Marian sermons begins with an exegetical reading of the biblical pericopes used in the mass of each feast, interpreting them in light of Mary's life.[205] But Honorius also concluded his sermons with examples of Mary's actions in the world, generally in the form of a miracle story or *exemplum*. "Exempla" have been defined as short edifying accounts that were incorporated into other texts—namely sermons—to provide a moral message; in the earlier history of the genre, the distinction was less clear between miracle stories and strictly edifying tales based in a recognizable setting.[206] The Cistercians became especially prolific at collecting exempla, particularly toward the end of the twelfth century.[207] But such collections were already attested in the eleventh and twelfth centuries, with Alfonsi creating one of the first such volumes in the *Disciplina clericalis*.[208]

Honorius's use of miracles in sermons as exempla made relatively early use of this new trend, although there are some early examples.[209] His Marian exempla fall into two categories. On the one hand, some of the miracles in his sermons describe the miraculous foundation of the feast day in question, thereby justifying the feast's celebration in the first place. On the other hand, they illustrate the rewards bestowed on those who were especially devoted to Mary, encouraging the listeners to act likewise. Given their common purpose, it is hardly surprising that almost all of Honorius's Marian exempla appear in the early miracle collections. He may even share a source with Dominic and William of Malmesbury: the Worcester Legendary.[210] Because Honorius was active at Christ Church and Worcester, it is entirely possible that he moved in the same circles as the earliest compilers and may have known them personally. Honorius's use of miracles as exempla may have inspired monks like Dominic and William to create their collections as a means to further facilitate such use in preaching. William, for one, recognized the potential role these stories could play in promoting Marian devotion among not just monastic but lay audiences, too, when he wrote that his miracles would be "beneficial for the minds of the simple in order to increase their love for our lady."[211] Sermons no doubt represented one of the ways in which William foresaw the laity hearing such stories. Sermons like those of Honorius thus provide a possible additional reason for the composition of the miracle collections, and insight into how what was originally a monastic message about religious practice came to be transmitted and shared on a much larger scale.

To offer an example of how Honorius wove miracles into his Marian sermons, combining them with monastic exegesis to make them relevant for the feast day in question, it is worth looking at his sermon for the feast of the Purification. After glossing Psalm 84:12 ("Truth has sprung out of the earth; justice has looked down from heaven"), Ezek. 44:2 ("This door will be closed forever, and only the King of Kings will cross through it"), and Num. 17 (the account of Aaron's flowering rod) as prophecies for the virgin birth—the latter two of which are found in the sequence *Concentu parili hic* for the Purification feast in the twelfth-century portion of the Caligula Troper (a Worcester manuscript)—the sermon comes to the Gospel account by which Christ was presented in the Temple by his mother (Luke 2:22–35)—the event that the feast was ultimately celebrating.[212] Honorius glossed Simeon's prophecy to Mary as described in Luke 2:35:

> [The sword] pierced the soul of Mary with great pain, as she saw him hanging on the cross, and she is therefore greater than any martyr. Christ was the ruin of the Jews and the cross, which the Jews and Gentiles opposed everywhere, was the

resurrection of the Gentiles, although the Jews went to ruin on account of their perfidy.[213]

In this way, Honorius pointed forward to the Passion, during which Mary suffered alongside Christ. The reference to the downfall of the Jews echoes Honorius's thoughts in the *Sigillum* about the preconversion Synagoga, discussed in the previous chapter.[214] But the Gospel narrative also allows Honorius to make a wider point about the need for the congregants to imitate Mary in making an offering to the church on this day, not of material goods, but of penitence. The sermon even provides a gloss on the ritual performed as part of the liturgical celebration. Honorius cited the Gospel text to explain the procession of candles, which took place on the Purification feast (hence "Candlemas"): it represents the priest and prophet Symeon carrying Christ, the light of the world. Finally, Honorius introduced a story: "It is pleasing now to hear briefly, to your delight, how much the Virgin Mary is used to relieve those who invoke her."[215] The tale involves a little Jewish boy who is thrown into an oven by his enraged father after taking communion in a church. The boy is ultimately saved by Mary and emerges unharmed—a fate not spared the father, who is thrown into the same oven by angry bystanders. The story became a staple of the miracle collections and will be the subject of more extensive analysis in the next chapter, but here it is important to note its links with the rest of the sermon. The tale picks up on the anti-Jewish sentiment articulated in Honorius's gloss on Luke, and shares with the texts and rituals of the Purification liturgy the features of the young child—the Jewish boy, the infant Christ—along with the element of fire—the candles, the oven. As such, the tale was not just a dramatic story illustrative of Mary's great powers of mercy and protection but instead resonated with the themes and imagery associated with the Purification feast in Honorius's multilayered interpretation.

The sermons for the feasts of the Annunciation, Nativity, and Assumption likewise use miracles as a rhetorical strategy to underline the significance of each day.[216] For the feast of the Annunciation, Honorius related the story of Mary of Egypt, the prostitute who was turned away from a church in Jerusalem and became a desert hermit, ultimately performing miracles herself.[217] Honorius's much-shorter sermon for the feast of Mary's Nativity contains several miracle accounts, including extracts from the Nativity Apocrypha concerning Mary's childhood, the foundation story of the feast found also in Dominic's collection of miracles, and a version of Odo's tale of the monk-thief of Cluny who had a vision of Mary as "mother of mercy."[218] The sermon for the Assumption likewise ends with a miracle story, this time the famous tale of Theophilus, the fallen cleric who prays fervently to Mary after he makes a pact with the devil. This popular story will also be discussed in much greater detail in the next chapter. The story's link with the Assumption feast is implicit by way of the narrative of Exodus, which is taken as an allegory for Mary's Assumption. Like the people of Israel, Honorius explained, Mary rose from the desert to escape the enemy hordes, or in Mary's case, the "tangle of Jews and demons submerged in the abyss."[219] The story of Theophilus also features a Jew entangled with the devil who acts as a go-between for the ambitious cleric. Honorius concluded his sermon with an exhortation to pray to Mary like Theophilus did in order to save his soul: "Let us all flee to her, my dearly beloved, with entire mind, let us bestow on her offerings of prayer and praise, to the point where we might see her with her son reigning over the hosts of angels, and obtain some small portion of her same joy and kingdom, with her aid."[220] The presence of miracle accounts in these sermons thus emphasized how effective Marian devotion could be, whether carried out through imitation of Mary's followers, performance of prayer, or celebration of her feast days.

The sermons of Honorius, like the legendaries and liturgical offices, illustrate the ways in which miracles were made an integral feature of the liturgy. Incorporated into the ritual life of the monastery—providing readings at meals, collatio, and matins—miracles took part in the very liturgical practices they described and sought to authorize. But the liturgy was not left unexplained. Sermons—a part of the liturgy themselves, and indistinguishable from the other read texts surrounding them in the order of the mass—supplied a gloss on the liturgy, clarifying the texts used in the chants and readings of the day as well as their connection to the feast in question. Most important, these sermons represent a bridge between monastic and lay culture. Directed to a lay as well as monastic audience, Honorius's sermons not only offered interpretation of the biblical text but also placed it within a wider framework of apocryphal legends, advice about proper religious practice, and evidence of Mary's miraculous actions. In this way, Mary's power to act in the world was reinforced with every delivery of a sermon, as was the importance of celebrating her through prayer and the liturgy. Miracles and liturgy entwined, as miracles bolstered and embellished the liturgy in equal measure.

CONCLUSION

The appearance of the first Marian miracle collections in England in the early twelfth century was witness to several cultural developments. On the one hand, they were just one more example of an abundant hagiographic corpus produced for many saints in England at the turn of the twelfth century. The fact that the compilers of the Marian miracle collections were responsible for other saints' lives allows us to consider the Marian genre as a natural extension of this literary activity, a further expression of the drive to record letters, laws, histories, and hagiographies that pervaded Anglo-Norman monastic culture. English monks were moved to complement the apocryphal stories with evidence of Mary's ongoing works from a wide variety of sources—written and oral, exotic and local, legendary and familiar—grouping them together in manuscripts. In discussing the literary heritage that gave rise to miracle collections in England, one scholar argued that these stories of saintly intervention were the defining feature of their cults—"the warm, pulsing evidence that a saint lived now, acted now, and was worthy of past and future veneration."[221]

The literary context that inspired the earliest compilers of Marian miracles is only part of the story, however. The collections were deeply embedded in religious practice, showcasing the need to perform particular acts of devotion to obtain Mary's boundless mercy. In the absence of shrines and relic cults, and therefore unconcerned with questions of fund-raising and attracting pilgrims, the English Marian collections instead privileged liturgical practices as the fundamental means of devotion. The main message of the stories is that Mary has the power to save, and will do so in return for chant, prayer, and commemoration on feast days. Mary's intervention to correct her own liturgies in the miracle accounts communicated her investment in their proper performance. It also emphasized that she was listening whenever liturgies were sung and prayers were made. The miracles reflect an interest in particular forms of Marian devotion and served to justify them at a time when they were just emerging or were subject to challenge. But the stories also promoted old practices alongside new ones, provided faraway examples as support for local traditions, and gave local precedents for universal practices. The picture that emerges from the collections is one of diversity in practice and encouragement for all available forms of liturgical expression in praise of Mary. Finding their way into the very liturgies they featured, as readings and in sermons, miracles became performative in their own right. Only the collections made this possible, for only once they were extracted from their diverse sources and compiled in volumes could the miracles be used more extensively in liturgical contexts. Reextracted for use in sermons, the miracle stories took their message of Marian devotion to even wider audiences, beyond the confines of the monastery. The collection of Marian miracles thus allowed for a new relationship to develop between Mary and her devoted followers, supplying the proof that she really was what she was praised as being: the mother of mercy.

CHAPTER 4

||||||||||||||||||||||

Enemies of Mary

JEWS IN MIRACLE STORIES

AMONG THE TALES THAT MONKS IN ANGLO-NORMAN ENGLAND selected for the Marian miracle collections they compiled, there is a recurring figure who plays an important role in highlighting Mary's greatness as merciful mother and heavenly queen: the Jew. In the previous chapter, we saw how miracles described the best way to obtain Mary's favor and the rewards available to those who showed the proper forms of devotion. In order to exemplify the right approach to praising and celebrating the Virgin, a significant number of miracle stories made use of the trope of the "bad guy" against which the good devotee is contrasted, and often this bad guy was depicted as Jewish. The Jewish characters in these tales generally carry out the opposite of what appropriate devotion should look like: desecration instead of veneration, doubt instead of belief, violence instead of mercy. Consequently, the stories invariably end in either the conversion of the Jews at the sight of Mary's miraculous actions, or their punishment for unrepentently seeking to oppose her and her followers. We have already seen how the Jew was used as a foil against which proper Christian belief about Mary was articulated in theological texts as well as in chants and liturgical readings. Stories about the rivalry between Mary and the Jews, her efforts to make them recognize the virgin birth and Incarnation, and their refusal to acknowledge it made the doubt underscored in the polemical and liturgical texts come to life. Such tales staged a drama of unbelief and its resolution through the display of Mary's power as she demonstrated the error of her doubters. While works of theology treated the Synagogue and unbelieving Jew as almost abstract categories, miracle stories represented Jewish hostility in stark literal terms, bringing them into the eternal present of the narrative. Miracle stories were polemic in action, presenting a memorable illustration of the Virgin's supremacy, with Jews acting as important witnesses to it.[1]

The prominence of Jews in Marian miracle stories has not gone unnoticed by scholars.[2] Geoffrey Chaucer's "Prioress' Tale," a particularly gory and sensational Marian miracle found in his *Canterbury Tales* (circa 1389), has guaranteed ongoing interest in the Marian miracle genre on account of the story's depiction of a group of sinister Jews who slit the throat of a schoolboy given to singing a Marian hymn.[3] Robert W. Frank embedded the tale in what was by Chaucer's time a pan-European tradition of Marian miracles, noting that "anti-Semitic tales are a commonplace in the genre, a standard constituent element."[4] Other scholars have remarked on the presence of Jews in the vernacular medieval miracle collections, such as the *Gracial* of Adgar, *Miracles de Nostre Dame* of Gautier de Coincy, *Milagros de Nuestra Señora* of Gonzalo de Berceo, and monumental *Cantigas de Santa Maria*, seeking explanations for the depiction of Jews in these works especially from the contemporary social and political circumstances of the collections' composition.[5] This has not been done to the same extent for the Latin collections, which were nevertheless the source for these later, more famous volumes.[6] It is to try to understand these seminal versions of the stories that this chapter will first explore the literary tradition that shaped them, comparing the twelfth-century versions with their sometimes much-older sources. Where no direct source exists, I will investigate the possible combination of influences that prompted the author to add to the corpus of stories about Jews.

What comes out of this study is that despite the lengthy literary tradition of which the Marian stories featuring Jews were a part, the monastic authors of the twelfth century did not simply repeat their sources but instead changed them in significant ways that deserve to be analyzed in the context of Marian devotion in Anglo-Norman England.[7] As this chapter will trace, the stories' redactors often exaggerated the evil nature of the Jewish figure along with the antagonism he bore Mary and her followers. It is tempting to see in this exaggeration a changing vision of Jews at the turn of the twelfth century. The depiction of Jews as avaricious moneylenders, devious magicians, and corrupt blasphemers could be seen in light of the emerging commercial economy, new scholarly interests in science, and the theological polemics mentioned in a previous chapter, all of which really did involve Jews to some extent. But this would be to ignore the stories' primary purpose, which was performative (as part of religious practice) and Marian. The miracle stories were "not a straightforward reflection of contemporary attitudes towards Jews," as Lipton has argued with respect to visual depictions of Jews, but rather they say something about the authors' vision of Christian values and religious practice.[8] Like the stories discussed in the previous chapter, those that involve Jews promoted particular acts of devotion—including prayer, charity, the veneration of icons, and the placing of wax effigies at saints' shrines—by illustrating how Jews did the opposite. If anything, in casting the Jews in recognizable terms and appealing to contemporary social dynamics, the redactors sought to amplify the urgent need to turn to Mary as the very embodiment of Christian virtue and an antidote to social ills, preserving Christian values in a changing world. The more malevolent they made the

Jews—treacherous, sacrilegious, blasphemous, avaricious, and even murderous—the greater seemed the imperative to side with Mary, who opposed the Jews' evil and sought to curb their negative influence on Christian society. These considerations provide an important additional lens through which to view the Marian miracle stories as they were rewritten in twelfth-century England, enhancing the role of the Jew to showcase just how worthy of praise and prayer Mary was thought to be.

FOUNDATIONS

The juxtaposition between Mary and the Jews in narrative had old roots. As is well known, the apocryphal legends about Mary's life already featured Jews as key figures of doubt and threat.[9] In the case of the narratives of Mary's early life, best exemplified by the *Protevangelium Jacobi* and the *Gospel of Pseudo-Matthew*, the polemical encounter takes place around the question of the virgin birth.[10] A first hint of polemic is apparent in a prophecy Mary herself makes just prior to giving birth. According to the *Protevangelium*, when Joseph saddles her on an ass to take her to Bethlehem for the census, she laughs and says, "I see with my eyes two peoples, one weeping and lamenting and one rejoicing and exulting."[11] The *Protevangelium* offers no comment, but the later fifth-century *Gospel of Pseudo-Matthew* has a beautiful boy appear to explain the prophecy:

> For she saw the people of the Jews weeping because they have departed from their God; and the people of the Gentiles rejoicing because they have now approached and are near to the Lord, in accordance with what he promised to our fathers, Abraham, Isaac and Jacob: for the time is at hand when in the seed of Abraham a blessing will be bestowed on all nations.[12]

The passage sees Mary herself become a prophet, foretelling not only the miraculous birth she is about to experience but also the supersession of Christianity over Judaism as its consequence. Mary is presented as the personification of Christianity's triumph over Judaism, foreseeing it before she enacts it by giving birth to Jesus. More significant, she recognizes that she stands at the crossroads between the two faiths, as the only character in the narrative to understand the magnitude and meaning of her own role at this point.

The polemical tenor of the Marian Nativity Apocrypha is also reflected in an episode involving a Jewish witness character who questions Mary's virginity and suffers the consequences. The narrative features two midwives, not found in the Gospels.[13] In the *Gospel of Pseudo-Matthew*, the first, named Zelomi, exclaims in wonder that "a virgin has conceived, a virgin has brought forth, and a virgin she remains," thereby articulating the doctrine of Mary's perpetual virginity.[14] She then calls out to her companion, Salome, who mistrusting Zelomi's claims, insists on medically checking Mary's virginity, at which point her hand is consumed with a burning pain. Salome is only restored to health by touching the baby and proclaiming her faith that he is the Messiah. If there were any doubt about Salome's Jewish identity, her prayer for healing asserts that she is "the seed of Abraham, Isaac and Jacob."[15] The passage was a narrative expression of the doctrine of Mary's virginity *in partum*, which would become hotly debated in the fourth century, especially between Helvidius and the ascetic Jerome.[16] Although this episode likely sought to address Christians who doubted that Mary could have maintained her virginity in the course of giving birth, the fact that it features a Jewish character in the position of witness illustrates how useful the idea of Jewish doubt and its resolution was to supporting contentious ideas about Mary.

The apocryphal narratives that deal with the end of Mary's life, the best known of which is the *Transitus* by Pseudo-Melito, include Jewish witnesses to affirm the miraculous power of Mary's body in a strikingly similar way.[17] In these tales, when Mary dies and the apostles carry her bier through Jerusalem, the Jews of Jerusalem rush out in order to seize her body and burn it, so as to prevent it from becoming a site of worship.[18] One Jew, in some versions named Jephonias, manages to reach the bier and makes an attempt to upset it, but his hands immediately stick to it and wither; in some tellings, an angel appears and smites them off. The rest of the Jews immediately go blind. "Let no one who loves God and my Lady Mary, who bore him, be a companion and friend to the Jews; for if he is so, the love of the Messiah is severed from him," runs the commentary of one version.[19] The story does not end with the violent act, however. It becomes a conversion narrative, with the apostles advising Jephonias to pray for the restoration of his hands. He does so and is saved, as are the blind Jews when they affirm their faith in Mary's sanctity. In one version, found in two twelfth- and thirteenth-century manuscripts, in order to be cured, Jephonias has to read from the "Books of Moses" (*libri Moysi testimonia*)—namely, the prophecies announcing the virgin birth.[20] This recitation stages a public performance of the traditional mode of Christian polemics. The story therefore played into theological traditions, depicting the Jews' misunderstanding of scripture as a physical blindness that is reversed only when they accept its Mariological message: the reading of prophecy literally opens their eyes to the truth of Mary's sanctity and power.[21] In a related scene that appears in the first full text that combined the different apocryphal lives of Mary, the *Life of the Virgin* by the seventh-century Byzantine scholar Maximus the Confessor, the Jews of Jerusalem try to burn Mary in her own home, although their attacks are turned back on them. The virulent animosity expressed between Mary and the Jews in this text draws from and exaggerates that found in the apocryphal narratives, although the degree to which it was known in the West remains uncertain.[22]

Debates about the veneration of icons in early medieval Byzantium helped to crystallize the notion of Jewish threat to Mary. Both during and shortly after the iconoclast controversy in the eighth and ninth centuries, the defense of icons against their opponents was vividly expressed in short narratives.[23] Accounts of miraculous icons were used by iconophiles to illustrate how worthy these objects were of veneration. Subject to attack, the image would come to life and/or take revenge on the perpetrator, thus showing the terrible consequences of iconoclasm. Challenging, threatening, and even trying to deface images, Jews frequently played the role of energetic iconoclasts. As Katherine Corrigan has shown in her study of iconoclastic Jews depicted in eighth- and ninth-century Byzantine art, it was not so much that Jews posed a direct threat to images (they were too few in number, in any case) but rather that iconophiles saw Jewish opposition to religious images as a convenient way to taint iconoclasts as unbelievers, defending "orthodoxy against more powerful enemies who seemed to be repeating the arguments of the Jews."[24] Making iconoclasm a "Jewish thing" placed it outside the realm of orthodox Christianity, thereby condemning Christian iconoclasts as unorthodox.[25] Just as in the apocryphal narratives, the active iconoclasm of the Jews was always resolved in favor of the images, thereby demonstrating the strength of the iconophile position. Such tales, then, had an important place in the theological debates about the appropriateness of venerating images, underlining the necessity for Christians to approach them with veneration. Although internal to Christian debates, such stories also linked Judaism with an active and violent anti-Marianism—in this case not against Mary herself but instead against her visual representations. This came to have crucial consequences when the stories were disseminated as part of the Marian miracle collections.

The tales of Jews opposing, threatening, and doubting Mary clearly appealed to the earliest compilers of the Marian miracles in early twelfth-century England. Many such stories appear in the collections, although the earliest redactors showed varying degrees of interest in them. The eighteen stories linked to Anselm include only one: the Jewish boy. Dominic's fourteen stories include two that feature Jews, the Jewish boy and Theophilus, although he added revealing comments about their perceived meaning. A further three image stories were added to the collections as they grew—Toledo, Lydda, and the Virgin's Image Insulted—alongside the ubiquitous Theophilus and a later original tale with an English setting—the conversion of Jacob/John, the Jew of London.[26] William of Malmesbury nevertheless stands out as most obviously interested in stories about Jews.[27] His collection includes six stories in which Jews are depicted as antagonists: Theophilus, the Jewish boy, Toledo, Toulouse, Theodore and Abraham, and the Virgin's Image Insulted. His versions of these stories are especially interesting given his own unique voice, for he altered many details and colored them to give a particular image of Jews. They represent an important source for understanding the evolving depiction of the Jew in Marian miracle tales as rewritten in Anglo-Norman England.[28]

This chapter will take each story individually, and examine how they evolved from their earliest-known sources. The twelfth-century redactors clearly had textual sources in some cases, but in others there is stronger evidence for oral transmission.[29] Sometimes the alteration of a written source is slight, and is reflected in minor details of character description or plot points. In other cases, the story has been radically transformed or lengthy commentaries have been added to explain the redactor's thoughts on the story's meaning. Some stories seem to have been entirely invented, with no known precedents. Such moments of creative license are revealing of the context in which William and the other redactors were writing, and suggest that they reframed their stories to resonate with contemporary readers and hearers. It was also in these forms that they became fixed. The stories found in the twelfth-century collections became the versions found in many dozens of manuscripts in subsequent centuries; "here was the nucleus of all later collections current in the Western Church," remarked Frank Barlow on the importance of these first compilations.[30] Gathering the stories into volumes opened up the possibility that they would be copied and circulated together, gaining a level of authority that individual stories would not have had. Easy to access in the new collections, the updated stories about the Jews' antagonism to Mary became readily available for use in sermons and liturgical reading, as we have seen in the previous chapter. The twelfth-century compilers of the Marian miracles thus helped to establish the juxtaposition between Mary and the Jews as part of Marian devotional culture in two ways: exaggerating Jewish evil in the stories themselves, and accumulating these negative images in volumes, multiplying their effect for eager consumers of the genre.

THEOPHILUS

Perhaps the best known and most widespread of all the Marian miracle stories that feature Jews is the tale of Theophilus.[31] The story describes the ambition and fall of the cleric Theophilus of Adana, who when removed from his position by a new bishop, seeks help from the devil through a Jewish intermediary. In order to be restored to his former post, he must deny Christ and Mary, which he does, and in this way receives his position back. But Theophilus comes to regret his act, and spends forty days of heartfelt prayer and fasting in a Marian church. Mary then appears to him and destroys the contract with which he had signed away his soul, and he dies a saved man.

The original version of the Theophilus legend was written in the sixth century by Eutychianus of Adana, and was translated into Latin by Paul, who is said to have sent his translation to Charlemagne.[32] In the tenth century, the nun Hrotswitha of Gandersheim set the story to verse, as did Pseudo-Marbod of Rennes.[33] Fulbert of Chartres included a version of the tale in his sermon for the Virgin's Nativity, which became a popular reading for the feast day throughout Europe.[34] The story was also "one of the most important texts inspiring devotion to Mary in late Anglo-Saxon England," according to Clayton.[35] The first Old English version appeared in one of Aelfric's homilies for the Assumption, and the Office of the Virgin in a Christ Church manuscript took its readings from it.[36] In addition, two psalters—from Winchcombe and Winchester in the second half of the eleventh century—contain prayers frequently used for the liturgy of the Assumption that are reminiscent of those addressed to Mary by Theophilus.[37] The story was thus one of the earliest miracle stories to be incorporated into commemoration of the Virgin, reminding hearers of the benefits of prayer to Mary. The Theophilus legend was certainly a dramatic and spectacular case of Mary's response to prayer: she could forgive and save even when the crime was to have openly denied her in order to gain favor from the devil.

The power of Marian prayer communicated by the Theophilus legend was not lost on the monks of the Anglo-Norman realm. The story was so ubiquitous that it could be mentioned in the miracle story *Sicut iterum* with the description, "I do not want to write about who this Theophilus was, or what he did, or by what miracle the mother of mercy freed him, because I know that it is well known to all."[38] A sequence that appears in a troper from St. Albans also refers to Mary as mother of mercy who reformed Theophilus by dragging him out of the "fetid lake of misery."[39] The version of the Theophilus legend by Paul with the incipit *Factum est autem priusquam* is found in a number of eleventh- and twelfth-century English legendaries.[40] One of these, the Worcester Legendary, may have served as the source for at least three known versions of the Theophilus legend produced in the early twelfth century: Honorius's sermon for the Assumption, Dominic's miracle collection, and William's collection.[41] This same version then made its way almost verbatim into many of the Marian miracle collections.[42] It was in helping to establish the image of Mary as *mater misericordiae* that the Theophilus legend gained such immense popularity, extracted from liturgical and homiletic sources to become a standard feature of the earliest miracle collections.

One way in which the Theophilus legend demonstrates Mary's merciful nature is by contrasting it with the sinister character of Theophilus's go-between with the devil. In most versions of the story, he is described as a Jew, either *Judaeus* or *Hebraeus*, although Gilbert Dahan has shown that the terms applied to him differ in the many medieval versions of the tale.[43] In the translation by Paul, Theophilus is described as "a most nefarious Jew, a most wicked worker of the diabolical arts, who had already plunged many into the pit and snares of perdition, through his impious arguments."[44] His skills include summoning the devil, whom he refers to as "my master" (*Patronum meum*). His allegiance to the devil necessarily makes him the enemy of Christ and Mary, for Satan demands that his followers deny "the son of Mary and she herself." The Jew's evil nature is further enhanced by the vivid description of the meeting with the Prince of Darkness. The night after Theophilus seeks him out, the Jew leads him by the hand to the Circus Maximus in Constantinople, where they find the devil enthroned.[45] Throughout this scene, the Jew acts as the devil's mouthpiece. Satan addresses not Theophilus but rather the magician, as if only able to converse with those who have sworn to follow him. Even after the pact is made, "the truly execrable Jew frequently sought out the *vicedominus* in secret and told him: 'Now you have seen what kind of benefits and quick solutions you've received from me and my master, to whom you pleaded.'"[46] If Theophilus emerges at the end of the legend in its earliest Latin version as a redeemed Marian devotee, the Jew is portrayed as his antithesis: an entrenched follower of Mary's greatest enemy.

Some redactors added elements to the depiction of the Jew that shifted the story's meaning, if in subtle ways. While otherwise remaining close to Paul, Dominic elaborated on the scene where Theophilus places his seal on the contract. He compared this act to Adam's fall from grace, likening the Jewish intermediator to the "ancient serpent" (*antiquo serpente*).[47] At this point, Dominic also inserted a commentary on what he felt was the root cause of Theophilus's perfidy: "O what an awful plague is avarice, with which you [the devil] compel the hearts of Christians to all kinds of shameful acts."[48] Dominic lamented the ubiquity of this vice, echoing the prologue to the story in which he urged his readers to follow Theophilus's example and not despair of God's compassion. By contrast, Theophilus and the Jew are originally described as lost (*utrique perditus*).[49] In making Theophilus's betrayal one of greed rather than ambition or pride, Dominic slightly changed the moral of the story, and expressed a concern we will encounter more explicitly in other stories.[50]

William recognized the long and varied history of the Theophilus legend even as he wrote his own version of it.[51] While keeping close to the versions by Paul and Dominic, William described the Jewish character as "a Hebrew, about whom a not trivial rumor spread that he was able to contrive what he wished with the aid of powerful evil incantations," and who was "adept at hunting innocent souls."[52] The Jew's address to Satan in William's account further emphasizes the hunting imagery. Expanding on the dialogue, William had the Jew say: "Behold, my lord, how eager I have been to serve you, and see what I have captured in the snares of my arts, a man who is not without some influence among Christians."[53] The Jew is therefore depicted as the reverse of the apostles; they are urged to become "fishers of men" for Christ (Matt. 4:18–20), whereas the Jew delivers his conquests to the devil. The antagonism the Jew feels toward both Mary and Christ is implied in the devil's own vitriolic statements about them: "Make him swear to me that he will abjure Christ and his mother Mary, whom I loathe equally in hatred to the death. For no one can be mine who does not spit on love and faith for them."[54] After the pact, the Jew does not stop promoting his master to Theophilus: "From the Jew there came almost daily reminders: look how far the speed of the devil outstripped the sloth of Christ! His mere nod had given Theophilus back his position!"[55]

William may only have subtly added to the Jew's agency in his account, but he did enhance the severity of the punishment the character receives. In the version translated by Paul, the following lament interrupts Theophilus's prayer of repentance to the Virgin: "Why did I have to meet that most nefarious Jew, who ought to be burned?"[56] Then, in an aside, it is explained that not long before, the Jew had been found guilty "by the law and a judge."[57] While Dominic did not mention this detail, William extrapolated on it:

> But the Jew was shortly afterward detected in his illicit ways. He was not long found out and convicted for his crimes, and trembling before the severity of the laws of the state, was beheaded. As for Theophilus, he saw the error of his ways, and cursed the devilish practices, which when exposed, resulted on earth in the public ruin of the devotee and cast him for the future into the everlasting fires.[58]

William judged that the Jew's actions merited not just condemnation by the law but also the harshest of punishments: beheading and hell. The Jew's retribution also seems to be the catalyst for Theophilus's repentance, signaling the turning point of the narrative.

William's alterations to the Theophilus legend, the emphasis on the Jewish magician's pursuit of Christians, and his subsequent punishment are an example of the distinct tone that redactors of Marian miracles could bring to the stories they reworked. In the case of William's version of Theophilus, it may reflect deeper concerns about the underlying conflict between the competing values of Jews and Christians, particularly on the question of necromancy. William's other works show that he was worried about the corrupting influence of meddling in magic. One of his other Marian stories involves a cleric who is given free rein by his bishop to study as much as he pleases, and ends up turning to black magic in order to seduce women.[59] When one particularly resistant girl catches his fancy, he "used the familiar whispered spells to summon the devil into secret conclave," but refuses to abjure Christ and Mary at the devil's request, and so is ultimately saved by Mary.[60] William elsewhere associated the practice of magic with non-Christians, as is evident in several passages of his *Gesta Regum Anglorum*. In one, he described the account of an old monk at Malmesbury who told about his time in Spain searching for the treasures of the Emperor Octavian with the help of a Jew practiced in the arts of necromancy.[61] In connection with this anecdote, William also recorded in his *Gesta Regum* the "black legend" of Gerbert of Aurillac, who became Pope Sylvester II (999–1003) allegedly thanks to a pact he made with the devil. Gerbert is said to have fled from the monastery of Fleury to Catalonia to learn the *quadrivium*, but most especially "astrology and other such arts from the Saracens," such that he was able eventually to call up the devil with incantations and "covenanted to pay him perpetual homage."[62] Gerbert's teacher throughout was a Muslim philosopher, whom William considered typical of his community for having at his disposal everything "that has been discovered by human curiosity . . . whether noxious or beneficial."[63] Relating the "black legend" in much greater detail than any of his predecessors or contemporaries, William was also the first to establish a connection between Gerbert's interest in studying the liberal arts in Muslim Spain and his practice of magic.[64]

William may have received some of his ideas about magic and its associated sciences from monastic circles in England, where a marked interest in scientific learning had recently emerged. In his *Gesta Pontificum*, William claimed to have heard that Gerard, Archbishop of York (1101–9), had been known to read Julius Firmicus's work of "curious arts"—the *Mathesis*, a treatise on astrology— in secret.[65] Even closer to William were scholars in the Southwest of England. Based especially at Hereford Cathedral but also at Worcester, these scholars were working on scientific subjects with the help of translators from the Arabic. Charles Burnett has identified the involvement of Peter Alfonsi, the Spanish convert from Judaism and physician to Henry I, as an important contributor to the transmission of Arabic scientific knowledge into England at these institutions.[66] In his letter to the "Peripatetics of Francia," Alfonsi lamented the poor knowledge of astronomy among Latin Christians and set himself out as a potential teacher; Burnett has pointed out that his offer was taken up only in England.[67] Alfonsi likely helped scholars such as Adelard of Bath and Walcher, the prior of Great Malvern, to translate astronomical works into Latin, including the astronomical tables of al-Khwarizmi, which survive in a Worcester manuscript from the early decades of the twelfth century.[68] Alfonsi's didactic work, the *Disciplina clericalis*, describes other liberal arts in addition to astronomy, which he may have taught, including necromancy. Still, elsewhere he distinguished between the science's more and less harmful incarnations: necromancy could involve the manipulation of natural elements, or the summoning of demons.[69] No doubt familiar with the work being undertaken at these nearby institutions, particularly at Worcester, where he had close ties, William may have feared that the pursuit of such knowledge by his fellow monks could lead to dabbling in the darker arts. The fact that former non-Christians, such as Alfonsi but perhaps other Iberian Jews, were responsible for the spread and normalization of this new learning may have made it appear all the more suspect, and stained it with the threat of sacrilege and apostasy.

While concern with scientific learning and magic among his contemporaries could have informed William's subtle exaggeration of the Jewish character in the Theophilus story, not to mention the Jew's worsened punishment, all versions of the tale ultimately juxtaposed two forms of achieving supernatural help. The one, necromancy, could obtain the devil's help in order to gain worldly wealth and power. But prayer to Mary was even more powerful, and could achieve salvation for the most damned of sinners. This message is found also in William's story of the cleric engaged in the black arts. The protagonist is saved, despite his experimentation with love spells, because he had said the Little Office on a daily basis. Necromancy is thus contrasted with prayer, and it is prayer that is the proper approach to receiving the rewards worthy of a proper Christian. This makes the Jewish necromancer in the Theophilus legend an effective counterexample. The Jew represents not just improper allegiance—to the devil, instead of to Christ and Mary—but the wrong way of achieving one's desired ends—through magic, not prayer; his violent end is therefore appropriate to his actions. Theophilus, on the other hand, realizes that not only were his goals misaligned (i.e., his desire for worldly goods) but that his approach was misguided as well. Only in turning to prayer can he receive real power from that most powerful of intercessors, Mary.[70] The conclusion in which Mary triumphs over the devil and Theophilus is saved, whereas the Jew is damned, provides the story with a fitting moral, and one that clearly reflects the same interest in Marian prayer found in other miracles stories.

JEWISH BOY

One of the most popular stories about Jews that circulated in the Marian miracle collections was that of the Jewish Boy.[71] In it, a Jewish boy inadvertently takes communion with his Christian playmates, then returns home and is thrown into an oven by his enraged father. This is not only a Eucharistic miracle but also a Marian one, for it is Mary who protects the boy from the flames and allows him to emerge unscathed to admiring crowds.

As scholars such as Miri Rubin and Caroline Walker Bynum have explained, the Eucharistic and Marian elements in this story are closely intertwined, for Mary shares Christ's flesh just as it is present in the consecrated host.[72] As a result, echoes of the Jewish boy story are found in the stories of Jewish desecration of hosts that emerged in the thirteenth century, whose history Rubin has traced.[73] But the Marian aspect of the Jewish boy story became increasingly dominant over the story's long history. The earliest-existing version, in Evagrius Scholasticus's (536–600) Greek *Historia Scholastica*, set during the patriarchate of Menas (536–552), features Mary only at the end.[74] After emerging from the oven where his glassblower father threw him, the little boy claims that he was able to survive for three days in the furnace thanks to "a woman wearing a purple robe [who] had visited him frequently and proffered water and with this he had quenched the adjacent coals and that she had fed him whenever he was hungry."[75] The father is ultimately impaled for his crime, whereas the boy and his mother receive baptism at the urging of Emperor Justinian.[76] A relatively faithful Latin version of Evagrius's account was produced in the early eleventh century by a so-called John the monk (*Johannes monachus*), a southern Italian monk who translated a volume of miracles—only some of them Marian—into Latin.[77] He embellished the story with dialogue and additional characters, and had the father being offered the chance of baptism multiple times, which he refuses, and the story ends instead in his death.

The transformation of the story into a Marian miracle was due in large part to Gregory of Tours, who also drew from Evagrius in his version of the narrative in *De Gloria Martyrum*. Gregory made the important addition of an image of Mary, which the boy sees in the church where he takes communion. This became an indispensable element of the story and was incorporated by Paschasius in his *Liber de Corpore et Sanguine Domini* to buttress his claims for the real presence of Christ in the Eucharist.[78] Paschasius perhaps unsurprisingly enhanced the Eucharistic elements of the story, but he also brought in more Marian ones, making the church where the boy had taken communion a Marian foundation and claiming that the image of Mary inside was seen to distribute the host alongside the priest.[79] He also highlighted the antagonism of the father toward the Eucharist as a feature of Judaism. The father of the boy is described as "inimical to Christ the Lord and his laws, and moved by the poison of bitterness." As the man tells his son before throwing him into the fire, "If you have taken communion with children of the Christian religion, to the punishable injury against Mosaic law, having forgotten your father's faith, I will harshly inflict murder (*parricida*) on you!"[80] Although the boy credits the Eucharist with saving him from feeling anything in the oven, he also thanks Mary for fanning the flames. Mary and the miraculous image she inhabits therefore act to legitimize and bolster the Eucharistic message that dominated the story in these early versions.

Twelfth-century England saw the adaptation of the Jewish Boy story in a number of contexts, first of all in sermons. Honorius used the tale as an *exemplum* in his sermon for the feast of the Purification and mentioned it in his *Sigillum*.[81] While shortening the narrative in both works, he nevertheless introduced some innovative features. The image of Mary that the Jewish boy sees in the church is described as painted on the church wall, as opposed to an icon or carved figure. It is tempting to think here of the wall paintings in the Worcester chapterhouse, among which there may have been a large-scale image of Mary on the central column.[82] Herbert of Losinga, abbot of Ramsey and later the first bishop of Norwich, also included a version of the Jewish boy in a sermon for Christmas. This story is set in an unnamed Greek city, and Herbert went into some detail portraying the context:

There was a certain city of the Greeks in which Christians and Jews dwelt and mingled with one another. Thence sprang familiarity and common dealings. The language of both was the same, while their religion differed. The children of the Jews were taught the learning of the Christians, and thus the sap of truth was by degrees distilled into the tender minds of the Jews.[83]

Despite the potential for conversions he saw in this kind of coexistence, Herbert emphasized the evil of the boy's mother and father, too, making both responsible for the crime: they kindle the fire with additional coals, and close it up with rocks and cement once their son is inside.[84] Herbert also saw the need for "a most just vengeance on the heads of the Jews; and they who would not believe in the incarnate word were all alike burned in the aforesaid furnace."[85] This collective blame of any unconverted Jews is unique to Herbert's sermon, and would have suggested to its hearers that unbelief was in and of itself worthy of punishment.

Circulation in monastic circles by the early twelfth century assured the Jewish Boy story a prominent place in the earliest Marian miracle collections. It is one of the most ubiquitous tales from early on in the collections' history. It appears in two of the earliest manuscripts with the incipit *Contigit quondam res*: Lambeth Palace Library MS 214 and Rome, Vatican Library Reginensis Latini MS 543.[86] A striking new detail found at the beginning of the story provides a possible idea of its source: "A certain event of this kind occurred in the city of Bourges, that Peter, a monk from St. Michael of Chiusa, used to tell, saying that he had been there at the time."[87] As Southern noted, Anselm, abbot of Bury St. Edmunds, had been a young monk at the monastery of St. Michael in Chiusa.[88] This is also the first version situated in Bourges—a detail repeated in the vast majority of subsequent collections. Dahan has suggested that mass conversions of Jews carried out in Bourges in the sixth and seventh centuries as referred to in the *Vita* of the bishop Sulpicius Severus may have influenced the choice of location.[89] Apart from the setting, the story deviates little from Paschasius's version and remains stable throughout the manuscript tradition. The boy sees a veiled image of Mary over the altar that distributes the Eucharist with the priest; there is no mention of a Christ child on her lap, and it is unclear whether this image is perceived as a sculpted figure, icon, or wall painting. The story ends with "those witnessing it, as much the Jews as the Christians, praised the Lord and his holy mother, and became, from that day on, zealous in the faith of God."[90]

Dominic also placed the events in Bourges, indicating he was familiar with Anselm's version, although perhaps from an oral source. While it is one of only two stories involving Jews in Dominic's short collection, the lengthy prologue Dominic added to it is especially revealing. The first in his "Elements" series, the story is meant to demonstrate Mary's power over fire. The attribution works both physically and allegorically, for the conclusion of his account urges the faithful to pray to the Virgin for liberation from the fires of hell, just as the boy received her protection from the flames in the oven.[91] Dominic expanded on the moral of the story:

> First of all, with the grace of Christ as our aid, let us let you off quickly with a few things about something we heard similarly committed by the infidel Jewish people, that we will expose in our anger. This most infidel Jewish people—because of the huge extent of their sins and above all the demand for the outpouring of Christ's blood, to their own damnation and perniciousness (about which it is stated "may his blood be on us and on our sons" (Matt 27:25)) after they rightly lost their land and kingdom in accordance with the divine sentence, that same most obstinate people, I say, because of the crimes—so great in number and magnitude—that they committed, this people, once beloved by God, are lost and now dispersed throughout the earth on account of their offenses. Their condition has been made clear to all people in the same way that the fratricide [of Cain] is given as a sign on all their flesh. What flesh or mind would not abhor to offend Christ, taking heed of how this people, once so lovingly chosen by God from among all men on Earth, is now cast down so low on account of its sins? Look at how every city, wherever it may be located, tolerates this people placed among them, and look at how wherever the Jewish perfidy resounds everywhere and when Christians have relations with many Jews, there is constantly doubt in the minds of the former with regard to the true faith. And because of this, a distinction should rightly be made as much on the basis of their faith as of their nature/kind and most perverse behavior.[92]

The opening of Dominic's story provides exceptional insight into his perception of Jews. The rhetoric against them is vicious, and resorts to tropes common in polemical literature, such as reference to the Jews' demands for Christ's blood in Matthew 27:25. Dominic also repeated the claim that the Diaspora was proof of the Jews' guilt, a punishment for their crimes, with reference to the mark of Cain that is meant to mark Jews as Christ killers.[93] Mention of the Crucifixion connects the story with the Gospel narrative, placing the father's violence toward his son in a long history of Jewish animosity toward Christians, following their supposed murder of Christ himself.

The threat of Jewish violence against Christians is made even more pressing by Dominic's appeal not just to the biblical past but also to the contemporary presence of Jews in Christian society. In the passage above, he lamented that Jews were allowed to live in Christian cities, such that "a Jewish synagogue is seen in very many towns."[94] He considered such freedom dangerous because Christians could come to question their faith through exposure to Jewish beliefs. This fear of coexistence may have been heightened for Dominic by the recent immigration of England's first Jewish settlers in the generation prior to his own. It is doubtful that there was already a synagogue in every English town by the 1120s, particularly at Evesham, but it has recently been argued that there were Jewish communities in many places, including London, Norwich, Lincoln, Cambridge, Winchester, Thetford, Northampton, Bungay, Oxford, Bury St. Edmunds, and possibly even York, by the reign of Stephen (1135–54).[95] As a result, Dominic may have knowingly referred to the settlement of Jews in "very many towns" in order to make the message of his story all the more pressing to listeners. Unlike Herbert, however, Dominic showed little faith in the power of the Christian message to convert Jews and saw only danger in their living in close proximity, instead wishing for some kind of separation or distinction between the two communities.[96] Seeing as this warning directly precedes the rest of the narrative, he seems to imply that if left unchecked, the Jews might commit an act such as the one described in the story. Read in light of the prologue, Dominic's version of the story comes across as a cautionary tale about the risks of allowing Jews to live among Christians, and he thus makes allegiance to Mary a greater imperative to help fight their growing and destructive influence.[97]

Without resorting to explicit commentary like Dominic's, William's version of the Jewish Boy story likewise established a firm connection with past Jewish violence to create a more dramatic, moving narrative.[98] William set the events in Pisa, the only known instance in which this specific location is used, and one he attributes to the particularly holy nature of the city.[99] William's reworking of the story also used the stock tropes of hagiographic literature to make the attempted murder appear all the more horrific, especially by emphasizing the boy's innocence. The boy is described as eager to play with his friends, who "went on with their games until mealtime," until hunger has him run home to find his parents already at the dinner table.[100] They ask him "playfully" (*ludibunda dulcedine*) where he has been, and he, in his boyish innocence, thinks nothing of telling them the whole truth, for how could a child of that age think he had done wrong?[101] But once he has told them, his father reveals his true nature, and "gasping out the Jewish perfidy (*perfidiam judaicam anhelans*)," throws his son into the burning flames he has stoked to cook their meal. The tale appears to be about Mary's protection of the innocent, for the boy was able "to see with the eyes of his body what we intuit in our secret thoughts."[102] The boy's supreme purity gives him powers as a visionary, and his ordeal is described as martyrdom (*parvulique martyrium*). Although the father's punishment deviates from that of the standard version—he is not thrown into the fire, but driven out of town—the contrast between the father and son is starkly drawn, antagonizing the one through praise of the other.[103] The boy's exaggerated qualities of innocence and youthfulness make him a kind of Christ-child figure, a fitting martyr who almost suffered death at the hands of the most nefarious enemy of Christ and his mother. We should remember that unlike the father, the mother in this and most versions of the tale is horrified by the events, and also quick to convert at the end, which aligns her with Mary as suffering mother of the crucified Christ.

William's stress on the innocent qualities of the Jewish boy also connects with the strong Eucharistic emphasis of the story, particularly in an alternative version of the tale he included in his work of history, the *Gesta Regum Anglorum*. He added the story here, together with a number of other Eucharistic miracles, to conclude a section on the errors of Berengar of Tours (ca. 999–1088). Berengar had been condemned for opposing the real presence of Christ in the consecrated host in a lengthy debate with Lanfranc.[104] In this exchange, Lanfranc put forward the doctrine of transubstatiation against Berengar's contentions that the host was merely a sign for Christ's body rather than his real flesh. Lanfranc's attempt at using Aristotelian language in his arguments— namely, in terms of essence and substance—reflect the same theological impulse behind much of Anselm's work on the Incarnation.[105] William certainly agreed with Lanfranc's position: "My own belief is that once blessed by the church, those mysteries are the very body and blood of the Savior," he wrote in his *Gesta Regum*.[106] William was also critical of the fact that Berengar "infected" many others with his ideas, although the accused heretic repented after the condemnation he received from Pope Gregory VII and went on to live a virtuous life. William's description of the recent controversy nonetheless reveals the force with which it had been conducted and high profile of those involved. The fact that he gave his own position on the matter in the *Gesta Regum* and supported it with examples from several Eucharistic miracles, including the one about the Jewish boy, suggests the debate still resonated when William was writing in the 1130s.

The twelfth-century transformation of the popular story of the Jewish boy offers glimpses of important emphases that explicitly relate to current theological and devotional trends. The story told a twofold message about the power of the Eucharist and that of the Virgin. In the first case, the story participated in contemporary Eucharistic debates, which involved individuals familiar to the redactors, namely Lanfranc. The use of the story in defense of the doctrine of transubstantiation by past writers, like Paschasius, may have drawn attention to the tale once more with revived interest in the debate. The story certainly illustrated the power of taking communion, but it was also very much about Mary's special relation with the innocent, not least her own son, whose flesh she shared.[107] The closeness of the Jewish boy with the Virgin in the story, underscored especially by William, may have reflected interest in exploring Mary's relationship with the child Jesus, as we have seen in *De excellentia* of Eadmer and the *Sigillum* of Honorius. The growing emphasis on Mary's role as a loving mother, then, could help to explain the interest in showcasing Mary's love for and protection of the Jewish boy.[108] Both of these developments would have provided the story with additional force that suggests why it became so popular precisely in the early twelfth century.

Part of the reason the Jewish boy tale was so successful in transmitting its Eucharistic and Mariological messages was because it featured a horrific assault committed by a memorable antagonist. The fact that it was attempted infanticide was only made worse by the similarity established between the child and Jesus. Reminding hearers of the Crucifixion, the story set up a striking rivalry between Mary as savior and protector and the Jewish father as would-be murderer, a man willing to kill his own son in the ultimate act of anti-Christian violence. The evil of the Jewish father therefore heightened the sense of Mary's mercy. By placing the story in the context of present-day interactions between Jews and Christians, redactors like Dominic made the danger seem all the more contemporary and pressing and stressed the need to side with Mary against the Jews. But the story also established another dichotomy, contrasting the boy's innocent belief in Mary with the savage disbelief of the Jews. This tale of simple faith and cruelty was a template for properly approaching Mary; with the former (faith), one would receive her protection, with the latter, one would find fitting punishment. As a result, the story presented an appealing paradigm for Christians, illustrating, through condemnation of the imagined anti-Christian behavior of Jews, how all Christians could become Mary's children.

LYDDA

The story of the image of Mary at Lydda is one of several popular image narratives, which like the Theophilus and Jewish boy legends, had roots in the Byzantine world.[109] It appears in a number of early Marian miracle collections, together with the story of Gethsemane that almost always directly follows it.[110] These two tales are linked by theme: the miraculous properties of an image of Mary. The legend of the image at Lydda is set during the lifetime of the apostles, but after Christ's Resurrection. The apostles buy a synagogue from the Jews of the town and convert it into a church. Hearing the use to which their former building is being put, the Jews regret their action and appeal to the emperor to reverse the decision so that they might have it back. In the meantime, the apostles approach the Virgin for help, and she assures them: "I am with you in this church, in aid of you."[111] When the parties gather at the building after forty days have passed to resolve the issue, the Jews notice an almost lifelike image of Mary (*quasi viva in carne sit*) on the western wall turn its gaze toward the East. Terrified by the sight, they leave the church to the apostles, saying that "truly, the woman is in this house."[112] They are not entirely deterred, however, for sometime later they manage to convince the emperor, Julian the Apostate, the so-called persecutor of churches (*persecutor ecclesiarum*), to allow them to remove the image from the marble. The image once again strikes such terror in their hearts that they leave it alone, where it remains until the present day.[113] The brief story of Gethsemane involves a similar image, also not painted by human hand, and this time fixed to one of four pillars that surround Mary's tomb on the Mount of Olives.

The story of the image at Lydda is an amalgam of tales first witnessed during the period of iconoclasm in eighth- and ninth-century Byzantium, when several successive eastern emperors banned religious images. The earliest-known source for these tales is the *Letter of the Three Patriarchs*. It is thought to have been written in 836, and is addressed to the Emperor Theodosius by a group of iconophiles.[114] A fierce apology for the veneration of icons, the *Letter* describes thirteen miracle-working icons, four of which are Marian, in support of its position. As discussed earlier, in many of these accounts, the icons are subject to abuse, at which point the perpetrator is punished miraculously by the religious figure depicted in the image.[115] Often this persecutor is a Jew. In order to make the account more poignant, the stories sometimes refer to a period where Jews were thought to have actually destroyed Christian buildings; Ambrose writes that during the reign of Julian, the Jews burned churches in Gaza, Ascalon, and Beirut as well as Alexandria.[116] But there is little evidence that Jews were active in the iconoclastic controversy, which suggests that these stories merely used the figure of the Jew to condemn and defame iconoclastic Christians.

One of the stories that was included in the *Letter of the Three Patriarchs* in defense of icons concerns an image of the Virgin found in the city of Lydda.[117] The location is derived from Acts 9:32, where Lydda is mentioned as the town in which Peter arrived to minister to the locals. The story describes that while there, he and the apostle John built a church with their own hands, and when they had finished it, asked Mary herself to give the edifice her blessing. She answered, mysteriously, "But I was there and I still am with you!"[118] Her image then appeared as if by divine intervention on one of the church's columns.[119] Emperor Julian heard about the image and had a group of Jewish painters investigate it. The painters were amazed at how lifelike it looked, "as if she were still looking at and speaking to them."[120] When they tried to remove the image, it only became more luminous, as if it were an integral part of the column.[121]

A similar story follows directly in the *Letter of the Three Patriarchs*, with further echoes of the twelfth-century version.[122] This time in an unnamed city near Lydda, Aeneas, the man whom Peter healed in Acts 9:33–35, is said to have built a church in honor of Christ's mother. As he finished the job, Jews and pagan Greeks of the city claimed it for their own. They approached the governor, who declared that the building should be shut and guarded for a period of three days, at which point it would go to the group that received a divine sign. On opening the doors, on the western wall of the church they discovered the image of a woman dressed in purple, with the words "Mary the mother of

Christ, King from Nazareth" written below. Both Jews and Greeks departed, ashamed and humiliated at the Christians' triumph, and the image went on to perform many miracles of healing and exorcism.[123] This story may in turn have influenced an account of events found among the records of the Council of Erfurt in 932.[124] In a letter to Emperor Henry I, the doge of Venice related an incident that had recently occurred in Jerusalem. It involved the testing of the Holy Sepulchre and a synagogue, which were placed under Muslim control until God gave a sign that he favored one over the other; the Holy Sepulchre won when it was opened to reveal the appearance of Christ himself on one of the columns surrounding his tomb (*dominus incarnatus et quasi crucifixus stantem in dextera columna intra suum sanctum sepulchrum*).[125] The account is reminiscent of the earlier Byzantine tale of Aeneas, although they differ with respect to the location and painted figure.[126]

The line of transmission from the *Letter of the Three Patriarchs* to the English manuscripts, which came to include the Lydda story, is hard to establish. A Greek version in a manuscript of unknown provenance from the third quarter of the eleventh century reproduces the story about the image of Lydda from the *Letter*.[127] Yet the Lydda story of the Western collections is clearly a conflation of the two stories in the *Letter* described above. While impossible to say exactly when the story about the miraculous image of Lydda was merged with the story about the testing of the church, it is nevertheless intriguing that the resulting account focused entirely on the Jews. The pagan Greeks disappear from the narrative, and only the Jews are portrayed as demanding ownership of the building. In fact, in the twelfth-century version, the church had once been a synagogue. Additionally, instead of Julian demanding the image's removal, it is the Jews who take the initiative in wanting to have the image destroyed. By the twelfth century, when the story was incorporated into the miracle collections, the message had become one of strictly Jewish iconoclasm and hatred of religious images.

The Jews' increased agency in the twelfth-century version of the Lydda story is one of the most notable changes it underwent. Rather than an allegory of Christianity's supersession over both paganism and Judaism, the story became an enactment of the conflict between Christians and Jews, specifically over the issue of images. The question of biblical exegesis was also at stake, as indicated by the peculiar behavior of the Marian image. The figure of Mary on the western wall of the church appears to one of the Jews to look toward the East (*Tunc unus ex Iudeis aspiciens in parietem vidit imaginem in occidentem positam respicientem contra orientem*).[128] This is a literal depiction of Ezechiel 44:1: "And he brought me back to the way of the gate of the outward sanctuary, which looked toward the East: and it was shut" (*et convertit me ad viam portae sanctuarii exterioris quae respiciebat ad orientem et erat clausa*). Ezechiel's vision was one of the key prophecies used in the Christian tradition, particularly from Jerome onward and especially in *Adversus Judaeos* literature, as a reference to the virgin birth.[129] Read allegorically, it was said to mean that Mary remained a virgin despite conceiving and giving birth.[130] The story of the miraculous image at Lydda thus made material what Ezechiel's prophecy points to metaphorically; Mary, in her pictorial version, literally looks eastward, where her biblical allegory—the closed gates of Jerusalem—faced East, in anticipation of the advent of Christ. This is especially resonant in the context of renewed interest in the polemical genre in twelfth-century England, as indicated in a previous chapter. Gilbert Crispin, for example, cited the text in his *Disputatio* against the Jews.[131] It is tempting to think that the Lydda story appealed to monks in Anselm's circles because of this stark representation of the Jewish-Christian theological debate. But the story's iconophilic roots complicate whether the Lydda story was transformed to reflect this theological trend. Clearly there was a wider fascination with stories about miraculous images, and particularly those attacked by Jews, of which Lydda is just one of several examples, and which I will now discuss in greater detail.

VIRGIN'S IMAGE INSULTED

As illustrated in the conclusion of the Lydda story, Jews in the miracle stories were imagined not only as passive skeptics toward the holiness of Christian objects but rather as actively seeking to destroy them. The Jews' aversion to images is powerfully depicted in a story connected in both theme and literary tradition to Lydda: the Virgin's Image Insulted.[132] This popular story was not part of the collections attributed to Anselm and Dominic but is still found in a large number of twelfth-century collections, including the one written by William.[133] The story recounts the theft of a painted icon of Mary by a Jew, who in a fit of fury throws it into a nearby cesspit. To add insult to injury, he proceeds to empty his bowels over it. A Christian finds the image and cleans it, and then the painting begins to emit a sweet-smelling oil. The first-known account of how the Jew desecrated the icon is found in the seventh-century travelogue *De locis sanctis*, written by Adomnán, the late seventh-century abbot of Iona (d. 704).[134] His work claims to describe the itinerary undertaken by Arculfus, a bishop from Gaul, on pilgrimage to holy sites in Byzantium and the Middle East. Arculfus's stop in Constantinople included a visit to the Marian icon, which "Arculfus, as he is wont to tell, saw with his own eyes."[135] Discussion of *De locis sanctis* has begun to question whether Adomnán had a real eyewitness account on which to base his text, and whether he did not instead build his narrative from literary sources.[136] David Woods suggests that the description of

Constantinople in *De locis sanctis* is based on a collection of now-lost Byzantine works, including a life of Constantine, miracles of St. George, and wonders in the style of Gregory's *De gloria martyrym*, that had made their way to England.[137] Perhaps reflecting this heritage, at some point the story became associated with Jerome, and his name is attached to it in certain manuscripts.[138] Although more recently other scholars have claimed Adomnán drew from a mix of oral and written sources, it is possible that his anecdote about the Marian icon was derived not from an account told to him but rather from a written Byzantine story, although no exact precedent survives.[139]

The story that inspired Adomnán's retelling may have resembled a series of popular tales that concern the destructive iconoclasm of Jews. One of these is first attested in the late ninth century, but was attributed to a fourth-century patriarch, Athanasius of Alexandria.[140] It relates how the Jews of Beirut find an image of Christ in a cell attached to a synagogue. They take it and subject it to the tortures Christ suffered at the Passion, including spitting and piercing with a lance, saying, "Whatever our fathers did to him, let us all do the same to this image." To the Jew's surprise, the image emits blood and water.[141] The tale is evidently related to a story in Gregory's *De gloria martyrum*, in which a Jewish man finds an image of Christ in his house and stabs it, at which point it bleeds.[142] Other similar stories are found in the *Letter of the Three Patriarchs*. In one, a prefect mocks an icon of Mary in Alexandria, and Mary comes to him in a vision, breaking his arms and legs "like leaves breaking off a figtree."[143] Another story with echoes of the Pseudo-Athanasian tale has a Jew throw an image of Christ he has just stabbed down a well. The blood it emits has him discovered, arrested, and eventually baptized.[144] This same tale is found in the account of an English pilgrim who traveled to Constantinople; we find it in an early twelfth-century manuscript probably from Winchester.[145] The stories share many features with that of the Virgin's Image Insulted, despite the change in image from one of Christ to one of Mary as well as the shift in the substance it oozes, from blood to oil.

A certain degree of confusion arose early on in the story's literary history regarding the location of the miraculous image in the story of the Marian icon. Arculf described it as hanging "on the wall of a certain house."[146] The reference to a house (*domus*) is surprising, and Woods has argued that this is in fact a mistranslation of the Greek word for church.[147] While his contemporaries largely accepted the domestic setting, William seems to have been less convinced of it. He constructed a different scenario by placing the image in the Constantinopolitan church of Blacherna as part of a longer account of the holy images of Constantinople in his miracle collection. William described the painting as the work of Nicodemus, who exercised a rare talent in portraying the Virgin. The Greeks flocked to the image, William related, because it continued to work miracles; not least of these is the one in which every Saturday, when the sun sinks into the sea, the veil is spontaneously raised and up to the ninth hour of the Sabbath hangs (as it were) in the air and reveals the image clearly to all who wish to see it. During this period it is open to view, but on all other days it is hidden. The veil is spontaneously replaced after the ninth hour on the Sabbath, just as it was previously drawn away without anyone's intervention.[148]

The miracle is one we have seen in a previous chapter, included at the end of the sermon in favor of the celebration of the Saturday office.[149] While there is no mention of a Jew or desecration of the image in that account, William is convinced by "men whose word we can take, [who] affirm that this same image, shrouded in a silk veil, is endowed with divine virtues."[150] It seems that William combined the story about the desecration by the Jew with that of the Saturday miracle, assuming they involved the same miraculous icon.[151]

William's change to the image's location has an important consequence in that it alters the severity of the Jew's action. The crime goes from the removal of an image from a private house (*domus*) to theft from a church. The increased gravity of the offense is reflected in the outcome of the story. In Adomnán's original version, the Jew's fate is left unclear: "After that disgusting purging of his stomach, that most hapless man went away, and what he did subsequently, how he lived, or what sort of end he had, is unknown."[152] In an alteration to what is otherwise a close copy of Adomnán, the version found in most of the twelfth-century miracle collections states that "he [the Jew] was consumed by a fittingly ignominious death, and was thereafter nevermore. From there it is to be believed that he was immediately and justly disposed of his evil spirit, because the crime he had committed against Christ and his mother, and was removed from the gaze of men."[153] The Jew's untimely death in this version becomes just as significant as the miracle of the oil emerging from the image, and in BL Cotton Cleo. C. x, the miracle ends when the Christian recovers it from the latrine, with no reference to the oil at all.

William put even greater emphasis on the Jew's punishment: "Sitting himself down over [the image], he broke wind, intending, by the emptying of his bowels, to insult our faith. But the sacrilege injured him with a deserved punishment, and his vitals were flushed out into the pit along with the disgusting torrent."[154] In describing the Jew's end, William may have been recalling the death of Arius, founder of the so-called Arian heresy, as depicted by Socrates Scholasticus in his fifth-century *Ecclesiastical History*. The account relates that as Arius approached the forum one Saturday, he was seized by a sudden need to empty his bowels, and when he sat down in the street to relieve himself, "together with the evacuations, his bowels protruded, followed by a copious haemorrhage, and the descent of the smaller intestines: moreover portions of his spleen and liver were brought off in the effusion of blood, so that he almost immediately died."[155]

The similarity here with William's tale of the Jew suggests that William know-ingly wished to link the Jewish iconoclast with Arius—an association that may have seemed natural to him from the fact that Arians and Jews both refused to embrace the Incarnation, and more important, shared the same skepticism about the veneration of images.[156] This skepticism is then contrasted with the zeal of the Greeks for holy images, which in his opinion, should serve as a model for those in the West.[157] The goal of William's story is thus clear: to high-light the proper attitude one must take toward devotional images by juxta-posing it with the violent iconoclasm of the Jew. In so doing, he presented the Jew's death as an especially severe warning about the dangers of following his example.[158]

The pressing need to demonstrate the power invested in Marian images and terrible consequences of their desecration expressed in the Marian miracles could be a reflection of new ideas arising about religious images in the eleventh and twelfth centuries. Despite the fact that not many such objects seem to have survived the Reformation period, sculpted images are mentioned often in En-glish written works, as surveyed by Jean-Marie Sansterre. References in a vari-ety of sources from the twelfth and thirteenth centuries provide evidence of carved Marian statues at Rochester, Finchal, Abingdon, Sempringham, Glaston-bury, Salisbury, Christ Church and St. Augustine's Canterbury, Worcester, and Westminster, suggesting they were common features of English churches in this period.[159] These may have been wooden and stone sculptures of Mary en-throned with the Christ child on her lap, the so-called *Sedes Sapientiae*, which spread throughout western Europe in this period and now survive especially from northern France.[160] Although there is little evidence that these statues were sites of popular lay pilgrimage in England on the same scale as relics of other saints or similar statues in Norman houses (e.g., Coutances and Saint-Pierre-sur-Dives), some are described as having thaumaturgic powers. In his *Gesta Pontificum*, William related the gift of a necklace that was to be hung around the neck of the Marian statue at Coventry by the noblewoman Godiva, circa 1067, as she lay dying.[161] This indicates that they were not seen as mere repre-sentations in wood of the Virgin but rather as infused with a sacral quality on par with relics—an understanding that Sansterre has argued was only begin-ning to emerge in the twelfth century.[162]

Despite the fact that they never became the sites of local cults, Marian im-ages may have been attributed a special *virtus* in England, as suggested by cer-tain liturgical rites in which they were involved. Sansterre has identified several liturgical blessings of Marian statues in pontificals from the mid-eleventh cen-tury onward—a practice that seems to have been unique to England.[163] One of these, found in a late eleventh-century manuscript and another mid-twelfth-century manuscript, both from Christ Church Canterbury, is especially elabo-rate and asks, among other things, that "wherever she should have been, all diabolical power and malign machination should be absent and pushed far away, and that the supplications of her faithful should be heard."[164] As a physical embodiment of Mary, the image was clearly seen as charged with divine power as a result of the liturgical rite, which included not just the verbal blessing but also censing and unction. Just as important, the statues were themselves the focus of liturgical practice, placed on altars and carried in procession such that every celebration of a Little Office or commemorative Saturday office in Mary's honor, not to mention the major feasts marking her life cycle, were in some sense directed at these objects.[165] Discussions of the doctrine of the bodily Assumption in this period may have given added impetus to the veneration of Marian images, since there was no body on earth to worship.[166] As such, religious images may have taken on increased significance for monks like William, who argued so forcefully for the bodily Assumption. This in turn could explain their interest in stories about miracle-working images, particularly ones that look and act like real women and come to life as if to illustrate the animate powers of the Virgin within. Allen Smith places special emphasis on the stories' emergence in clerical circles, where they served "to validate the clerical culture of performative piety" and urged clerics and nuns alike toward celibacy.[167] As the objects of liturgical and theological devotion, miracles presented religious images as effective and efficacious stand-ins for Mary, and therefore proper objects of praise and prayer in religious practice.

The growing popularity of images as objects of worship seems to have brought with it an interest in Jewish approaches to religious objects, as Lipton has recently asserted.[168] Twelfth-century theologians such as Rupert of Deutz reflected on the relationship of Christians with religious images, and in so doing, discussed proper and improper means of engaging with them by contrasting Christian attitudes with Jewish ones.[169] The same approach was taken in England, where Anselm's friend and abbot of Westminster, Gilbert, concluded his polemical dialogue the *Disputatio contra Judaeo* with a section on religious imagery.[170] In it, the Jew accuses the Christian of venerating graven images against the law laid out in Exodus 20:4–5. "The Christians carve out, make, and paint these effigies, from whatever they can, and wherever possible, they adore and worship them," he complains.[171] He sees the crucifix as a particularly flagrant contravention of the commandment, maintaining that it is also just horrid to depict God as a miserable man hanging from nails.[172] The Christian retorts that if the creation of images were forbidden, Moses would have sinned in making the brazen serpent, as would God in commanding him to do so (Num. 21:8–9).[173] To reconcile God's seemingly contradictory positions on images, the Christian appeals to Augustine in distinguishing between reverence and worship or idolatry. He explains that images are not made for adoration or worship but instead to act as representations of events and figures that are the real objects of veneration, like Christ and the Passion; Christians worship the signified, not the sign.[174] Still, images are worthy of honor for what they represent and must be shown respect: "A Christian in no way worships the representation of a particular thing through divine veneration, but rather, reveres and honors sacred sculpted and painted images of holy things, in an act of obligatory respect."[175]

In placing this passage in his dialogue, Gilbert indicates that the polemic over images continued to be relevant at the turn of the twelfth century. Twelfth-century England may not have experienced an iconoclastic controversy like eight-century Byzantium, where stories such as the Virgin's Image Insulted first originated. But the place of images in religious culture was undergoing change, and once more drew attention to the Jews' rejection of their creation and use.[176] Walker Bynum has remarked on host desecration that Jews "like dissidents who did in fact occasionally attack statues, were in this sense essential to a religion that needed a divine that was visibly, suddenly, and often violently present in the stuff of the physical world."[177] As the production and veneration of painted and sculpted figures grew in the twelfth century, stories about Jews opposing and even attacking them became of interest once more, and also helped to justify their popularity. Projected onto Jewish characters, opposition to images could be condemned and resolved miraculously by the punishment Mary meted out to the desecrators; the greater the opposition, the greater the triumph for Mary and her material representations, and the greater the encouragement to venerate them. We see this clearly in the enhanced role given to the Jews in stories of desecration as they were rewritten for the twelfth-century miracle collections. In the tale of Lydda, only Jews end up challenging the Marian image and desire its destruction. In the Virgin's Image Insulted story, the Jewish character is no longer just an agent in the miracle of the oil, but becomes the subject of the equally important miracle of his own humiliating death. The twelfth-century adaptations of old stories about iconoclasm thus reveal how Jews continued to be considered valuable counterpoints for exploring the appropriate approach toward religious images, not just in theological discussion, but in vivid narratives, at a time when images were gaining prominence in the Marian cult.

TOLEDO

The retribution Mary helps to bring about against the perpetrators of violence toward another kind of image, this time of her son, is the basis for the story of the Jews of Toledo.[178] This tale is found in many manuscripts, almost without exception in the same version (with the incipit *Ad excitandum humilium corda*); the only other extant twelfth-century version is William's, which had less success, but made important interventions in the narrative.[179] The story is set on the feast of the Assumption in Toledo, when during mass, a voice is heard from the heavens crying out,

> Woe, woe, how terrible and worthless the perfidy of the Jewish mind has proven to be! Woe, what an awful catastrophe that even while he remains shepherd of the chosen flock in the life-giving sign of the cross of the world's redeemer (my son), the fury of the Jewish people reigns, and they even now taunt a second time my only son, the light and salvation of the faithful, and seek to destroy him with the punishment of the cross.[180]

Seeking out the perpetrators of this mysterious crime, the Christians of the city come across the Jews in the synagogue torturing a waxen image of Christ by spitting on, slapping, and piercing it. The Jews are put to death on the spot. The most popular version then urges the readers/listeners to venerate Mary, who on this day suffered her son's Passion at the hands of the Jews as if for a second time, and as a result seeks to help liberate Christians from their enemies just as she saved them from the fires of hell.[181]

The Toledo story may have been based on an oral account, as the author claims in the prologue to have heard the tale from pious men.[182] Carter noted that there are records of attacks on Toledo's Jewish community following the death of Alfonso VI of Castille in 1109, albeit now only in thirteenth-century sources.[183] The *Annales Toledani* relate that "they killed the Jews of Toledo on the Sunday, eve of the Assumption," which chimes with the narrative.[184] Perhaps rumors of this event had reached England, by which point the riots may have been attributed to some sinister act perpetrated by the Jews, such as that described in the Toledo story.

William did not set his account in a recent past, however, but rather in the Visigothic period, in an attempt to provide the story with what he considered a more appropriate historical context. He opened his version by observing that

> reliable histories assert that Spain was at one time overburdened by the number of Jews there; and unambiguous rumor insists that it is no less polluted by them nowadays too. For instance, it has more than once been reported that at Narbonne they have a supreme pope, to whom Jews run from all over the world, piling gifts on him, or deciding by his arbitration any dispute arising among them that requires someone to resolve it. Such a great number of them swamped Toledo in the time of Reccared, king of the Goths and ruler of Spain, that they attempted to claim equal rank with Christians in all respects, and used bribery to try to bring about the annulment of regulations passed against them by councils at Toledo. They tested the mettle of the pious king, but the unbelievers could find nothing in his breast that encouraged their arts: their cash was beneath the notice of the self-controlled king. Hence the compliment to him in a letter he received from the blessed Gregory, that he did not sell justice for gold; rather, he

rated justice above gold. The letter is to be found in the ninth book of the *Registrum*.[185]

William then related the events at Toledo as an explanation for the persecution of the Jews, who had previously been allowed considerable freedom. He was clearly impressed with the Visigothic response to the Jews, and at the end of the story praised King Sisebut (612–21) for giving the Jews who had escaped the Toledan attacks a choice between conversion and expulsion. This, in William's opinion, was the only way to prevent them from becoming so powerful that they came to have their own pope (*Summum papam*) resident in Narbonne, as he described in the above passage. Legends of a Jewish prince (*nasi*) in Narbonne had circulated since approximately 1000, and probably referred to the Kalonymides, a dynasty that had led the Jewish community of southern France and represented their interests to the Christian secular authorities.[186] Yet William's account of the Toledo story contains the earliest evidence of the transmission of this legend into England. He may have learned it from Julian of Toledo (d. 690), who cited Narbonne as the site of the "prostitute of the blaspheming Jews."[187] The legend became more widespread by the mid-twelfth century, when it was included in the first accusation of ritual murder of a Christian committed by Jews, recorded by the English Benedictine Thomas of Monmouth in his *Life and Passion of William of Norwich*.[188] In William's version of the Toledo story, the reference to the Jewish pope indicated the danger of leaving Jewish populations to flourish unchecked. William saw the abuse of the image by the Jews of Toledo as the culmination of what could happen when Jewish communities were permitted to purchase favor from the authorities—a concern evident in other stories, as we will see. Although he placed the account in the ancient Visigothic past, William provided it with a crucial moral about Mary's desire to limit the powers of Jews in Christian society—a desire shared by praiseworthy rulers.

Despite the possibility of a historical basis, it is apparent that the Toledo story also had strong literary roots, particularly in the stories of Jewish iconoclasm by Pseudo-Athanasius and Gregory, described above. There are key differences with these narratives, though. First of all, contrary to Gregory's account, the Toledo story features an act of desecration committed by the entire Jewish community and ends with the mass persecution of all involved. The second major change is to the nature of the image itself. Whereas Gregory and Pseudo-Athanasius described a painted icon, the Toledo account refers to a waxen image (*imago cerea*), depicted as almost lifelike (*quasi viventem*), that was intended "for the disgrace of the Christian religion and faith" (*ad Christianae professionis et fidei dedecus*).[189] William wrote similarly that it was a "wax model caricaturing Lord Jesus" (*ad domini Jesu ludibrium*).[190] We should note that the image does not appear to have been stolen from Christians but rather to have been made by the Jews themselves; it is described as "the artifice and falsehood of the fraudulent Jews."[191] This is a significant difference from other tales of Jewish iconoclasm against Christian images, all of which are understood as being originally produced by Christians. Here, there is intentionality on the part of the Jews versus the accidental discovery of a preexisting image, which adds a further ritual element to the desecration.

As Katelyn Mesler and I have discussed, the idea that Jews desecrated wax images of Christ was an invention of the twelfth century, and the story of Toledo one of its earliest witnesses.[192] Jews had been accused of mocking the Passion by vandalizing images of Christ on the cross since the fifth century—an accusation that may have been linked to Purim celebrations, as Elliott Horowitz has argued.[193] Such images were not described as being made of wax until the period in which the Toledo story was first redacted, however. This change coincided with the growing tradition of placing votive offerings made of wax at shrines throughout western Europe. Sculpted to represent limbs or entire bodies, such offerings were left at saints' shrines to give thanks for a miracle or plead for healing. Several studies indicate that while known to some degree since antiquity, the fabrication of votives out of wax was strongly proscribed by ecclesiastical authorities prior to the ninth century and only began to appear in a Christian context at the end of the tenth.[194] Anne-Marie Bautier has identified over fifty accounts of anatomical ex-voto objects in miracle collections, most of which were made of wax, from the period 800 to 1200.[195] Pierre André Sigal compiled statistics for the twelfth to fifteenth centuries, from northwestern Mediterranean regions, noting that representational figures make up 62 percent of all wax offerings at saints' shrines.[196] As an example, the late twelfth-century miracles of Notre-Dame of Rocamadour refer four times to waxen figures of babies presented at the Marian shrine by previously infertile parents as thanks; these weighed approximately the same as their living equivalents, which gives us an idea of how like their models they must have looked.[197] If such objects were increasingly used as shrine offerings, the depiction of Jews subjecting one to an act of desecration, with miraculous results, would have been a strong indication of its efficacy. Just as in the iconoclastic miracles, Jews showed the incorrect way of treating the votive, but also illustrated just how powerful it was. It may have been a desire to defend the relatively novel practice that explains why Jews came to be accused in the twelfth century of desecration of wax figures in accounts similar to that of Toledo, but located all over western Europe, at Trier, Pescara, Rouen, and Le Mans / Lyon.[198]

The fact that wax votives were understood as stand-ins for those who placed them at shrines has important implications for the meaning of the Toledo story. The waxen image of Christ would not have been seen just as an object of veneration but instead as a very real replacement for Christ, because the relation of identity between a waxen figure and the person it represented had become so firm. The Eucharistic overtones here are strong, pointing once more to the debates concerning the "real presence" in the Eucharist of the late eleventh and early twelfth centuries. Brigitte Bedos-Rezak has indicated that these debates played an important role in shaping the understanding of wax seals in terms of their semiotic function, as reified signs of their owners. She indicates that twelfth-century scholars such as Peter Abelard underlined the close principle of identity between a wax image and the thing it was made to represent.[199] This places the Toledo story in a framework of twelfth-century semiotics and technological developments that saw wax take on multiple roles—seals, votives— linked to an increasingly strong concept of identity.

For Mary in the story, the identity of the wax image *as* Christ is clearly indicated by her lament: "[The Jews] taunt now *a second time* my only son . . . and seek to destroy him with the punishment of the cross." As a result, she understood the act not as one of desecration but instead as a reenactment of the Crucifixion. Given these prominent Passion overtones, growing interest in the Virgin as weeping, suffering mother, *mater compatiens*, at the foot of the cross is an important context for understanding the Toledo story as it appeared for the first time in the Anglo-Norman miracle collections. Contemporary works such as Anselm's Prayer to Christ on the cross, Eadmer's *De excellentia*, and Honorius's Marian sermons all emphasize Mary's role during the Crucifixion as cosufferer and coredemptrix, as we have seen in previous chapters. Fulton has shown that these works were instrumental in making Mary an indispensable feature of the Passion scene as an eyewitness and hence a model for devotees who were encouraged to put themselves in her place while seeking to empathize with the dying Christ.[200] The Toledo story evoked this sense of cosuffering—of the reader or hearer alongside Mary—and exaggerated it with the addition of the threatening Jews.[201] Presenting the Jews as Mary's particularly vicious rivals—because of their responsibility for Christ's Passion—the monastic redactors concluded the tale with encouragement to venerate the Virgin since she, "in her suffering, teaches the Christian people about the abovementioned Passion and wants to free them from the treacheries of demons and enemies of the human race."[202] The result would have been heightened belief in Mary's unique work in countering the evil of the Jews as enemies not just of her and her son but also of all Christians.

Making the threat all the more urgent, when Mary as grieving mother laments the injustice and harm done to her son by the Jews, she does so not in the biblical past but also in the timeless present of the story. In this way, the threat of the Jews to Christ was shown to be ongoing. The Toledo story can be considered perhaps the first instance where Jews were accused of ritually subjecting Christ, normally via proxy, to abuse—an act that was eventually extended from waxen images to Christian children in the ritual murder accusation.[203] As indicated above, the first record of the ritual murder accusation was made in England, circa 1150, by a Benedictine monk in the well-known case of William of Norwich.[204] As Uri Shachar has argued, this hagiographic narrative relied heavily on establishing a mimetic relation between the murdered body of the boy William and that of Christ, which again speaks to the semiotic shift pointed to by Bedos-Rezak in which material objects (seals, votives, bodies) became increasingly valued not just as referents but as closely identified with their signifiers.[205] The Toledo story may therefore have exercised an important function in establishing narratives about Jews committing violence on Christian bodies (and their proxies), not just in imitation of the Crucifixion, but as real attempts to repeat it.[206]

THEODORE AND ABRAHAM

Another tale in which Mary is shown to counter the vices embodied by Jews revolves around a Jew who lent to a Christian.[207] The story had precedents in Byzantium going as far back as the seventh century, but an obscure history up to the twelfth century when it was incorporated into the Marian miracle collections. The original legend featured the "Antiphonetes" icon, an image of Christ that served as surety for a loan in a business transaction.[208] The tale made its transition into Latin in the late tenth or early eleventh century by the southern Italian monk John, who claimed that he took it from a collection of Greek miracle stories.[209] In one line of transmission, the image is described as that of St. Nicholas, whose statue is used as surety by a Christian taking a loan from a Jew; the Christian's deviousness in attempting not to repay it is then revealed by Nicholas' miraculous intervention.[210] This story was known in England and appears in Honorius's sermon for the feast of Nicholas in the *Speculum Ecclesiae*. A rhymed version appears in a late eleventh-century manuscript from Battle Abbey.[211] It eventually became a staple of the lives of Nicholas from the twelfth century onward.[212]

At around the same time, two alternative Latin adaptations that feature a similar plotline, this time with Marian images, appeared. One was written by William of Malmesbury.[213] The other version is anonymous, with the incipit *Fuit quidam religiosus Ecclesiae Leodicensis Archidiaconus*.[214] The prologue of this latter version describes how a certain archdeacon of Lyon arrived at a Byzantine church on his travels east and found celebrations under way for a miraculous icon. The reference to Lyon could be explained by the fact that Hugh of Die, archbishop of Lyon (ca. 1040–1106) and a close friend of St. Anselm, had traveled to the East in 1100 in the wake of the First Crusade.[215] He may have told the story to Anselm or someone in his entourage during Anselm's exile in Lyon.[216] Although aware of Anselm's time in Lyon, William does not mention anything about the archdeacon in his version of the story, and launches directly into the narrative, providing no indication of his source.²¹⁷ This seems to be symptomatic of a general lack of interest in the Crusades among the twelfth-century compilers of Marian miracles.²¹⁸

The differences between the surviving versions of the story are considerable, if not so much in terms of the general story line as in the way the characters are described. John's original Latin translation tells of Theodore, a pious merchant unlucky in business, who lives in Constantinople during the reign of Emperor Heraclius (r. 610–41). After receiving no support from his friends to regain his wealth, Theodore seeks out as a last resort a Jewish friend, Abraham, and offers him as surety an image of Christ found on one of four columns in the city. Abraham is surprised, asking Theodore, "Do you not know the enmity we Jews have toward you Christians on account of this image? For do you not say that our forefathers crucified him? How could I therefore accept it as surety?"²¹⁹ But Abraham demonstrates his goodwill by striking the deal and he even provides Theodore with money a second time when the first installment is lost in a ship-wreck.²²⁰ When faced with the risk of not being able to pay the money back on time, Theodore commits a chest to the sea, together with a note and prayer for Christ's help. Both men have a dream that foretells the success of the plan, and Abraham rises to discover that the chest has reached him in the night. At this point, although he recognizes the miraculous nature of the events, Abraham wishes to "test" Theodore, telling him on his return that the loan never reached him, "not because he wanted to refuse him, but because he wanted to know in the end whether the Christian faith was firm or not."²²¹ Swearing to this in front of the image of Christ, he sees a great flame emerge from it that nearly kills him. On coming to, he converts with his entire household and gives up his fortune to found a church to house the icon, of which he becomes the priest.

The miracle stories in the twelfth-century collections differ significantly from John's version. First and foremost, the image becomes Marian. William described it as "not sculpted, as is the case in our lands, but painted on wood" and located in Hagia Sofia.²²² The other twelfth-century version of the tale initially refers to an image of Christ, but at the end, the miracle is said to have been performed by "a venerable image of the Holy Mother of God holding in her lap a venerable image of her Son," which makes it sound like a *Sedes Sapientiae* statue rather than an icon.²²³ The miracle the image performs is also significantly different. Instead of producing a miraculous burst of flame, the Marian image reveals Abraham's lie by coming to life and speaking the truth. William compared the miracle to that of Balaam's speaking ass (Num. 22:28), exclaiming, "A pretty wonder that an inanimate object should utter words like a human—and show up an unbeliever!"²²⁴ In presenting the miracle as performed by a "living" statue of Mary, the twelfth-century versions reflect a growing interest in miracles performed by Marian images that act in human fashion. Although there is at least one tenth-century miracle of this kind, Sansterre's survey of such accounts has revealed that they did not become popular until the late eleventh and twelfth centuries.[225] He attributes this to the rise in the popularity of images more generally in this period, as discussed above in the context of the Virgin's Image Insulted.

Together with the identity of the icon, both twelfth-century versions of the Theodore and Abraham tale alter the character of the protagonists. While John depicts Theodore as a virtuous but unlucky merchant, and Abraham as a generous and faithful friend, the twelfth-century redactors established a rather different picture of the two. In the version attributed to the archdeacon of Lyon, the Christian merchant comes across as a proud and materialistic man: "a certain citizen who, wanting to extend the fame he had on the basis of his great wealth, began to spend a great deal on luxuries."[226] His irresponsible spending habits bring him to bankrupcy, and the friends he had only gained through his wealth and fame abandon him. After obtaining the loan from the Jew, the Christian nevertheless manages to forget about repayment.[227] Nor is his panic to repay the loan due to any sense of honor, but to the fact that he had promised to become the Jew's slave were he to be late paying his creditor back.[228] This contrasts with the Jew, who explicitly says that "[he] does not believe that Jesus Christ is the Lord, although [he] does not doubt that [he] was a just man and a prophet," and so accepts to take the image as loan without hesitation (*indubitanter*).[229] This statement makes him sound more Muslim than Jewish, which might make sense if a former crusader had narrated the story, given that he would have been more familiar with the beliefs of the former than the latter. Yet these words also maintain the open-mindedness of the character from the earlier version, even more so because he has nothing bad to say regarding Christ, contrary to John's Abraham. The discovery of the chest is in this case more fortuitous than in the original, for the Jew's servant is said to have been walking along the beach when he spied it. The Jew then only denies having received the money after finding out that the Christian has greatly multiplied his treasure during his travels.[230] If John drew a sympathetic picture of both Theodore and Abraham, this twelfth-century version places the Christian in a somewhat less generous light, if not so much the Jew.

William, on the other hand, made a considerable effort to convince his reader that Theodore was a worthy protagonist. He went to great lengths to mitigate Theodore's profession by emphasizing his good and pious nature:

> Of this city Theodorus was a citizen, a layman of praiseworthy modesty, though he made his living by a means that especially seduces men into sullying the truth. He was in fact a trader: you can see almost no one in this line who is afraid to expose his sworn word to perjury if he can turn a penny or two. What is more, when open cheating does not serve, they take advantage of the unwary by craft. Theodorus was not like that at all. He knew nothing whatever about cunning, for

he chose to know nothing; and he regarded lying as morally wrong. He did not try to beat down a price or wipe out a buyer's profit. If he gave, he did so gladly and liberally, from a full hand. If he made a promise, he fulfilled it duly and swiftly: to a tender conscience it is a kind of lie to be tardy in doing what one has promised.[231]

Theodore's virtuous nature ultimately brings about his financial ruin, but like Job, Theodore takes his hardship well, laughing at the tricks played on him, and when he is so poor that he can barely sustain himself, he places his faith in God while acknowledging that God helps those who help themselves. Theodore continues to prove his uprightness with Abraham, assuring his friend that he "should rather die keeping my word than be branded as a perjurer."[232] Having regained his fortune, surprisingly without recourse to deception (remarked William), a storm threatens to prevent him from repaying the loan, leaving Theodore to fear Abraham will curse the naive faith of Christians.[233] He adds more than the necessary amount to the chest he sets on the waves, and is patient when his friend denies having received it, promising to pay him again should the Jew's oath in front of the statue leave him unscathed.[234] Theodore remains resolute in his generosity and faith in the power and mercy of the Virgin, which makes him a worthy recipient of her miraculous help.

The Jew gets worse treatment in William's version of the story. Initially, Abraham is the merchant's friend. Abraham is said to suffer at the sight of Theodore's distress such that "he went so far as to weep himself."[235] Despite this initial display of friendship between the two characters, Abraham ends up behaving far worse than Theodore's Christian friends. While Theodore is increasing his fortune, Abraham harasses the man's wife, his anxiety about the repayment of the loan turned to resentment and anger; "creditors are so ill disposed to poor friends that he did not imagine that Theodorus was unable to put to sea," remarked William in an aside.[236] Abraham is described as going down to the shore the morning of the planned repayment to identify Theodore's ship. Abraham then sneaks the chest away and hides it under his bed, not even informing his wife of the remarkable event.[237] His former acceptance of the icon gives way at this point to open mockery, for he "thought it a trivial matter: it would, he imagined, bring him no harm if he stained our rites by perjury. And he at once forswore himself in front of the image, asserting that the money had not been returned."[238] But when the image of Mary reveals the truth, Abraham's conversion is complete, and he gives away all his money to charity.[239]

William contrasted his two characters more than any previous adaptation of the tale. Theodore is the virtuous, patient hero, and Abraham, seemingly friendly at the outset, is revealed to be greedy and deceitful as the story unfolds. But William's exaggeration seems to stem from his ambivalence about their profession, which placed both characters in a moral gray zone. The pursuit of business, he seems to say, left little room for virtue. William made great efforts in showing that Theodore was nevertheless successful in fighting the sinful nature required for the successful practice of the trade, while Abraham embodied it to the fullest degree. Herein lies the most striking difference between William's redaction and the original version. The Byzantine miracle story presents trade and money lending in a neutral and even positive light. In their study of the tale, Benjamin Nelson and Joshua Starr explain that in the Byzantine world, the pursuit of wealth was not censured by religious authorities; on the contrary, "the God of our Byzantine story is, indeed, the bestower of profitable returns."[240] Much had changed by the time the story was reworked by William.

The epilogue of the Theodore and Abraham story in William's version reveals that William read the events differently:

> From that day on in Constantinople the wild fanaticism of the Jews grew cold, though previously it had been rampant agianst us. Mary was to hand, mercifully angry with pretense, showing up faithlessness, and ensuring that by the judgment of the townspeople, traitors were stripped of their properties if they did not think they should avoid sacrilege. Yes, she is so unwearying in distributing her mercies that those who are unwilling to be won by benefits are brought over by blows. Some she raises up by honors in the present, [and] others she brings low, according as she sees it to be expedient; for she is aware of all future events in advance. Injuries inflicted upon her faithful she avenges with high spirit; yet soon she mercifully shows pity even to the injurers, if she sees they are penitent. She does not despise men of low rank or condition, so long as she sees that their minds are warm in venerating her. In this way, she shows how far from right is the arrogance of rich men who do not receive services from the poor gratefully but extort them without a word of thanks. For in the eyes of mortals only wealth recommends a man; anyone who lacks it is dirt. Religious fervor is measured by the standard of treasure, [and] riches are thought to tip the balance in oratory: rare (or rather nonexistent) is eloquence that is clothed in rags. Once a man thrived on knowing something; now the real mark of the uncouth is to possess nothing. For instance, only money is nowadays thought to relieve human cares and soothe men's minds with an appearance of tranquillity. An ugly and false state of affairs! The superior mind should not be judged according to the whim of fortune: even a great man does not seem cheaper in his people's eyes if he has found himself lodging in some beggar's hovel.[241]

It seems that in William's view, the pursuit of wealth came necessarily at the expense of piety. Perhaps for this reason a Jew came to embody the sins of the profesion for him. In his *Commentary on Lamentations*, William had observed that Jews were "longing only for the riches of the present life" rather than eternal salvation.[242] The idea that Jews were vulnerable to greed and corruption because they rejected the spiritual nature of Christianity (in its exegesis and its promise of spiritual rewards), would become a common trope of theological polemics, which accused Jews of being mired in carnality.[243]

It is tempting to see in William's condemnation an indictment of Jewish involvement in money lending in William's time. Scholars have underlined the heavy involvement of Jews in financial services and predominantly money lending in England as compared to other parts of western Europe.[244] These services were essential for the elaborate building programs initiated by the Normans after the conquest, which required considerable sums both in the secular and religious spheres.[245] We know of Jews lending money to religious institutions for building works already in the late eleventh century, which may be behind Gilbert Crispin's claims of having engaged both in business and conversation with a Jew.[246] Osbert of Clare complained of being personally indebted to Jews and asked several of his friends, including Anselm, for help in paying off his debts.[247] By the end of the twelfth century, monastic debts to Jews reached considerable proprotions as described in Jocelin of Brakelond's *Chronicle of Bury St Edmunds*.[248] The Jewish moneylender, as exemplified by William's Abraham, was becoming a familiar figure among English monasteries.[249]

Certainly not all moneylenders in England at this time were Jewish, and William's critique of the profession recognizes this, since he condemns Christian practitioners as fiercely. If anything, it was the spread of such financial practices throughout *Christian* society that seems to have worried him.[250] The popularity of the anonymous version of the Theodore and Abraham story, in which Theodore comes out much worse, might reflect a greater concern with the unreliable and devious Christian merchant than with his Jewish counterpart. The moral implications of charging interest—money begetting money smacked of theft and was defined as such starting in the late eleventh century— were ringing alarm bells for some ecclesiastical leaders, which led to a proliferation of canon law banning the practice.[251] At the same time, William's attempt to make Theodore a fitting hero while tarring Abraham's character points to a now-familiar rhetorical strategy: condemning undesirable behavior by associating it with Jews. For William, it seems that business and faith were inherently uncomfortable bedfellows, but the Jewish moneylender could be pictured as an embodiment of the worst kind of faithless entrepreneur, willing to cheat and lie in ways that reflected his rejection of Christian values.

Considered within this context, William's comments about the descent of society into materialism and greed reflect an important aspect of his vision not just of Jews but also of Mary's place in the world. In addition to the miracle Mary performs to set Abraham on the right path, William's epilogue to the story credits her alone with saving Constantinople, and rectifying the imbalances between rich and poor, while punishing the recalcitrant who refuse to give up their wealth. Only the Virgin could stop the downward trajectory of his society, since she embodied every virtue, as William had established in the prologue of his miracle collection. Her mercy, honesty, and beneficence were a counterbalance to the avarice and sacrilege William saw growing around him. Her commitment to countering the troubling changes in society was thus both literal and metaphoric: she intervened to perform miracles that reestablished the proper social order, but also provided an example to Christians, inspiring virtue in her devotees as well as encouraging proper values and behavior. As a result, William's story presented devotion to Mary as a corrective for the evils of modern society by reducing a complex situation into a simple moral tale with archetypal characters: the virtuous, generous Christian; the crooked, deceitful Jew; and the formidable Virgin who sets everything right.

TOULOUSE

Like his version of the tale of Theodore and Abraham, William's story of the Jews of Toulouse appealed to contemporary concerns in order to give a more general message about Christian mores.[252] Yet it is unlike any other story in his collection. The miracle tale appears for the first time in his volume of miracles and went on to make only an occasional appearance in the manuscript tradition, and then only in a much-altered form.[253] William's original version recounts how on one Easter Sunday in Toulouse, a Jew and Christian are standing outside the church while the Christian listens intently to the Gospel reading. The Jew begins to mock Christ and the saints, so the Christian knocks him down, killing him. When the Jews of the town angrily demand justice from the count, although he is tempted by their bribes at first, he is finally convinced instead to instate a tradition by which a Jew is to be publicly slapped in the church square every Easter—a "privilege" auctioned off to the highest bidder.

William's description of the annual Toulousan custom incredibly has a basis in the historical record. An early legend that Charlemagne had ordered Jews to be boxed on the ears as punishment for their betrayal of Toulouse to the Saracens appears in the *Vita* of ninth-century St. Theodardus, even though there is nothing further to confirm what is now found only in a seventeenth-century edition.[254] The *Chronicon* of the early eleventh-century French Benedictine monk Ademar of Chabannes provides a more immediate source, however. It relates an episode in which the chaplain of the nobleman Aimery de Rochechouart killed a Jew in 1020, having paid to slap him publicly in what is portrayed as an Easter tradition:

> At this time, Hugo, the chaplain of Aimeric, the viscount of Rochechouart when he was with that same man in Toulouse at Easter, as Easter is always commemorated there, he delivered a slap to a Jew, whose eyes and brain spilled out of his perfidious head onto the ground; the Jew died immediately, and having been car-

ried to the synagogue of the Jews from the cathedral of St. Stephen, was buried.[255]

Further suggesting Ademar was his source, William placed his account of the events during the reign of Count William III of Toulouse (ca. 950–1037), the same period depicted in the *Chronicon*.[256] As for William's comment that the tradition still continued in his day (*est ergo consuetude ibi usque ad hanc diem*), the cartularies of the Cathedral of Toulouse describe that the twelfth-century bishop Amelius (d. 1139) reattributed the customary payment "in exchange for / in lieu of the slap of the Jews" (*pro colapho Judaeorum*) to the canons and deacons of the cathedral.[257] The preposition "pro" leaves it unclear whether the act was still carried out, or the equivalent amount was simply paid by the bishop without an auction. William nevertheless thought of it as a living custom, and in this he may have been right.

What makes the appearance of the Toulouse tale in William's collection all the more extraordinary is that it is not really a Marian miracle at all. William made some attempt in the final draft to suggest that Mary's intervention had convinced the count to punish the Jews, but this is not developed in the story and comes across as an afterthought.[258] William seems to have had other reasons for including it: "For as I am speaking of Jews, I want to tell of something that happened in connection with the Jews of Toulouse: a proper joke (*iocundum sane*) and one to make the reader laugh (*legentium torqueat ora risu*)."[259] The story was therefore included here because it involved Jews, showing just how enmeshed Jewish antagonism had become to thinking about Mary. In addition to this, to William and probably his readers too, the story was apparently funny.

As I have argued elsewhere, the obvious amusement with which William relays how the Toulousan tradition began can be explained by his vision of Jews in Christian society.[260] First, William had deep reservations about the relationship between Jews and the monarchy. He claimed that only bribery could explain the presence of so many Jews in Toulouse in the first place: "It was here that a large number of the accursed race lived. . . . [T]he Jews were so out of control that in the wantonness of their wealth, they took advantage of the prince's mildness."[261] During the events in Toulouse, the Jews again sought to bribe the count to help them, "promising gold." The count's advisers confronted him, arguing that he would not only set a bad example, but if he did not punish the Jews themselves, "he should be abandoned by them all, as someone who overlooked injuries to Christ, a half-Jew (*semi-Judaeus*) in fact."[262] Here, William may have been appealing to a situation that was familiar to his readers, namely the favor shown by King William Rufus (d. 1100) to the Jews, as described in William's *Gesta Regum*. In an attempt to showcase Rufus's shortcomings, William provided the following anecdote:

Let me give an example of his [Rufus's] arrogance, or rather ignorance, toward God. Some London Jews, whom his father [William the Conqueror] had transferred there from Rouen, came to him on some feast day or other bearing gifts. Prompted by their flatteries, he dared encourage them—no less—to debate against the Christians, saying that "by the holy Face of Lucca," if they prevailed he would become a Jew himself. The contest was therefore held, to the great alarm of the bishops and clergy, who were filled with fear in their pious anxiety for the Christian faith. And from this dispute, at any rate, the Jews got nothing but confusion, although they have often boasted that they were beaten by party passion and not argument.[263]

William makes the same accusation against Count William of Toulouse as against Rufus for accepting "gifts" from the Jews in exchange for allowing them to mock the Christian faith in the public debate he staged. Because English law stipulated that the Jews were the direct responsibility and property of the king, the ties William described between Rufus and the Jews may have looked disturbingly like collusion and conspiracy.[264] The echoes between William's depiction of Rufus's closeness to the Jewish community in England and the Count of Toulouse's susceptibility to their wiles supports Thomson's assessment that "William's irony has a serious moral undertone, and is directed against contemporary or near-contemporary leaders in Church and State."[265]

A satirical reading of the Toulouse story seems fitting, but does not capture the story's principal message.[266] Although the count is clearly shown to be a weak leader, the Jews are ultimately the butt of the joke. Their punishment is highly ironic: instead of seeing the Christian punished for killing their coreligionist, the Jews receive punishment themselves in an identical form to that suffered by the murder victim. To us this seems cruel, but that would be to ignore William's perception that the real crime had been the Jews' mockery in the first place. For example, the Jew who ended up murdered had mocked the Christian by telling him that Christ was a wizard who deserved to be killed, and that Christians "were dustmen, fixated on the embers from funeral pyres, worshipping as we did men dead and gone."[267] The Jew who provoked the Christian was apparently not alone in his irreverence, either, for the Jews of the town went so far "as to mingle with the Christians and force their way into the church on feast days, greet what they heard there with guffaws, and take the tale back home."[268] With this in mind, the humor in the story comes from the Jews' comeuppance for their hubristic belief that they could get away with laughing at Christian beliefs *and* have a Christian punished for it.

The timing of events, then, is highly significant. The Easter setting suggests that the *collaphus* tradition was meant to reverse the Passion narrative to which the Christian was listening at the beginning of the story: instead of the Jews of Jerusalem insulting, slapping, and spitting on Christ, the Jews of Toulouse became the victims of this very treatment.[269] The derisory laughter of the Jews in the Gospels at the expense of Christ and his followers thus becomes the joyful laughter of Christians on righting the social and spiritual order. The resolution of the story involves rejoicing at Christ's triumph over his tormentors and the Toulousan Christians' triumph over the Jews.[270] Mary hardly need figure in a narrative that provides such a clear message of Christian victory over Jewish evil, and this is probably why William decided to include it in his collection.

THE JEW OF LONDON

While the story of the Jews of Toulouse requires some reading between the lines, the tale of the Jew of London is more explicit in its reflection of contemporary ideas about Jews and Judaism.[271] The tale begins with a Jew named Jacob who travels from his home in London to Winchester. On the way, he is captured by robbers, tied up, and fed with only bread and water for three days in the hopes of receiving a significant ransom. On the third night, however, Jacob has a dream in which he sees a woman in a white gown come to him; he sees her not just in spirit but also with his own eyes (*non iam in spiritu ut prius sed corporeo visu*), we are told. She introduces herself to him as Mary, "whom you and your kind abuse out of your evil, and deny that I brought forth the world's redeemer."[272] She admits that she has come to bring Jacob out of his error, and show him what awaits him if he persists in it. She then proceeds to show him a deep and terrible pit in which he sees people being roasted, screaming such that he himself almost dies at the horrific sound. "These prisons, these fires, these torments of every kind will befall you and your followers if you do not deny the Jewish impiety very quickly and come running to the sacraments of the Christian faith, therefore follow me that I might show you what good you are missing out on as a result of your blindness," she warns him, urging him to follow her to see what he and other Jews are missing because of their blindness.[273] She then takes him to a beautiful palace atop a hill, where he sees the joyful faces of those who believed that Christ had taken his flesh from her. After returning to himself, Jacob heeds Mary's advice "to do what you ought" (*quid tibi agendus sit sollicite propende*), and flees to the nearest town, where he seeks out a monastery and has himself baptized as John. Found only as of the late twelfth century, the story was a later addition to the Marian miracle collections, but the original story is set sometime in the mid-twelfth century, which is why I am considering it here; Carter identified the bishop who baptized Jacob as Robert of Bath (1136–66), placing the story's setting in approximately the time frame of the earliest collections.[274] The story became popular, and was incorporated into famous collections such as the *Cantigas de Santa Maria*. This is especially significant given the uniquely English setting of the story—the only one of the Marian stories about Jews to be located in England.

The story of Jacob's conversion is in many ways unoriginal. Quite apart from its Passion overtones—the three days of captivity and subsequent release—it follows a long literary history of accounts of journeys to the otherworld, be it heaven or hell, or both, with some of the most famous being St. Patrick's Purgatory and the vision of the monk of Eynsham.[275] Mary herself is treated to a tour of heaven and hell in a narrative tradition that dates back to eighth-century Byzantium and circulated later in Ireland.[276] In the story of Jacob, though, she is depicted as the tour guide rather than the tourist. Jacob's journey is also unique in featuring a Jew in this latter role. The story's main message is one of conversion, but the involvement of a Jew makes it a starker form of conversion than the usual search for penitence after a sinful life; in fact, nothing is mentioned about the quality of Jacob's character, and we must remember that he is the victim in this tale as opposed to the perpetrator of any evil. The only reason he might merit the flames is that he is Jewish. Mary is explicit about this, and also about the transformation that Jacob must undergo to save himself from the fires of hell: he must open his eyes to the truth of the Christian message. This message is summarized as the fact that Christ redeemed humanity and was born of her, a human woman. The criteria for Jacob's salvation are therefore very much in keeping with the themes of twelfth-century theological polemics: he must accept the Incarnation and virgin birth.

The conversion of the Jews, while generally a matter of some importance for medieval Christians, may have been a particularly pressing issue in twelfth-century England, such that a story like that of Jacob of London appeared precisely in this context.[277] We have seen the ways in which Honorius made the conversion of Synagoga a central feature of his interpretation of the Song of Songs in his *Sigillum*.[278] But Honorius was speaking eschatologically, imagining such an event taking place near Judgment Day. There is some suggestion, however, that more immediate and present forms of conversion did occupy the minds of some of the monastic authors now familiar to us. William, for example, describes Jewish attempts to apostatize after their conversion to Christianity in a later recension of the passage from the *Gesta Regum Anglorum* cited earlier: "The Jews in [King William II's] time gave a display of arrogance toward God, on one occasion at Rouen trying by bribes to recall to the Jewish faith some who had abandoned their mistaken ways."[279] The event referred to in this passage is drawn from the *Historia Novorum* by Eadmer, a known friend of William's.[280] In Eadmer's more extensive account, he noted that some Norman Jews approached Rufus while in Rouen to force some of their coreligionists, who had converted to Christianity, to return to their former faith: "They asked that for a price paid to him he should compel them to throw over Christianity and to return to Judaism."[281] As Eadmer portrayed it, Rufus complied, taking the money and making them, "broken by threats and intimidation, deny Christ and return to their former error."[282] Eadmer then went into great detail about one particular case that involved a young Jew who converted after seeing a vision of St. Stephen, the protomartyr. The boy's father came to the king in despair and paid handsomely to have his son forced back to his former faith. Rufus agreed, and instructed the boy to return to his father and Judaism. The boy then hotly refused, prompting the king's rage but also his shame at having been exposed as a terrible Christian, in Eadmer's words. The father came back just as angry that his son was merely more entrenched in his new faith, but Rufus declined to give back more than half the fee, scoffing, "I am certainly not going to have worked for nothing!"[283]

Eadmer's vivid story was no doubt intended to support his bleak view of Rufus, who had been embroiled in ongoing conflict with Archbishop Anselm. Yet it also illustrated the aftermath of an event that must have had ripples in early twelfth-century England. The call to the First Crusade by Pope Urban II in 1095 unleashed waves of violent persecution against Jewish communities, most famously in the Rhineland, but also in northern France. Guibert of Nogent tells of the violence inflicted on the Jews of Rouen by local fighters on their way east, who spared only those individuals who submitted to baptism. One young Jewish boy was rescued when a Christian nobleman snatched him away and placed him in his own family; the boy was then deposited in the monastery of Fly to prevent his relatives from taking him back, as they had tried to do several times already, and this is where Guibert came to know him personally.[284] The echoes here with Eadmer's account are striking, suggesting it may not have been such an unusual situation. Norman Golb has argued that the brutality perpetrated in this area would have made emigration to England an especially attractive prospect, although we cannot know how many left.[285] As such, some of the first Jewish settlers in England may have been forcibly baptized, like the Jews in Eadmer's account who then returned to their former faith or chose not to, as indicated in a letter written by Archbishop Anselm. In 1105 or 1106, Anselm wrote to Ernulf and William, prior and deacon of Christ Church Canterbury, respectively, asking that they use the revenues of the archdiocese to support Robert, a convert from Judaism, in order that "this man, with his little family, may not suffer harsh poverty but may rejoice in having passed from falsehood to the true faith and experience through our loving kindness that our faith is nearer to God than Judaism."[286] Anselm seems to have been concerned that converts tended to apostatize because they were not taken care of, either financially or spiritually, and he sent another letter to Gundulf, the bishop of Rochester, asking him to make sure that Ernulf and William were held to account.[287] The monks of twelfth-century England did not perhaps know quite what to make of the difficult status of the baptized Jews of northern

France who found their way to the newly conquered territory. They would have been clear about the need to maintain baptized Jews in the Christian faith, however, and it may have been through stories like the one about Jacob the Jew that they expressed the ideal of true conversion, what that conversion should involve, and what would be the ultimate result.

We have seen that conversion could be an important conclusion to stories about Mary's miraculous interactions with Jews. Although many of the stories discussed here show the punishment of violent and recalcitrant Jews, some, like the Jewish Boy as well as Theodore and Abraham, also illustrate Mary's powers to lead Jews to Christianity. In the case of Jacob, Mary plays the part of missionary; she is not just the subject of Christian belief (i.e., the virgin birth) but also its active agent. She has the same role here as in Honorius's *Sigillum*, actively seeking to bring the members of the synagogue into the Christian fold. William also wrote about Mary's missionizing efforts in the introduction to his story about the Jewish boy: "It is a significant proof that I will tell, of how much Mary's efforts go toward the conversion of her own people."[288] Mary is not just a *mediatrix* for penitent Christians; she acts as mediator in the conversion of the Jews, too, namely by performing miracles. Her own Jewish heritage and the fact that she was the first to recognize Christ as the incarnate God at her Annunciation additionally made her an effective example for them to follow—something that William recognized. It is highly unlikely that such stories were ever intended to actually convert Jews, and they were no doubt meant for circulation among Christians, just as was the case with the polemical dialogues. But the conversion of Jews was an especially powerful means of showing Mary's ability to act in the world, specifically with mercy. If many of the Marian miracle stories show the antagonism the Jews harbored toward Mary—their refusal to believe in the virgin birth along with their desire to harm her, her son, her images, and her devotees—stories about their conversion demonstrated Mary's powers in bringing them on side, extending her famously merciful nature to those who had once rejected her.

CONCLUSION

Mary's role in the Marian miracle stories was manifold, and so too was that of the Jew. Mary protected her devotees, wrenched their souls back from the devil, warned them of evil, and brought about the punishment of the persistently wicked. She sought the conversion of unbelievers and correction of the sinful. Jews, on the other hand, attacked images of Mary, carried out mock crucifixions, cheated their friends, and bribed the authorities. They had to be convinced of the Christian faith through miracles, but even then sometimes persisted in their unbelief.[289] Jews came into allegiance with the devil and performed black magic; they resisted Mary's efforts and clung to their materialistic, carnal, icon-oclastic ways. Marian miracle stories thus dramatized the conflict between faith in the Virgin's power and Jewish resistance to believe anything they could not see with their own eyes. Giving narrative form to the controversy between "spiritual" Christianity and "carnal" Judaism, miracle stories provided neat resolutions to complex theological problems, as Mary stepped in to demonstrate the truth of the Incarnation and virgin birth. Jews were the ideal witnesses, with their conversion or punishment—for there was no other alternative—a memorable drama as well as potent symbol for Mary's power in heaven and on earth. Miracle stories supplied Mary with a stage on which to display her greatness, and Jews provided her with an antagonist against whom to exercise her mercy and justice. The more malevolent and stubborn the Jew, the greater was Mary's triumph over his unbelief.[290] Just like the Jewish interlocutors of the polemical dialogues, the Jews in miracle stories were particularly useful for demonstrating Mary's worthiness of veneration. Jewish opposition to Christian ideas about her was thus integrated into and made an essential part of miracle accounts, the most explicit expression of her dominion over heaven and earth.

Marian miracles were not timeless, however. Rather than fixed in form from their origins, the accounts changed over time. As they were rewritten in the twelfth century for incorporation into the collections, some stories that were not Marian at the outset came to involve her, and others gave Mary greater authority and power to act. They conversely, almost systematically, worsened the depiction of the Jewish characters, especially under the pen of William. We have traced through the various redactions of the tales, from their Byzantine origins to their twelfth-century versions, how the figure of the Jew was increasingly vilified, his nature more destructive, and his punishment proportionately more drastic. Many of these embellishments could be interpreted as reflecting contemporary concerns. The immigration of the first Jews to England, along with their success in financial professions and closeness with the monarchy, were part of a significant social and economic shift in post–Conquest England. So too was the interest shown in new forms of learning and the problem of forced baptism. But these social factors at most help to explain the ways in which authors tried to make their stories resonate with contemporary audiences. Ultimately what really mattered was the form of devotion being promoted, and what Christians *ought* to do in contrast with what Jews were imagined as doing. Given this, we should understand the ongoing interest in miracles performed by Marian icons and statues as part of a wider proliferation of religious images and votives. The figure of Mary as *mater dolorosa* and missionary among her own people was also being developed in the writings of Anselm, Eadmer, and Honorius. More generally, the growing devotional fervor for Mary urged on by the monks of Anglo-Norman England—through their liturgical, theological, and literary production—gave impetus to the vilification of the Jew as a means to exalt her even further.

Whatever the multiple influences and motives behind the compilers' interest in composing stories about Jews and rewriting older ones, the very act of compilation gave the figure of Mary's Jewish antagonist new currency. As argued earlier, collecting stories in volumes allowed them to play a significant role in the liturgy, since they could be used as readings during the office and at mealtimes, not to mention excerpted in sermons. Once compiled together, the Marian miracles were far more accessible than the isolated stories scattered through a myriad of sources, which is evident in the immediate popularity of the collections. In this way, the Jew as Mary's enemy became a familiar figure as the collections spread throughout Europe and became integral to the Marian canon. This explains the prevalence of the stories discussed in this chapter as part of the famous vernacular collections produced in later centuries, most of which were translated from Latin collections similar to those produced in Anglo-Norman England. Formed in a particular context—that of early twelfth-century England—these tales were transmitted widely, passing on their message about Jewish unbelief, and Mary's miraculous correction of it. Moved by their love of Mary and desire to see her recognized for her powers to protect her faithful followers, English compilers thus made considerable strides in the establishment of the idea of the Jew's evil as the corollary of their true interest—Mary's mercy.

Conclusion

|||||||||||||||||||||||||||||||||||

THE MARIAN MIRACLES REVEAL MARY'S TWO FACES in the cult developed for her by monks in the Anglo-Norman sphere. As much as she was shaped as the mother of mercy and queen of heaven, she was understood to be the bane of the Jews, tirelessly seeking their conversion and punishment. In the former role, Mary saved. She was the source of salvation by having brought Christ into the world for the redemption of humanity. She also saved individual souls, those who sang her praises in the liturgy and prayed for her intercession to sway the all-powerful Judge. Jews became useful witnesses to her soteriological powers, demonstrating that even her most obstinate enemies could be overcome in the end. The Jews who converted in these tales did so through her: recognizing her presence in icons and images as well as seeing her ability to effect tangible change in this world and the next. For those who did not, Mary also punished. The recalcitrant Jews who refused to acknowledge Mary brought out the reverse of her merciful side, for she made sure they suffered the consequences. As a result, Mary emerged all the more powerful from her battle with the unbelieving Jews. The evil of the Jews underscored her victory, and the greater the challenge they were thought to pose, the greater was Mary's triumph in turning their arrogance to hubris. This serves to remind us that for all that these sources demonized Jews, they were not produced with an eye to forming particular discourses about them. Their aim was to create new ways of understanding Mary. But because Jews were part of the Marian story in Christian theology and narrative, the growth of her cult drew Jews into the limelight.

Jews were themselves one-half of a two-sided coin. They were not just distinguished from Mary—in her merciful, truth-revealing, salvific role—but also from the devotees who venerated her. Ultimately, the monks who helped to consolidate the juxtaposition between Mary and the Jews in devotional sources wanted to present good devotional behavior by showcasing the Jews' evil. Jews, by desecrating images, blaspheming against Mary, and assaulting her followers, provided a useful contrast with the monks, nuns, clerics, and virtuous laypeople of the miracles who diligently performed the liturgy in her honor, prayed to her, venerated her images, and visited her churches. These actions were the appropriate means to approach Mary, not through perjury or abuse, but through liturgy and prayer. The message concerned not just the need to believe in Mary and her role as immaculate mother of God; for most of the miracle stories, simple belief was not enough. What was at stake was how to *show* belief and, more important, love. This came by way of the many liturgical and devotional practices performed in Mary's honor. The Jews fell outside this scheme and actively attacked it, not merely through their unbelief, but through their acts of sacrilege. This conception of Jews is reflective of a cult in which the onus was as much on praxis as on belief. Jews were useful in thinking about both aspects, but whereas polemical literature privileged their role in testing belief, the miracle stories were clearly interested in promoting practice.

As their involvement in marking out correct practice from bad conduct shows, Jews in the Marian miracle stories participated in broader discourses about Marian devotion. In many ways, these were unique to Anglo-Norman England. Although the miracle stories depicted universal forms of approaching Mary, ones that were not limited to England, there was a particular impulse in the period that followed the Norman Conquest to foster the Marian cult by unusual means. The miracle collections were just such an example. Spurred on by the literary fashion of recording the histories and miracles of the saints, an elaborate hagiographic corpus was created for Mary just as it had been for other saints, with the collection of her miracles, together with the redaction of many new ones, representing the most novel contribution. The liturgy was of central significance to this project. Miracles promoted and justified controversial forms of venerating Mary as much as theological treatises and exegetical commentaries did, and gave memorable examples that could reach large audiences. Hardly surprising, then, that miracle and liturgy were to be found in mutual interaction. The stories had a performative role in readings and sermons, and as exempla became an important means of communicating devotional and moral messages. The divine sanction the miracles provided liturgical practices—from antiphons, to offices, to feast days—made them potent tools for justifying these practices to both the individual and community. Miracles, liturgy, and theology all combined to give Mary unprecedented signficance, which the opposition of the Jews only emphasized.

Bringing together these diverse materials reveals something about the individuals involved in the movement to promote and venerate Mary. It suggests that while Archbishop Anselm made a notable contribution to the cult of the Virgin with his prayers, helping to develop a new way of speaking and thinking about Mary, he may not have played as central a role in its flourishing as other individuals in his immediate circle who were willing to take their interest in the Marian cult to extremes in which he had no part—in the promotion of the Conception feast, creation of the feast of Anne, and development of the doctrines of the Immaculate Conception and bodily Assumption. Anselm of Bury,

Osbert of Clare, William of Malmesbury, Eadmer of Canterbury, Dominic of Evesham, and Honorius Augustodunensis played crucial parts in the elaboration of the Marian cult with new liturgical texts, sermons, theological treatises, and miracle colletions as well as the adoption of feast days and liturgical practices. It was not a question of national allegiance, as it was a mixed group— English, Norman, French, and Lombard; Marian devotion cannot be claimed as an exclusively English interest. Yet it took particular hold in England as a result of the creative energy and polemical engagement that a time of social and cultural upheaval brought about. These men knew each other, read each other's work, and were familiar with each other's ideas; they copied and borrowed from each other, and pushed each other further; they were joined ultimately by a love of Mary and a desire to see her gain a greater place in devotional culture.[1] It was from varying backgrounds but a unified aim that the cult of the Virgin was given an especially powerful boost by monks active in England in the first half of the twelfth century.

Despite the strong monastic impetus behind the sources discussed in this book, the monks who helped develop her cult did not keep Mary for themselves. While the theological doctrines were limited to intellectual spheres, the feasts for which they were developed spread widely, bringing with them the view that Mary was to be celebrated in her own right, as second in power only to God. Through chant, prayer, and sermons, Mary's capacity for universal intercession was communicated to wide audiences, laypeople as well as clerics, and she provided them with an almost all-powerful guardian and patron. She was also a point of emotional contact with the divine—a figure with whom to sympathize in her sufferings and rejoice in her triumphs. In this, she was presented as an ideal role model. But the fact that she was the very embodiment of chastity, humility, charity, and obedience did not mean she was pictured solely as an example for monks and nuns. If anything, Mary helped to establish these fundamentally monastic virtues for everyone in Christian society. This vision of Mary as powerful patron and example for Christians, so greatly developed in the monasteries of the Anglo-Norman world, would therefore become the standard understanding of her place in Christian society. As the sources explored in this book traveled outside the monastic milieu, what was at root a monastic cult was transformed into something far more universal.

This has considerable implications for the vision of Jews formulated as part of the Marian cult, and with which I will conclude this book. The more Anselm's heirs made Mary out to be the universally accepted virgin queen of heaven, conceived without sin, and assumed to heaven in her immaculate body and soul, the starker grew the distinction between those who chose to follow her and those who did not. Once her preeminent status among the saints was established in such bold terms, it became increasingly difficult to dispute her centrality to the narrative of Christian salvation, even if the details of the doctrines of the Immaculate Conception and bodily Assumption remained contentious. The Jews were the inadvertent victims of this process. By casting Jews in familiarly antagonistic roles against those who showed Mary due reverence, and making these images available for easy dissemination, monks in England helped to further consolidate the dichotomy between Christian and Jew more generally, as Marian devotion rose to prominence in subsequent centuries. Thanks to Mary's growing importance in medieval society, the Jews quickly came to seem inimicable not just to Mary herself but to her devotees. "They were Mary's enemies and so the enemies of each and every Christian," writes Rubin.[2] Jews were no longer just to be seen as passive unbelievers; they were active threats to Mary's growing number of followers. We might consider that English monks helped advance a particular language about Jews—a language of violence and antagonism that was then transmitted beyond the monastery walls. It was expressed in hymns, architecture, paintings, sermons, treatises, and stories, all with a view toward praising Mary. Wherever these were reproduced, recited, and repeated, their message of Marian mercy and Jewish danger, of belonging and exclusion, was reinforced.

The tendency to see Jews as willfully violent toward Mary and her followers raises an interesting question about the culture in which such images were developed, and from which they were then circulated.[3] The compilers and redactors of the miracles shared the same circles as the theologians who were interested in the hermeneutic possibilities of presenting the Jewish position in their work. The Jews in these treatises were useful as "devil's advocates," but only in a metaphoric sense; in the miracles, they really did advocate for Satan himself.[4] There seems at first to be a fundamental disjunct between the fact that learned men so committed to rational exploration could at the same time make up wild stories about Jewish violence toward children, clerics, and images of the Virgin. Scholars have tended to draw clear lines between the "rational anti-Judaism" of the polemical literature from "irrational anti-Semitism" of legends.[5] The first is presumably the domain of intellectuals, men like Anselm who dedicated themselves to the pursuit of reason. The second was the result of irrational or "chimerical" visions of Jews that "became embedded in the mentality of millions of normally rational Christians," in the words of Gavin Langmuir.[6] This book has shown that a rational mind-set did not preclude a love of the legendary. The image of Jews in the miracle stories—nefarious, sacrilegious, dangerous, and violent—could coexist happily with the "hermeneutic Jew"—the figure useful for theological argument because he rejects Christian dogma—in the minds of highly educated monks in Anselm's circles. These men who exercised their reason in the writing of theological treatises also perpetuated myths about Jewish behavior that had no known grounding in reality. We might understand this seeming incongruity by considering that both images of Jews—irrational and rational—were contrasted with the right thinker and right doer, the monastic

Marian devotee who expressed his allegiance to Mary and Christ in theological reflection as well as in nonrational forms, such as liturgy and devotional practice; both were ultimately expressions of one and the same faith. In fact, images and narratives of Jewish doubt often served to graphically illustrate points of theology (as in the Eucharistic debates), transcending the boundaries of the legendary and functioning as empirical evidence, hence participating in the same symbolic system. As such, the two figures of the Jew were the product of the same cultural context, shared by a common circle of monks, for whom liturgy, theology, and literature were merely different strands of one religious endeavor and forwarded their particular conception of theological truth and proper devotion at the expense of those who did not comply with it.[7]

So were the Jews presented in the Marian materials thought of as "real Jews"? Did monks and the audiences to whom these sources were disseminated really think that Jews, in addition to refusing the virgin birth, committed the acts of infanticide, murder, and violence depicted in them? It is difficult to peer behind the veil of rhetoric at the thoughts of the monks discussed here, although we have hints that their concerns about the presence and activities of Jews in contemporary society were real. The popularity of the legends certainly opened up the possibility that such fears could spread and be applied to Jews in society. As Rubin has pointed out, "The argument was that just as Jews acted *then* [in this case, the fictional context of the stories], they still act *now*."[8] The twelfth century saw the emergence of rumors about Jewish violence against Christians that took various forms. It was briefly mentioned in the final chapter that the actual abuse by Jews of waxen images in rituals of desecration was first alleged in the mid-twelfth century, in a number of sources from Italy, Germany, and France, soon after the Toledo story was in circulation. With considerably more impact, however, was the first-ever accusation of the ritual murder of a Christian child by a community of Jews, leveled in the 1150s by Thomas of Monmouth in his *Vita et Passio Willelmi Norwicensis*.[9] The text set out to explain how a young boy and tanner's apprentice, William, was abducted by the Jews of Norwich in 1144, subjected to tortures resembling crucifixion, and dumped in the woods nearby. Thomas was a newcomer to the monastic community of Norwich Cathedral in the 1150s, and became interested in the story of William's death in his attempt to develop a cult of the boy as Norwich's own saint and martyr. Although the accusation against the Jews was not generally believed in Norwich itself, it spread and was repeated numerous times over the next centuries, first in England, and soon after in France and Germany. Intriguingly, the first account from Norwich that described William's abuse at the hands of the Jews contains echoes of several Marian miracle stories: the Jewish boy thrown in the oven for having taken communion, crucifixion of the waxen image in Toledo in derision of Christ's crucifixion, and attempts of the Toulousan Jews—like their Norwich counterparts in the *Passio*—to bribe the authorities.[10] Thomas even included the same report of the Jewish leader in Narbonne that William of Malmesbury recorded in his version of the Toledo story. Sharing the same monastic circles as those individuals who first compiled the miracle accounts, it would hardly be surprising that Thomas was inspired by what he heard about Jewish behavior from listening to the vivid tales.[11]

The path from myth to accepted fact is nonetheless slippery. How and why people come to believe things without any factual evidence is not a straight-forward process. David Nirenberg has been wise to warn that "any inherited discourse about minorities acquired force only when people chose to find it meaningful and useful and it was itself reshaped by these choices. . . . [S]uch discourses about minorities was but one of those available and its invocation in a given situation did not ensure its acceptance."[12] In the case of the ritual mur-der accusation, not all of Norwich's monastic community believed the charges, nor should we imagine a credulous population ready to jump at the first men-tion of Jewish wickedness in order to satisfy some latent hatred of difference. If anything, the ways in which the stories were altered illustrate that what later came to be stereotypes were at one point carefully crafted to speak to a particu-lar context. Still, in the very act of hearing, retelling, and internalizing these images of antagonism, through years of exposure to liturgy, sermons, and art, there was a risk that an underlying belief might develop that what they said about Jews was true. Once part of the collective imagination, narratives such as those that appear in the miracle collections could then be mobilized for a given purpose with the understanding that they would considerably worsen public perception of Jews in a given situation, thus becoming part of an arsenal of rhetorical weapons with which to inflict damage on Jews, if and when the need arose. We cannot underestimate the potential power of the kinds of images examined in this book to inform ideas about what Jews were at least *capable* of doing.

The ritual murder accusation illuminates how inherited narratives could be made useful in special circumstances. Formulated for the first time in a mind filled with the kinds of stories found in the miracle collections, its purpose at the outset was to support and forward the cult of a local saint. Yet it took on a life of its own; Thomas may have wanted to believe the rumors about the Jews of Norwich because he desperately wanted a martyr, but in writing as if they were true, he irreparably damaged the perception of Jews for his contempo-raries. "Narrative has a mimetic function: narrative prefigures and refigures ac-tion," giving sense to violence in local frames of reference, writes Rubin.[13] The charge of ritual murder was certainly used to explain the death and disappear-ance of other children and adults. It was even put to use in justifying Europe's first-ever expulsion of Jews from a territory: the Île-de-France by Phillip Au-gustus in 1182.[14] Although we do not know that anyone actually believed the charge to be valid in this case, it cannot have been intended to fall on deaf ears.

In providing a template for Jewish behavior called on by anyone who wished to justify anti-Jewish action, the narratives discussed in this book may have created fertile ground for the acceptance of such accusations; over thirty Jewish men and women were burned at Blois in 1171 because presumably some people believed them capable of killing a Christian child. Images take on meaning in the contexts in which they are deployed—"discourse and agency gain meaning only in relation to each other," as Nirenberg puts it—and the ones encoded by early twelfth-century English monks were at risk of being interpreted in ways that went far beyond their initial scope.[15]

This is not a story about the clerical control of images in the Middle Ages, although it is about how these images were shaped in monasteries.[16] The idea that images were the domain of a select few, to be manipulated at the will of those who recorded and interpreted them, is only partly true when applied to the fashioning of ideas about Jews in early twelfth-century monastic culture. The notion of control comes uncomfortably close to the idea of propaganda, implying that the process was purposeful and that English monks consciously set out to disseminate a particular understanding of Jews because that was their intention. It has become apparent that the means by which such a thing occurred were far more complex. It included a renewal of cultural expressions in Benedictine monasticism. Part of this involved the proper commemoration of the Virgin, with Mary acting as a figurehead for English monks and nuns in liturgy and prayer. There was also an emphasis on literary production, especially hagiographic, that turned to Mary just as it turned to the Anglo-Saxon saints. The context was one of conquest and occupation, in which certain local customs were challenged and justifications were sought using current theological trends. We also see an impulse to argue theological problems dialectically, notably among them the Incarnation and virgin birth. Within many of these elements, we find Jews inscribed: in the apocryphal literature that informed the liturgy, liturgical sources that inspired the art and architecture, polemical literature that sparked debate as it recorded it, and sermons and miracle stories that shared old narratives made new. The Jews were there, in all these sources, not to say something about Judaism, so much as to highlight the perceived truth of Christianity in all its manifold expressions (liturgy, theology, art, and literature). The intention was to glorify the Virgin, but it just so happened that Jews were part of her story. As Mary's star rose, so fell the Jew, such that wherever she rejoiced, the "miserable Jew blushed with shame," as went the song.[17]

Mary's popularity continued to rise in the mid-twelfth century, where this book ends. The sources I have discussed—theological treatises, sermons, miracle stories, and liturgical texts—had a long and successful afterlife as Mary was increasingly understood to be a universal queen, shared among all spheres of medieval society. The liturgical practices became widespread and transcended the monastic milieu to become standard customs: the Little Office became the basic text of Books of Hours, which began to appear in the early thirteenth century; and the Conception feast spread, as did the feast of Anne, becoming incredibly popular in urban centers in the fourteenth and fifteenth centuries.[18] The theological arguments for the Immaculate Conception were taken up in the thirteenth-century universities, while the doctrine of the bodily Assumption gained widespread approval thanks to the visions of the late twelfth-century German nun Elizabeth of Schönau. New polemics that defended the Incarnation and virgin birth against the Jews were written in France by prominent thinkers like Peter Abelard, Peter the Venerable, and Walter of Châtillon, among many others.[19] The Marian miracle collections perhaps had the most widespread success, first rewritten in verse by Nigel of Canterbury and translated into Anglo-Norman by Adgar of London.[20] The universal nature of the collections—with stories set everywhere in the world—ensured their appeal and longevity not just in England but throughout Europe as well. Having first crossed the channel into France, where they were versified in French by Gautier de Coincy, they also made their way to the Low Countries, where Caesarius of Heisterbach appropriated them for the Cistercian cause, and to Spain, where in the thirteenth century, Gonzalo de Berceo composed his Castillian translation and King Alfonso X of Castile set them to music in his enormous Galician-Portuguese *Cantigas de Santa Maria*.[21] Several individual miracles were incorporated into the *Golden Legend*, ensuring their ongoing popularity in sermons disseminated to even wider audiences.[22]

Even more strikingly, we get further glimpses of that slippery slope between rhetoric and reality. Matthew Paris used his chronicle of circa 1250 to accuse a Jew named Abraham, a moneylender form Berkhamsted, of desecrating an image of Mary and then murdering his wife when she tried to rescue it from the latrine.[23] The anecdote can be traced to real individuals, but is also inflected with the miraculous tales of Jews desecrating Marian images and attacking her devotees. We can see Matthew's narrative as part of wider social processes; in the mid-thirteenth century, Henry III dedicated his *Domus conversorum*, the house for converted Jews, to Mary, and in 1240, the Talmud was placed on trial in Paris at least in part for containing blasphematory material against Mary and her son.[24] By this point, the imagined antagonism between the Jews and Mary was having very real consequences. The legacy of the Marian sources therefore deserves far greater attention for the ways in which they shaped attitudes toward Jews.[25] It is beyond the scope of this book, however, to look past the English shores to France, Spain, Germany, and eastern Europe, where these materials traveled and flourished. Still, it has great promise for a wider study that would allow the full complexity of the connection between Mary and the Jews to be explored in different regions of Europe and over the *longue durée*.

Notes

||||||||||||

Introduction

1. This has been remarked notably in Rubin 2009a; 2009b, 158–76.

2. Cunningham 1999; Shoemaker 1999.

3. This was the case in the large number of Christian treatises articulated against the Jews, surveyed in Williams 1935; Dahan 1990; Cohen 1999.

4. Corrigan 1992.

5. Fassler 2009.

6. Remensnyder 2014.

7. Fulton 2002; Rubin 2009a, 2009c. For another major cultural study, see Pelikan 1996. For a more theological study, see Graef 2009.

8. Clayton 1990.

9. This is through the Old Hispanic Office project funded by the European Research Council at the University of Bristol, where I am working with Emma Hornby and Rebecca Maloy on the Marian liturgy in early medieval Iberia. My gratitude goes out to them and the entire team.

10. Cf. Morgan 1999.

11. Clark 2007, 9.

12. There is little surviving Marian material from Augustinian houses, as noted in Morgan 1999, 119. On the importance of southern English houses, see Burton 1994, 17.

13. Barrow 1994, 25–39.

14. Clark 2007, 147. For a list of the manuscripts produced in English monasteries, see Ker 1969, which can be supplemented by Gameson 1999.

15. Tinti 2015.

16. Knowles 1943, 147.

17. Reilly, forthcoming. My sincere thanks to Diane Reilly for sharing her unpublished material. For previous assessments of Bernard's Mariology, see Roschini 1953.

18. Waddel 1999, 124–29. This tempers, for example, Leclercq 1954.

19. Ibid., 129.

20. On Cistercian readings, see Martimort 1992, 97–100; Webber 2010, 41. For an introduction to the Benedictine material, see Leclercq 1952.

21. Roper 1993; Morgan 1999; Gransden 2004; Pfaff 2009; Heslop 1981, 2001, 2005. Another formative scholar was Edmund Bishop (1918a, 1918b). Helpful in identifying additional sources have been Ker 1969; Gameson 1999.

22. Lamy 2000; Fulton 2002; Mayr-Harting 2004.

23. Southern 1958; Ward 1982. Rachel Koopmans (2011, 93, 101) only briefly mentioned them.

24. The authorship exercised by English monks in the Latin collections was perhaps not emphasized enough in a recent doctoral dissertation by Jennifer Shea (2004), who nevertheless did remark on the critical role attributed to Jews in the miracle stories collected in Anglo-Norman England.

25. Rubin 2009c, 164. See also Rubin 2009b.

26. The "hermeneutic Jew" is a term that has become popular in the scholarship on medieval Christian ideas about Judaism. See, for example, Markus 1995; Cohen 1999, especially 3. For the term's history, see ibid., 3n3.

27. Most recently, see Shuve, forthcoming. My thanks to Karl for letting me see this before publication.

28. Heisy 2013.

29. Scheck 2008, 97.

30. On Odo, see Cousin 1949. On Odilo, see Garand 1979. On William of Volpiano, see Gazeau and Gouillet 2008. On Odilo's reforming activities, see ibid., 110–15; Bulst 1984; Diard 2003, 206. See also Gazeau 2000, 135. On Peter, see Fulton 2002, 124–25.

31. Clayton 1990, 137.

32. For a summary of the arguments, which are too numerous to mention in their totality, see Chibnall 1999; Bates 2005.

33. The sheer number of monks and nuns grew exponentially, from perhaps a thousand in 1066 to about ten times that in 1200. See Constable 1996, 89. On bishops, see Bethell 1969; Brooke 1975; Brooke and Brooke 1999.

34. Barlow 1979, 190. See also Burton 1994, 21–28.

35. For their biographies, see Gibson 1978; Southern 1990.

36. See especially the work of Antonia Gransden, but also Rodney M. Thomson (1983, 7–9), writing in response to Richard Southern (1970). On book production, see the summary in Thomson 1983, 15–17; Gameson 1999, 5–8. With reference to individual monastic houses, see ibid., 14–19. This was not limited to England, however, as emphasized by Teresa Webber (1997).

37. See Koopmans 2011. On the relationship between liturgy and hagiography, see Parkes 2014.

38. Noted in Abou-el-Haj 1983; Chibnall 2000; Hayward 1998, 2004, 2005; Thomas 2005; Yarrow 2006; Bates 2014.

39. Winterbottom 2010; Afanasayev 2013; Thomson 2015.

40. Although articulated negatively, this was noted by Southern (1970), and countered to some extent by Thomson (1983) and G. R. Evans (2007). The subject has had renewed interest, such as in Clark 2007.

41. Highlighted in Ortenberg 1992.

42. Constable 1996, especially 6.

43. Cf. ibid., 7.

44. Stephen Vanderputten (2013) is nevertheless wise to warn us that reform is rarely the result of single enterprising individuals, but a process undertaken over generations.

45. For Anselm's attitude toward simony as well as monastic ownership of property, see Gasper and Gullbekk 2012, 159–60.

46. The councils of 1125, 1127, and 1129 all centered on the problem of clerical marriage, in addition to canons issued in 1076, 1102, and 1108 on the matter; additionally, forty-four of the sixty-nine papal decretals of the twelfth and thirteenth centuries referring to clerical celibacy were related to England. Cf. Whitelock, Brett, and Brooke 1981; Parish 2010, 106–8. On this question, see also Brooke 1956a, 1956b.

47. Constable 1996, 93–94, 229.

48. Ibid., 199–208.

49. Fassler 1985.

50. Clayton 1990, 138–39.

51. For a description, see Forsyth 1972.

52. Clayton 1990, 139–41. This study argues that the evidence for ascribing it an earlier date of 1061 is tenuous, based on Dickinson 1956.

53. For the place of liturgy among reforming ideals, see Waddell 1991.

54. Cf. Shea 2004.

55. The public performance of prayer in the liturgy was not discussed in ibid.

56. Fulton 2002.

57. Brooke 1956a, 3; Parish 2010, 108–13.

58. Huntington 2003; Bale 2009; Goscelin 2004; Slocum and Brown 2012.

59. For other similar trends in Germany, see especially Power 2001. See also Mews 2001. On the genre, see Newman 1995; Morton and Wogan-Browne 2003. For its influence on the Marian cult, see Barlow 1979, 195.

60. See Kauffmann 2001; Fulton 2006.

61. For the digitized manuscript, see http://www.bl.uk/manuscripts/Viewer.aspx?ref =lansdowne_ms_383_f002r (accessed February 21, 2016). See also Kauffmann 2001, 267–69; Thomson 1982, 125; Pfaff 2009, 342.

62. Geddes 2005.

63. On the scarcity of sources from women's religious houses in the twelfth and thirteenth centuries, see Thompson 1991. Although Anne Bagnall Yardley (2006) has done much to illuminate the musical lives of nuns in England, most of the evidence she cites is from the later medieval period.

64. On the higher literacy rates in England compared to other areas, see Baun 2004.

65. Yardley 2006.

66. Warner 1976.

67. William of Malmesbury 1998, 563. See also Golb 1984, 1998.

68. Hyamson 1928; Roth 1951; Lipman 1984; Susser 1993; Hillaby 1995, 2003.

69. See Stacey 1995. See also Mundill 2010; Abulafia 2013.

70. Mundill 2010.

71. Abulafia 2011, 2013.

72. See, for example, the studies collected in Jones and Watson 2013.

73. Schäfer 2007; Schäfer, Meerson, and Deutsch 2011. See also Biale 1999.

74. Jordan 1992.

75. Abulafia 1985, 2011; Rubin 2009b, 165–67. For more on these sources, see Chazan 1987, 2002.

76. Resnick 1996, 97.

77. Yuval 2006. An exception might be found in a story about the Jews of Toulouse by William of Malmesbury (2015, 28), who accuses a Jewish character of calling Jesus a wizard and Christians worshippers of ashes, which could refer to the Toledot Yeshu tradition or Alenu prayer, discussed in chapter 4. This was suggested by Anna Sapir Abulafia (2011), 198–99. For more see chapter 4.

78. For this tradition, see chapter 2.

79. Scheil 2004, 3. For after the expulsion, see Bale 2007.

80. Anna Sapir Abulafia (1993) articulated the link between reforming ideals and the condemnation of Jewish beliefs and practice for Rupert of Deutz and Hermann of Tournai.

81. Iogna-Prat 2002.

82. This is discussed more in the conclusion.

83. Vanderputten 2012, 242. This relates mostly to rituals as demonstrations of power, be they episcopal or royal, which have been the main focus of attention of scholars of medieval ritual. His observation could nevertheless also relate to the more regular elements of the liturgy, such as the celebration of feast days and performance of votive offices.

84. For context and bibliography, see Adams and Hanska 2015, especially the introduction, 1–20. Cohen (1984, 2002) has also explored preaching, though not exclusively or extensively. Frizzell and Henderson (2005) look at the liturgical use of the Hebrew Bible, passing over the fact that it would not have been considered Jewish by Christian practitioners.

85. This was attempted in Abulafia 2002b, especially 2002a; Cohen 2002. See also Chazan 1997, 2004; Langmuir, 1990a, 1990b, 1992. The importance of theological polemics has been stressed through the work of Abulafia; see chapter 2. Scholars almost universally assume a downturn or hardening in Christian attitudes toward Jews during the twelfth and thirteenth centuries, which they seek to explain, although some are attempting to rethink it (Elukin 2009).

86. Rubin 1991, 1992, 2004.

87. These issues lie at the heart of the studies in Gittos and Hamilton 2016. Constable (1994) nevertheless emphasizes the use of both vernacular and Latin in preaching, and studies are suggesting that the liturgical use of the vernacular was more widespread than previously thought (Lenker 2005; Symes 2016).

88. This was argued also for miracle collections in Koopmans 2011.

89. Gittos 2016, 23.

90. Bradford Bedingfield 2005; Symes 2016. On the dramatic and participatory dimension of medieval dramatic ritual, see the seminal work of Flanigan (1991, 2001) and Flanigan, Ashley, and Sheingorn 2005.

91. These tendencies are addressed in Gittos 2016, 13–14, bibliography.

92. See the articles by Hamilton, Chave-Mahir, Birkedal Bruun, and Hamilton in Gittos and Hamilton 2016. For an instructive defense of the study of the liturgy, see Gittos 2013a, 8–1, 2016; Gittos and Bradford Bedingfield 2005. On liturgy as constructing institutional identity, see especially Boynton 2006; Fassler 2009.

Chapter 1: Praising Mary:
Liturgy and Prayer

1. Discussed in Leclercq 1961.

2. Boynton 2007. Echoed in Parkes 2014, 132.

3. On the place of the Psalms in monastic culture, see Dyer 1999.

4. On the mediation of the Bible via sermons, see Poleg 2013, 152–97.

5. The similarities between the Divine Office and private devotion are underscored in Black 2001.

6. On the liturgy as transmitting faith, see Palazzo 1998. On the liturgy as mediating the Bible, see Boynton 2011; Poleg 2013, 14–58.

7. Morgan 1999.

8. Roper 1993, 47.

9. Clayton 1990.

10. Clayton 1990, 128–29; Gransden 2004, 629–33. Compiled with the help of Knowles and Hadcock 1971. For the building of smaller, secondary Marian churches, see Blair 2005, 200.

11. Clayton 1990, 135.

12. On the early development of Marian feasts, see Maître 1996, 47; Jeffery 1995, 217; Palazzo and Andrews Johansson 1996, 17–18; Fassler 2001; Avner 2011; Bradshaw and Johnson 2011, 212; Shoemaker 2008a, 2008b. For their history in Rome, see Klauser 1972, especially 123; Guilmard 1994; Palazzo and Andrews Johansson 1996, 16; Pfisterer 2002, 121; MacGregor 2008. On the origins of the Conception and Presentation feasts, see Kishpaugh 1941; van Dijk 1954.

13. Some proponents of the "rupture" theory of the Norman Conquest, with respect to the English church, have been Frank Stenton (1943, articulated at 664), David Knowles (1966, 119), Southern (1966, 246–53), John Scott (1981, 3), Antonia Gransden (1974, 105–6), and Arnold William Klukas (1984, 138–40). For a summary of the arguments, see Brett 1981, 125. For the corrected view, see Ridyard 1987; Gransden 1989; Gibson 1995, 42–45; Heslop 1995; Pfaff 2009; Koopmans 2011, 89.

14. Gittos 2013b, 45–49. See also Hiley 1993. For a tempered view, see Pfaff 1992b; 2009, especially 123–24.

15. "Multaque de Christianae religionis cultu servanda instituit." Whitelock, Brett, and Brooke 1981, 597, 607. See also Brett 1975.

16. Vaughn 1981b, 100.

17. Heslop 1995, 53–62. Richard Pfaff (1992b, 104) refers to these as "distinctively Anglo-Saxon." For the Presentation feast, see Kishpaugh 1941.

18. Heslop 1995, 57–59; Rubenstein 1999, 295; Gittos 2013b, 48.

19. See especially Hayward 1998.

20. Macray 1863, 96.

21. On this episode, see Hiley 1986.

22. Ridyard 1987, 205.

23. Barrow 1992; Rubenstein 1999; Thomas 2005, especially at 293; Yarrow 2006; Koopmans 2011, 102–6.

24. Rubenstein 1999.

25. Compare this to dedications to Peter (7), the Trinity (5), and Nicholas (5), as the next top three between 1066 and 1100, and James (14), the Trinity (10), and Peter (9) between 1101 and 1150. These data do not include Cistercian institutions, which were all dedicated to the Virgin. See Binns 1989, 18–27.

26. Lanfranc 2002, 82–83. On its use at Westminster, St. Albans, Evesham, Eynsham, Durham, St. Augustine's, Rochester, Dover, Christ Church, Battle, and various others, see Klukas 1984. For reservations, see Lanfranc 2002, xxxi. Even if present at other houses, they were not necessarily followed closely; see Pfaff 2009, 118, 157.

27. Gittos 2013a, 47, 112–22.

28. Epistle 41, in Anselm of Canterbury 1990, 234.

29. Articulated in Bishop 1918a, but also noted in Gasquet and Bishop 1908, 43–53; Fournée 1984, 713; Haney 1986, 38.

30. Pfaff 1992b, 104.

31. From calendars in the late eleventh century, Oxford Bodleian Library (hereafter Bodl.) MS 579; Corpus Christi College, Cambridge (hereafter CCCC) MS 391. See also Davis 1954, 380; Clayton 1990, 44–46.

32. The earliest post–Norman Conquest Christ Church calendar is in Oxford Bodl. Add. MS C. 260. See also Lawrence 1982, 106.

33. British Library (hereafter BL) Arundel MS 60; Wormald 1946, 141–53; Gameson 1999, 95. See also Oxford Bodl. Auctarium MS D. 2. 4; Coates 1999, 49; BL Cotton MS Nero C. iv. Relatedly, see Haney 1986. The artwork in the latter manuscript nevertheless betrays an interest in the theme, as will be discussed later in this book.

34. CCCC MS 146. See also Gameson 1999, 61; Pfaff 2009, 122. For its history, see Teviotdale 1992, 408.

35. The lack of liturgical manuscripts from this period makes it particularly difficult to draw conclusions, as frequently repeated in Hiley 1994.

36. For Eadmer's biography, see Southern 1966, 229–40. See also Southern 1990, 404–22.

37. On Eadmer's attitude toward minor saints, see Rubenstein 1999; Koopmans 2011, 102–6. For his role as precentor, see Fassler 1985.

38. Rubenstein 1999.

39. "Mihi considerare volenti occurrit hodierna solemnitas, quae de conceptione beatae Matris Dei Mariae multis in locis festiva recolitur. Et quidem priscis temporibus frequentiori usu celebrabatur, ab iis praecipue in quibus pura simplicitas et humilior in Deum vigebat devotio. At ubi et major scientia et praepollens examinatio rerum mentes quorumdam imbuit et erexit, eamdem solemnitatem, spreta pauperum simplicitate, de medio sustulit; et eam quasi ratione vacantem redegit in nihil. . . . Quorum sententia eo maxime in robur excrevit quod ii, qui eam protulerunt, saeculari et ecclesiastica auctoritate divitiarumque abundantia praeeminebant. . . . [F]estum scilicet de conceptione ipsius sacratissimae dominae sua qua se pollere gloriabantur auctoritatis ratione abolere non timuerunt." Eadmer of Canterbury 1904, 1, 5.

40. For a summary of these arguments, see Lamy 2000, 19. See also Corbin 1967, 433.

41. Eadmer of Canterbury 1962, 50.

42. Lanfranc 2002, xxix.

43. Found in Elliott 1993. See also Smid 1965, 11, 22–23; Gijsel and Beyers 1997. For the earliest testimony of the *libellus*, see Fulbert of Chartres, *Approbate consuetudinis* sermon, in *Patrologia Latina* (henceforth PL) 141:322. Cf. Gijsel and Beyers, 140–46; Fassler 2009, 81–82. For its attribution to Paschasius, see Lamy 2000, 31.

44. "Benedictio in die conceptionis sanctae Mariae: Caelestium carismatum inspirator terrenarumque mentium reparator, qui beatam Dei genitricem, angelico concipiendam praeconavit oraculo, vos benedictionum suarum ubertate dignetur locupletare et virtutum floribus. Amen." BL Harley MS 2892, f. 161. For a transcription, see Eadmer of Canterbury 1904, appendix D. On this manuscript, see Pfaff 2009, 92–93.

45. Clayton 1998. For Aelfric's reaction, see Clayton 1990, 244. See also Clayton 1986, especially 287; 1998.

46. Cf. Vaughn 1981a, 190. Of course, the Assumption feast also had apocryphal roots, but had been part of the liturgical calendar for centuries across western Europe, contrary to the Conception.

47. The *Protevangelium* is found in the Glastonbury manuscript, Oxford, Balliol College MS 240, ff. 107v–9r. The *Pseudo-Matthew* is in BL Cotton MS Nero E. I, ff. 116v–18, from Worcester. On this second manuscript, see Jackson and Lapidge 1996. The Malmesbury manuscript is in Oxford Bodl. MS 852, a collection of Saints' Lives, to which was added a Latin version of the *Gospel of Pseudo-Matthew* (ff. 68–72v) in the twelfth century.

48. For the Bury manuscript (Cambridge, Pembroke College MS 25 [P]), Gransden 2004, 642–43; Webber 1998, 188; Clayton 1998, 129–30.

49. Clayton 1998, 138, 165–91. See also Clayton 1986.

50. Younge 2013, 112–13.

51. The extract of Haymo of Halberstadt's universal history dealing with the life of Anne is found in Cambridge St. John's College MS 35 [B. 13]. Thomas N. Hall (2002, especially 113–14) attributes this work to the abbacy of Baldwin (†1097), although Teresa Webber (2014a, 185) has placed this section in the early twelfth century. For the *Trinubium*'s origins, see Iogna-Prat 1996, 74. For its interest in terms of Mary's incorporation into biblical genealogies, see Geary 2006, 71–72.

52. Eadmer of Canterbury 1904, 1.

53. "Istius vero tempore coepit primum celebrari apud nos in Anglia solemnitas conceptionis beatae genitricis Mariae." Hart 1863, 1:15.

54. Luard 1869, 377. Most of the Worcester annals are actually a copy of a Winchester manuscript in a thirteenth-century hand. The entry for the Conception feast does not appear in this manuscript at all, suggesting that it was an interpolation by the Worcester scribe who copied the original. Cf. ibid., xxxv; Hart 1863. These references were first noted in Bishop 1918a.

55. "Ipso anno primum coepit celebrari apud nos solennitas concepiionis sanctae Mariae." Hayward 2010.

56. Vacandard 1897; Bouman 1958, 128–30. For a summary of the arguments, see Lamy 2000, 36–37. For arguments against them, see Fournée 1960, 164.

57. The Sherborne Cartulary (BL Add. MS 46487, f. 71) from circa 1146 contains a prayer specifically for the Conception feast. On this manuscript, see Pfaff 2009, 176–79. At St. Augustine's, a martyrology from circa 1100 (BL Cotton MS Royal 2 B. iv, f. 153ᵛ)

refers to the Conception feast, although there is no accompanying text. On this manuscript, see Gameson 1999, 105; Pfaff 2009, 117. At Ely, two calendars produced by the end of the twelfth century both contain the feast (Trinity College, Cambridge, MS 1105 [O.2.1], f. 12ᵛ; BL Arundel MS 377, f. 5ᵛ). On these calendars, see Wormald 1946, 19. On the manuscripts, see ibid., 1–7.

58. These are BL Cotton MS Tiberius B. iii, f. 7ᵛ; Trinity College Cambridge MS 987 (R.17.1), f. 4 (the "Eadwine Psalter,"); Oxford Bodl. Add. MS C. 260, f 6ᵛ See Wormald 1946, 63, 79; Gasquet and Bishop 1908, 68–69 (with commentary), 116–17. See also Pfaff 1992a, 74–85; 2009, 122. All three calendars also have the Presentation feast, *Oblatio Sanctae Mariae*, falling on November 21.

59. For the St. Albans Psalter, see Geddes 2005, 89; Pächt, Dodwell, and Wormald 1960, 278–80; Thomson 1982, 1:25, 120. Three other psalters contain the feast in the calendar. See Wormald 1946, 45; Thomson 1982, 101. On Geoffrey more generally, see Thomson 1982, 20–22.

60. For the appearance of the feast in calendars, see Wormald 1946, 30 (Abingdon–Cambridge University Library (hereafter CUL) MS Kk. i. 22, f. 7), 111 (Chester–Oxford Bodl. Tanner MS 169, f. 14); 19 (Ely–BL Harley MS 547, f. 7; Cambridge Trinity College Library MS O. 2. 1, f. 13; Milan Biblioteca Nazionale Braidense MS AF XI. 9, f. 4), 38 (Evesham–Oxford Bodl. Barlow MS 41, f. 163b; B: Add. MS 44874, f. 5v), 55 (Gloucester–Oxford Jesus College MS 10, f. 6v), 75 (Westminster–Oxford Bodl. Rawlinson MS lit. g. 10, f. 6v; BL Royal MS 2. A. xxii, f. 10v).

61. The feast is found in the calendar of the Winchester Psalter (BL Cotton MS Nero C. iv; Wormald 1973), and several calendars from St. Augustine's Canterbury (see Wormald 1946, 47–48, 61).

62. Gransden 2004, 644.

63. See chapter 3.

64. Ibid., 647. He is credited with developing the scriptorium as well; see MacLachlan 1986.

65. "Anselmus duas apud nos solemnitates instituit, scilicet conceptionem sanctae Mariae quae iam in multis ecclesiis per ipsum celebriter observatur, et commemorationem eius in adventu quam Hildefonsus episcopus instituit." Gransden 1973, 122.

66. On this feast, see Garcia Rodriguez 1966; Fassler 2013; Ihnat, forthcoming b.

67. Sharpe, Carley, and Thomson 1996, 53, 79. On Anselm's development of the Bury library, see Thomson 1972, 630–36; Webber 2014a. Other monasteries also had copies of Ildefonsus's treatise—for example, Glastonbury—although there is no parallel evidence for the celebration of the Old Hispanic feast day. Cf. Sharpe, Carley, and Thomson 1996, 193–94.

68. The calendar is found in BL Cotton MS Cleopatra B. iii, f. 42v. See also Gransden 2004, 647n100; 2007, 108.

69. Gransden 1973, 96–99. See also Gransden 2004, 648–49.

70. Ibid.

71. On Osbert's biography, see J. Armitage Robinson to Osbert of Clare in Osbert of Clare 1929, 1–20; Mason 1996, 89–91; Briggs 2004b, 3–61.

72. These are found in one single manuscript probably from Osbert's lifetime: BL Cotton MS Vitellius A. xvii; see Osbert of Clare 1929. On the dating of the manuscript, see Briggs 2004b, 3, 7–10, 194–96.

73. In Epistle 1, Osbert of Clare (1929, 47) says himself: "If my appointment had prevailed with the king" (*si mea olim coram rege praevaluisset electio*), indicating that he had been put forward and it seems elected for the position by the monks. For Osbert's exile, see Epistle 4, in Osbert of Clare 1929, 8 (translation), 60, and Mason 1996, 33; Briggs 2004a.

74. On Osbert's attempts to promote Westminster, see Briggs 2004b, 42–54. For his involvement in forgery, see ibid., 55–97. On Edward's canonization, see Mason 1996, 89.

75. Osbert composed a number of hagiographic texts, all for Anglo-Saxon saints: Edburga (for Ely), Edmund (for Bury St. Edmunds), Aethelbricht (for Hereford), and Edward the Confessor (for Westminster). See Briggs 2004b, 22–23.

76. Epistle 7, in Osbert of Clare 1929, 65.

77. Ibid.

78. This led Marielle Lamy (2000, 38–39) to question Osbert's discussion about the feast in his letter.

79. "Nos tamen coepto diei insistentes officio cum gaudio gloriosam festivitatem exegimus et solenni tripudio. Postremo vero aemuli mei et qui canino dente bona invidentes rodunt aliorum, qui vanas suas ineptias semper nituntur approbare, et dicta et facta religiosorum moliuntur improbare, nescientes secundum apostolum neque quae loquuntur neque de quibus affirmant, evomuere venenum iniquitatis suae, et in me sagittas linguae pestiferae iaculantes asseverarunt tenendam non esse festivitatem cuius primordia Romanae ecclesiae non habent auctoritatem." Epistle 7, in Osbert of Clare 1929, 65–67. Translation slightly adapted from Robinson 1911, 12.

80. "Cumque usu atque experimento consuetudines Romanae noveritis ecclesiae, si quid aliquando in ea dignum auctoritate de hac genitricis Dei veneranda conceptione vel potuit vel poterit inveniri per vos nobis petimus revelari." Epistle 7, in Osbert of Clare 1929, 65.

81. Bayo 2004, 857.

82. Charter 112, in Douglas 1932, 112–13.

83. "Quoniam diligentia sollicitudinis vestrae per diversa mundi spatia multos ad amorem beatae et gloriosae Dei genitricis Mariae ferventer accendit, quae castis visceribus perpetuae virginitatis auctorem caeli et terrae Christum dominum concepit et peperit, et in multis locis celebratur eius vestra sedulitate festa conceptio." Epistle 7, in Osbert of Clare 1929, 65.

84. John of Worcester 1995, 186.

85. Luard 1864, 45. For a look at the similarities with the Worcester Chronicle, see John of Worcester 1995, 188.

86. Two other accounts of the council—the Anglo-Saxon Chronicle and *Historia Anglorum* of Henry of Huntingdon—say nothing about the reinstatement of the feast. Cf. Whitelock, Brett, and Brooke 1981, 750; Henry of Huntingdon 1996, 482–485.

87. Epistle 7, in Osbert of Clare 1929, 67, as indicated in Bale 2009, 5. For further evidence of Anselm's political prowess, see Hahn 1991.

88. For evidence of Hugh's devotion to the Virgin, I would like to thank Thomas Waldman for sharing his essay "Hugues 'D'amiens' et la Vierge Marie" (forthcoming). On the connections between Cluny and St. Pancras, see Steiner 1993.

89. Osbert of Clare 1929, 67.

90. Fournée 1981, 125, 129, 131. See also Fournée 1960, 164. Denis Hüe (1991, 41–42) agrees. Some have argued that it would have been unusual for Hugh to himself have promoted it since he did not support the doctrine of Mary's Immaculate Conception, but this does not preclude his approval of the feast day. Cf. Burridge 1936, 574. For Osbert at Lewes, see Epistle 1, in Osbert of Clare 1929, 47.

91. It is found in several liturgical manuscripts from the abbey of Fécamp: calendars, a lectionary, a collectar, a breviary, and a missal. Cf. Fournée 1960, 164–68. The office in the breviary (Rouen, Bibliothèque municipale MS 244) is found also in a manuscript from Saint-Martin-des-Champs, which will be discussed below. Solange Corbin (1967, 418–19) recorded eight other twelfth-century offices, all from French monastic houses, including Annecy, Grand Séminaire originally from Lyon, Paris, Bibliothèque nationale de France [hereafter BnF] Latin [hereafter lat.] MS 1688 from Moissac; Verdun, Bibliothèque municipale MS 10 from Saint-Airy de Verdun; Rouen, Bibliothèque municipale MS 213 from Jumièges. On the manuscript tradition in Normandy, see Avril 1975.

92. These are: Annecy, Grand Séminaire, BnF MS lat. 1688, Verdun, Bibliothèque municipale MS 10, and BnF MS lat. 18168, respectively. These are all from the first part of the twelfth century, with all the remaining ones being from the late twelfth century, including one from Jumièges and another from Fécamp.

93. BnF MS lat. 18168, 105v–10v. On this manuscript, see Denoël 2011, 76, 85, appendix 3.

94. Saint-Martin-des-Champs was a royal priory, formerly of canons, but placed under the jurisdiction of Hugh, abbot of Cluny, who reformed the house and filled it with monks. Cf. Huguet 1859, 4–5. For the links between Cluny and Reading, see Coates 1999, 7–8. For the connections to other English monasteries, particularly as reflected in the liturgy, see Steiner 1993.

95. Freeburn 2011, 44. Matthew of Albano was seen as the ideal Cluniac, particularly by his biographer, Peter the Venerable, himself a famous abbot of Cluny; Matthew vocally opposed reformers who would restrict liturgical commemoration. Cf. Freeburn 2013, 185, 192–93.

96. For William's possible identity, see Waldman, forthcoming; Freeburn 2011, 27n9. For the Marian poem, which is also found in Worcester Cathedral Library MS F. 92, f. 286v, see Freeburn 2011, 37–38, 233. See also the corresponding entry in Thomson and Gullick 2001, 58–62; Gameson 1999, 156. Another Mariale (Paris, Mazarine 201) was produced at Saint-Martin in the twelfth century; see Barré 1967, 387.

97. The prayer is *Deus ineffabilis misericordiae*. It may have served as a source for the bull *Ineffabilis Deus*, issued by Pope Pius IX in 1854, and establishing ex cathedra the dogma of the Immaculate Conception.

98. Cambridge UL MS Ii. 4. 20, ff. 197–97v, ff. 292–92v; see Pfaff 2009, 283n33. See also Corbin 1967, 420.

99. This can be verified by comparing the chants with those found in the database on CANTUS, http://cantusdatabase.org/ (accessed February 25, 2016).

100. The hymn emphasizes Mary's Davidic lineage and her miraculous virgin motherhood, but does not discuss her conception in any great detail. BnF MS lat. 18168, f. 105v.

101. This sequence begins with the same words (*Concinat orbis*) as the sequence for a weekday after Easter Sunday, *Concinat orbis cunctus*, found in a number of eleventh- and twelfth-century manuscripts from Normandy and England, as discussed in Hiley 1993, which indicates it was Norman in origin (ibid., 153). *Concinat orbis orians* is not the same sequence but may have been related.

102. This was indicated in a comparison of the text in BnF MS lat. 18168 and the two texts mentioned in Zamberlan, n.d. While not peer-reviewed, this article nevertheless provides a useful textual comparison. For reference to the sermon, see also Canal 1962; Fassler 2009. For the diverse readings across manuscripts, see Corbin 1967, 418–19.

103. These are Rouen, Bibliothèque municipale MS 471 ff. 86v–91; Trinity College Cambridge MS 315 [B.14.30] ff. 20–22; CCCC MS 332 ff. 180–94; CCCC MS 451 ff. 189–94v. For a list of manuscripts, see Canal 1962, 42. For a list of provenances, see Gameson 1999, 64, 72.

104. The genealogy laid out in Matthew is actually that of Joseph, although theologians were attempting to reconcile it with Mary's; see Geary 2006.

105. For example, the chapter for Sext is drawn from Eccles. 24:5, 21–22. Mary's role as Wisdom is explored for earlier sources in Barker 2011.

106. "Sanctissime namque Dei genitricis corpus ante saecula ad generandum Dei saeculum praedestinarum prope finem mundi." BnF MS lat. 18168, f. 106v. Translated here in Fassler 2009, 114.

107. "Deus qui beatae Mariae virginis conceptione angelico vaticinio praedixisti praesta huic presenti familiae tuae eius praesidiis muniri cuius conceptionis sacra solemnia congrua frequentatione veneratur per dominum." BnF MS lat. 18168, f. 105v.

108. For the early development of the cult of Anne, see Kleinschmidt 1930, 13–23; Bannister 1903, 109; Leclercq 1921–53. For the Naples text, see Hall 2002, 108. The Saint-Vivant text is in Vatican MS 651, which appears to have been an addition to the original manuscript; see Wilmart 1928, 262. Studies of the later cult include Reames 2004; Brandenburg 1995; Sheingorn 2003; Sheingorn and Ashley 1990; Nixon 2004; Brusa 2012.

109. In Epistle 12, Osbert of Clare (1929, 77) quotes Simon as having said to him: "For it is almost more famous in our time for being celebrated with two privileges: I eat the solemn meal with the brothers on the first day, and the dean who is present ministers during the octave." (*Duobus enim privilegiis in observando celebrior pene nos cunctis temporibus extitit; ego praelibo solennem fratribus refectionem in die prima, decanus vero praesens luce ministrat octava.*)

110. While mentioned, these texts are not described in any great detail in Briggs 2004b, 136–37.

111. See Ihnat 2014.

112. Ibid.

113. Ibid.

114. His interest is noted in Briggs 2004b, 141–52.

115. Others include Peter Abelard to Heloise, Peter the Venerable to his nieces, Ivo of Chartres to the nuns of the monastery of Saint-Avit, and Goscelin of Saint-Bertin to the recluse, Eva. On this tradition, see Newman 1995; Morton and Wogan-Browne 2003; Goscelin of St. Bertin 2004.

116. On the literature of English nuns more generally, see Bell 1995, 2007.

117. See, for example, Prov. 31:22; cf. Ihnat 2014, 33–35.

118. Cited in Morton and Wogan-Browne 2003, 22–23.

119. "Sub gratia benedicitur, materque filias Judae domino et regi parturit Emmanuel." Ibid., 23.

120. Ibid., 40. This text was often used in late antique advice literature for virgins, such as that written by Ambrose, Augustine, and Jerome. On this tradition, see Shuve, forthcoming; Clark 1986.

121. The litany in the Shaftesbury Psalter (BL Lansdowne MS 383, ff. 146v–49v), with Anne (spelled *Agna*, but distinct from Agnes), is edited in Morgan 2013, 85.

122. For the litany in the Portiforium, see CCCC MS 391, f. 223. See also Heslop 2007, 67; Gameson 1999, 64; Pfaff 2009, especially 126–29, 226–27. The litany is not edited in Hughes 1960. Nor is it included in Morgan 2013, which nevertheless includes several thirteenth-century litanies from Worcester that also feature Anne; see ibid., 127, 131.

123. BL Cotton MS Caligula A. xiv, ff. 71^v–72^v. Although it is found in *Analecta Hymnica* (henceforth AH), 34:156, the prose text has not been discussed in conjunction with Osbert's texts. On this manuscript, see Teviotdale 1992; Heslop 2007; Jonsson 2005.

124. Frank Lawrence has pointed out that the neumes were used at centers such as Rouen, Fécamp, and Jumièges, suggesting a Norman scribe recorded the music in this part of the manuscript. My thanks goes out to Frank Lawrence for his help regarding this text, especially its music.

125. Epistle 13, in Osbert of Clare 1929, 80.

126. Nigel Morgan (2012, 26) remarked on the Evesham litany (in BL Add. MS 44874), noting the Worcester influence. For the other litanies from Winchester (Oxford Bodl. Auctarium MS D. 4. 6, ca. 1175–80), Bury St. Edmunds (BL Harley MS 5309, ca. 1250), Christ Church Canterbury (Oxford Bodl. Ashmole MS 1525, ca. 1210–20), and Carrow (Madrid Bib. Nac. MS 6422, ca. 1250–70), see, respectively, Morgan 2013, 106; 2012, 66, 74, 91. For descriptions, see Morgan 2012, 13, 15, 20. For Shrewsbury (York Cathedral Library MS XVI.O.19, ca. 1250–75) and Wilton (London, Royal College of Physicians MS, ca. 1245–55), see Morgan 2013, 92, 100. For manuscript descriptions, see Morgan 2013, 25–26, 29–30. It also appears in a late twelfth-century glossed psalter from Reading (Oxford Bodl. Auctarium MS D. 4. 6, f. 247v). See also Coates 1999, xx–xxi, 25, 48, 53–55, 59, 113, 142, 152–53.

127. The feast was added in the thirteenth century to an eleventh-century Winchester calendar (BL Cotton MS Vitellius E. xviii, f. 5; see also Wormald 1973, 162). The Evesham calendar (BL Add. MS 44874) also features the feast; cf. Wormald 1946, 33. On the mass text, added to a St. Augustine's sacramentary, see CCCC MS 270, ff. 181–81v. See also Gameson 1999, 62; Pfaff 2009, 113–17; Hall 2002, 128.

128. Osbert's texts had a considerable legacy. See Baugh 1932; Reames 2004.

129. See Heslop 2007.

130. The banner held by the angel reads *Noli timere Joachim . . . angelus Domini*. BL Cotton MS Nero C. iv, f. 4. For the image, see http://www.bl.uk/manuscripts/Viewer .aspx?ref=cotton_ms_nero_c_iv_fs004r (accessed February 26, 2016). Kristine Haney (1981; 1986, 36–46) read this image as Joachim and the angel like the one in the Caligula Troper. The figure was identified as Joseph in Witzling 1984, 20–22.

131. BL Cotton MS Nero C. iv, f. 8. For the image, see http://www.bl.uk/manuscripts/Viewer.aspx?ref=cotton_ms_nero_c_iv_fs008r (accessed February 26, 2016).

132. Klein 1998, 37.

133. Roper 1993, 42–43.

134. On the early history, see Bishop 1918b; Leclercq 1960; Hallinger 1957; Canal 1961; Clayton 1990, 68; Roper 1993, 95–96.

135. Bishop 1918b, 228; Hallinger 1957, 23; Rosenwein 1971, 139. For Marian devotion at Cluny, see Iogna-Prat 1993; Marino Malone 2005.

136. "Quicquid dicit conventus dicunt [infirmi] et ex praecepto, domni abbatis Hugonis insuper omnes horas de sancta Maria." Bernard of Cluny (1726) 1999, 1:23, 189. "Statutum est, ut sicut ex consuetudine, aliae horae sanctae Virginis matris Domini in ecclesia infirmorum, quae in honore ipsius consecrata est, quotidie decantantur, et ejusdem ibi completorium cantaretur, et in omnibus horis ante psalmos praemitteretur versus: Memento, salutis auctor, cum gloria sua. Causa instituti huius fuit, honor matri domini super omnem creaturam singulariter exhibendus, et ut quia eius horae in conventu publico propter fratrum numerositatem et officiorum multiplicatem, brevitate temporis prohibente cantari non poterant, saltem in capella ipsius a paucioribus ex integro cantarentur." Charvin 1965, 35. It is also mentioned obliquely in the Customary of Ulrich, circa 1060: "Canunt psalmodiam quae remansit, et, si voluerint, horas de S. Maria." Ulrich of Cluny PL 149:758. For the customaries more generally, see Boynton 2005.

137. Epistle 17, in Damian 1989–98, 1 1:158. An office was ascribed to him in Ulrich of Cluny PL 145:935–36, as noted in Leclercq 1960, 89. For a transcription, see Graef 2009, 206–7.

138. Epistle 142, in Damian 2004, 141.

139. For example, BnF MS lat. 13570; Avranches, Bibliothèque municipale MS 101; Monte Cassino MS 434; Vatican Library Chigi MS C VI 173. On these offices, see Leclercq 1960.

140. On the alleged decree, see Somerville 1972, 127–30.

141. "In the year of our lord 1095: Pope Urban coming to Gaul through Burgundy and Francia, in the manner of the councils, renewed and confirmed the decrees of Pope Gregory. He excommunicated Philip, king of France, who, with a living wife, took another wife of another living man. Here, the Pope celebrated a council in Clairmont, in Auvergne, in the month of November this following year, in which it was established that the Hours of Blessed Mary should be said daily, and her office performed on Saturdays. From this, the custom grew in certain churches to perform nine lessons with nine responsories and all the other necessary elements, except in Lent, or unless it is a duplex feast which has its own lessons and responsories, or on the vigils of Easter, Pentecost, All Saints, Christmas, Epiphany and the Vigils of the Apostles that have a fast, and on the feasts of the Ember Days, except during the Advent of the Lord, because on the Wednesday, *Missus est* is read, and on the Friday, *Exargens Maria*, and on Saturday, because all of them belong to the Virgin Mary; and therefore many perform on these three days dedicated to the Virgin Mary six lessons and homilies belonging to the day, which is itself of the Virgin Mary. Others perform the ferial office with one Nocturn. But do as you wish. But first, I believe it better to do as the argument of that constitution of Pope Urban in the Council of Clermont." (*Anno Domini MXCV. Urbanus Papa in Gallias veniens per Burgundiam & Franciam, habitis Conciliis, Gregorii Papae decreta renovat, & confirmat.*

Philippum Regem Franciae, qui vivente uxore alteram induxerat alterius viventis uxorem excommunicat. Hic Papa Claromonte in Arvernia Concilium celebrat mense Novembris hoc anno sequenti, in quo statutum est ut horae B. Mariae quotidie dicantur, officiumque ejus diebus Sabbati fiet. Ex quo mos in quibusdam ecclesiis inolevit, facere novem lectiones cum novem responsoriis, & aliis necessariis, nisi in Quadragesima, vel nisi adsit festum duplex, vel quod habeat lectiones & responsoria propria, vel in vigiliis Paschae, Pentecostes, Omnium Sanctorum, Nativitatis, Epiphaniae, & vigilis Apostolorum habentium jejunium, & feriis quatuor temporum, exceptis in Adventu Domini, quia in feria 4. legitur, 'Missus est,' & feria sexta exargens Maria, & Sabbato, quia omnia sunt de Virgine Maria; & ideo plures faciunt illis tribus diebus de Virgine Maria sex lectiones, & homilias de feria, quod ejusdem B. Mariae est. Alii faciunt officium feriale cum nocturno. Sed fac ut volueris. Sed primum credo melius faciendum argumento illius constitutionis Urbani Papae in Concilio Claromontensi.) Geoffrey of Vigeois 1657, 27:292–93.

142. Other sources mention only that Urban instated a particular preface of the mass for Marian feast days; cf. Somerville 1972, 129–30.

143. Symons 1953, 7–9. These antiphons, together with versicles and collects, are found in at least two eleventh-century manuscripts, from Exeter and Durham: the Leofric Collectar (BL Add. MS 2961) and Durham Collectar (Durham MS Rc. A. IV. 19). See, respectively, Roper 1993, 310, 301–2. On the former, see Pfaff 2009, 132–34.

144. Dewick 1902, ix; Clayton 1990, 65–81; Roper 1993, 65–68.

145. See Clayton 1990, 43, 68; Roper 1993, 66–68, 219, 306–7.

146. BL Cotton MS Titus D. xxvi. II. See also Roper 1993.

147. BL Cotton MS Tiberius A. iii; BL Royal MS 2. B. v. For a general discussion, see Dewick 1902, xvii, xiii–xiv. For descriptions of the manuscripts, see Roper 1993, 71–74, 303–4, 308. For a description specifically of the Tiberius manuscript—whose origins this study places at Christ Church in the mid-eleventh century—see Gneuss 1997. For the complete transcriptions and translations, see Clayton 1990, 66–76.

148. Lapidge 1991, 71.

149. Dewick 1902, xvi; Roper 1993, 72–73.

150. Roper 1993, 50, 294. Edited in Hughes 1960, II:60–61; translated in Clayton 1990, 77–78. Henri Barré (1967, 376–77) edited the readings for the matins in the office. Barré argued this office has an earlier source in Cambrai, although the manuscript he cited was produced around the same time as the Portiforium. This was pointed out by Clayton (1990, 79–81), who supports the idea of an English precedent.

151. William of Malmesbury 2002, 111–13.

152. Bishop 1918b, 227.

153. For many references to daily offices for All Saints and the dead, see Lanfranc 2002, 10–11, 16–17, 20–21, 32–33, 42–43, 74–75, 184–85. See also Roper 1993, 69.

154. For the pre–Norman Conquest structure of the cathedral, see Brooks 1984, 37–49. For the oratory of Mary, see ibid., 44–46. For Lanfranc's church, see Klukas 1984, 148–49.

155. Private masses have an important role in Lanfranc's *Constitutions*. Cf. Roper 1993, 43–44. On Lanfranc's architectural changes to Christ Church more generally, see Klukas 1984, which argues that a number of other English churches followed Christ Church's new layout, although there is no mention of Marian altars or chapels.

156. Confirmed in Roper 1993, 69.

157. Morgan 1999, 122–25; Roper 1993, 181–283. For descriptions of manuscripts, see Roper 1993, 287–324.

158. Gerald of Wales 1861–91, 4:202. See also Roper 1993, 41, 46–47; Morgan 1999, 122–23.

159. For a schematic description and discussion of the Winchcombe manuscript, Valenciennes, Bibliothèque municipale MS 116, ff. 135–140v, see Roper 1993, 102–3, 247–48, 324. See also Morgan 1999, 123; Pfaff 2009, 173–76.

160. Riley 1867, 1:76. For a transcription, see Roper 1993, 244–46.

161. "Hic etiam processionem in commemoratione beatae Mariae, quae singulis hebdomadibus in albis celebretur, ad altare eiusdem virginis fieri statuit." Riley 1867, 1:107.

162. "Twelve lessons are nevertheless read on that same night of the blessed Virgin, which are done by memory and without candles (on which day laborers are accustomed to pass through with their families), after which follow the responsories by the weak evening light through the transparent glass." (*Legebantur autem duodecim eadem nocte de beata Virgine lectiones, quas corde tenus, sine candela, bajuli transcurre consueverunt cum suis, quae sequuntur responsoriis, tenui tamen lumine cruciboli per vitrum diaphanum translucente.*) Ibid., 1:231.

163. "Licet in nostra ecclesia, quod non fit in aliis, qualibet septimana, die Sabbati, nisi obstet causa rationabilis, fiat commemoratio de beata Virgine, totaliter per diem et noctem in albis solemniter." Ibid., 1:284–85.

164. For an insightful introduction to the Little Office, although with a focus on thirteenth-century Paris, see Baltzer 2000.

165. BL Royal MS 2. A. x. See Roper 1993, 98–100; Thomson 1982, 94; Morgan 1999, 123; Pfaff 2009, 170–72.

166. These are BL Add. MS 21927 (see Roper 1993, 311; Morgan 1999, 124) and Cambridge Jesus College MS 68 C. 18 (for a short description of the manuscript, see Roper 1993, 297). While the Wherwell Psalter may have been intended for personal use, this does not rule out communal performance of the practice. See ibid., 70.

167. Gransden 1973, 83. Although recorded circa 1234, the Customary supports other evidence of Anselm's Marian devotion.

168. See Roper 1993, 309.

169. Ibid., 57.

170. BL Add. MS 21927.

171. This office differs considerably from the thirteenth-century Little offices from Paris surveyed by Rebecca Baltzer (2000). They in turn have more elements in common with the Saturday commemorative office found in the St. Albans breviary, discussed above.

172. As cited in BL Add. MS 21927, f. 101v (Drèves 1886–1922, 50:86–88):

Quem terra pontus aethera
colunt adorant predicant
trinam regentem machinam
claustrum Mariae baiulat.
Cui luna sol et omnia
deserviunt per tempora
perfusa coeli gratia

gestant puellae viscera.

Beata mater mundere,
cuius supernus artifex,
mundum pugillo continens,
ventris sub archa clausus est.
Benedicta celi nuntio,
fecunda sancto spiritu
desideratus gentibus,
cuius per alvum fusus est.
Gloria tibi domine
qui natus es de virgine
cum patre et sancto spiritu
in sempiterna secula. Amen.

173. These included Advent, from Christmas through the octave of Epiphany, from Passion Sunday through the octave of Easter, and from Ascension through Trinity Sunday. See Baltzer 2000, 464–65.

174. "O beata virgo Maria omni laude dignissima regina caelorum domina angelorum interventrix peccatorum . . . tuis domina intercessionibus tuoque patrocinio nos committimus, obsecrantes ut dum humili te obsequio frequentamus in terris tu gloriosa domina sedula prece nos digneris adiuvare in caelis." BnF MS lat. 10433, f. 231. Adapted slightly from the translation in Clayton 1990, 73, which points out that it appears as the final reading in the pre–Norman Conquest Marian office found in BL Cotton MS Tiberius A. iii. For more details, see ibid., 70–74.

175. "Obsecramus ergo lachrymosis suspiriis, ut nunc ad gemitum nostri meroris aurem inclines." BL Royal MS 2. A. x, f. 135v.

176. "Non enim est aliquid in nobis tam pravum si tibi placet quod orando abolere non possis." Ibid., f. 136.

177. Dewick 1902, x–xi. On the basis of script features, Roper (1993, 72), however, attributes it to late eleventh-century Christ Church, where it may have been copied for Nunnaminster.

178. "Tu quoque sancta Maria semper virgo angustiae nostrae et vere de manu inimici nostri possessionem huic sanctae ecclesiae tuae oblatam et in tuorum famulorum alimoniam collatam. Presta igitur domina ut non gaudeat inimicus qui non timuit tuam invadere possessionem. Redde ei secundum opera malitiae suae quia nostra in te sperantia corda perturbavit et domus tuae reverentiam pro nihilo reputavit. Annue quoque ut omnes ei consentientes ultionis tuae vindictam sentient et quia te contempserunt cum obprobriis et suppliciis intellegant. Te quoque sancto Machute confessor et te virgo veneranda sancta Eadburga oramus quatinus nostram Deo commendetis tribulationem et inimicorum nostrorum prava consilia ad perpetuam sibimet ipsis dampnationem commutetis nobisque eternam misericordiam eius impetretis." BL Royal MS 2 B. v, ff. 1–1v. For a transcription, see Dewick 1902, cols. 1–2.

179. As suggested in ibid., xi.

180. See also Roper 1993, 308. This counters Lester K. Little's (1993, 125) claim that no curse formulas exist from Anglo-Saxon or Anglo-Norman England.

181. Epistle 142, in Damian 2004, 141–42. See also Fulton 2002, 224.

182. Parkes 2014, 151.
183. For general surveys, see Cottier 2001; Wilmart 1932.
184. Boynton 2007.
185. Ibid., 898.
186. Ibid., 902.
187. Lanfranc 2002, 10–11. For additional examples, see Boynton 2007, 903.
188. Constable 1996, 203–4.
189. Fulton 2002.
190. The formula is the offertory: "Ave Maria, gratia plena, Dominus tecum, benedicta tu in mulieribus, et benedictus fructus ventris tui." It is found in Hesbert's *Antiphonale Missarum Sextuplex* as formulary nos. 005, 007.2, and 033. See the database online at http://www.uni-regensburg.de/Fakultaeten/phil_Fak_I/Musikwissenschaft/cantus/ (accessed February 27, 2016). Collated in McKinnon 2000, 182. For discussion, see ibid., 182–85.
191. Leclercq 1932, especially cols. 2051–53.
192. BL Lansdowne MS 383, ff. 166–66v. See Beck 1924; Morgan 1999, 126.
193. In terms of manuscripts containing identical or similar prayers, Morgan (1999, 126–27) identified both the Winchester Psalter (BL Cotton MS Nero C. iv) and the Winchcombe Breviary (Valenciennes, Bibliothèque municipale MS 116).
194. It was included as a work of Anselm in Anselm of Canterbury 1853, cols. 1040–46; PL 158:1036–46. The hymn was cataloged as number 1926, in Chevalier 1892, 114. It appears also in *Analecta Hymnica* (henceforth *AH*), 35:254. Cataloged under Pseudo-Anselm, it was attributed instead to Thomas Becket in Meersseman 1960, 16.
195. Drèves 1886–1922, 35:254.
196. As indicated in Morgan 1999, 125.
197. Southern 1966, 42–47. For another work that upholds this idea, see Reynolds 2012, 136, 213.
198. Fulton's (2002, 195–203) argument emphasizes the figure of the weeping Mary at the foot of the cross, as depicted by Anselm, as the principal novelty. See also Fulton 2006, 2013.
199. This goes back to the seventh-century *Life of the Virgin* by Maximus the Confessor (2012).
200. Bestul 1977, 27–31. On a survey of prayer to Mary in Anglo-Saxon England, see most especially Clayton 1990, 90–121.
201. The abbot of Fécamp between 1028 and 1078, and nephew of reformer William of Volpiano, John of Fécamp wrote considerable contemplative works, particularly focusing on meditation on the cross, which may have inspired Anselm; John wrote no known prayers to the Virgin, however. Fulbert of Chartres, on the other hand, did, and provides an important additional witness to Marian prayer in the eleventh century. See McNamer 2010; Fulton 2002.
202. "Sed quid ago obscenitates meas referens auribus illibatis? Horresco, Domina, horresco, et, arguente me conscientia, male nudus coram te erubesco. Cui vero moribundus offeram vulnus meum? Ad quem ibo, apud quem deplorabo dolorem meum? Aut quando aliunde sperem beneficia sanitatis, si mihi clauditur unicum illud reclinatorium aeternae pietatis? Audi igitur, Domina, audi propicia, audi et exaudi civem per-

ditum de sorte hereditatis tuae post longa exilia, post seva ludibria, post multa supplicia revertentem ad ubera consolationis tuae." Barré 1963, 183.

203. Morgan (1999) listed the eleven monastic psalters and prayer books from late eleventh- and early twelfth-century England that contained the prayer: Cambridge St. John's College MS 18; BL Cotton MS Vespasian D. xxvi; BL Harley MS 863; BL Lansdowne MS 383; BL Royal MS 8 D. viii; Society of Antiquaries MS 7; Madrid Biblioteca Nacional Vit. MS 23–28; Oxford Bodl. Auctarium MS D. 2. 6; Oxford Bodl. Laud Miscellania MS 79; Rouen, Bibliothèque municipale MS 231; Verdun, Bibliothèque municipale MS 70. Cf. Morgan 1999, 126.

204. In the discussion following his paper, scholar Thomas H. Bestul (1984, 411) denied any direct influence of Maurilius's prayer on Anselm. Yet Bestul (1977, especially 33–34) does argue for both Anglo-Saxon influence on Anselm's prayers and Norman devotional culture. Barré (1963, 288) argues for Anselm's originality.

205. Epistle 28, in Anselm of Canterbury 1973, 106; 1990, 121. On the prayers, see also Wilmart 1924, 1930.

206. "Feci igitur orationem unam unde fueram postulatus; sed in ea me non satisfecisse postulanti cognoscens, alteram facere sum invitatus. In qua quoniam similiter nondum satisfeci, tertiam quae tandem sufficeret perfeci." Epistle 28, in Anselm of Canterbury 1853, 136.

207. "I composed a prayer, as I was asked to do, but I was not satisfied, knowing what had been asked, so I started again, and composed another. I was not satisfied with that either, so have done a third which at last is all right." Cited in Gransden 1973, 106.

208. Ibid., 59.

209. My own translation is confirmed by that in Cottier 2001, lxxxii, n52: "Je fis donc une prière selon ce qui m'avait été demandée; mais apprenant que par cette prière je n'avais pas satisfait celui qui me l'avait demandée, je fus engagé à en faire une autre. Celle-là non plus ne donna pas satisfaction, j'en achevai une troisième qui put enfin convenir."

210. For the dedication of Bec to Mary, see Orderic Vitalis 1980, 12–13.

211. Epistle 99, Anselm of Canterbury 1990, 249.

212. Eadmer of Canterbury (1964, 192–94), Anselm's biographer, does describe Anselm as treasuring a relic of Mary's hair. But when the Christ Church monks asked to celebrate the octave of Mary's Nativity, it was not because Anselm himself insisted but rather by their own will. Epistle 41, Anselm of Canterbury 1990, 134.

213. But McNamer (2010) contends that female religious culture, specifically, provided the impetus for the development of new, more affective forms of prayer. Here it seems to be male monks.

214. Most historians have pointed out the characteristic emotional tone of the prayers and their profoundly personal qualities as something Anselm brought to them. See, for example, Cottier 2001, lxvii.

215. Southern 1966, 34. See also Wilmart 1930.

216. Anselm of Canterbury 1973, 106; 1990, 121.

217. McCord Adams 2004, 35.

218. Anselm of Canterbury 1853, 3:13–14; 1973, 108.

219. Barré 1963, 299.

220. Anselm of Canterbury 1853, 3:16; 1973, 112.

221. Ibid. 1853, 3:16–17; 1973, 112–13.

222. Ibid. 1853, 3:16; 1973, 112.

223. Fulton 2002, 234.

224. Anselm of Canterbury 1853, 3:19; 1973.

225. Ibid. 3:21–22; 1973, 120–21.

226. Fulton 2002, 236. Fulton wants to explain this approach to Mary by suggesting the penitent identifies in his pain of sin with Mary in her pain for the crucified Christ. The problem in reading these prayers to Mary in this way is that the Crucifixion is not mentioned, nor is Mary's suffering during it.

227. Anselm of Canterbury 1973, 106; 1990, 121.

228. Fulton 2002, 205.

229. Anselm of Canterbury 1973, 96.

230. The earliest-surviving manuscripts are from Saint-Martin-de-Troarn (Normandy), Saint-Arnoul-de-Metz, Saint-Vaast-d'Arras, and Saint-Amand-les-Eaux, followed soon after by Christ Church Canterbury and St. Albans, and later Eynsham, Harrold, Reading, Durham, and Winchester. For lists of manuscripts, see Bestul 1984, 359–61; Cottier 2001, lxxxiv–ci; 1996, 282–95. For a further example, which closely echoes Anselm, see BL Arundel MS 60, a Christ Church manuscript from the first quarter of the twelfth century, discussed in Bestul 1977, 31–32, 39–41; 1981.

231. Bestul 1977, 35.

232. Bestul 1984, 360–61.

233. Southern 1966, 236–37.

234. For two exceptions, see Graef 2009, 215–18; Fulton 2002, 246–47. Both these sources, though, tend to critique Eadmer for his lack of sophistication rather than emphasizing his novelty.

235. "Deus fili huius felicissimae matris, qui es virtus et vera sapientia summi patris, oramus te quatenus ipsa misericordia, qua factus es homo pro nobis, insinuare digneris cordibus nostris que animo, qua cogitatione tenebatur haec dulcissima tua mater cum te, inquam talem ac tantillum in brachiis suis exsultans et laeta teneret, cum tibi ut infantulo gestienti dulcibus osculis atque frequentibus congauderet, cum te lacrymantem super genua sua quibus poteratur modulis consolaretur, cum denique aliis et aliis studiis, ad quae ipsam materna pietas informabat, tibi pro qualitatum vicissitudinibus sedula blandiretur?" Eadmer of Canterbury PL 159:564.

236. Anselm of Canterbury 1853, 3:8; 1973, 96.

237. "Itaque si tam utilis est in subveniendo memoria nominis matris Dei, non mirum si magnae salutis afferet fructum frequens meditatio sancti amoris eius, si plenam jucunditatem dabit dulci studio cogitata et recogitata immensitas gaudii eius." Eadmer of Canterbury, PL 159:570.

238. This was the general argument in Fulton 2002.

239. "Excedat omnem altitudinem quae post Deum dici vel cogitari potest." Eadmer of Canterbury, PL 159:559.

240. "Sicut ergo Deus sua potentia parando cuncta pater est et dominus omnium, ita beata Maria suis meritis cuncta reparando mater est et domina rerum; Deum enim est dominus omnium, singula in sua natura propria jussione constituendo; et Maria est domina rerum, singula congenitae dignitati per illam quam meruit gratiam restituendo." Ibid., PL 159:578.

241. "Quis, inquam, tam miram, et omni prorsus rei praeter hanc inauditam gratiam huius mulieris oculo mentis aspiciens, non obstupescat, et non modo elinguis, verum etiam a tantae rei comprehensione prorsus immunis fiat?" Ibid.

242. "Quapropter ea quae nobis sunt impenetrabilia intermittentes, precibus impetrare nitamur ut, quod intellectu capere nequimus, salutari saltem affectu obtinere mereamur." Ibid.

243. "Cur itaque non juvabis nos peccatores, quando propter nos in tantum celsitudinem es elevata ut te dominam habeat et veneretur omnis pariter creatura? . . . Si ergo, quae plena salute es potita, non intendis ut eadem salus pro modulo nostro etiam ad nos usque pertingat, jam tuorum sufficiens commodorum, nostrorum negligens esse videberis, et quae pro totius mundi salvatione meruisti fieri mater altissimi, cum nos proposueris, quos obvolvit finis saeculi, quod, quaeso, proderit nobis tua gloriosa et felix exaltatio, et quam inde habemus, dulcis et affectuosa exsultatio?" Ibid., PL 159:579.

244. "Velociorque est nonnunquam salus memorato nomine eius quam invocato nomine Domini Jesu unici filii eius . . . Invocato autem nomine matris suae, etsi merita invocantis non merentur, merita tamen matris intercedunt ut exaudiatur." Ibid., PL 159:570.

245. Klein 1998, 36–39.

246. BL Landsdowne MS 383, ff. 13v, 14.

247. On the St. Albans Psalter, see Geddes 2005. On the importance of Mary in the image cycle, see ibid., 102. See also Collins, Kidd, and Turner 2013. For the full images, see https://www.abdn.ac.uk/stalbanspsalter/english/index.shtml (accessed February 28, 2016). On the Winchester Psalter, see especially Haney 1986; Uhlig Crown 1975.

248. Klein 1998.

249. On the possibility of artists working in England having visited the eastern Mediterranean and learned Byzantine techniques, see Thomson 2010.

250. Klein 1998, 31–33.

251. For a discussion of this, see Morgan 1999, 129–30.

252. For interpretations of these objects, see Heslop 1978; 1980; 1981, 56–58; 1984.

253. It should be noted that apart from Reading, a Cluniac foundation, and Kelso, founded under the Tironesian Order, the other houses are all Benedictine foundations. Cf. Heslop 1981, 53.

254. On the semiotic meaning of seals and their importance in medieval culture, see Bedos-Rezak 2011.

255. Bedos-Rezak 2000, 1513–14.

256. Ibid., 1490.

257. On Proclus, see Cunningham 2004, 53. See also, more generally, Constas 2003. On the sixth- and seventh-century homilists, see Allen 2011. For examples of the others, see Cunningham 2008. See also Shepardson 2008.

258. Cunningham 1999.

259. For an edition, see Braun 1976, 227–58; Sepet 1867–68.

260. *Sermo de mysterio Trinitatis et Incarnationis*, PL 39:2196–98. On the use of this and the *Contra Judaeos* in the Advent liturgy, see Lagueux 2004, 2009.

261. For example, the Roman *OR XIIIA*, dated to 700–750, gives the vigil readings for the entire Advent season as Isaiah. Cf. Andrieu 1961, 485.

262. See Jugie 1923; Fassler 2000b, 2001.

263. BnF MS lat. 10433. This office may have served as the liturgical basis for all Marian feast days, since four sets of prayers for the Annunciation, Assumption, Nativity, and Purification follow the text. It was dated at one point to the abbacy of Gervase (1138–ca. 1157), but recently to a later date. See Pfaff 2009, 485, 486; Stirnemann 2013, 102–3. For the manuscript, see http://gallica.bnf.fr/ark:/12148/btv1b85388041/f457.image.r= 10433.langEN (accessed March 2, 2016).

264. BnF MS lat. 10433, ff. 226–46. This office has the psalms 8, 18, 23, 44, 45, 86, 95, 96, and 97 in matins, compared to 8, 18, 23, 44, 45, 47, 84, 86, 95, 96, 97, and 98 in the Worcester Antiphonal. For lists of the psalms used in these offices, see Roper 1993, 227–35. For evidence that the monastic office influenced the secular equivalent, see Baltzer 2000, 466. For the secular structure of the monastic office, see Roper 1993, 74. The Westminster office shares lessons with other monastic offices, including a mid-twelfth-century St. Albans commemorative Marian office. See BL Royal MS 2. A. x, ff. 135–40v. For a list of incipits of these, see Roper 1993, 244–46.

265. "Magnae devotionis et fidei hec mulier ostenditur quae Scribis et Phariseis dominum temptanibus simul et blasphemantibus tantam eius incarnationem per omnibus sinceritate cognoscit tanta fiducia confitetur ut et presentium procerum calumniam et futurorum hereticorum confundat perfidiam." BnF MS lat. 10433, f. 232. See also Bede PL 92:479.

266. "Te laudant angeli sancta Dei genitrix quae virum non cognovisti et dominum in tuo utero baiulasti concepisti per aurem dominum nostrum ut benedicta dicaris inter omnes mulieres." BnF MS lat. 10433, f. 232.

267. "Nam sicut tunc Judaei Spiritus Sancti opera blasphemando verum consubstantialemque patri Dei filium negabant sic haeretici negando Mariam semper virginem Spiritus Sancti operante virtute nascituro ex humanis membris unigenito Deo carnis suae materiam ministrasse verum consubstantialemque matri filium hominis fateri non debere dixerunt." Ibid., f. 232^v. See also Bede, PL 92:479.

268. "Gaude Maria virgo cunctas haereses sola interemisti quae Gabrielis archangeli dictis credidisti. Dum virgo dominem et hominem genuisti et post partum virgo inviolata permansisti." BnF MS lat. 10433, f. 232^v.

269. "Gabrielem archangelum scimus divinitus te esse affatum uterum tuum de spirito sancto credimus inpregnatum erubescat Iudeus infelix qui dicit Christum ex Ioseph semine esse natum." Ibid., ff. 232^v–33.

270. CCCC MS 473, f. 194. See Huglo 1993. For the history of the responsory, see Brou 1948.

271. Respectively, BL Cotton MS Tiberius A. iii, f. 111v; BL Royal MS 2 B. v, f. 5. See Dewick 1902, xviii.

272. Avranches, Bibliothèque municipale MS 101, f. 112; Rome, Vatican Library Chigi MS C VI 173, f. 5. For transcriptions, see Leclercq 1960, 91, 95.

273. Huglo 1993, 54.

274. "Non sunt audiendi qui legendum putant natum ex muliere factum sub lege." BnF MS lat. 10433, f. 233. See Bede PL 92:480.

275. "Christi virgo dilectissima virtutum operatrix opem fer miseris subveni domina clamantibus ad te iugiter." BnF MS lat. 10433, f. 233v.

276. Ibid.

277. On the role of matins readings in the monastic cult of saints, see Snijders 2011.

278. BL Royal MS 2 B. iv. ff. 178–78ᵛ. See Thomson 1982, 94–95; Pfaff 2009, 166.

279. Guéranger 2000, 2:220. Max Harris (2011, 44, 91, 145) mentions it as a "popular Christmas season sequence" appearing not only at Freising but also thirteenth-century Notre Dame in Paris and Bayeux, although with no indication about its origins.

280. BL Royal MS 2 B. iv. ff. 178 78ᵛ. Translated in Guéranger 2000, 220–21.

> Laetabundus exultet fidelis chorus alleluia.
> Regem regum intacte profudit thorus res miranda.
> Angelus consilii natus est de virgine sol de stella.
> Sol occasum nesciens stella semper rutilans valde clara.
> Sicut sydus radium profert virgo filium pari forma.
> Neque sydus radio neque virgo filio fit corrupta.
> Cedrus alta Libano conformatur Ysopo calle nostra.
> Verbum ens altissimi corporari passum est carne assumpta.
> Ysaias cecinit, synagoga meminit nunquam tamen desinit esse caeca.
> Si non suis vatibus credat vel gentilibus sibillinis versilibus hec predicta.
> Infelix propera, crede vel vetera cur damnaberis gens misera quam docet
>   littera.
> Natum considera, ipsum genuit puerpera.

281. See Harris 2011, 46–47.

282. It is often divided up into readings for the office of matins in the manuscripts described in Ildefonsus of Toledo 2007, 91–120. See also Rucquoi 1997. On the polemical aspect of the office, see Ihnat, forthcoming.

283. These are based on figures in Jerome's polemical works. See Ildefonsus of Toledo 2007, 27–36.

284. Barré 1957. The sermons are *Vos inquam convenio* and *Legimus sanctum Moysen*, both from the fifth century. For an edition of the former, see Braun 1976, 227–58. On the importance of the two sermons in later liturgical traditions, see Lagueux 2009. Tovar Paz (1994, 219) noted the tendency of seventh-century Visigothic bishops to reuse older sermons rather than compose their own.

285. "Quicquid enim in insigni genealogia Christi ad evangelicam respicit hystoriam, totum ex abundanti recurrit ad Annam ut ipsa sit quasi quaedam meta legis et gratiae, per quam dignitas humanae videtur in Christo refloruisse naturae." Wilmart 1925–26, 17.

286. AH, 15:186.

> O parentis parens Dei, apud ipsum memor mei
> Quibus deprimor meorum, terge sordes peccatorum.
> Et ipsa quam genuisti, casta mater aula Christi
> Tua tecum sancta prece: me ab omni purget fece.
> Felix archa testamenti, quae Judea non credenti.

287. Ibid.

> Sicque fieres multorum: consolatrix miserorum.
> Consolare me lugentem, et conforta penitentem.

Et reduc ad vite viam, et videre da Messiam.
Quem venisse nescit rea, sed venturum gens Hebrea
Astruit et asseverat: perfidiaque est ut erat.

288. Noted in Palazzo 1998, 1138.
289. For lay participation in the liturgy, see Tinti 2015, 244–45.

Chapter 2: Understanding Mary: Theological Treatises

1. Used in the opening of the *Proslogion*, in Anselm of Canterbury 1998, 87. On this theme in Anselm's theology, see Gasper 2004, 107–43. Of course, Anselm was not the first to apply dialectic to theological problems; this was already occurring in the eleventh century with figures such as Berengar of Tours and Anselm of Besate. See Holopainen 1996. On Anselm's originality, see Marenbon 1988, 94–104. On knowledge and faith in monastic culture more generally, see Leclercq 1961.

2. Anselm was no doubt inspired to some degree by his teacher, Lanfranc, but Lanfranc also expressed worries about the lack of authoritative support Anselm included in his work. See Gibson 1978, 61–62; Gasper 2004, 129–30.

3. For classic works, see de Ghellinck 1948; Chenu 1976; Holopainen 2004. On the renewed interest in logic, see Wei 2012, 17–33. On Anselm's contribution, although with a focus on the ontological argument, see ibid., 53–59. On the school of Bec, its educational program, and Anselm's key role within it, see Gibson 1978, 44–60; Vaughn 1993; Novikoff 2011, especially 397–401; 2013, 35–52.

4. On Anselm's approach to the Incarnation, see Leftow 1995.

5. Articulated in the *Proslogion*, in Anselm of Canterbury 1998, 82–104. For the argument, see ibid., 87–88.

6. For a brief discussion of Anselm's ideas about Mary, see Graef 2009, 210–15.

7. See Southern 1966, 89–91. For a general schema of the *Cur Deus Homo*, see ibid., 92–93.

8. *Cur Deus Homo*, II.6, in Anselm of Canterbury 1998, 319.

9. Ibid., 320.

10. Ibid., 323.

11. For a discussion of Anselm's appeal to "fittingness" in his arguments, see Leftow 1997, especially 91. For a contrasting position, see Visser and Williams 2009, 214–23.

12. See Dunthorne 2012, 157–64.

13. *Cur Deus Homo*, II.16, in Anselm of Canterbury 1998, 337.

14. See the prologue to *De virginali conceptu*, in ibid., 357.

15. For a discussion, see Visser and Willliams 2009, 242–46.

16. *De virginali conceptu*, XIII, in Anselm of Canterbury 1998, 373.

17. For a discussion of this mechanism, see Visser and Williams 2009, 242–46.

18. Southern and Schmitt 1969, 302–3. As Anna Sapir Abulafia (1989b, 115–17) has indicated, this analogy can be traced all the way to the sermon *Legimus Sanctum Moysen*; see also Southern and Schmitt 1969, 101.

19. *De virginali conceptu*, XVIII, in Anselm of Canterbury 1998, 376.

20. On the purity of Mary through her faith in the Annunciation, see Deme 2003, 167–69.

21. *Cur Deus Homo*, II.16, in Anselm of Canterbury 1998, 340.

22. Gasper 2004, 144.

23. Southern 1966, 236–37. A. W. Burridge (1936, 581–83), in contrast, placed it between 1109 and 1123–24.

24. For a limited study on the treatise, including a schematic outline, see Burridge 1936. For other limited studies, along with questions of dating, see Lamy 2000, 34–35, 118–19; De la Chapelle 1962.

25. For a list of the contents, see Southern 1966, 367–74.

26. "[Ego et priscorum simplicitatem et modernorum ingenii sublimitatem mecum revolverem, cecidit in mentem quaedam divinae Scripturae verba in medio ponere] et quid judicii de singulis gerant, pro meo sensu pia consideratione perpendere, quatenus sua auctoritate probetur quid cui attribuendum, quid mei similibus sit certa magis ratione sequendum." Eadmer of Canterbury 1904, 2.

27. "Et hi quidem ut nulla memoria de conceptione virginis matris in ecclesia filii ejus fiat, non sibi rationis videri affirmant, eo quod ex nativitate illius quae ubique festive recolitur, conceptionis ejus exordium satis memoretur, nec enim, aiunt, nata esset, si concepta non fuisset, et cum in lucem ex materni uteri secreto prodivit, clarum fuit quod in alvo parentis concepta in humanam formam concrevit. Cum itaque corporis ejus specificata compositio, et in hujus mundi latitudine exhibitio veneretur a cunctis, supervacue illa adhuc informis materia coleretur, quae in nonnullis saepe, priusquam plene in humanam effigiem transeat, deperit et adnihilatur." Ibid., 3.

28. For example, in *De virginali conceptu*, VII, in Anselm of Canterbury 1998, 366–67. It was also reflected in the contemporary exegesis of Exodus 21:22–23, which stipulated that if someone causes a woman to abort, it only counts as murder if the child is fully formed, thereby implying it has yet to be infused with a soul. On the history of this issue, see Dunthorne 2012, 165–80.

29. "Nec enim ecclesia Dei inconcussae auctoritatis ducit ipsam scripturam, quae ortum illius ab angelo praenuntiatum refert. Nam licet beatus Hieronymus, juxta alterius cujusdam scripturae materiam, quam in adolescentia sua legisse, et cujus auctorem se fatetur ignorare, eam fecerit; dicit tamen non eo pacto se scripsisse quod scripsit, ut aliquam descriptae rei certitudinem ecclesiis vellet inferre, sed hoc solo ut rogantibus amicis simpliciter morem gereret. Unde, quaemadmodum dixi, scriptum illud in auctoritatem ecclesia suscipere noluit, videlicet indecens esse reputans de beata matre Dei quid dubitabile in laudem ejus recitari." Eadmer of Canterbury 1844–55, 159:560.

30. See Gijsel and Beyers 1997.

31. See ibid., 35–36.

32. "Sed utrum ita proxime nascitura quovis oraculo aut angelo nuntiata sit . . . in divina pagina non habetur, in canonica scriptura non reperitur." Eadmer of Canterbury 1904, 5.

33. For the blessing, see Gijsel and Beyers 1997, 35. He was precentor near the end of his life, after 1122. Cf. Southern 1966, 237.

34. "Multis saeculis ante ortum ejus vel conceptum, Isaiam Spiritu Sancto afflatum dixisse constat: Egredietur virga de radice Jesse, et flos de radice ejus ascendet; et re-

quiescet super eum spiritus domini, spiritus sapientiae et intellectus, spiritus consilii et fortitudinis, spiritus scientiae et pietatis, et replebit eum spiritus timoris domini (Isa. 11:1–3). Haec itaque virga quae talem ex se protulit florem, nullo dissentiente, virgo Maria fuit, et flos, qui de radice ejus ascendit, benedictus filius, super quem et in quo omnis plenitudo divinitatis essentialiter requievit. Haec igitur virgo, tanti filii dignissima parens, cum in alvo suae parentis naturali lege conciperetur, quis non concedat Dei sapientiam a fine usque ad finem pertingentem, cuncta implentem, cuncta regentem, novo quodam et ineffabili gaudio coelum, terram, et omnia quae in eis sunt, perfudisse; ac inestimabili jubilatione pro sui reintegratione, quam per illam sibi eventuram divina et occulta inspiratione praevidebant, perlustrasse? Sed cum ipsa conceptio fundamentum, ut diximus, fuerit habitaculi summi boni, si peccati alicujus ex primae praevaricationis origine maculam traxit, quid dicemus?" Eadmer of Canterbury 1904, 7–8.

35. "De Joanne quoque angelus, qui eum nasciturum praenuntiabat, asseruit quod Spiritu Sancto repleretur adhuc ex utero matris suae (Luke 1:15). Si igitur Jeremias, quia in gentibus erat propheta futurus, in vulva est sanctificatus, et Joannes, dominum in spiritu, et virtute Eliae praecessurus (Luke 1:17), Spiritu Sancto est ex utero matris repletus, quis dicere audeat singulare totius saeculi propitiatorium, ac filii Dei omnipotentis dulcissimum reclinatorium, mox in suae conceptionis exordio Spiritus Sancti gratiae illustratione destitutum?" Ibid., 9. This passage resembles Damian's (PL 144:628) Sermon on the Nativity of John the Baptist (no. 23), which Lamy (2000, 47) has ascribed to Nicholas of Clairvaux, meaning Eadmer's could have been the original.

36. "Fundamentum siquidem et quasi quoddam seminarium civitatis et habitaculi summi boni in eo ponebatur; et mansio lucis aeternae, et templum quod corporaliter inhabitaret ille incorporeus et incircumscriptus et creans simul et vivificans omnia spiritus parabatur." Eadmer of Canterbury 1904, 5–6.

37. "Ab re tamen et contra fidem esse non aestimo, si exordium conceptionis ipsius tanti a simplicibus ecclesiae filiis aestimetur, ut tam sublime, tam divinum, tam ineffabile fuerit, ut in illud mens humana nulla perspicacitate assurgere possit." Ibid., 5.

38. "Quod si quis eam primae originis peccato non omnimode expertem fuisse pronuntiat, cum illam ex legali conjugio maris et feminae conceptam verissime constet, si sententia catholica est, ego a catholicae et universalis ecclesiae veritate nulla ratione volo dissentire. Magnificentiam tamen operationum virtutis divinae quadam quasi mentis lippitudine pro posse considerans, videor mihi videre quia si quid originalis peccati in propagatione matris Dei et domini mei extitit, propagantium et non propagatae prolis fuit." Ibid., 9–10 (adapted slightly from the translation in Southern 1966, 294).

39. Although Paschasius Radbertus seems to have said something quite similar in his De partu virginis, it is almost certain that the passage mentioning it was interpolated in the twelfth century. See Lamy 2000, 48. The doctrine was also unknown in the East, despite its celebration of Mary's Conception. See Jugie 1952, 40.

40. "Castaneam nucem attende: cum de sui generis arbore prodit nascitura, involucrum illius totum hispidum et densissimis aculeis undique septum apparet. Intus castanea concipitur, primo quidem nucleum lactei liquoris, nihil hispidum, nihil asperum, nec aliquibus aculeis noxium in se habens aut circa se aliquatenus sentiens. Illic in summa lenitate nutritur, fovetur et alitur, ac formata in sui speciem et habitudinem

jam adulta, rupto involucro ab omni spinarum punctione et onere liberrima, matura egreditur. Si Deus castaneae confert ut inter spinas remota punctione concipiatur, alatur, formetur, non potuit haec dare humano quod ipse sibi parabat templo in quo corporaliter habitaret, et de quo in unitate suae personae perfectus homo fieret, ut licet inter spinas peccatorum conciperetur, ab ipsis tamen spinarum aculeis omnimode exsors redderetur?" Eadmer of Canterbury 1904, 10.

41. "Angelos, aliis peccantibus, bonos a peccatis servavit, et feminam, matrem suam mox futuram, ab aliorum peccatis exsortem servare non valuit? In aeternitate consilii sui fixum statuit eam dominatricem et reginam fore angelorum, et nunc inferiorem gratiam angelis natam, in consortium conceptam esse credemus omnium peccatorum?" Ibid., 16.

42. "Potuit plane, et voluit; si igitur voluit, fecit. . . . [V]oluit enim te fieri matrem suam, et quia voluit, fecit esse." Ibid., 11.

43. "Quia ergo ita fieri oportebat, matrem de qua talis crearetur, mundam esse ab omni peccato decebat." Ibid., 13.

44. On the development of doctrine about Mary's sinlessness from Anselm to Eadmer, see Fournée 1984.

45. "Necesse igitur fuit ut natura, de qua se hominem facere volebat, et humana et munda ab omnis peccati contagio esset; quod ubi inveniret, cum, ut dixi, nihil incorruptum vitiata cunctorum radice existeret, sed qui humanae perditioni subvenire disponebat, Dei virtus et Dei sapientia nuncupatur. . . . Poterat ergo de massa peccatrice naturam humanam ab omni labe peccati immunem facere, unde in unam personam sui susciperet, ut homo integer esset et divinitati suae nihil minueret." Eadmer of Canterbury 1904, 21.

46. De virginali conceptu, VIII, in Anselm of Canterbury 1998, 367–68. Irven Resnick (1996, 70–71) points out that Anselm was the first medieval author to state this explicitly.

47. De virginali conceptu, X, in Anselm of Canterbury 1998, 368.

48. "Sed cum eminentiam gratiae Dei in te considero, sicut te non intra omnia, sed supra omnia quae praeter filium tuum acta sunt, inaestimabili modo contueor, ita te non lege naturae ut alios in tua conceptione devinctam fuisse opinor, sed singulari et humano intellectui impenetrabili divinitatis virtute et operatione ab omnis peccati admixtione liberrimam." Eadmer of Canterbury 1904, 12–13.

49. De virginali conceptu, X, in Anselm of Canterbury 1998, 369–70. See Resnick 1996, 76–77.

50. As Southern (1966, 293) put it: "If this link between natural conception and the taint of Original Sin could be broken in one case, then the necessity of Christ as a redeemer of the whole human race would be jeopardized." See also Graef 2009, 211.

51. Cur Deus Homo, II.16, in Anselm of Canterbury 1998, 340.

52. Ibid., 337.

53. "La doctrine de saint Anselme est résolument anti-immaculiste," comments Jean Fournée 1984, 713. See also Gasper 2004, 147–49.

54. De virginali conceptu, XVI, in Anselm of Canterbury 1998, 345.

55. "Quod si aliquis ipsam Dei genitricem usque ad Christi annuntiationem originali peccato obnoxiam asserit ac sic fide qua angelo credidit inde mundatam, iuxta quod dicitur "fide mundans corda eorum", si Catholicum est non nego, licet altior consider-

atio mentem meam ab hoc divellat. Nam, ut dixi, matrem domini super omnia praeter Deum esse perpendens, sublimiori gratia dei quam apostolos vel aliud quid quod extra Deum filium suum creatum asseritur ipsam irradiatam protestor. Igitur si primordia creationis illius alio intuitu quam aliorum de propagine Adae prodeuntium considero, precor nemo vultum subsannando avertat, nemo, quae pietatis et quam Deus dat purae devotionis affectu in Dei genitricem permotus dico, suo sensu aliqua animositate ductus, evertere temptet, nisi fidei Christianae penitus contraria esse certus existat." Eadmer of Canterbury 1904, 13–14.

56. Ibid.

57. "Si ergo aliquid excellentius et quod humanum intellectum supervolet, conceptionem B. Mariae designasse aestimandum est, excellentior gloria et major dignitas in ejus quam in Christi domini conceptione divinitus enituisse verisimili ratione videtur." Ibid., 6.

58. "I do not say this, but rather the son of God, the brightness of eternal light and the unreachable light himself, who emptied himself and took on the form of the servant, arranged his own advent in this way for human minds so that it might be grasped and understood . . . it cannot be absurd to believe that the beginnings of her conception were marked with such sublimity of divinity that her conception was not able to penetrate entirely into human minds." (*Non hoc dico. Sed filius Dei, candor lucis aeternae et ipse lux inaccessibilis, formam servi accepturus semetipsum exinanivit, suumque adventum ita humanis mentibus contemperavit ut capi posset et intelligi. . . . non absurde credi potest primordia conceptionis ejus tanta deitatis sublimitate praesignata, ut humanarum conceptio mentium ea plene penetrare non valeret.*) Ibid., 7.

59. "Estimet hoc qui vult, argumentis suis probet qui vult, iis quae dicimus adversetur qui vult . . . quae scripsi non muto." Ibid., 16. Burridge (1936, 580) argues for Eadmer's moderation compared to later defenders.

60. Epistle 7, in Osbert of Clare 1929, 65–68. J. Armitage Robinson (1911) dated the letter to between January 22, 1128, and August 1129.

61. Ibid., 66.

62. "Non impossibile fuisse credimus ut . . . beatam virginem Mariam sine contagione peccati in ipsa conceptione sanctificaret." Ibid.

63. "Et quia controversiae schismata facientium, scandala moventium, haeretice garrientium, obstruendae sunt in domo Dei catholica veritate et ecclesiastica defensione fidelium, ad hoc tendit stilus meus ut cum talibus religiosis personis et litteratis de hac invidiorum calumnia et genitricis Dei conceptione gloriosa vel scripto vel verbo loquamini, qui et subtilia sanctae scripturae argumenta non ignorant et vobiscum defendere contra inimicos veritatis causam beatae virginis Mariae non formident." Ibid., 67.

64. Southern 1966, 240.

65. On the council where it was approved, see chapter 1.

66. "For when the Holy Spirit, through whom the Virgin administered the substance of flesh to the Word of God, descended into Mary, all stain of original sin at once fled." Dialogus, I.16, 1152. Translation from Freeburn 2011, 74.

67. For an edition of the sermon, see Eadmer of Canterbury 1904, appendix A, 65–83. Scholar E. W. Williamson claimed it was interpolated into the manuscript of Osbert's letters (BL Cotton MS Vitellius A. xvii), which he edited, but it is clearly written in the same hand as the rest of the letters.

68. "Dicere tamen non audeo quod de hac sancta generatione corde concipio ut aliquis aemulus cynico me dente incipiat rodere et detractionibus perversis integritatem fidei meae lacerans infestare." Epistle 13, in Osbert of Clare 1929, 80.

69. "Desinant ergo infideles et haeretici de hac sancta sollennitate in sua vanitate multiplicia loqui, et discant quia filii matris gratiae non de actu peccati celebritatem faciunt, sed de primitiis redemptionis nostrae multiplicia sancte novitatis gaudia solenniter ostendunt." Ibid., 80.

70. "[Utinam] universa de mea credulitate expertum haberet ecclesia quo me sibi praesidio vendicet et tueatur catholica fides et orthodoxa. Corde autem credo et ore confiteor quod ante secula temporalia Deus sibi matrem praeelegit virginem, de cuius aula virginalis uteri faceret egredi mortalitatis humane piissimum redemptorem." Ibid.

71. See ibid., 44.

72. "Et haec est solennitatis hodierne laetitia ineffabilis, in qua angelo nuntiante matrem domini Mariam genitrix Anna concepit, sicut eam ante tempora secularia ut ex ea asceretur in sapientia suo sol iustitiae praeelegit." Eadmer of Canterbury 1904, 74.

73. "Et bene olla spei nostrae dicitur beata virgo Maria, quia fictilis, quia testacea, quia ex massa praevaricationis Adae plasmata." Ibid.

74. Ibid.

75. For this letter, see Lamy 2000, 42–53.

76. Anselm spent considerable time there while in exile between 1098 and 1107. See Eadmer of Canterbury 1964, 94–95, 116; Evans 2004, 20–24; Vaughn 2012, 42, 107–8. For the manuscript, now in the Grand Séminaire library at Annecy, see Corbin 1967, 418.

77. Epistle 215, in Bernard of Clairvaux 1953, 290.

78. Ibid. On Bernard's contribution to the debate, see Lamy 2000, 49–52.

79. Bernard of Clairvaux 1953, 292.

80. On the development of the debate into later centuries, see Lamy 2000.

81. For this account, see Elisabeth of Schönau 2000, 209–11.

82. Mayr-Harting 2004, 103.

83. Ibid., 104.

84. On its history, see Fulton 1998.

85. Elliott 1993, 714. For editions of several of the narratives, and commentary on all, see Shoemaker 2002. See also Mimouni 1996, 480–509.

86. For some of the earlier history, see Milburn 1993.

87. Fulton 1998.

88. There are only a handful of manuscripts that contain the treatise itself. See William of Malmesbury 2015, xxiii–xxix.

89. On the importance of the cantor, see Fassler 1985.

90. Pfaff 1980.

91. William of Malmesbury 2015, 1.

92. This was remarked in Carter 1959, 302.

93. William of Malmesbury 2015, 2.

94. Ibid., 6–7.

95. On William's indebtedness to Anselm, see Carter 1959, 306–7. See also Sønnesyn 2012, 65–66.

96. *De virginali conceptu*, XVIII, in Anselm of Canterbury 1998, 376.

97. William of Malmesbury 2015, 7.

98. Ibid., 9.

99. Ibid., 10.

100. Ibid.

101. Fulton 1994, 1998.

102. Jane Elizabeth Huber (2013) questions this idea, suggesting that the liturgy was derived from the consecration of virgins, which makes extensive use of the Canticle's marriage imagery.

103. Fulton 1998.

104. Iogna-Prat 1996, 89, 96–97.

105. "But how, or when, or by what persons her holy remains were removed from this sepulchre, or where she awaits the resurrection, no one as it is said, can know for certain." Adomnan of Iona 1958, 56–59.

106. "What more shall we tell you about this feast day, except that Mary, mother of Christ, was on this day taken from this toilsome world up to the kingdom of heaven to her dear son. . . . If we say more about this feast day than we read in the holy books, which were set down through God's command, then we would be like those heretics who wrote, according to their own agenda or dreams, many false accounts. But the believable teachers, Augustine, Jerome, Gregory, and many others have turned away from them through their wisdom." Thorpe 1843–44, 1:436–38. Translation by Scheck 2008, 100. Aelfric 's attitude to Mary's Assumption is also discussed by Clayton (1990, 235–40). His skepticism is shared by the Blickling homilies, as described in Scheil 2004, 270.

107. For the poem, see Clayton 1987.

108. "Exaltata est super choros angelorum, repletum est in bonis desiderium suum; videt Deum facie ad faciem sicuti est, gaudet cum filio in eternum." Kienzle 1997, 27.

109. Eadmer of Canterbury PL 159:572–73.

110. "Veneranda nobis huius diei festivitas opem conferat sempiternam in qua sancta Dei genitrix mortem subiit temporalem, nec tamen mortis necis deprimi potuit quae filium tuum dominum nostrum de se genuit incarnatum." It is found in the Leofric Collectar (BL Harley MS 2961, f. 133) and St. Albans breviary (BL Royal MS 2. A. x, f. 86^v, 115^v) for both the feast of the Assumption and its octave. In the Portiforium of Wulfstan (CCCC MS 391, f. 478), the collect is found for the office of sext for the feast of the Assumption, in the section added to the end of the manuscript; it has additionally been augmented with the following: *cuius intercessione quas ut mortem evadere possimus animarum*. Hughes 1960, 1:106. For a French translation, see Palazzo and Johansson 1996, 36–37, which claims it was probably composed when the procession for the Assumption feast was instated during the papacy of Sergius I (687–701), although there is nothing to confirm this.

111. "[Subveniat domine plebi tuae Dei genitricis oratio quam et] si pro conditione carnis migrasse cognoscimus in caelesti gloria apud te pro nobis orare sentiamus." It is found in the St. Augustine's missal, dated circa 1095 (CCCC MS 270, ff. 111–11^v); Wulfstan's Portiforium (CCCC MS 391, f. 479); Hughes 1960, 1:106; Leofric Collectar (BL Harley MS 2961, f. 134v). See Palazzo and Johansson 1996, 36.

112. "[Dormitio Sanctae Mariae]: Cuius sacratissimum corpus et si non invenitur super terram tamen pia mater ecclesia venerabilem eius memoriam sic festivam agit ut pro conditione carnis eam migrasse non dubitet. Quo autem illud venerabile Spiritus

Sancti templum nutu et consilio divino occultatum sit plus elegit sobrietas ecclesiae cum pietate nescire quam aliquid frivolum et apocrifum inde tenendo docere." BL Cotton MS Vitellius C. xii, f. 136.

113. On the use of the martyrology for reading in the chapterhouse, see Webber 2010, 8.

114. Herbert of Losinga 1878, 2:352–53. See also Fulbert of Chartres, *Approbate consuetudinis sermon, in* PL 141.322, Damian PL 144:861; Jugie 1944, 381; Abelard PL 178:541.

115. BnF lat. 1987, ff. 368v–69v. For a digital version, see http://gallica.bnf.fr/ark: /12148/btv1b9066918m/f371.zoom (accessed March 4, 2016). The text has not been edited apart from *De Assumptione Beatae Virginis Mariae, Liber Unus* PL 40:1141–48. See Quadrio 1951, particularly 32–34, 41–45. On authorship, see Canal 1959; Graef 2009, 222–23.

116. CCCC MS 332; Worcester Cathedral Library MS F. 94. See Gameson 1999, 64, 157; Thomson and Gullick 2001, 65–68. For William's travels, which included Worcester and Rochester, see Thomson 2003b, 73.

117. Dominique Iogna-Prat (1996, 91) attributed it to the time of Anselm. J. M. Canal (1959) pointed out the earlier Saint-Martial manuscript, making this impossible. See also Barré 1949, 902.

118. "Sunt etiam quaedam, quae quamvis commemorari ex toto omissa sint, vera tamen ratione creduntur." *De Assumptione Beatae Virginis Mariae, Liber Unus*, PL 40: 1144.

119. "Si quis autem refragari his elegerit, cum dicere non velit, haec non posse Christum: proferat quare non conveniat velle, ac per hoc non esse. Et si se veraciter consilium Dei de his nosse manifestaverit, incipiam ei credere, de quibus aliter non praesumpsi sentire: . . . Si ergo vera sunt quae scripsi; tibi gratias ago, Christe, quia de sancta virgine matre tua nisi quod pium est ac dignum visum sentire non potui. Si ergo dixi ut debui, approba, Christe, obsecro, tu et tui: sin autem ut non debui, ignosce tu et tui?" Ibid., PL 40:1148.

120. William of Malmesbury 2015, 10.

121. Ibid., 1–5.

122. It is missing from the Patrologia Latina edition of the sermon, but was noted in William of Malmesbury 2015, 13n82.

123. Schmitt 2006.

124. See Klein, 1998.

125. Ibid, 30, referring to Crown 1975, 121. Most Byzantine images depict a footstool, not a tomb.

126. Klein 1998, 36.

127. Glasgow Special Collections Hunter MS U.3.2, ff. 18–19v. It has traditionally been associated with York, but this is still debated. For a description and commentary, see Boase 1962, 8–14. See also Greenland 1996. For a potential earlier source, see Kurth 1945, 118; Hawkes 1995, 252–53, 265–67; Zarnecki 1984, 159.

128. Schmitt 2006, 162–63.

129. For Honorius's biography, see Flint 1972a, 1972b, 1977, 1995. On Honorius's Song of Songs commentaries, see Flint 1974.

130. Flint has made the claim that Honorius may have been a kinsman of Anselm's, and that his name "Augustodunensis" refers to his life as a canon of the *alte Kapelle* at Regensburg rather than any provenance from Autun, as it is often translated. Honorius did much to obscure his own identity. See Flint 1982; 1995, 19, 31.

131. Anselm's influence on Honorius's work has been noted by Flint (1995, 31), who states that "Honorius' concentration upon the literary and theological output of Anselm of Canterbury is without parallel in the late eleventh and early twelfth centuries." See also Fulton 2002, 248–49; Novikoff 2011, 415–16. On Honorius's reforming tendencies, see Flint 1977; 1995, 122–25. On the *Offendiculum*, see Flint 1995, 132–33.

132. Another series of Marian sermons is found in the late eleventh century CCCC MS 332, from Christ Church Canterbury; see Barré 1957, 11.

133. For the address to the monks of Christ Church, see Honorius Augustodunensis, *Speculum Ecclesiae*, PL 172:813. See also Flint 1995, 104.

134. Honorius wrote several works intended for the pastoral training of monks, including the polemical *That Monks Should Be Allowed to Preach*. On these, see Flint 1975; 1977; 1995, 102, 127.

135. John H. Van Engen (1983, 291) downplays the novelty of Honorius's contribution, instead describing Rupert of Deutz's more systematic interpretation of the Song of Songs as the first to apply the text to Mary. Although Honorius's work is more cursory, it is prior to Rupert's and gives the same fundamental message about the nature of the Song of Songs; see Flint 1972b. As Fulton (1998) has noted, it goes to show the exegetical power of the liturgy as a lens through which to interpret scripture rather than the other way around.

136. For a detailed history of the use of the Song of Songs for the Assumption liturgy, see Fulton 1998.

137. Honorius Augustodunensis 1991, 47. We know that monks in this period were interested in liturgical commentary, as attested by Honorius's contemporary William of Malmesbury's reworking of Amalarius of Metz's liturgical commentary, the *Abbreviatio Amalarii*. For a discussion and transcription, see Pfaff 1980. For Fulton's comments, see Fulton 2002, 248–49.

138. On the image of bride as church, see Matter 1990, 86–122. On the image of bride as soul, see ibid., 123–50.

139. Flint 1974, 203.

140. The Evesham manuscript (Oxford, Jesus College Library MS 54) is the earliest-existing copy of the *Sigillum*. On the English manuscripts, see Flint 1995, 9.

141. Shuve, forthcoming, 272–76.

142. Aldhelm 2009, 106.

143. Honorius Augustodunensis 1991, 53.

144. Flint 1995, 19, 31; Southern 1966, 209–17.

145. Honorius Augustodunensis 1991, 59.

146. Ibid., 76.

147. Ibid., 86.

148. Ibid., 60.

149. Ibid., 86.

150. For this tradition, see Matter 1990, 25–31. See also Origen's prologue in Norris

2003, 1–7. Bede especially developed the dramatic aspect with the addition of rubrics; see Matter 1990, 99–100.

151. Fulton 2002, 275–80. For the narrative quality of the Song of Songs commentaries, see Astell 1990, 61–72.

152. Honorius Augustodunensis 1991, 62.

153. Ibid., 62.

154. Ibid.

155. Elliott 1993, 709, pointed out in Fulton 2002, 276.

156. Honorius Augustodunensis 1991, 87.

157. Elliott 1993.

158. "Haec prima inter mulieres vovit Deo virginitatem, et ideo sola inter mulieres meruit virgo summae prolis fecunditatem." *Sermo de Nativitate*, in Honorius Augustodunensis, *Speculum ecclesiae*, PL 172:1001.

159. Honorius Augustodunensis 1991, 51.

160. Ibid., 70.

161. The combination of an Old English version of Ralph d'Escures's sermon together with materials encouraging monastic celibacy in a twelfth-century manuscript (BL Cotton Vespasian D. xiv) also suggested to scholar George Younge (2013, 12–13) that Mary served as a monastic example.

162. For an edition and discussion of the sermon, see Kienzle 1997. On Honorius, see ibid., 22–23. See also *Sermo in Assumptione*, in Honorius Augustodunensis, *Speculum Ecclesiae*, PL 172:497; 1991, 48–49; Constable 1995, 45–46.

163. Honorius Augustodunensis 1991, 48.

164. Constable 1995.

165. Honorius Augustodunensis 1991, 67.

166. Flint 1995, 136.

167. Honorius Augustodunensis, PL 158:585–92. Flint (1974, 200–201) has erroneously attributed this to Ralph d'Escures as well.

168. Honorius Augustodunensis 1991, 50.

169. Ibid., 52.

170. Ibid., 50.

171. Winchester Cathedral Library, Winchester Bible , f. 270v. For a color plate, see Donovan 1993, 20. For a description, see ibid., 54–55. Donovan does not mention Mary as a potential identification for the female figure in the image, citing only the church and Queen of Sheba.

172. Heslop 1981, 53; Morgan 1999, 130–31.

173. Morgan 1999, 132–34.

174. Reilly 2001, 160–62; Schmitt 2006.

175. Zarnecki 1951, 36. This discovery overturned earlier assumptions that the iconography originated in the monumental architecture of northern French churches, which has regardless continued, as evidenced in Gold 1985, particularly 51n18–19, 61–65, where the important English witnesses are omitted.

176. For Heslop's virtual reproduction of the chapterhouse and roundels that decorated the chapterhouse's ceiling, see http://www.uea.ac.uk/~t042/ (accessed March 5, 2016). The design and layout of the chapterhouse would have been undertaken circa

1095. Heslop 2005, 790. See also Heslop 2001. On the dating of the chapterhouse, see Barker 2005, 175.

177. Eton College MS 177. The fact that this manuscript shares titles and captions with the flyleaf of a twelfth-century Worcester manuscript (Worcester Cathedral Library MS F. 81)—drawn from the chapterhouse walls—suggests that the Eton illuminations reflect the now-lost cycle of wall paintings. On this manuscript, see Henry 1990. On its relation to Worcester, see ibid., 32–43.

178. A later English example is found in a tympanum at St. Mary's, Quenington, circa 1140–50; see Heslop 2005, 796–97. Philippe Verdier (1980, 17–18) also suggested the English origins of the iconography, but only with reference to Reading and Quenington.

179. Links between imagery of the Assumption and that of the so-called Triumph of the Virgin, although with no reference to the Worcester image, are discussed in Gold 1985, 57–61.

180. Heslop 2005, 792–93.

181. Skubiszewski 1988.

182. *Cur Deus Homo*, II.22, in Anselm of Canterbury 1998, 355.

183. *Cur Deus Homo*, I.3, in ibid., 268.

184. Southern (1954, 82, 83, 86) argued that contact with Jews may have inspired Anselm via Gilbert Crispin, the latter of whom claimed to have written his own polemical dialogue because of discussions he had with a Jewish businessman. See also Dahan, 1984; Abulafia 1990, 1992a.

185. See, for example, Williams 1935; Blumenkranz 1963; Dahan 1990, 1998; Abulafia 1995; Cohen 1999; Limor and Stroumsa 1996.

186. This is the main claim of Abulafia (most generally in 1995), although opposed by Dahan (1994). For a recent discussion of the Anselmian inheritance of these authors, see Dunthorne 2012, 82–107.

187. There has been considerable attention on this movement, including Funkenstein 1971; Abulafia 1984b, 1984c, 1990, 1992a, 1992b, 1995, 1996a; Schreckenberg 1988; Dahan, 1990, 1994, 1998; Cohen 1999; Chazan 2004; articles collected in Signer and Van Engen 2001.

188. Pseudo-William of Champeaux, who wrote a further work of polemic influenced by both Gilbert and Anselm, dedicated his work to Alexander, bishop of Lincoln (1123–48), indicating ties to England; see Abulafia 1989a.

189. See Gilbert 1986, xxvii– xxx, with discussion in Abulafia 1984a, 1984b, 1984c, 1992a; Blumenkranz 1948.

190. Tolan 1993, 10; 1996, 385.

191. Cohen (1999, 207) refuses to venture whether Alfonsi met any of Anselm's school, although he underscores the Anselmian tone of certain sections of the *Dialogue*.

192. There are twenty-two manuscripts of Gilbert's *Disputatio* from the twelfth century alone, and twenty-one of Alfonsi's, from Rochester (although in a Christ Church hand), Bury St. Edmunds, St. Albans, Lanthony priory in Gloucester, Westminster, and Hereford Cathedral. For a complete list of *Disputatio* manuscripts, see Gilbert 1986, xi–xx. For a full list of Peter's *Dialogue* manuscripts, see Tolan 1993, 102.

193. Van Engen (1983, 241–42) has emphasized the Lotharingian connection of Odo, Guibert, and Rupert. Rupert may prove the exception to the rule, influenced by his ex-

egetical interests and discussions with Jews in the Rhineland. Still, Rupert's treatise, the *Anulus sive dialogus*, is of a later date than all those discussed here: 1120/21. For the treatise, see Rupert of Deutz 1979.

194. For Odo, see Odo of Tournai 1994. See also Rubin 2009b, 162–63; Abulafia 1989a. For Guibert, see Abulafia 1996b, 166; Ziolkowski 2001; Rubenstein 2002, 116–24. See also Rubin 2009b, 163–64. On Guibert, see Rubenstein 2002, 116–24; Abulafia 1996b, 166; Labande 1984. See also Dahan 1984, 530–31; Rubin 2009b, 163–64.

195. Odo of Tournai 1994, 96. Guibert of Nogent (PL 156:492) articulated something similar. For translation, see Rubenstein 2002, 118–19.

196. Odo of Tournai 1994, 97. See also Guibert of Nogent PL 156:494.

197. PL 156: 499–500.

198. For explorations of the polemical angle of Honorius's gloss of the Song of Songs, but with a focus on Honorius's later *Commentary on the Song of Songs*, which does not feature Mary, see Cohen 2004; Monroe 2007. For a more in-depth discussion of the *Sigillum*'s polemical dimension, see Ihnat 2015.

199. On this, see Matter 1990, 25–31.

200. This may have been formative for Bernard's similar reading of the Song of Songs in his sermons on the text. See, for example, Berger 2010; Cohen 1999, especially 231–33.

201. Honorius Augustodunensis 1991, 77.

202. Ibid.

203. Ibid.

204. Ibid.

205. Ibid.

206. Ibid., 81.

207. Ibid., 82.

208. Ibid.

209. Ibid., 84.

210. Ihnat 2015.

211. Cf. Heslop 2005, 790. Heslop took this from a Worcester manuscript (Worcester Cathedral MS F. 8.1, f. 234) related to the Eton manuscript in which the roundels are found, with a slightly truncated version of this verse. For the relation between the manuscripts, see Henry 1990, 32–43.

212. Heslop (2005, 794) thinks rather that a more likely source is a Worcester manuscript containing Bede's *Commentary on the Song of Songs*, reworked in the twelfth century, which attributes this line to *Synagoga ad fidem Christi conversa*. Nevertheless, this is essentially the same character as *Ecclesia convertenda*, so the *Sigillum* is an equally likely source.

213. Ibid., 791.

214. Ibid., 795–97.

215. For a discussion of the anti-Jewish tenor of the Eton roundels, which may reflect the chapterhouse paintings, see Henry 1990, 42–43. Heslop (2001, 297), on the other hand, maintains that the tone of these is conciliatory, given the stress on the union between the two peoples. For the union, however, the Jews must convert, arguably begging the question of what kind of reconciliation this really is.

216. On the collatio, see Webber 2010, 10n17.

217. Lambeth Palace Library MS 3, f. 198. For the manuscript's dates and place of origin, see Shepard 2007, 4–8. For a description of the image, see ibid., 143–51.

218. Lambeth Palace Library MS 3, f. 307, in Kauffmann 2003, 86–87.

219. On the development of the image, see Fassler 2000a.

220. Contemporary depictions are found in three French manuscripts from the first half or even quarter of the twelfth century: the Citeaux Lectionary, Dijon Bibliothèque municipale MS 641 (f. 40v), Dijon Bibliothèque municipale MS 129 (f. 4v), and the Saint-Bénigne Bible, Dijon Bibliothèque municipale MS 2+ (f. 406). The Virgin is depicted in these as Theotokos, with Christ on her lap, not independently as she is in the English manuscripts. For the Winchester and Eadwine Psalter images, see Gibson, Heslop, and Pfaff 1992; Dodwell 1993, 336–40. For English originality in depicting the Jesse Tree, see Shepard 2007, 146; Kauffmann 2003, 130.

221. BnF MS lat. 16743–46 (f. IV:7v), possibly from the Capuchins of Saint-Honoré, from circa 1175–200, and BL Add. MS 15452 (f. 331v), from northern France or England, circa 1210. On the ties to these manuscripts, see Shepard 2007, 144n5.

222. Kauffmann 2003, 87.

223. Lipton 2014, 61–63.

224. Kauffmann 2003, 133.

225. This was also argued by the anonymous author of the Assumption sermon: "Si igitur natura matris est filius, conveniens est ut sit et filii mater, non quantum pertinet ad aequam administrationem, sed quantum pertinet ad eamdem reciprocam substantiam: ut homo de homine, caro de carne, mater a filio, filius a matre, non ad unitatem personae, sed ad unitatem corporalis naturae et substantiae." *De Assumptione Beatae Virginis Mariae, Liber Unus* PL 40:1145.

226. Pfaff 1980.

Chapter 3: Hagiographies of Mary: Miracle Collections

1. See especially Ward 1982. See also Philippart 1996; Boyarin 2010.

2. This was noted in Shea 2004.

3. Most explicitly in Signori 1996.

4. For more on the apocrypha, see chapter 4.

5. Ibid.

6. Guibert of Nogent 1996, 173–81; see Yarrow 2006, 70–75.

7. Hermann of Tournai, PL 156:961–1017.

8. Although these studies do not discuss the religious dimension so much as the social and political aspects of these pilgrimage accounts, see Signori 1995; 1996, 599–604. For a review, see Remensnyder 1999. The French collections are also the main subject of Benedicta Ward's (1982, 142–55) survey of Marian miracles. For an edited version of the Coutances miracles, see Pigeon 1876, 367–83. These miracles have been dated between 1106 and 1135, and probably closer to 1130; see Signori 1995, 90–91. For the Saint-Pierres-sur-Dives miracles, recorded for the occasion of the abbey's construction in 1145, see Brunat 1974; Signori 1995, 152–73. For the Chartres miracles,

see Fassler 2009, 171. The Fassler book establishes a link between the collections' compiler, Walter of Cluny, and Henry of Blois, a former monk of Cluny and then bishop of Winchester; perhaps the impetus to record the Chartres miracles was provided by the English precedent. For the Rocamadour miracles, see Bull 1999. For the little-known Dormans miracles, composed by Gautier of Compiègne sometime after 1133, see *De miraculis beatae virginis Mariae*, in PL 173:1379–86; Sansterre 2011b, 69–71.

9. On the importance of miracles for pilgrimage sites, see Finucane 1977, 1995; Sigal 1977, 1985; Yarrow 2006. For an exploration of the complex social and theological dynamics at work in the cult of saints, although not strictly focused on this phenomenon, and responding specifically to the work of Peter Brown, see Hayward 1999. On the Marian tradition, especially from a sociopolitical perspective, see Signori 1995. See also the introduction in Bull 1999.

10. According to Benedicta Ward (1982, 134), the universal collections came later. The English collections nonetheless appeared sometime between 1120 and 1150, with only the Coutances and Laon collections produced earlier or simultaneously (between 1106 and 1135 for the former, and between 1112 and 1113 for the earliest version of the latter).

11. See the introduction.

12. Yarrow 2006, 63–99.

13. Southern 1958. First put forward in Mussafia 1887–91; largely confirmed by a survey in Ward 1883, 586–600.

14. Macray 1863, 320. On Dominic, see Southern 1958, 182; Jennings 1962. Although J. C. Jennings is not explicit about the dating of Dominic's collection, Philip Shaw (2006, 398) places it between 1125—the year he became prior—and 1130.

15. These are Oxford Balliol College MS 240 and private owner F. Wormald. J. C. Jennings (1962, 300) identified two more: BL Cotton MS Cleopatra C. x, Aberdeen University Library MS 137 and Toulouse, Bibliothèque municipale MS 482.

16. "Mead" is taken from the Life of Dunstan, though seemingly not from either "B's," Eadmer's, or Osbern's versions. The story of "Eulalia" concerns the abbess of Shaftesbury, with whom Anselm exchanged many letters, and is said to have been told by a monk of Bec. Southern 1958, 189–91.

17. "The Pilgrim to Santiago de Compostela" and "Two Brothers in Rome" were adapted from the *Dicta Anselmi*. See Southern 1958, 189–91, 193, 199; Southern and Schmitt 1969, 25–26; Thomson 1972, 631.

18. On the story about Anselm, see also Williamson's appendix to the letters in Osbert of Clare 1929, 191–200; Thomson 1972, 630–31.

19. New York, Pierpont Morgan MS 736. See Thomson 1982. For Anselm's involvement in its production, see Hahn 1991, 132. For a description and discussion, see Wormald 1952. For its dating, see Thomson 1971, 212–20; Parkes 2014. On Anselm's development of Bury's scriptorium, see Webber 1998, 189. This was made more pressing by the long vacancy at Bury (1102–21); see Abou-el-Haj 1983.

20. Southern based his understanding of Anselm's collection on Chicago UL 147. For a transcription of the manuscript, see Dexter 1927. The tales in the second part of this manuscript vary a great deal in tone and register, are generally longer, and contain more specific geographic and biographical details; they have short introductions, and

long doxologies as epilogues; some are in verse, especially toward the end of the collections—all of which suggests they were not written by the same author.

21. This has been the terminology used to describe the various sections of the collections since the first discussion by Adolfo Mussafia 1887–91. Southern (1958) was the first to claim that Anselm composed both HM and TS.

22. I make no claims for his authorship, though, and accept that he may have merely acted as supervisor or patron.

23. Peter Carter (1959) produced an edition, and J. M. Canal (William of Malmesbury 1968) published another one, but recently, Michael Winterbottom and Rodney Thomson edited and translated a version (William of Malmesbury 2015).

24. Ibid., xvi. Philip Shaw (2006) argued for a longer period of writing, with some of the stories already composed by 1125.

25. William wrote about the lives of saints Wulfstan, Dunstan, Patrick, Benignus, and Indract at the request of Prior Warin of Worcester and the monks of Glastonbury, for whom he also wrote a history of their abbey. This type of commission was not unusual, as most other hagiographers of the period attest. For Aldhelm, see book 5 of William of Malmesbury 2007, 501–79. For his other hagiographic works, see William of Malmesbury 2002.

26. CCCC MS 42, found at Dover, a priory of Christ Church, but written in a Christ Church hand. The first twenty-six miracles are almost an identical copy of those found in Chicago UL MS 147, the first section of which is a complete HM series. For William's visit to Bury, see Thomson 2003b, 73.

27. William's authorship is supported by attribution of a series of miracles in Salisbury Cathedral MS 97, as pointed out in William of Malmesbury 2015, xv–xvi. For dating, see Shaw 2006.

28. Koopmans 2011, 93, 101. See also Southern 1970, 172.

29. Koopmans 2011, 97–98. Pierre-André Sigal (1977, 244) has noted the trend as widely European. Michael Clanchy (1993, 7) has shown that the special circumstances in England after the conquest may have added further impetus.

30. Koopmans 2011, 97.

31. Published in Southern and Schmitt 1969.

32. For the famous account of this type of phenomenon, see Geary 1990.

33. See Hayward 1998, 2005; Rubenstein 1999; Yarrow 2006.

34. See Yarrow 2006, 24–62. See also Bates 2014.

35. "Ad omnipotentis Dei laudem cum saepe recitentur sanctorum miracula quae per eos egit divina clementia, maxime sanctae Dei genitricis Mariae debent referri preconia, quae sunt omni melle dulciora. Ergo ad roborandas in eius amorem fidelium mentes et ad excitanda corda pigritantium ea que fideliter narrari audivimus, largiente deo recitare studeamus." Dexter 1927, 15.

36. "[Quae licet] quaedam [miracula] sint praecedentium patrum stilo exarata tamen quia ita sunt in diversis codicibus disgregata ut difficillime vel nullomodo a quibusdam queant inveniri iccirco studium fuit disgregata congregare quatinus facilius possint in unum volumen redacta reperiri." Dominic of Evesham 1998, 256.

37. Ibid.

38. Ibid., 257.

39. "Verum enimvero sic nequaquam oportet fieri, sed multo amplius nova cum antiquis diligentissime perscrutari ut quemadmodum diversis cibis corpus, sic variis virtutibus et miraculis animus affectuosius inhereat cum omnibus ratione vigentibus sit in propatulo nullum bonum alteri nocere sic e diverso scimus nullum malum alteri prodesse. Ista est materialis causa qua licet longe infra pedes aliorum positi, tamen co-acti sumus ad hoc opus accedere ac deprecantibus fratribus et amicis multorum pro velle morem gerere, docti magis in Dei sapientia quam in aliqua scintilla secularis scien-tiae confidere. Subsequitur etiam finalis causa qua spes maxime appetenda praecipitur tam scriptores quam lectores et auditores in die tremendi examinis ab ira iusti iudicis per merita gloriosissimae matris eiusdem iudicis protegi cuius cognoscimus virtutes tum scribendo tum legendo et audiendo venerari." Ibid.

40. On the tropes in the hagiographic prologue more generally, see Goodich 1981. For other contemporary examples, see Gransden 1990, especially 61–62.

41. This was remarked in Carter 1959, 302.

42. William of Malmesbury 2015, 13–14.

43. Ibid., 14.

44. Gregory the Great, *Homilies on Ezekiel*, 11.7, in 6:1014.

45. Sønnesyn 2012, 61.

46. Allen Smith 2006.

47. William's miracles are set in twenty-five different locations, as noted in William of Malmesbury 2015, xxi.

48. See Southern 1958, 189–91.

49. In later copies, these varied collections would be combined, and the miracles of Soissons, Rocamadour, and Chartres were incorporated into volumes that also con-tained universal Marian miracles.

50. William of Malmesbury 2015, 21.

51. Respectively, CCCC MS 42, Lambeth Palace Library MS 214; BL Cotton MS Cleopatra C. x, Oxford Balliol College MS 240; BnF MS lat. 18168; BnF MS lat. 12169, 12606; BL Add. MS 35112; BnF MS lat. 14463; BnF MS lat. 2769. These are only the man-uscripts linked to identifiable locations, from the twelfth century. A large number are simply ascribed to England (BL Add. MS 15723; BL Egerton MS 2947), France (Chicago University Library [henceforth Chicago UL] MS 147; BnF lat. MS 2873), or unknown (Oxford Bodl. Laud Miscellania MS 410; Oxford Bodl. Canonici Liturgical [hereafter Canon. Liturg.] 325; Copenhagen Thott MS 128.2; Copenhagen Thott MS 26.8; BnF lat. MS 2672).

52. It was also noted for miracles more generally in Palazzo 1998, 1145–46.

53. Ward 1982, 162.

54. There is also a striking lack of miracles related to cures, as noted in ibid., 155. This is perhaps unsurprising because they do not deal with local shrines.

55. For a classic study, see Finucane 1977, 1995.

56. Guy Philippart 1996, 571–77), for example, has noted the strong soteriological nature of Marian miracles from the eleventh century onward.

57. See ibid., 79–80.

58. Lambeth Palace Library MS 214 f. 151; BL Add. MS 15723 f. 67v; BL Add. MS 25112 f. 22; BL Arundel MS 346 f. 60v; BL Cotton MS Cleopatra C. x f. 116; BL Royal

MS 6. B. xiv f. 91v; BnF MS lat. 2672 f. 14; BnF MS lat. 2873 f. 21v; BnF MS lat. 12169 f. 116; BnF MS lat. 14463 f. 5v; BnF MS lat. 18168 f. 80; CCCC MS 42 f. 91; Copenhagen Thott MS 26.8 f. 53; Copenhagen Thott MS 128.2 f. 2v; Oxford Balliol College MS 240 f. 148v; Oxford Bodl. Laud Misc. MS 410 f. 78v; Oxford Bodl. Canon. Liturg. MS 325 f. 161v. See Dexter 1927, 17.

59. Lambeth Palace Library MS 214 f. 151v; BL Add. MS 15723 f. 68v; BL Add. MS 35112 f. 22v; BL Arundel MS 346 f. 61; BL Cotton MS Cleopatra C. x f. 117v; BL Royal MS 6. B. xiv f. 96v; BnF MS lat. 2672 f. 15; BnF MS lat. 12169 f. 116v; BnF MS lat. 12606 f. 172; BnF MS lat. 14463 f. 6; BnF MS lat. 18168 81; Copenhagen Thott MS 26.8 f. 54v; Copenhagen Thott MS 128.2 f. 3v; Oxford Balliol College MS 240 f. 149; Oxford Bodl. Laud Misc. MS f. 79v; Oxford Bodl. Canon. Liturg. MS 325 f. 163. See Dexter 1927, 18.

60. Lambeth Palace Library MS 214 f. 154v; BL Add. MS 35112 f. 29v; BL Arundel MS 346 f. 63v; BL Cotton MS Cleopatra C. x f. 123; BnF MS lat. 2672 f. 21; BnF MS lat. 2873 f. 24v; BnF lat. MS 12169 f. 119v; BnF MS lat. 12606 f. 172v; BnF MS lat. 14463 f. 17; BnF MS lat. 18168 f. 87; CCCC MS 42 f. 84v; Copenhagen Thott MS 26.8 f. 63v; Copenhagen Thott MS 128.2 f. 10v; Oxford Balliol College MS 240 f. 152; Oxford Bodl. Laud Misc. MS 410 f. 83; Oxford Bodl. Canon. Liturg. MS f. 169v. See Dexter 1927, 28.

61. On Eulalia, see Knowles, Brooke, and London 2001, 219.

62. Dexter 1927, 36.

63. " Et nos fratres karissimi, qui digni non sumus ut illius vocemur servi, si eius servicium post hanc admonitionem, iuxta illius voluntate celebrare studuerimus, credo quod illius sanctimonialis feminae fratres nos in eterna beatitudine dignabitur facere." Ibid.

64. BL Lansdowne MS 383, in Beck 1924. See also Morgan 1999, 126.

65. Constable 1996, 206–7.

66. See, for example, CCCC MS 42 f. 87; BL Cotton MS Cleopatra C. x f. 136v; BL Royal MS 6. B. xiv f. 97; BnF MS lat. 14463 ff. 40v–41. Chicago UL MS 147 (Dexter 1927, 36) and BnF MS lat. 2873 f. 64v, despite being French in provenance, have a number of stories with English settings including Eulalia, and may have been based on an English source.

67. Cf. William of Malmesbury 2015, 75–76. This antiphon is derived from a story found in BL Add. MS 35112 f. 54v; BL Arundel MS 346 f. 70–71; BnF MS lat. 2672 60v; BnF MS lat. 14463 ff. 25v–26v; BnF MS lat. 18168 ff. 100v–101v; Copenhagen Thott MS 128.2 ff. 46v–48.

68. William of Malmesbury 2015, 73–74.

69. The most standard version is found in Dexter 1927, 19. But it is also found in BL Add. MS 35112 f. 22v; BL Arundel MS 346 ff. 61–61v; Balliol College MS 240 ff. 149–49v; BnF MS lat. 2672 f. 15v; BnF MS lat. 12169 f. 116v; BnF MS lat. 12606 f. 172; BnF MS lat. 14463 f. 6v; BnF MS lat. 18168 ff. 82–82v; CCCC MS 42 f. 82v; Copenhagen Thott MS 26.8 ff. 55–56; Copenhagen Thott MS 128.2 ff. 4–5; BL Cotton MS Cleopatra C. x f. 118v; Lambeth Palace Library MS 214 f. 152; Oxford Bodl. Laud Misc. MS 410 f. 80; Oxford Bodl. Canon. Liturg. MS 325 ff. 163v–64.

70. Ibid., 19.

71. Damian 1844–55, PL 145:588.

72. BnF MS lat. 1085 from the abbey of Saint-Martial-de-Limoges contains the antiphon, as does an antiphoner showing Aquitanian influence from the cathedral of Toledo (Toledo Biblioteca Capitular MS 44.2) from circa 1095. G. G. Meersseman (1960, 192) placed it in the twelfth century.

73. The first is found in BL Cotton MS Tiberius A. iii, f. 111. See Dewick 1902, xlv; Clayton 1990, 73–74. The second is found in BL Royal MS 2 A. x, f. 116v. While in no way complete, the CANTUS database contains only fifteen entries for the antiphon, mostly from the fourteenth century or later.

74. William of Malmesbury 2015, 67.

75. "Gaude Maria virgo cunctas haereses sola interemisti quae Gabrielis archangeli dictis credidisti. Dum virgo dominem et hominem genuisti et post partum virgo inviolata permansisti."

76. William of Malmesbury 2007, iv.177, 8–9, 476–79.

77. On the votive offices, see chapter 1.

78. William of Malmesbury 2002.

79. William of Malmesbury 2015, 33.

80. This hymn was originally composed by Sedulius, although without the lines referring to Mary; ibid., 34. See also AH 50:53.

81. "Hic ipsa praecelsa parens altissimi saepius visa, et cum dulcimodo virginum choro ineffabili suavitate coelestis harmoniae noscitur audita. [Huic candidissimo contubernio angelum domini exercituum, et post Augustinum suosque consortes nitidissimum decus Anglorum, familiarius ac frequentius interfuisse beatissimum constat Dunstanum]." Capgrave 1874, 116. On this anecdote, see Hiley 1994, 31.

82. For Osbern's account, see Capgrave 1874, 117–19. For William's, see ibid., 315–17. I was unable to find the hymn either in CANTUS or AH, suggesting that it was an English innovation.

83. See Gransden 1989.

84. William of Malmesbury 2015, 104–5.

85. Carter 1959, 545. For the evolution of the building, see Gransden 2004.

86. It is found also in CCCC MS 42 f. 82; BL Cotton MS Cleopatra C. x f. 133v; Oxford Bodl. Canon. Liturg. MS 325 f. 191–91v; BnF MS lat. 2672 f. 36v; BnF MS lat. 14463 ff. 22v–23; Copenhagen Thott MS 128.2 ff. 30–30v; Oxford Balliol College MS 240 ff. 145v–46; BL Royal MS 6. B. xiv f. 96v.

87. This is part of the popular hymn *Ave maris stella*, which is found as early as the ninth century. Here, we are given the first line of the last three verses of the hymn, which are as follows:

Virgo singularis,	O unique Virgin,
inter omnes mitis,	Meek above all others,
nos culpis solutos,	Free us from our sins,
mites fac et castos.	Make us meek and chaste.
Vitam præsta puram,	Bestow a pure life,
iter para tutum,	Prepare a safe way,
ut videntes Jesum,	That seeing Jesus,
semper collætemur.	We may ever rejoice.

Sit laus Deo Patri,	Praise be to God the Father,
summo Christo decus,	To the Most High Christ (be) glory,
Spiritui Sancto,	To the Holy Spirit,
tribus honor unus. Amen	(Be) honor, to the Three equally. Amen.

88. Dexter 1927, 15. The passage in the manuscript contains only the incipits, but I have supplemented them with the complete text in square brackets, from the CANTUS online database.

89. BL Add. MS 21927, ff. 105–5v. For an edition, see Roper 1993, 235. Although the presence here of the *Nunc dimittis* canticle would suggest a secular cursus, almost all the votive offices surveyed in Roper (ibid., 235) include it.

90. "Primum et ultimum psalmum, pro consuetudine interponendo: In te, Domine, speravi, dices. Capitulum vero et collectam ac cetera ex Annuntiatione dominica assumes." Dominic of Evesham 1998, 278.

91. *Deus qui de beata* appears as a collect for vespers of the Annunciation feast in the Leofric collectar (BL Harley MS 2961, f. 29v) from the third quarter of the eleventh century, and together with *Ecce virgo concipiet* as a chapter for lauds and second vespers of the Annunciation feast in a twelfth-century St. Albans breviary (BL Royal MS 2 A. x, f. 121, 122).

92. For some twelfth-century manuscripts that contain it, see BL Add. MS 35112 f. 32v; BnF MS lat. 2672 f. 46v; BnF MS lat. 2873 f. 29; BnF MS lat. 14463 ff. 20–21; CCCC MS 42 f. 89; Copenhagen Thott MS 26.8 ff. 77–79v; BL Cotton MS Cleopatra C. x f. 142; Oxford Bodl. Laud Misc. MS 410 ff. 93–93v; Oxford Bodl. Canon. Liturg. MS 325; Chicago UL MS 147 (Dexter 1927, 52).

93. Cf. Dexter 1927, 52. No abbot named Leofric appears in Knowles, Brooke, and London 2001, 38.

94. William identifies the introit's composer as Sedulius (d. 450) in his version. Cf. Dominic of Evesham 1998, 83. This is in fact true insofar as the *Salve sancta parens* introit is drawn from Sedulius's *Carmen Paschale* (II.l, 63–64).

95. BL Add. MS 15723 f. 76; BL Add. MS 35112 f. 57; BnF lat. MS 2672 f. 66v; BnF lat. MS 2769 f. 66; BnF 14463 ff. 33–33v; Copenhagen Thott MS 128.2 ff. 51v–53; Oxford Balliol College MS 240 ff. 156–56v; Oxford Bodl. Canon. Liturg. MS 325 ff. 207–8v.

96. "Dominus presul hoc Herbertus / Norwicensis est expertus / Qui dicebat se vidisse / hanc et manu contigisse." BL Add. MS 15723, f. 65v, as indicated in Ward 1883, 623.

97. See, for example, CCCC MS 270, ff. 149–49v; Oxford Bodl. Rawlinson MS lit. c. 1, f. 138v; see Pfaff 2009, 158–65.

98. Including Chicago UL MS 147 (Dexter 1927, 48–51); BnF MS lat. 2672 f. 51; BnF MS lat. 14463 ff. 21–22v; Copenhagen Thott MS 26.8 ff. 103–7; BL Cotton MS Cleopatra C. x f. 139v; BL Royal MS 6. B. xiv f. 85v; BL Add. MS 35112 ff. 17–18, where it appears separately as an actual sermon titled *Sermo quare in Sabbatis fit memoria beatae Marie.*

99. "Sollempnem memoriam sanctae Mariae virginis matris domini decet filios ecclesiae sollempni officio celebrare quippe cum multis sanctorum concessum sit quadam speciali dignitate familiaritatis ut quicumque celebratores extiterint non fraudenter salute ipsorum patrocinii. [Quis quem sanctorum poterit quis unquam laudis sacrificio promere potentiorem in subveniendo miseris quam dominam Mariam mundi reginam,

miserorum miseratricem utpote ipsius misericordiae misericordem matrem?]" Dexter 1927, 48. The term "memoria" could refer to the office itself, as is the case in the Portiforium of Wulfstan; cf. Hughes 1960, 2:vi.

100. The miracle about the miraculous image of Mary in Constantinople circulated separately in, for example, BL Egerton MS 2947.

101. Dexter 1927, 50.

102. "Hac spe roboratae plures in mundo ecclesiae, quia non possunt omnes, elegerunt vel unam in ebdomada diem in tantae virginis matris honore. Quae autem dies sic festiva Mariam deceret, quam septima sabbati, livera ab omni senario opere diei? Igitur in hac die multi fideles accensi zelo Mariae ad gratiam reddunt sollempne servitium gratiose matri. Sed ne fastidium generet festivitas per singulas horas, donec et illud confirmet sinodalis auctoritas, missam tantum cantare sollempniter, nec sine gloria in excelsis deo. Et hoc probant ratione, sumentes argumentum de minore. Si rex inquiunt vel imperator advenerit, quae ecclesia est quae non statim solitas procrastinet ferias, faciem templi coronis aureis adornans, thuribulis et ceteris ad processionem ordinatis? Igitur si ad terreni principis presentiam quodammodo renovatur paschalis sollempnitas, dignum et religiosum valde est ut mundi domina gloriosa Maria in suo Sabbato honoretur sollempni officio, ad filii honorem qui diligit et honorat bonam matrem. Iam vero ne dicant insipientes apud se non recte confitentes quiescere faciamus omnes festos dies Mariae a Sabbato, quia non vidimus signum Dei est opere preciosum, referre quid operetur Deus in Constantinopolitana urbe, quo signo defendat Sabbata Mariae." Ibid.

103. The miracle is found detached from the sermon in a number of miracle collections, including William of Malmesbury's, which was not among those noted in Barré 1967, 390–91.

104. For some of the earliest, see ibid., 388–90.

105. The sermon *Sollempnem memoriam* may be later, because it is in a different hand from the pieces around it. Ibid., 380. For Barré's claims of Lietbert's authorship of the sermon, see ibid., 392.

106. Somerville 1972, 127–30, and more in chapter 1.

107. Trinity College, Cambridge, MS 315 [B.14.30], ff. 55–56v; see Gameson 1999, 72. For a digital version of the he manuscript, see http://sites.trin.cam.ac.uk/manuscripts /B_14_30/manuscript.php?fullpage=1&startingpage=1 (accessed March 8, 2016).

108. Clayton 1990, 79–81.

109. Ibid., 80–81.

110. See Riley 1867, 1:284–85.

111. "Constituit et unusquique clericus ordinatus sive monachus per singulos dies horas sanctae Mariae decantaret. Adiunxit etiam hanc institutionem ut in singulis hebdomadibus semper in Sabbato commemoratio ipsius santissimae virginitatis ac fecunditatis fieret, quemadmodum in dominica fit commemoratio resurrectionis filii sui. Dominic of Evesham 1998, 277.

112. BL Royal 6. B. xiv, ff. 84v–85. Although this manuscript dates from circa 1200, the story is also found in the twelfth-century English miracle collection, Toulouse MS 482, which itself contains many of William of Malmesbury's tales. See Ward 1883, 638. For the Toulouse manuscript, see Mussafia 1887–91, 2:24.

113. "Qui sanctae Dei genitrici placere studebat, vel salutando, vel horas eius canendo, vel etiam multis formis servicium eius agendo." Dexter 1927, 26.

114. Ibid., 27.

115. For the former, see ibid., 54. For the latter, see Lambeth Palace Library MS 214, ff. 158–59.

116. BnF MS lat. 2672 f. 63v; BnF MS lat.14463 ff. 42–43; Oxford Balliol College MS 240 ff. 144v–45v; BL Royal MS 6. B. xiv, f. 90v.

117. Dexter 1927, 30.

118. "[Hic sicuti de pluribus retulimus, sanctae virginis Mariae mundi reginae, servitium devota mente reddebat,] horasque diei que tunc temporis a paucissimis dicebantur in eius honorem decantabat." Ibid.

119. Damian 1989–98, 1:157. See also Fulton 2002, 224.

120. William of Malmesbury 2015, 77.

121. Ibid., 79–82.

122. Ibid., 39.

123. Ibid., 73–74.

124. John of Worcester 1995, 223–25.

125. William of Malmesbury 2002, 111–13.

126. William of Malmesbury 2007, 451.

127. John of Salerno 1844–55, 133:72.

128. William of Malmesbury 2015, 62.

129. On the celebration of the Little Office at Cluny, see chapter 1.

130. Coates 1999, 6.

131. On the Little Office in England, see chapter 1.

132. For some of the manuscripts in which it is found, see BL Add. MS 35112 f. 24v; BL Arundel MS 346 ff. 66v–67; Oxford Balliol College MS 240 ff. 158–58v; BnF MS lat. 2672 f. 50v; BnF MS lat. 2873 f. 27; BnF MS lat. 12606 f. 174; BnF MS lat. 18168 ff. 93–93v; CCCC MS 42 ff. 88–88v; Copenhagen Thott MS 26.8 ff. 74–75v; BL Cotton MS Cleopatra C. x ff. 138v–39v; Oxford Bodl. Laud Misc. MS 410 ff. 88–88v; Oxford Bodl. Canon. Liturg. MS 325 ff. 175v–77; BL Egerton MS 2947 f. 36. See also the transcription of Chicago UL MS 147 (Dexter 1927, 37–38).

133. For a discussion of this story, see Thurston 1904; Bishop 1918a; Southern 1958; Lamy 2000, 90–93. See also Clayton 1990, 47–50. Scholars have tended to take the tale at face value, including in Corbin 1967, 430–31.

134. Translated in Clayton 1990, 48–49.

135. See Lamy 2000, 91. For Southern's explanations, see Southern 1958, 196.

136. Lamy 2000, 91–92; Southern 1958, 196. For the immigration of disgraced clerics to Scandinavia, see Niblaeus 2010, 157–60.

137. The version that appears in a Heiligenkreuz manuscript is notably pro-Norman: "In that time, in which it pleased the divine benevolence to correct the English of their evils and to control more tightly their servile duties by the most glorious Duke of the Normans, William, he subjected that same kingdom through war, and by William's strength and efforts, entirely reformed for the better the state of ecclesiastical dignity. The devil, enemy of all good things, envying the works of the Duke's pious intention, first by the deceptions of his close associates, then by the incursions of foreigners, in

many ways tried to impede his successes." (*Tempore illo, quo divinae placuit bonitati, Anglorum gentem de malis suis corrigere, et suae servitutis officiis arctius astringere, gloriosissimo Normannorum Duci Wilhelmo eandem patriam debellando subegit, ejusque virtute et industria totius ecclesiasticae dignitatis statum in melius reformavit. Cuius piae intentionis operibus invidens ille bonorum omnium inimicus diabolus, tum familiarum fraudibus, tum extraneorum incursibus multotiens conatus est ejus obsistere successibus.*) Crane 1925, 22.

138. Marielle Lamy notes the same incongruity, but with reference to St. Augustine's, where the feast was not actually celebrated before the Norman Conquest. Lamy 2000, 93n174.

139. Southern 1958, 198–99. In arguing that the author must have had access to the Ramsey chronicles, Southern seems to preclude oral transmission, yet Koopmans (2011, 70) points to oral transmission as the source of errors (i.e., à la Broken Telephone).

140. On the purposeful "selectivity" of memory for the construction of institutional histories, see Geary 1994.

141. Bishop 1918a, 249; Southern 1958, 194; Boyarin 2010, 20.

142. This was put forward in Boyarin 2010, 22. Alternatively, she suggested Stigand, who had presided over both Winchester and Christ Church, two institutions that celebrated the feast pre–Norman Conquest. It would seem odd, however, to justify a feast to Norman ecclesiasts by way of a rebel Anglo-Saxon bishop.

143. Ibid., 20.

144. Lambeth Palace Library MS 214; Rome, Vatican Library Reginensis Latini MS 543.

145. The earliest manuscript known so far to contain it is Chicago UL MS 147.

146. For links between the abbeys, starting in the tenth century with Ramsey's commission of Abbo of Fleury's *Passio Sancti Edmundi*, see Gransden 1981, 71.

147. This was noted by Southern (1958, 194), but without resolution.

148. Another version of the legend, found in an anonymous sermon for the Conception, has been dated to the late twelfth century by Lamy (2000, 91, 103).

149. For Bernard's letter, see ibid., 51–52.

150. The abbot Odilo of Cluny commissioned a copy of Ildefonsus's treatise, *De perpetua virginitate*, together with his *Vita*; see Garand 1979. See also Ferreiro Alemparte 1970, 252.

151. "Fuit in Toletana urbe quidam archiepiscopus qui vocabatur Hildefonsus, religiosus valde et bonis operibus ornatus qui inter cetera bonorum operum studia sanctam Mariam Dei genitricem valde diligebat et prout poterat omni reverentia eam honorabat. In cuius laudem volumen insigne de eius sanctissima virginitate stilo elegante composuit quid ita eidem sanctae Mariae conplacuit ut illi ipsum librum manu tenens appareret et pro tali opere gratias referret. Ille vero cupiens eam altius honorare constituit ut celebraretur sollempnitas eius singulis annis octavo die ante festivitatem natalis ita videlicet ut si sollempnitas annuntiationis dominice circa passionem vel resurrectionem evenerit in predicto die sub eandem sollempnitatem congrue restitui possit." Dexter 1927, 16. Lambeth Palace Library MS 214 f. 150v; BL Add. MS 15723 f. 66v; BL Add. MS 35112 f. 21v; BL Arundel MS 346 f. 60; BL Cotton MS Cleopatra C. x f. 115v; BnF MS lat. 2672 f. 13; BnF MS lat. 2769 f. 63v; BnF MS lat. 2873 f. 21; BnF MS lat. 12169 f. 116; BnF MS lat. 12606 f. 171v; BnF MS lat. 14463 f. 5; BnF MS lat. 18168 f. 79; CCCC MS

42 f. 82; Copenhagen Thott MS 26.8 f. 51; Copenhagen Thott MS 128.2 f. 1; Oxford Balliol College MS 240 f. 148; Oxford Bodl. Laud Misc. MS 410 f. 78; Oxford Bodl. Canon. Liturg. MS 325 f. 160.

152. William gets the council wrong, citing Toledo IX (655) instead of Toledo X (656); see Martínez Díez and Rodríguez 1992, 517–21. Rodney M. Thomson (2003b, 64–66, 131–32) has indicated that William would have been familiar with the *Pseudo-Isidorean Decretals*, which contain the acts of the council.

153. Cf. William of Malmesbury 2015, 45–49. For the historical background of the text, see de Gaiffier 1970.

154. William of Malmesbury 2015, 47.

155. See ibid., 45–49.

156. Dominic of Evesham 1998, 274.

157. William of Malmesbury 2015, 37. This attribution is also found in William of Malmesbury 1998, 518–19.

158. For Fulbert's responsories, see Drèves 1886–1922, 50:280. Cf. William of Malmesbury 1968, 82; Fassler 2009.

159. The feast of the Purification was actually instated by Pope Sergius I (687–701). Cf. Palazzo and Andrews Johansson 1996.

160. William of Malmesbury 2015, 130–31.

161. See, for example, Signori 1996, 612.

162. Koopmans 2011, 132.

163. Bull 1999, 42. The only exception to this is discussion of the Aelfsige legend, which is widely recognized as having featured in liturgical celebrations for the feast of the Conception. See, for example, Bishop 1918a, 249.

164. This would change significantly in the later twelfth century with respect to relic cults, in which we know that miracle accounts were read aloud by the shrine as pilgrims visited. For the later collections, see Koopmans 2011, 112–200.

165. The reverse is the case in one of the earliest-surviving manuscripts of the HM collection, Lambeth Palace Library 214 ff. 150v–64v, which follows from two sermons by Hildebert of Lavardin (d. 1133) in a different hand (PL 171:751–58, 947–50); neither of these is Marian, however, making the choice of manuscript into which to insert the Marian collection a mystery. Still, Hildebert had important ties to Bec, connecting him to the circle of Anselm. Vaughn 2012, 112.

166. The lives of Eustachius, Brendan, Drithelm, and Salvius as well as the vision of Wettin by Walafrid are in one hand, and the fragment of a missal in another hand appears to have been added to them. The sermons that follow the miracle collection were added much later, judging from the hand.

167. BnF MS lat. 2769 ff. 55–84v. The pairing of William of Jumièges's *History* just following the miracle collection might indicate something about the Anglo-Norman content of the miracles, but this would have been only in the late twelfth century, when the *Historia Normannorum* was copied.

168. CCCC MS 42 (Marian miracles on ff. 82–99v); see Gameson 1999, 86.

169. An early example of a Mariale, BnF MS lat. 3781, possibly from the monastery of Ripoll in the early twelfth century, was used as a lectionary according to the original markings of division of texts into lessons; it contains only two single miracle stories.

170. Éric Palazzo (1990, 21) has noted the existence of *libelli* with a variety of prayers, formulas for particular feasts, and readings, especially in honor of the Virgin.

171. The Mildred manuscript is BL Harley MS 3908. The Edmund manuscript is New York, Pierpont Morgan Library MS 736. For a description and discussion, see Wormald 1952, 215. On the liturgical contents of this later book, see Parkes 2014. Another example is New York, Pierpont Morgan Library MS S926, containing five booklets, each from the second half of the eleventh century, and containing liturgical and hagiographic materials associated with St. Alban, St. Dunstan, Ethelhard, and St. Birinus that were only much later bound together, on which see Thomson 1982, 8–9, 15–116.

172. Wormald 1952, 262.

173. Beverly Kienzle (1997) argues that it was written when Ralph was abbot of Séez (between 1088 and 1107), as it is addressed to Abbot William of Fécamp (d. 1107). For an edition and discussion, see Kienzle 1997. For Honorius as the source, see ibid., 22–23. See also Constable 1995, 45–46.

174. For a recent German translation, see von Schönau 2006.

175. The miracle collection starts on f. 137, in a completely different hand from the homilies. Cf. Anselm of Canterbury 2007.

176. Of course, without knowing when the whole codex was assembled, it would be impossible to know when the miracles were inserted.

177. For the sermons in this collection (ff. 1–65v), which were once attributed to Ildefonsus of Toledo, but whose attribution has since been revised, see Barré 1957, 11. A similar set is found in Worcester Cath. Lib. MS F. 94.

178. See Bacci 2002.

179. BnF MS lat. 14463. There is no change in hand between the three texts.

180. BL Egerton MS 2947. For the hymns, see Dreves 1886–1922, 35:137–49. What is referred to as an *oratio* in the manuscript is actually a hymn: *Imperatrix reginarum et salvatrix animarum.* Cf. ibid., 20:154, 157. *Ecce ad te confugio virgo nostra salvatio* may also be a hymn, but one I was unable to locate. The version of the Theodore and Abraham story in the miracle collection has the incipit *Fuit quidam religiosus Leodicensis,* and the one added to the end is *In illo tempore erat quidam nauclerus.*

181. The first part, in a Carolingian minuscule, includes a number of sermons for the feast of the Assumption, including a number attributed to Ildefonsus of Toledo (PL 96:239–59, 269–72, on which see Barré 1957) and Paschasius's *Cogitis me.* These are followed by a number of Marian hymns with a prologue as well as a hymn for the Ascension.

182. The original text continues on f. 111, with sermons for the feast of Peter and Paul.

183. This is the office in the manuscript linked to Saint-Martin-des-Champs discussed in chapter 1.

184. BnF lat. 12606.

185. Ibid., f. 174.

186. Ibid., f. 171ᵛ.

187. Gransden 1963, 112. Sally Roper (1993, 82) has pointed out that many houses observed the collatio, but the Eynsham example of a *collatio Dei genitricis* is unique.

188. BnF lat. MS 3809A, ff. 67v–78v. It has both the *Gospel of Pseudo-Matthew* and a fairly extensive collection of thirty-nine miracles for the feast of the Nativity. For the As-

sumption, we find the *Transitus* of Pseudo-Mellitus along with several texts by Pseudo-Ildefonsus and Pseudo-Augustine. On the manuscript, see the *Catalogue général de manuscrits latins* 7 (3776–835): 284–95; for a description of the miracles, see ibid., 287. On the use of books for monastic reading, see Webber 2014b.

189. On the collation, see Webber 2013, 235–36. On the refectory readings, see ibid., 236–39. Diane Reilly (2011) has also made a study of reading materials for matins and the refectory of the late eleventh and early twelfth centuries, specifically underscoring the role of Giant Bibles in these contexts. None of the twelfth-century miracle collections are of an even comparable size or include such lavish illustration.

190. For example, the book list circa 1175 from Burston-on-Trent, BL Add. MS 23944, f. 157v, includes a collection that has been likened to BL Add. MS 57533, which is nevertheless later. See Sharpe, Carley, and Thomson 1996, 38. For one dated 1247/48 from Glastonbury, see ibid., 193. In this case, it is in a section of books related to Mary that includes several theological treatises and collections of sermons; for a discussion of the list, see ibid., 167–68. See also one dated 1192 from Reading abbey, ibid., 441; for a discussion, see ibid., 419–21. See also Coates 1999, 31; for a discussion, see ibid., 19–24. In the same list from Reading's cell Leominster, see ibid., 455. An entry for a book containing miracles was added to the book list of Rochester cathedral priory dated circa 1122/23, but before 1202 when another book list was compiled; see ibid., 491, 507; for a discussion, see, respectively, ibid., 469–70, 497–98. On a late twelfth-century book list from Whitby, see ibid., 633–634, 637.

191. Webber 2013, 229–30.

192. Webber 2010, especially 41–46.

193. Ibid., 46.

194. Corbin 1967.

195. These are Walter Howard Frere and Langton E. G. Brown (1915), and Hereford Cathedral Library MS O.iii.9, as listed in Corbin 1967, 421. For use of nonbiblical text as lections, see Webber 2015.

196. Corbin 1967, 433.

197. See Flint 1995, 102, 127. On the significance of preaching in English monastic culture from the tenth-century reform movement, see Tinti 2015, 245–46.

198. Ibid., 239–40.

199. Another manuscript that suggests the pastoral care provided by the Christ Church monks is BL Cotton MS Tiberius A. iii, which has been the source of considerable study because of its unusual combination of monastic texts with pastoral ones. See ibid., 242–43, especially 242n53.

200. For a study of this sermon, see Muessig 2002, 259–65. For a brief introduction to *ad status* sermons, see Poleg 2011, 213–16.

201. "Ad omnes sermones debes primum versum Latina lingua pronunciare, dein patria lingua explanare." Honorius Augustodunensis, *Speculum Ecclesiae*, PL 172:829.

202. "Hodie juvenes et virgines, senes cum junioribus laudent nomen Domini, quia venit exaltare regnum populi sui. Virgines exultent et Christo devotis laudibus persultent, quia virgo Maria mundo salvatorem edidit qui castis virginibus coelestia munera tribuit. Viduae gaudeant et Christo votive plaudant, quem vidua Anna hodie cum Symeone templo intulit, qui continentes coeli templo inducit. Conjugatae jocundentur et Christo laudes consono ore modulentur, ad cujus matris ingressum, Elisabeth mari-

tata, Spiritu sancto repleta, prophetavit, qui in legitimo conjugio viventes in coelesti thalamo sibi copulabit. Grata infantilis aetas laudes Christo concrepando voces extollat, quia quem coeli capere non poterant, in cunis infans jacebat. Hunc Johannes infans in matris utero salutabat. Hunc milia infantium ejus causa ab Herode sua morte laudabant. Florens puerilis aetas Christo ovando jubilet, qui puer in medio doctorum residet et formam discendi pueris praebet. Fervens juvenilis aetas gratulando Christo plaudat, qui juvenis factus mundum miraculis illustrat." *Sermo in Purificatione,* in Honorius Augustodunensis, *Speculum Ecclesiae,* PL 172:851.

203. Goodich 2007, 33.

204. On the importance of sermons as the key means of mediating the biblical text, see Poleg 2011, 2013.

205. On the structure of twelfth-century monastic sermons, see Kienzle 2000, 281–85. On the use of the Bible in preaching, see Poleg 2013, 152–97.

206. On the criteria for the genre, see Bremont and Le Goff 1982, 36–41. See also Goodich 2007, 34–35. On the later sermons, see the useful introduction in Bériou 2000.

207. Intriguingly, there are fifty-eight surviving exempla collections from thirteenth-century England, the most of any area of Europe, with forty from France. See Bremont and Le Goff 1982, 72. On the development of the genre through the end of the twelfth to the thirteenth century, see ibid., 54–56; Berlioz and Polo de Beaulieu 1998.

208. On this text and its reception, see Tolan 1993.

209. Aelfric cited the example of Theophilus in his sermon for the Assumption. See Thorpe 1843–44, 1:448; Clayton 1990, 241. Fulbert of Chartres (PL 141:323) also cited the Theophilus legend in his sermon for Mary's Nativity.

210. Flint 1974, 202.

211. William of Malmesbury 2015, 14.

212. BL Cotton MS Caligula A. xiv, f. 52.

213. "Qui animam Mariae transivit cum eo magno dolore in cruce pendentem vidit, unde etiam magis quam martyr extitit. Christus autem fuit ruina Judaeorum et resurrectio paganorum, cum Judaei per infidiam corruerunt crux erat, cui Judaei et gentes ubique contradicebant." *Sermo in Purificatione,* in Honorius Augustodunensis, *Speculum Ecclesiae,* PL 172:850.

214. See chapter 2.

215. "Qualiter beata virgo Maria se invocantibus subvenire soleat, dilectionem vestram breviter nunc audire libeat." *Sermo in Purificatione,* in Honorius Augustodunensis, *Speculum Ecclesiae,* PL 172:852.

216. *Sermo in Annunciatione,* in Honorius Augustodunensis, *Speculum Ecclesiae,* PL 172:901–8.

217. *Sermo in Annunciatione,* in Honorius Augustodunensis, *Speculum Ecclesiae,* PL 172:904, 906–8. The story exists in an Old English version and is found in the Worcester Legendary in a Latin translation by Paul that may have been Honorius's source; see Flint 1972a, 76–78. For the Old English version, see Magennis 1996. On Mary of Egypt as a cultural figure, see Karras 1996, 123–24.

218. *Sermo de Nativitate Sanctae Mariae,* in Honorius Augustodunensis, *Speculum Ecclesiae,* PL 172:999–1002.

219. "Quaemadmodum populus Israel de Aegypto confusis adversariis, hostibus in mari Rubro obrutis, in exultatione educitur et per desertum in terram desiderabilem

cum cantico laeticiae intorducitur, sic gloriosa virgo Maria cuius hodie sollemnia recoli-
mus votiva, de hoc mundo confusis Judaeis, daemonibus in abyssum submersis, in laetitia et exultatione educitur, et per desertum aeris cum concentu angelorum et jubilatione
sanctorum in coeleste palacium regina coelorum introducitur." *Sermo in Assumptione*,
in Honorius Augustodunensis, *Speculum Ecclesiae*, PL 172:991.

220. "Ad hanc omnes, karissimi, tota mente fugiamus, vota precum, hostias laudum
ei reddamus, quatenus eam cum filio suo coetibus angelorum imperantem videamus
et aliquam particulam gaudii ejusdem regni ea favente obtineamus." *Sermo in Assumptione*, in Honorius Augustodunensis, *Speculum Ecclesiae*, PL 172:994.

221. Koopmans 2011, 25.

Chapter 4: Enemies of Mary:
Jews in Miracle Stories

1. For a work centering on this argument, see Blumenkranz 1954. On Jews as important witness figures, see Lipton 2014, especially 63–66.

2. Blumenkranz 1954; Limor 2005, 2006.

3. The bibliography on the anti-Semitism of the "Prioress' Tale" is too extensive to
be covered adequately here, although the roots of the story in the Marian miracle tradition have not always been sufficiently emphasized. For important studies, see Friedman
1974–75; Zitter 1991; Despres 1994; Fradenburg 1996; Bale 2007, 55–104.

4. Frank (1982) estimated that they represent approximately 7.5 percent of all
stock Marian stories, although he fails to mention how he reached this number.

5. These include Bagby 1971; Marcus 1996; Shea 2007; Bollo-Panadero 2008;
Boyarin 2010; Daas 2011. Other scholars have shown interest in the Marian miracles
for their potential social impact, including Abulafia 2011, 171–75. This potential impact
will be raised in the conclusion.

6. For a partial exception, see Boyarin 2010, which does look at the Latin versions
of Theophilus, but only to compare to the later Middle English versions.

7. This type of contextualization is absent in Stone 1999, although addressed for
earlier versions by Limor 2005, 2006. On the need to look to the immediate context, see
Blumenkranz 1954, 418. This approach was taken by Bale 2003, 2007.

8. Lipton 2014, 94.

9. Harm Reinder Smid (1965, 15–16) has suggested that the *Protevangelium Jacobi*
had an apologetic purpose, written to counter the objections to Christian doctrine of
Jews and pagans in second-century Syria or Egypt, where the text may have originated.
Stephen Shoemaker (1999) has made similar claims for the early Dormition narratives.
For a more general study of the apocryphal literature, see Shoemaker 2002. For a brief
survey of extant versions of the *Protevangelium*, see Cullman 1991, 421–25.

10. See Elliott 2008. For Anglo-Saxon England, see Clayton 1986, 1998.

11. Elliott 1993, 63.

12. Ibid., 93.

13. Cf. Toubert 1996, especially 327–28.

14. Elliott 1993, 93.

15. Ibid.

16. See Hunter 2007, especially 188–92.

17. A shortened version is also found in Gregory of Tours 1988, but without reference to the Jews. For versions in England, see Clayton 1998; Scheil 2004, 270–74.

18. Apart from one homily attributed to Modestus of Jerusalem, every legend of Mary's Dormition contains this scene. See Elliott 1993, 712–13.

19. Shoemaker 2004, 788.

20. "De libris Moysi testimonium dans quam scriptum est de ea quia ipsa futura est templum Dei vivi." BnF MS lat. 3809A, f. 4ᵛ; see chapter 3. A similar phrase is found in a twelfth-century Mariale, BnF MS lat. 2672, f. 11ᵛ.

21. On later traditions of the Transitus narrative, see Bradbury 2013.

22. It survives now only in a Georgian version, which has been edited and firmly attributed to Maximus the Confessor (2012) by Shoemaker. Yet there is no evidence for knowledge of this text in England.

23. Corrigan 1992.

24. Ibid., 61.

25. Ibid.

26. While it could be argued that some of these additions may reflect French interest—since many of the surviving twelfth-century manuscripts are French—the presence of many stories among these additions that are of English origin, more so than in Anselm's original group, suggest that the majority were added as the collections circulated in England, only then crossing the English Channel.

27. Scholars have remarked on William's anti-Semitism on account of his comments in other works. See Carter 1981, 153; William of Malmesbury 2013, xii; 2015, 22; Thomson 2003a, 123. See also Ihnat, forthcoming a.

28. They were also the main source of the section on Latin miracles in Shea 2004, although they were not contextualized and discussed only briefly.

29. This could have been directly from Greek and Italian monks, such as the monk Constantine at Malmesbury, or Anselm of Bury who had come from St. Sabas in Rome, a house formerly populated by Greek monks fleeing the East. For links between England and Byzantium, see Ortenberg 1992, 200–204.

30. Barlow 1979, 195.

31. Although these do not represent the only versions of the miracle stories, I will provide the numbers attributed to these stories in Poncelet 1902. The list compiled in Poncelet is of incipits, not of the entire tales, so there is still considerable work to be done comparing different versions. For an online search, see http://csm.mml.ox.ac.uk/index .php?p=pon_list (accessed March 14, 2016). For Theophilus, see Poncelet 1902, 74.

32. For its early history, see Dasent 1845; Plenzat 1926. For a rudimentary stemma, see Texier 1998, 782. The version by Paul appears as *De Theophilo penitente*, in *Acta Sanctorum*, February 4, 483–87; for a discussion, see ibid., 480–83.

33. For the text, see Hrotsvit von Gandersheim 1970, 154–55. For discussion, see ibid., 147–53.

34. For a translation, see Fassler 2009, appendix E, 426–28.

35. Clayton 1990, 118.

36. For Aelfric, see ibid., 240–41.

37. Cambridge University Library MS Ff. I. 23; BL Arundel MS 60. For the text of the former, see Clayton 1990, 109. For the latter, see ibid., 114–16. See also Boyarin 2010, 46–47.

38. "De hoc Theophilo, quis fuit vel quid fecit, vel quali miraculo mater misericordiae eum liberavit, ideo hic scribere nolui quia hoc notum fere omnibus novi." Dexter 1927, 43.

39. "Tu mater es misericordiae. De lacu foecis et miseriae Theophilum reformans gloriae." BL Royal MS 2 B. iv, ff. 183–83v. This sequence would have been sung at a general votive mass in honor of Mary. It appears under the rubric "In veneratione sanctae Dei genitricis Mariae."

40. BL Harley MS 3020, ff. 113–32; BL Cotton MS Nero E. i, ff. 157–60; BL Harley MS 4719 ff. 122v–25. All these are listed in Ward 1883, 595–98. On the Cotton manuscript, see Gameson 1999, 101; Pfaff 2009, 222n74.

41. Flint 1974, 202. Dominic included two other stories from the same legendary, about Julian Apostate and Mary of Egypt, both of which are also shared with Honorius's works. For Dominic's sources, see Jennings 1962. For William's sources, see Shaw 2006, 392–93.

42. See, for example, Lambeth Palace Library MS 214 ff. 159–64v; BnF MS lat. 2672 ff. 12–80 (with a break in the middle where a different quire was inserted); BnF MS lat. 12606 ff. 95v–96v; BnF MS lat. 14463 ff.; CCCC MS 42 ff. 97v–99v (unfinished); Copenhagen Thott MS 26.8 ff. 37–51.

43. Only in much later versions, such as Rutebeuf's late thirteenth-century play, would he be pictured as a quasi-Muslim; see Dahan 1977.

44. "[Erat denique in eadem civitate] Hebreus quidam nefandissimus et diabolice artis operator nequissimus qui iam multos in infidelitatis argumentis et in foveam perditionis immerserat baratro." *Acta Sanctorum*, February 4, 484.

45. Frugoni 2008, 132–33.

46. "Execrabilis vero Hebreus frequenter pergebat occulte ad vicedominum et dicebat ei: Vidisti quemadmodum beneficium et celere remedium ex me et patrono meo in quibus deprecatus es invenisti." *Acta Sanctorum*, February 4, 484.

47. Dominic of Evesham 1998, 263.

48. "O quam dira pestis avaritia! Quae ad omnia flagitia cogis Christianorum pectora." Ibid.

49. Ibid.

50. Moshe Lazar (1972, 49–50) argued that a transition from Theophilus's concern with recovering his honor to a desire for financial wealth is evident only as of Ruteboeuf's dramatic adaptation of the Theophilus story. Here we see it predate the play by over a century.

51. William of Malmesbury 2015, 15.

52. Ibid., 16.

53. Ibid., 16–17.

54. Ibid., 17.

55. Ibid.

56. "Quae mihi fuit necessitas cognoscendi nefandissimum et comburendum illum Hebraeum?" *Acta Sanctorum*, February 4, 484, E.

57. "[Erat enim ante paululum Hebraeus ille] a lege et iudice condemnatus." Ibid.

58. William of Malmesbury 2015, 17.

59. Ibid., 79–82.

60. Ibid., 79. This story eventually came to feature a student in Paris, who in falling lovestruck, engaged a wizard to try to obtain his love from the devil, but refusing to abjure Mary and Christ, the devil disappears, taking the wizard with him. He and a friend then become monks at Clairvaux. Cf. BL Add. MS 15723, ff. 80v–81.

61. William of Malmesbury 1998, 170:6, 291.

62. Ibid., 170:280, 282.

63. Ibid.

64. Escobar Vargas 2011, particularly chapter 2 on the legend of Gerald of Aurillac.

65. William of Malmesbury 2007, iii.118.2ß; see Hayward 2011, 77.

66. On these circles, see especially Burnett 1997a, 38–40; 1997b.

67. Burnett 1997a, 39.

68. Ibid.

69. For the inclusion of necromancy among the seven liberal arts, see Alfonsi 1977, 9–10, 114–15. For the distinction between necromancy as manipulation of natural elements versus of demons, see Alfonsi 2006, 150.

70. Adrienne Williams Boyarin (2010) saw later translations into Middle English as reflecting the growing importance of legal culture—namely, because of Mary's advocacy.

71. Poncelet 1902, 95. Various versions are collected in Wolter 1879.

72. Rubin 1991, 2004. See also Bynum 1987; Despres 1998, 269–74.

73. Rubin 2004.

74. This time frame was preserved in a considerably shortened version of the story included by Sigebert of Gembloux in his *Chronicon* for the year 552. See Wolter 1879, 42.

75. Evagrius Scholasticus 2000, 241–42.

76. Evagrius Scholasticus's (2000, 4:36, 242) editor Michael Whitby has seen a possible source for this tale in Georgius Monachus's *Life of Sabas*. The fact that Anselm was formerly the abbot of St. Sabas in Rome makes it tempting to suggest that this was the version with which Anselm himself had been familiar. The Marian story has only tenuous links to the legend of Sabas, however, and has much stronger echoes of the biblical story of the three Hebrew youths in the furnace (Daniel 3:1–100).

77. Johannes Monachus 1913, 44–45.

78. Paschasius Radbertus 1969, 60.

79. Ibid.

80. "At ille Christo Domino et suis legibus inimicus, felle amaritudinis commotus, ait ei: Si cum infantibus Christianorum religioni communicasti, ad ulciscendam Mosaicae legis injuriam, oblitus paterna pietate, parricida in te durus existam." Ibid.

81. See chapter 3.

82. On the Worcester wall paintings, see chapter 3.

83. Herbert of Losinga 1878, 2:31. For contemporary writings on Constantinople, see Sansterre 2011a, especially 702–3.

84. Herbert of Losinga 1878, 2:31.

85. Ibid., 33.

86. The same version is found in BL Arundel MS 346 ff. 65–65v; BnF MS lat. 2672 f. 39; BnF MS lat. 3809A, f. 73v; BnF MS lat. 12169 f. 122; BnF MS lat. 14463 f. 68v–69;

BnF MS lat. 18168 ff. 90v–91; Copenhagen Thott MS 128.2 ff. 15–15v; Chicago UL MS 147 ff. 7. For the version by Paschasius, see BL Add. MS 35112 ff. 33v–34; Oxford Bodl. Laud Miscellania MS 410 f. 93v; BnF MS lat. 2873 f. 30.

87. "Contigit quondam res talis in civitate Bituricensi quam solet narrare monachus quidam Sancti Michaelis de Clusa nomine Petrus dicens se illic eo tempore fuisse." Dexter 1927, 32.

88. Southern 1958, 199.

89. Dahan 1980, 43.

90. "Quod videntes tam Judei quam Christiani, Deum et sanctam eius genitricem collaudaverunt, et ex illa die in Dei fide ferventes extiterunt." Dexter 1927, 33.

91. "Oremus itaque piissimam dominam nostram et omnium Christianorum dulcissimam matrem Mariam ut quemadmodum prelibatum puerum ad incendio clibani misericordissime liberavit sic nos famulos suos in die tremendi exanimis a Gehennalibus flammis liberare dignetur." Dominic of Evesham 1998, 259.

92. "Ac primum Christi iuvante gratia paucis absolvamus quod in infideli genere Judaeorum eodemodo factum audivimus sicuti inferventi declarabimus. Postquam infidelissima gens Judaeorum gravissima mole peccaminum et maxime effusione sanguinis Christi exigente de qua ad sui dampnum ac perniciem constat proclamatum sanguis eius super nos et super filios nostros, ipsa inquam obstinatissima gens postquam merito locum et regnum completis tot tantisque facinoribus iuxta dominicam sententiam perdidit, populus olim Deo dilectus ubique terrarum pro suis criminibus diffusus cunctis gentibus ostentus habitus quaemadmodum fratricida eam omni carni insignum est datus. Quae enim caro aut quae mens non abhorreat Christum offendere cernens populum quondam deo tam dilectum a cunctis terrarum hominibus electum nunc pro suis peccatis ita deiectum esse? Ecce enim omnis civitas quocumque locorum sit hanc gentem infra se positam sustinet ubique Iudaica perfidia intonat et cum inter Christianos sit multorum Judaeorum conversatio iugiter tamen permanet in mente eorum vere fidei dubitatio. Ac per hoc iustissimum discrimen meruere quam fide tam specie et perversissima operatione." Ibid.

93. For the exegetical interpretation of the episode of Cain with respect to Jews, see Dahan 1982.

94. "Veluti in plurisque cernitur sinagoga Judaeorum esset." Dominic of Evesham 1998, 260.

95. Albert Hyamson (1928, 14–17) argues for Jews in Oxford already by 1075, Cambridge by 1073, and Winchester by 1115. Cecil Roth (1951, 2) pushes this forward to 1130–54. 4. More recent works put the presence of Jews earlier in the twelfth century in various cities, as far north as York: Dobson 1974; Pollins 1982, 16; Susser 1993; Hillaby 1995, 2003; Rutledge 2012; Jones and Watson 2013.

96. Dominic's proposed solution presaged by almost a century the decree that ordered Jews to wear distinguishing clothing; the decree was first issued in England in 1218, following a similar decree at Lateran IV in 1215. See Vincent 1994–96; Tolan 2015.

97. For the idea that the story functioned as a corrective to contemporary notions about the boundaries between Jewish and Christian communities, although without explicit reference to the role of Mary, see Abulafia 2011, 172.

98. William of Malmesbury 2015, 97–98.

99. Ibid., 97. Carter (1959, 530) suggests that this rather-curious setting may be due to a misreading of *Quale de pusione judaico*, found in the *Gesta Regum*, for *Quale de pisane judaico*, in *De laudibus*. William nevertheless rationalizes why events took place in Pisa, indicating that it was not merely a scribal error.

100. William of Malmesbury 2015.

101. Ibid.

102. Ibid., 98.

103. Ibid.

104. William of Malmesbury 1998, iii.286.2, 520–21. For the larger section, see ibid., iii.284.1–286.2, 512–21. On the main texts of the debate—Lanfranc's *Liber de corpore et sanguine Domini* (ca. 1063–68) and Berengar's *De sacra coena* (1070)—see Rubin 1991, 13–25. For a work that contextualizes the debates in philosophical and linguistic trends, see Stock 1983, 252–315.

105. On Lanfranc's arguments, see Stock 1983, 295–309; Holopainen 2004, 2012.

106. William of Malmesbury 1998, iii.286.1, 518–19.

107. On this increased agency of Mary and her significance in protecting the boy from his father, see Patton 2014, especially at 65–66, which nevertheless does not stress the fact that these elements were found in the English collections; it mistakenly attributes the Bourges setting to Gautier de Coincy.

108. The same is true in the popular miracle story of "Musa," the little girl whose vision of Mary encouraged her to live a particularly virtuous life until she died and was taken to live with Mary forever; see de Vogüé 1986, 87–91.

109. Poncelet 1902, 808.

110. It is found in BL Add. MS 35112 ff. 51–51v; BL Arundel MS 346 f. 68; BnF MS lat. 2672 f. 27v; BnF MS lat. 3809A f. 77v; BnF MS lat. 14463 ff. 35–35v; BnF MS lat. 18168 ff. 96–96v; BL Cotton MS lat. Cleopatra C. x ff. 128v–29; Chicago UL MS 147 ff. 10v–11; Dexter 1927, 43–45.

111. "Ego vobiscum sum in ipsa ecclesia in adiutorium." Dexter 1927, 44.

112. "Vere, mulier est in hac domo." Ibid.

113. Ibid., 45.

114. Munitiz et al. 1997.

115. On Marian Byzantine icons, see Brubaker and Cunningham 2007.

116. Epistle 2, in Ambrose 1967, 12–13.

117. Munitiz et al. 1997, 7.4, 36–39.

118. Ibid., 36–37.

119. Ibid.

120. Ibid., 38–39.

121. The same story appears in a shorter form of the same text, the *Letter to Emperor Theophilus on the Holy and Venerated Icons*, attributed erroneously to John Damascene, and for which Martin Jugie (1901–2) has identified Andrew of Crete as a possible author. Munitiz et al. 1997, liv, 4b, 150.

122. Ibid., 7.6, 38–41.

123. Ibid., 40–41.

124. My thanks to Jesse Sherwood for the reference to this council. See Hehl and Fuhrmann 1987, 6.1:113–14.

125. Ibid.

126. On the imagined hostility of Jews to the Holy Sepulchre, see Jestice 2007.

127. BnF MS gr. 1474, ff. 237v–47v. See Dobschütz 1903; Pentcheva 2011.

128. Dexter 1927, 44.

129. This dates back to Jerome. Jerome (ibid., 646–47) glossed Ezechiel 44:1–2 in his commentary on it: "Pulchre quidam portam clausam per quam solus dominus Deus Israel ingreditur et dux cui porta clausa est, Mariam virginem intellegunt, quae et ante partum et post partum virgo permansit."

130. Jerome 1964, 646–47.

131. Gilbert 1986, 29.

132. Poncelet 1902, 20.

133. BnF MS lat. 2672 ff. 51v–52v; BnF MS lat. 2873 ff. 30v–31; BnF MS lat. 14463 f. 22v; CCCC MS 42 f. 90v; Copenhagen Thott MS 26.8 ff. 94v–95; BL Cotton MS Cleopatra C. x ff. 129v–30; BnF MS lat. 18134 ff. 140v–41; Chicago UL MS 147 ff. 11–11v (see Dexter 1927, 45–46); Dahan 1980, 46.

134. *De locis sanctis*, 3:15, in Adomnan of Iona 1958, 88:813–14.

135. Ibid.

136. See, for example, Woods 2002.

137. In a complex explanation, Woods (ibid., 46–51) argues that Arculf was carrying relics and literary materials from his trip to the East and probably met with Adomnán.

138. BnF MS lat. 2873, f. 30ᵛ has the rubric *Sermo beati Iheronimi* preceding the tale. BnF MS lat. 18134, f. 140v also attributes it to Jerome, stating *Narrat Iheronimus quod*.

139. Robert G. Hoyland and Sarah Waidler (2014, 804) make this argument, pointing to Adomnán's claim that Arculf saw the Marian icon with his own eyes.

140. The Pseudo-Athanasian tale and this citation are both found in a ninth-century text by Theodore the Studite (1981, 55). For a detailed discussion of the history of the legend, see Bacci 2002. See also Sansterre 1999. The tale was also included with Marian miracle collections, such as BL Add. MS 35112 ff. 87–90v; BnF MS lat. 2873 ff. 50–52; BnF MS lat. 14463 ff. 1v–5.

141. Reported in Theodore the Studite 1981, 55. See Corrigan 1992, 32.

142. Gregory of Tours 1988, 40. Both Gregory's and the Pseudo-Athanasius text are found in several of the manuscripts containing Marian miracles.

143. Munitiz et al. 1997, 7.9, 44–45.

144. Ibid., 7.12, 7.13a, 46–47.

145. Oxford Bodl. Digby MS lat. 112, ff. 17–28ᵛ. For a discussion of provenance, see Ciggaar 1976, 212. For a look at dating, see ibid., 225.

146. "[Imago beatae Mariae in brevi tabula figurata lignea] pariete cuiusdam domus [suspensa pendebat]." Adomnan of Iona 1958, 118–19.

147. Woods 2002, 37–38.

148. William of Malmesbury 2015, 127. On the story, see Grumel 1931.

149. The miracle was extracted from the sermon in at least two early examples, both probably Norman in origin: BnF MS lat. 2628 and Rouen, Bibliothèque municipale MS 1418. See Poncelet 1904 209–10.

150. William of Malmesbury 2015, 127.

151. For a description of the typology of versions, see Dahan 1977.

152. "Et post turpissimam illam ventris purgationem ille infelicissimus discessit homo, quid vero postea gessit, aut quomodo vixit, vel qualem vitae terminum habuit, incompertum habetur." Translation altered from the sanitized one in Adomnan of Iona 1958, 118–19, which omits the purgation, instead calling it a "disgraceful action."

153. "Digna quippe et ignominiosa consumptus est morte et post ea nusquam conparuit. Unde credendum est quod cito pro scelere quod in Christum matremque eius commiscrat, a maligno spiritu iure manciparetur, qui hominum subtraheretur obtutibus." Dexter 1927, 45.

154. William of Malmesbury 2015, 127.

155. Socrates Scholasticus 1891, 34–35. This is reminiscent of the later iconography of the hanged Judas with his bowels hanging out. The late twelfth-century *Historia Scholastica* by Peter Comestor depicted Judas dying of burst bowels after hanging himself, since his damned soul could not exit via the mouth that kissed Christ in betrayal. Cf. Weber 2002, 169.

156. Evidence for the skepticism and even abuse of the cross, for example, is found in the accounts of the early eleventh-century so-called heretic Leutard and his followers as well as in Rodulphus Glaber's *Historiarum libri quinque*, 2.11:91, discussed in Frassetto 2007, 50; Fulton 2002, 81.

157. William of Malmesbury 2015, 128.

158. For another similar story featuring the fall of a Jew, see Bayless 2003.

159. Sansterre 2006, 274–92.

160. For the most thorough description and study, see Forsyth 1972. Although some of these were carved out to accommodate relics, their perceived power does not seem to have come from their role as reliquaries, since many of them were not. See ibid., 31–38.

161. William of Malmesbury 2007, 4.175, 311.

162. Sansterre 2011b. See also Sansterre 2013.

163. Sansterre 2006, 292.

164. Edited with commentary in ibid., 286–87.

165. Palazzo 1996, 317–22; Forsyth 1972, 38–45.

166. Allen Smith 2006, 186.

167. Ibid., 187.

168. Lipton 2014.

169. Lipton 2005; 2014, 63–94.

170. Gilbert 1986. See Robinson 1911, 54; Blumenkranz 1948; Southern 1954; 1966, 89–91; Abulafia 1984a, 1984b, 1984c, 1992b. For a similar though less cautious discussion of the legitimacy of religious images, see Rupert of Deutz 1979, 232–36. See also Abulafia 1993, 48–49. Rupert's work, from 1120/21, postdates Gilbert's.

171. "Has effigies Christiani exculpunt, fabricant et depingunt, unde possunt et ubi possunt, adorant et colunt." Gilbert 1986, 51.

172. Ibid., 50–51.

173. Gilbert (ibid., 51–52) cites Exodus 28:36, 28:9–11, 3 Kings 6:23, 6:29, 7:23–25, 8:6, and 8:11 as biblical proofs.

174. Ibid., 53.

175. "Nullam omnino Christianus divino cultu rei alicuius adorat effigiem, debito tamen honoris cultu sacratas sacrarum rerum colit et honorat effigies et picturas." Ibid.

This echoes the decree at the Synod of Arras (1025), at which it was recommended that images be placed in churches for the illiterate. Mansi 1759–98, 14:455.

176. Bernard was especially critical of devotional imagery, although the Cistercians quickly embraced it soon after him. On Bernard, see Reilly 2012, 128.

177. Walker Bynum 2011, 258–59.

178. Poncelet 1902, 283.

179. BL Arundel MS 346 f. 67; Oxford Balliol College MS 240 ff. 154–54v; BnF MS lat. 2873 f. 27v; BnF MS lat. 3809A f. 74v; BnF MS lat. 14463 ff. 34–35; BnF MS lat. 18168 93v–94v; Copenhagen Thott MS lat. 26.8 ff. 68–69; Copenhagen Thott MS 128. 2 ff. 17v–18v; BL Cotton MS Cleopatra C. x ff. 127v–28v; Chicago UL MS 147 ff. 9–9v (see Dexter 1927, 39–40); BL Add. MS 35112 ff. 77v–78; Oxford Bodl. Laud Miscellania MS 410 ff. 88v–89. William's version is found in BnF MS lat. 2769 ff. 64v–65v.

180. "Heu, heu quam inmanissima et inanissima probatur esse perfidia Iudaicae mentis. Heu quam dira calamitas quod intra mei nati mundi redemptoris crucis salu- tifere signaculo signati gregis ovilio manet et regnat insania Iudaicae gentis quae meum unicum filium lumen et salutem fidelium iam secundo conviciatur et crucis supplicio mortificare conatur." Dexter 1927, 39.

181. "Veneremur omnis dignissimam Mariae Dei genitricis excellentiam integrita- tem virginitatis et opem salutiferam misericordiam adiuti per eius unicum filium ge- neris humani reformatorem collati saluti qui quasi filii sui passionem secundo male mo- litam a Judaeis perfidis doluit et dolendo prescriptam passionem plebem Christianam docuit et a demonum humani generis inimicorum fraudibus liberari voluit. Sic nos suae pietatis affectu filii sui sinu representat beatissimo et a perpetuo Gehenne infernalium incendio liberavit." Ibid., 40.

182. "[Ad excitandum humilium corda ut percipiant gaudia celestia sub brevitate sermonis ut in proverbio dicitur in paucis constringere multa,] magna mater salvatoris quoddam descripturis miraculum quod auribus spiritualibus praelibatum meis auribus narrabo." Ibid., 15.

183. Carter 1981, 145.

184. Baer 1992, 51.

185. William of Malmesbury 2015, 26. It is worth mentioning that the Assumption feast was not celebrated in the Visigothic period, as noted in Carter 1981, 146.

186. On the Kalonymides, see Graboïs 1973, especially 50; Schatzmiller 1985, 52–58; Dahan 1995, 100–101. Later accounts include Peter the Venerable 1985, 70; Benjamin of Tudela 1907, 4. Norman Golb (1998, 202–7) deems the legend credible, describing it and its sources at some length, although without mention of William.

187. "Judaeorum blasphemantium prostibulum habebatur." Julian of Toledo, *Histo- ria Rebellionis Paulis adversus Wambam Gothorum regem*, PL96:766. Thomson (2003b, 42–43) indicates that William owned a collection of Julian's letters.

188. See Thomas of Monmouth 2014. For the dating of the text, see McCulloch 1997, 706–9.

189. Dexter 1927, 39–40.

190. William of Malmesbury 2015, 27.

191. "Perfidiam Judaeorum fraudulentorum [deleverunt ipsosque Judaeos eadem hora neci tradunt]." Dexter 1927, 40.

192. Mesler and Ihnat, forthcoming.

193. Horowitz 2006; Linder 1987, 236–37. See also Chapman 2008, 236–38.

194. Kriss-Rettenbeck 1972; Bisogni 2001, 98–115; Bautier 1977.

195. Bautier 1977.

196. Sigal 1983, 19.

197. Ibid., 20.

198. Mesler and Ihnat, forthcoming. Interestingly, in England, the idea that such figures could become the objects of magical practices is found in the *Laws of Henry I* (1114–18), in which murder by *invultuatio*—a term used for the creation of wax figurines for magical purposes—is condemned together with murder by potion, spell, and sorcery. Cf. Downer 1972, c. 71.1, 226–27. Mesler has indicated that this is the first known occurrence of the accusation.

199. Bedos-Rezak 2000, with discussion of Abelard specifically at 1522–24.

200. This was explored in great detail in Fulton 2002.

201. This was pointed out in Rubin 2009b.

202. "Et dolendo prescriptam passionem plebem Christianam docuit et a demonum humani generis inimicorum fraudibus liberari voluit." Dexter 1927, 40.

203. On the evolution of the accusation, see Stacey 1998; Utz 2005; Hames 2007.

204. Thomas of Monmouth 2014. More on this will be said in the conclusion.

205. Shachar 2015.

206. This could easily lead to the understanding that Jews consciously and willfully killed Christ, rather than put him to death in ignorance, because they continue to commit the same act even in post-biblical times. Cohen (2007) argued that this idea emerged only at the end of the twelfth century.

207. Poncelet 1902, 41, 559.

208. For the Greek and Latin history of the story, see Nelson and Starr 1939–44.

209. Now known as Munich Bayerische Staatsbibliothek Clm MS 4625. See Monachus 1913, 6–34, no. 1.

210. Harris 2008, particularly 123.

211. BL Cotton MS Tiberius B. v, ff. 55–56, 73–73v.

212. Honorius Augustodunensis 1844–55, 172:1035–36. For the eleventh-century version, see Harris 2008, 128–29.

213. William's story was considerably shortened in Oxford Balliol College MS 240, ff. 161v–62v and BL Add. Royal MS 6. B. xiv, f. 87v.

214. For this version, see Oxford Bodl. Canon. Liturg. MS 325, ff. 188–91; BnF MS lat. 14463 ff. 41–42; BnF MS lat. 2672 ff. 41–43v; Copenhagen Thott MS 128.2 ff. 30v–33v; Crane 1925, 41–44.

215. On Hugh of Die, see Riley-Smith 2003, 31.

216. Anselm stayed in Lyon multiple times during his various periods of exile between 1098 and 1107. See Vaughn 1994, 255, 257, 265. See, more generally, Staunton 2004.

217. William knew about Anselm's close relationship with Hugh, having written about it in William of Malmesbury 2007, 148–51. William could have heard the story directly from a Greek monk who visited Malmesbury, as described in the *Gesta Pontificum*. Ibid., 261.

218. The only story that directly concerns the Crusades in the twelfth-century collections is William of Malmesbury's (2015, 126) tale of the "Saracens of Ascalon," which is set in Ascalon during the reign of Baldwin II (1118–31).

219. "Nescis quia inimicitiam habemus nos Hebrei vobiscum, qui estis Christiani, propter imaginem istam? Numquid non vos dicitis quia patres nostri crucifixerunt eum? Et quomodo possum eum accipere antiphonitin?" Johannes Monachus 1913, 15.

220. Ibid., 15–17.

221. "[Haec autem faciebat Abramius,] non quia volebat negare illi, sed ut cognosceret finem rei, utrum firma esset fides Christianorum an non." Ibid., 31.

222. William of Malmesbury 2015, 92–96.

223. "Sanctae Dei genitricis venerandae imagini, Filii sui ipsam venerandam imaginem in gremio tenentis." Crane 1925, 42.

224. William of Malmesbury 2015, 95.

225. Sansterre (2013, 79–87; 2015) notes that living images of Christ were mentioned much earlier and with more frequency until the thirteenth century.

226. "Civium quidam, qui nominis sui famam volens extendere, largas quas habebat opes, largos in sumptus expendere coepit." Crane 1925, 41.

227. "Dies transeunt plurimi, dies per singulos negotia meditantur, dies pecuniae reddendae memoria elabitur." Ibid., 43.

228. "Quod si diem a te constitutum praeteriero, servus tuus certe in posternum ero." Ibid., 42.

229. "Jesum, ait, Christum Dominum esse non credo, sed quia eum hominem justum et Prophetam fuisse non dubito." Ibid.

230. "Audiens Judaeus, quia is, cui suam prestiterat pecuniam, regressus fuerat, et quia sibi Domino favente peregrinis eam mercibus admodum multiplicaverat more impatiens ad eum accessit, et praemissis aliquibus gratulabundis verbis improperando subintulit." Ibid., 44.

231. William of Malmesbury 2015, 92.

232. Ibid., 93.

233. Ibid., 93–94.

234. Ibid., 94.

235. Ibid., 92.

236. Ibid., 94.

237. Ibid.

238. Ibid., 95.

239. Ibid.

240. Nelson and Starr 1939–44, 294.

241. William of Malmesbury 2015, 95–97.

242. "[At Judaei] presentis solummodo vitae lucris inhiantes [nichil de cetero expectant]." William of Malmesbury 2013, 98.

243. On this idea of carnality, particularly on the interaction between exegesis, rational disputation, and social dynamics, see especially Abulafia 1992b, 1998.

244. See Stacey 1995; Abulafia 2011, 88–93; Pollins 1982; Mundill 2010.

245. It was the most remarkable wave of reconstruction in western Europe, as claimed in Brooke 1975, 43. For rebuilding as "the most conspicuous sign of the reform of an existing house," see Constable 1996, 222.

246. Hunter 1833, 146. See Mason 1996, 34.

247. Epistles 24 and 28, in Osbert of Clare 1929, 100, 107.

248. In the end, one Jew, presumably Benedict, was owed £1,200 by the sacrist. Jocelin of Brakelond 1989, 4.

249. On the emergence of this stereotype, see especially Little 1969; Lipton 1999, 31–53.

250. On this trend, see Gasper and Gullbekk 2012, 161–63.

251. See Little 1983.

252. Poncelet 1902, 1780.

253. It is virtually unrecognizable in versions from the thirteenth century (e.g., *Cantigas de Santa Maria*, no. 286), illustrating just how bizarre it must have seemed even to its contemporary readers.

254. *Acta Sanctorum*, May 1, 143.

255. Ademar of Chabannes 1999, 3.52:1–14, 132–36.

256. Carter (1981, 190) has pointed out errors; for example, Count William III was in fact Raymond of St. Gilles's grandfather not his father, as William claims.

257. "The fee given between the feast of All Saints [November 1] and the feast of St. Saturnin, bishop of this city [November 29], in lieu of/in exchange for the slap of the Jews, has been taken away unjustly from the canons and deacons. I release them from the charge and return and distribute it to the clerics of St. Saturnin, present and future" (*Leddam etiam quam a festivitate Omnium Sanctorum usque ad festum beati Saturnini episcopus in borgo pro colafo Judeorum datam, iniuste canonicis et decano auferebat, absolvo, reddo, et dimitto clericis beati Saturnini praesentibus et futuris*). Douais 1887, 200–201.

258. He added the following: "Dominum nostrum Ihesum Christum cuisque piissimam et dulcissimam genitricem Mariam in primis precibus totius devotionis ad adiutorum Christianorum flecti dein communi omnium procerum totiusque populi auctoritate et favore apud comitem agi ut non solum nobilis Christianus sicut laude dignus ab omni reatu iudicii sit liber verum etiam ut cunctorum iudicio quasi pro lege decernatur omni anno in posterum unum ex Judaeis per vindicta eo die exhibendum qui exponeret Christiano collum passurus vel alapam vel colaphum ut discerent Judei quam stultulm esset Christo improperare convicium." Oxford Balliol College MS 240. f. 155v.

259. Translation slightly adapted from William of Malmesbury 2015, 27, which calls it "a pleasant story and one to make the reader smile." The language suggests to me that William found this more comical than this translation allows.

260. Ihnat 2012, 408–23.

261. William of Malmesbury 2015, 28.

262. Ibid., 29.

263. William of Malmesbury 1998, 563.

264. Golb 1998, 114. For the risks involved for the Jews thanks to this arrangement, see Mundill 1998, 2010; Abulafia 2011, 89–95.

265. Thomson 2003a. For William's stance on Rufus, see Sønnesyn 2012, 213–27.

266. On the possibility of such stories having different effects on different audiences in the Anglo-Norman context, see Townsend 1993, 402–3.

267. William of Malmesbury 2015, 28.

268. Ibid. Abulafia (2011, 198–99) has indicated that the words of the Jewish murder

victim echo a Jewish liturgical prayer (Alenu), although we have no indication that William knew this.

269. Later legislation would try to curb this by forcing Jews to remain indoors throughout Easter week, but no such law existed in William's day, as far as is known; see Chazan 1980, 6.

270. The laughter produced by the joy of Christ's triumph over his enemies is referred to as the *risus paschalis*, described in Bayless 1997, 198.

271. Poncelet 1902, 982, 1411.

272. "[Ego sum inquit Maria] cui tu et genus vestrum malo vestro insultatis meque redemptorem mundi edidisse negatis." BL Add. MS 15723, f. 83.

273. "Hi carceres, hi incendia, his omnimoda tormenta te tuosque sequentes expetant nisi Iudaicam impietatem celerius dimiseritis et ad fidei Christiane sacramenta confugeritis. Autem sequire me ut ostendam tibi quid etiam boni per vestra caecitate perditis." BL Add. MS 15723, f. 83v.

274. BN MS lat. 3177 ff. 143–5 (late twelfth century; at the abbey of Beaupré by the thirteenth century); BL Add. MS 15 723 ff. 83–83v (thirteenth century; probably English and Cistercian from an unknown house). See Carter 1981, 152.

275. On these narratives, see Wilson 2012; Carozzi 1994.

276. Donahue 1942, 53.

277. This goes against Robert Stacey's (1992, especially 266) claim that conversion only became a pressing issue in thirteenth-century England. Although there is no evidence of missionary activity here, monks were interested in Jewish conversion to Christianity.

278. See chapter 2.

279. William of Malmesbury 1998, 563.

280. See Thomson 2003b; Brett 1981.

281. Eadmer of Canterbury 1964, 103. For the whole story, see ibid., 103–5.

282. Ibid., 103.

283. Ibid., 105.

284. Guibert of Nogent 1996, 111–12.

285. Golb 1984, 149–60.

286. Letter 380, in Anselm of Canterbury 1990, 135.

287. Letter 381, in ibid., 136.

288. William of Malmesbury 2015, 96.

289. Frustration with this is explicit in the polemical treatise (ca. 1147) of Peter the Venerable (1985, 122–24).

290. For a discussion of the fact that Jewish men are demonized far more than women in art (but also in literature), see Lipton 2008.

Conclusion

1. On the links between Benedictine monks, see Brett 1981.

2. Rubin 2009a, 83.

3. For an exploration of such ideas for the later Middle Ages, see Bale 2010.

4. For an exploration of the development of the idea of Jews as associates of the devil, see Trachtenberg 1943.

5. Langmuir 1990a.

6. Langmuir (1990a, 275–305, especially 291, 297–305) separates the two, attributing rational approaches to questions of religion to the likes of Anselm, and "irrational fantasies," such as the ritual murder accusation, to individuals trying to supress their doubts about their ability to answer these same questions. Another critique is Resnick 2012.

7. This opposes the assumptions of scholars (e.g., Chazan 1997) who argue that negative portrayals of Jews came especially from popular culture. There is nevertheless sometimes a tendency to conflate negative images and attitudes with active persecution and violence, and claiming that protection of Jews by the authorities means the "masses" were responsible for antagonism toward Jews generally.

8. Rubin 2009a, 83.

9. Thomas of Monmouth 2014. The literature on this narrative is extensive, but the main works are Langmuir 1990c; McCulloch 1997; Yuval 2006, especially 168–70, 185–86; Yarrow 2006, 122–68.

10. For a brief discussion of the influence of the Marian miracles on the ritual murder accusation, see Abulafia 2011, 171–75.

11. The influence of liturgical sources on the *Passio* has been explored by Blurton (2014), although drawing a connection between the *Passio* and *Planctus Mariae* Good Friday tradition risks anachronism, given that the latter emerged some decades later.

12. Nirenberg 1996, 6.

13. Rubin 2004, 2.

14. See Stow 2006.

15. Nirenberg 1996, 6.

16. This question underlies Palazzo 1998, 1153–54, which makes a stronger case for clerical control, as does Moore 1992 and 2007.

17. From the responsory, *Gaude Maria virgo*, discussed in chapter 1.

18. On liturgy and lay learning in late medieval England, see Zieman 2008. On the Books of Hours, see, among others, Duffy 2006.

19. Peter Abelard 2001; Peter the Venerable 1985; Walter of Châtillon, *Tractatus sive Dialogus Magistri Gualteri Tornacensis et Balduini Valentianensis contra Judaeos*, PL 209:423–58.

20. Kjellman 1977; Gautier de Coinci 1955–70; Nigel of Canterbury 1986.

21. Fidalgo 2004.

22. These are not mentioned, however, in Renna 2007.

23. Matthew Paris 1880, 114–15. On the anecdote, see Bale 2003.

24. On the former, see Stacey 1988; 1992, especially 267; 2013, especially 124–27; Vincent 2004; Fogle 2007. On the latter, see Jordan 1992. For a critique, see Hames 2004, 280–81.

25. This approach was taken in Shea 2004, which emphasized the *Miracles* of Gautier de Coincy as an important means of transmitting ideas about Jews and Mary between clerical and aristocratic audiences—the latter of which had influence over policy making. This follows the ideas of Moore 2007.

References

||||||||||||||||||||||||

Primary Sources

Ademar of Chabannes. 1999. *Chronicon*. CCCM 129. Turnhout, Bel.: Brepols.

Adomnan of Iona. 1958. *De Locis Sanctis*, edited by Denis Meehan. Dublin.

Aldhelm. 2009. *The Prose Works*. Edited and translated by Michael Lapidge and Michael Herren. Woodbridge, UK: Boydell and Brewer.

Alfonsi, Peter. 1977. *The Disciplina Clericalis*. Edited by E. Hermes. London: Routledge and Kegan Paul.

———. 2006. *Dialogue against the Jews*. Translated by Irven Resnick. Washington, DC: Catholic University of America Press.

Ambrose. 1967. *Fathers of the Church: Saint Ambrose, Letters (1–91)*. Translated by Mary Melchior Beyenka. Washington, DC: Catholic University of America Press.

Anselm of Canterbury. 1853. *Opera Omnia*. Edited by Franciscus Salesius Schmitt. 6 vols. Edinburgh: Thomas Nelson.

———. 1973. *Prayers and Meditations*. Translated by Benedicta Ward. Harmondsworth, UK: Penguin Books.

———. 1990. *Letters*. Translated by Walter Fröhlich. Kalamazoo, MI: Cistercian Publications.

———. 1998. *The Major Works*. Edited by Brian Davies and G. R. Evans. Oxford: Clarendon Press.

———. 2007. *Basic Writings*. Translated by Thomas Williams. Indianapolis: Hackett Publishing.

De Assumptione Beatae Virginis Mariae, Liber Unus. 1844–55. In *Patrologia Latina cursus completus, series latina*, edited by Jacques Paul Migne, 40:1141–48. Paris.

Bede. 1844–55. *Commentary on Luke*. In *Patrologia Latina cursus completus, series latina*, edited by Jacques Paul Migne, 92:301–634. Paris.

Benjamin of Tudela. 1907. *The Itinerary of Benjamin of Tudela*. Translated by E. N. Adler. London: Henry Frowde.

Bernard of Clairvaux. 1953. *The Letters of Bernard of Clairvaux*. Translated by Bruno Scott James. London: Burns Oates.

Bernard of Cluny. (1726) 1999. *Ordo Cluniacensis*. Edited by Marquard Herrgott. *Vetus disciplina monastica*, Paris: Osmont repr. Siegburg: Franz Schmitt.

Braun, René, ed. 1976. *Opera Quodvultdeo Carthaginiensi Episcopo Tributa*. CCSL 60. Turnhout, Bel.: Brepols.

Capgrave, John, ed. 1874. *Memorials of Saint Dunstan, Archbishop of Canterbury*. In *The Chronicles and Memorials of Great Britain and Ireland during the Middle Ages*, directed by Master of the Rolls. RS. 63. London: Longmans, Green, and Co.

Chevalier, Ulysse. 1841–1923. *Repertorium Hymnologicum*. 6 vols. Leuven: Inprimerie Polleunis et Ceuteric and Bruxelles: Sociéte des Bollandistes.

Crane, Thomas, ed. 1925. *Liber de Miraculis Sanctae dei Genitricis Mariae (Published at Vienna, in 1731, by Bernard Pez)*. Ithaca, NY: Cornell University Studies in Language and Literature.

Damian, Peter. 1844–55. *Sermo Lxiii de Sancto Johanne Apostolo et Evangelista*. In *Patrologia Latina cursus completus, series latina*, edited by Jacques Paul Migne, 144:857–66. Paris.

———. 1989–98. *Letters, 1–120*. Translated by Owen Blum. Washington, DC: Catholic University of America Press.

———. 2004. *Letters, 121–150*. Translated by Owen Blum and Irven Resnick. Washington, DC: Catholic University of America Press.

Dexter, Elise F., ed. 1927. *Miracula Sanctae Virginis Mariae*. Madison: University of Wisconsin.

Dominic of Evesham. 1998. *El Libro de Miraculis Sanctae Mariae de Domingo de Evesham (M.C. 1140)*. Edited by J. M. Canal. *Studium Legionense* 39:247–83.

Downer, L. J., ed. and trans. 1972. *Leges Henrici primi*. Oxford: Oxford University Press.

Drèves, Guido Maria, ed. 1886–1922. *Analecta Hymnica Medii Aevi*. 55 vols. plus indexes. Leipzig.

Eadmer of Canterbury. 1844–55. *De Excellentia Virginis Mariae*. In *Patrologia Latina cursus completus, series latina*, edited by Jacques Paul Migne, 159:558–80. Paris.

———. 1904. *Tractatus de Conceptione Sanctae Mariae*. Edited by Thomas Slater and Herbert Thurston. Freiburg: Sumptibus Herder.

———. 1962. *The Life of St Anselm, Archbishop of Canterbury*. Translated by Richard W. Southern. Oxford: Clarendon Press.

———. 1964. *History of Recent Events in England*. Translated by Geoffrey Bosanquet. London: Cresset Press.

Elisabeth of Schönau. 2000. *The Complete Works*. Translated by Anne L. Clark. New York: Paulist Press.

———. 2006. *Die Werke der Heiligen Elisabeth von Schönau*. Edited by Peter Dinzelbacher. Paderborn: Verlag Ferdinand Schöningh.

Elliott, J. K., ed. 1993. *The Apocryphal New Testament*. Oxford: Clarendon Press.

Evagrius Scholasticus. 2000. *The Ecclesiastical History*. Edited and translated by Michael Whitby. Liverpool: Liverpool University Press.

Fidalgo, Elvira, ed. 2004. *As Cantigas de Loor de Santa María (edición e comentario)*. Galicia : Xunta de Galicia, Centro Ramón Piñeiro para a Investigación en Humanidades.

Gautier de Coinci. 1955–70. *Les Miracles de Nostre Dame*. Edited by V. Frederic Koenig. Geneva: Droz.

Geoffrey of Vigeois. 1657. *Chronica Gaufredi Coenobitae Monasterii D. Martialis Lemovicensis ac Prioris Vosiensis Coenobii*, edited by Philippe Labbé. Paris: Sebastian Cramoisy.

Gerald of Wales. 1861–91. *Giraldi Cambrensis Opera*. Edited by John Sherren Brewer. London: Longman and Co.

Gijsel, Jan, and Rita Beyers, eds. 1997. *Libri de Nativitate Mariae*. CCSA 9–10. Turnhout, Bel.: Brepols.

Gilbert Crispin. 1986. *Works*. Edited by Anna Sapir Abulafia and G. R. Evans. London: British Academy.

Goscelin of St. Bertin. 2004a. *The Book of Encouragement and Consolation (Liber Confortatorius)*. Translated by Monika Otter. Woodbridge, UK: Boydell and Brewer.

———. 2004b. *The Hagiography of the Female Saints of Ely*. Translated by Rosalind Love. Oxford: Clarendon Press.

Gransden, Antonia, ed. 1963. *The Customary of the Benedictine Abbey of Eynsham in Oxfordshire*, edited by Antonia Gransden. Siegburg, Ger.: Franz Schmitt.

———. 1973. *The Customary of the Benedictine Abbey of Bury St. Edmunds in Suffolk*. London: Henry Bradshaw Society.

Gregory of Tours. 1988. *Glory of the Martyrs*. Translated by Raymond Van Dam. Liverpool: Liverpool University Press.

Guibert of Nogent. 1844–55. *Tractatus de Incarnatione Contra Judeos*. In *Patrologia Latina cursus completus, series latina*, edited by Jacques Paul Migne, 156:489–527. Paris.

———. 1996. *A Monk's Confession: The Memoirs of Guibert de Nogent*. Translated by Paul J. Archambault. University Park: Pensylvannia State University Press.

Hart, William Henry, ed. 1863. *Historia et Cartularium Monasterii Sancti Petri Gloucestriae*. ARS 33. London: Longmans, Green, and Co.

Hayward, Paul Antony, ed. and trans. 2010. *The Winchcombe and Coventry Chronicles: Hitherto Unnoticed Witnesses to the Work of John of Worcester*. Tempe: Arizona Center for Medieval and Renaissance Studies.

Henry of Huntingdon. 1996. *Historia Anglorum (History of the English People)*. Edited and translated by Diana Greenway. Oxford: Clarendon Press.

Herbert of Losinga. 1878. *Life, Letters, and Sermons of Bishop Herbert de Losinga*. Edited by Edward Meyrick Goulburn and Henry Symonds. 2 vols. Oxford: James Parker and Co.

Hermann of Tournai. 1844–55. *De Miraculis S. Mariae Laudunensis*. In *Patrologia Latina cursus completus, series latina*, edited by Jacques Paul Migne, 156:961–1017. Paris.

Honorius Augustodunensis. 1844–55. *Speculum Ecclesiae*. In *Patrologia Latina cursus completus, series latina*, edited by Jacques Paul Migne, 172:807–1107. Paris.

———. 1991. *Sigillum Beatae Mariae: The Seal of Blessed Mary*. Translated by Amelia Carr. Toronto: Peregrina Publishing.

Hrotsvit von Gandersheim. 1970. *Hrotsvithae Opera*. Edited by H. Homeyer. Munich: Verlag Ferdinand Schöningh.

Hughes, Anselm. 1960. *Portiforium of Saint Wulfstan*. 2 Vols. London: Henry Bradshaw Society.

Hunter, Joseph, ed. 1833. *Magnum Rotulum Scacarii vel Magnum Rotulum Pipae de anno Tricesimo-Primo Regni Henrici Primi*. London: Commissioners of the Public Record.

Ildefonsus of Toledo. 2007. *De Virginitate Sanctae Mariae; de Cognitione Baptismi; de Itinere Deserti*. Edited by Valeriano Yarza Urquiola. CCSL 114A. Turnhout, Bel.: Brepols.

Jerome. 1964. *In Ezechielem*. Edited by F. Glorie. CCSL 75. Turnhout, Bel.: Brepols.

Jocelin of Brakelond. 1989. *Chronicle of the Abbey of Bury St Edmunds*. Translated by Diane Greenway and Jane Sayers. Oxford: Oxford University Press.

Johannes Monachus. 1913. *Liber de Miraculis*. Edited by P. Michael Huber. Heidelberg: Carl Winter.

John of Salerno. 1844–55. *Vita Odonis*. In *Patrologia Latina cursus completus, series latina*, edited by Jacques Paul Migne, 133:931–44. Paris.

John of Worcester. 1995. *The Chronicle of John of Worcester*. Edited by Reginald R. Darlington and Patrick McGurk. Oxford: Clarendon Press.

Kulp-Hill, Kathleen, trans. 2000. *Songs of Holy Mary of Alfonso X: A translation of the Cantigas de Santa Maria*. Tempe, AZ: Arizona Center for Medieval and Renaissance Studies.

Lanfranc. 2002. *Monastic Constitutions*. Edited by Christopher N. L. Brooke and David Knowles. Oxford: Oxford University Press.

Luard, Henry Richards, ed. 1864. *Annales de Theokesberia, 1066–1263*. In *The Chronicles and Memorials of Great Britain and Ireland during the Middle Ages*, directed by Master of the Rolls. RS 36. Annales de Monastici 1. London: Longmans, Green, and Co.

———. 1869. *Annales Prioratus de Wigornia*. In *The Chronicles and Memorials of Great Britain and Ireland during the Middle Ages*, directed by Master of the Rolls. Annales Monastici 4, RS 36. London: Longmans, Green, and Co.

Macray, Willian Duncan, ed. 1863. *Chronicon Abbatiae de Evesham ad Annum 1418*. In *The Chronicles and Memorials of Great Britain and Ireland during the Middle Ages*, directed by Master of the Rolls. RS 29. London: Longmans, Green, and Co.

Matthew Paris. 1880. *Chronica Majora*. Edited by Henry Richards Luard. 7 vols. RS 57. London: Longman and Co.

Maximus the Confessor. 2012. *Life of the Virgin*. Translated by Stephen Shoemaker. New Haven, CT: Yale University Press.

Munitiz, Joseph A., J. Chrysostomides, Eirene Harvalia-Crook, and Ch. Dendrinos, eds. 1997. *The Letter of the Three Patriarchs to Emperor Theophilus and Related Texts*. Camberley, UK: Porphyrogenitus.

Nigel of Canterbury. 1986. *Miracles of the Virgin*. Edited by Jan Ziolkowski. Toronto: Pontifical Institute of Medieval Studies.

Odo of Tournai. 1994. *On Original Sin and a Disputation with the Jew, Leo, concerning the Advent of Christ, the Son of God: Two Theological Treatises*. Translated by Irven Resnick. Philadelphia: University of Pennsylvania Press.

Orderic Vitalis. 1980. *The Ecclesiastical History*. Edited and translated by Marjorie Chibnall. Oxford: Clarendon Press.

Osbert of Clare. 1929. *Letters*. Edited by E. W. Williamson. Oxford: Oxford University Press.

Paschasius Radbertus. 1969. *De Corpore et Sanguine Domini*. Edited by Paul Bede. CCCM 16. Turnhout, Bel.: Brepols.

Peter Abelard. 1844–55. *Sermo in Assumptione Beatae Mariae*. In *Patrologia Latina cursus completus, series latina*, edited by Jacques Paul Migne, 178:539–47. Paris.

———. 2001. *Collationes*. Translated by John Marenbon. Oxford: Clarendon Press.

Peter the Venerable. 1985. *Adversus Iudeorum Inveteratam Duritiem*. Edited by Yvonne Friedman. CCCM 58. Turnhout, Bel.: Brepols.

Riley, Henry Thomas, ed. 1867. *Gesta Abbatum Monasterii Sancti Albani.* 2 vols. in *The Chronicles and Memorials of Great Britain and Ireland during the Middle Ages*, directed by Master of the Rolls. RS. 28. London: Longmans, Green, and Co.

Rupert of Deutz. 1979. *Anulus seu Dialogus inter Christianum et Iudaeum.* Edited by Maria Lodovica Arduini. Rome: Instituto storico italiano per il medioevo.

Sermo de mysterio Trinitatis et Incarnationis. 1844–55. In *Patrologia Latina cursus completus, series latina*, edited by Jacques Paul Migne, 39:2196–8. Paris.

Socrates Scholasticus. 1891. *The Ecclesiastical History.* Translated by A. C. Zenos. Oxford: Parker and Company.

Somerville, Robert, ed. 1972. *The Councils of Urban II.* Vol. 1. *Decreta Claromontensie Annuarium Historie Conciliorum, Internationale Zeitschrift fur konsiliensgeschichts forschung.* Amsterdam: Adolf M. Hakkert.

Theodore the Studite. 1981. *On the Holy Icons.* Translated by Catharine P. Roth. Yonkers, NY: St Vladimir's Seminary Press.

Thomas of Monmouth. 2014. *The Life and Passion of William of Norwich.* Translated by Miri Rubin. London: Penguin Classics.

Ulrich of Cluny. 1844–55. *Antiquiores Consuetudines Cluniacensis Monasterii.* In *Patrologia Latina cursus completus, series latina*, edited by Jacques Paul Migne, 149:635–778. Paris.

William of Malmesbury. 1968. *De Laudibus et Miraculis Sanctae Mariae.* Edited by J. M. Canal. Rome: Alma Roma Libreria Editrice.

———. 1998. *Gesta Regum Anglorum (the History of the English Kings).* Edited and translated by R.A.B. Mynors, Rodney M. Thomson, and Michael Winterbottom. Oxford: Clarendon Press.

———. 2002. *Saints' Lives.* Edited and translated by Michael Winterbottom and Rodney M. Thomson. Oxford: Clarendon Press.

———. 2007. *Gesta Pontificum Anglorum (the History of the English Bishops).* Edited and translated by Michael Winterbottom and Rodney M. Thomson. Oxford: Clarendon Press.

———. 2013. *On Lamentations.* Edited by Michael Winterbottom and Rodney M. Thomson. CCCM 244. Turnhout, Bel.: Brepols.

———. 2015. *The Miracles of the Blessed Virgin Mary.* Edited and translated by Rodney M. Thomson and Michael Winterbottom. Woodbridge, UK: Boydell and Brewer.

Secondary Sources

Abou-el-Haj, Barbara. 1983. "Bury St Edmunds between 1070 and 1124: A History of Property, Privilege, and Monastic Art Production." *Art History* 6:1–29.

Abulafia, Anna Sapir. 1984a. "Gilbert Crispin's Disputations: An Exercise in Hermeneutics." In *Les mutations socio-culturelles au tournant des XIe–XIIe siècles*, 511–20. Paris: Centre national de Recherche Scientifique.

———. 1984b. "The Ars Disputandi of Gilbert Crispin, Abbot of Westminster (1085–1117)." In *Ad Fontes. Opstellen Aangeboden Aan Prof. Dr. C. Van De Kieftes*, edited by C. M. Cappon, 139-52. Amsterdam: Verloren.

———. 1984c. "An Attempt by Gilbert Crispin, Abbot of Westminster, at Rational Argument in the Jewish-Christian Debate." *Studia Monastica* 26: 55-74.

———. 1985. "Invectives against Christianity in the Hebrew Chronicles of the First Crusade." In *Crusade and Settlement, Papers Read at the First Conference of the Society for the Study of the Crusades and the Latin East*, edited by Peter W. Edbury, 1–14. Cardiff: University College Cardiff Press.

———. 1989a. "Christian Imagery of Jews in the Twelfth Century: A Look at Odo of Cambrai and Guibert of Nogent." *Theoretische Gechiedenis* 16:383–91.

———. 1989b. "Jewish-Christian Disputations and the Twelfth-Century Renaissance." *Journal of Medieval History* 15:105–25.

———. 1990. "St Anselm and Those Outside the Church." In *Faith and Identity: Christian Political Experience*, edited by David Loades and Katherine Walsh. Woodbridge, UK: Ecclesiastical History Society.

———. 1992a. "Christians Disputing Disbelief: St Anselm, Gilbert Crispin, and Pseudo-Anselm." *Religiongespräche im Mittelalter*, 131–48.

———. 1992b. "Jewish Carnality in Twelfth-Century Renaissance Thought." In *Christianity and Judaism*, edited by Diana Wood, 59–75. *Studies in Church History*, 29. Oxford: Blackwell Publishers.

———. 1993. "The Ideology of Reform and Changing Ideas concerning Jews in the Works of Rupert of Deutz and Hermannus Quondam Iudeus." *Jewish History* 7:43–63.

———. 1995. *Christians and Jews in the Twelfth-Century Renaissance*. London: Routledge.

———. 1996a. "Twelfth-Century Humanism and the Jews." In *Contra Iudaeos: Ancient and Medieval Polemics between Christians and Jews*, edited by Ora Limor and Guy G. Stroumsa. Tübingen: Mohr Siebeck.

———. 1996b. "Twelfth-Century Renaissance Theology and the Jews." In *From Witness to Witchcraft: Jews and Judaism in Medieval Christian Thought*, edited by Jeremy Cohen, 125–39. Wiesbaden: Harrassolvitz Verlag.

———. 1998c. "Bodies in the Jewish-Christian Debate." In *Framing Medieval Bodies*, edited by Sarah Kay and Miri Rubin, 123–37. Manchester: Manchester University Press.

———. 2002a. "The Intellectual and Spiritual Quest for Christ and Central Medieval Persecution of Jews." In *Religious Violence between Christians and Jews: Medieval Roots and Modern Perspectives*, edited by Anna Sapir Abulafia, 61–85. New York: Palgrave Macmillan.

———, ed. 2002b. *Religious Violence between Christians and Jews: Medieval Roots and Modern Perspectives*. New York: Palgrave Macmillan.

———. 2011. *Christian-Jewish Relations, 1000–1300: Jews in the Service of Medieval Christendom*. Harlow, UK: Longman and Co.

———. 2013. "Notions of Jewish Service in Twelfth- and Thirteenth-Century England." In *Christians and Jews in Angevin England: The York Massacre of 1190, Narratives and Contexts*, edited by Sarah Rees Jones and Sethina Watson, 204–21. York: York Medieval Press.

Adams, Jonathan and Jussi Hanska, eds. 2015. *The Jewish-Christian Encounter in Medieval Preaching*. New York: Routledge.

Afanasayev, Ilya. 2013. "Biblical Vocabulary and National Discourse." *Anglo-Norman Studies* 36:23–38.

Allen, Pauline. 2011. "Portrayals of Mary in Greek Homiletic Literature (6th–7th centuries)." In *The Cult of the Mother of God in Byzantium*, edited by Leslie Brubaker and Mary B. Cunningham, 69–90. Farnham, UK: Ashgate.

Allen Smith, Katherine. 2006. "Bodies of Unsurpassed Beauty: 'Living' Images of the Virgin in the High Middle Ages." *Viator* 37:167–87.

Andrieu, Michel. 1961. *Les Ordines Romani du Haut Moyen Âge*. Vol. 2. Leuven: Peeters.

Astell, Ann W. 1990. *The Song of Songs in the Middle Ages*. Ithaca, NY: Cornell University Press.

Avner, Riva. 2011. "The Initial Tradition of the Theotokos at the Kathisma: Earliest Celebrations and the Calendar." In *The Cult of the Mother of God in Byzantium*, edited by Leslie Brubaker and Mary B. Cunningham, 9–29. Farnham, UK: Ashgate.

Avril, François. 1975. *Manuscrits Normands, XIe–XIIe siècles*. Rouen, Fr.

Bacci, Michele. 2002. "'Quel Bello Miracolo onde si fa la Festa del Santo Salvatore': Studio sulle metamorfosi di una leggenda." In *Santa Croce e Santo Volto: Contributi allo Studio dell'origine e della Fortuna del Culto del Salvatore (Secoli Ix–Xv)*, edited by Gabriella Rossetti, 7–86. Pisa: Edizioni ETS.

Baer, Yitzak. 1992. *A History of the Jews in Christian Spain*. Vol. 1. Philadelphia: Jewish Publication Society.

Bagby, Albert. 1971. "Jews in the Cantigas of Alfonso X." *Speculum* 46 (4): 670–88.

Bale, Anthony. 2003. "Fictions of Judaism in England before 1290." In *The Jews in Medieval Britain: Historical, Literary, and Archaeological Perspectives*, edited by Patricia Skinner, 129–44. Woodbridge, UK: Boydell and Brewer.

———. 2004. ed. *St Edmund, King and Martyr: Changing Images of a Medieval Saint*. York: York Medieval Press.

———. 2007. *The Jew in the Medieval Book: English Antisemitisms, 1350–1500*. Cambridge: Cambridge University Press.

———. 2009. "Introduction: St Edmund's Medieval Lives." In *St Edmund, King and Martyr: Changing Images of a Medieval Saint*, edited by Anthony Bale, 1–25. York: University of York Press.

———. 2010. *Feeling Persecuted: Christians, Jews, and Images of Violence in the Middle Ages*. London: Reaktion Books.

Baltzer, Rebecca A. 2000. "The Little Office of the Virgin and Mary's Role at Paris." In *The Divine Office in the Latin Middle Ages*, edited by Margot Fassler and Rebecca A. Baltzer, 463–84. Oxford: Oxford University Press.

Bannister, H. M. 1903. "The Introduction of the Cultus of St. Anne into the West." *English Historical Review* 18 (69): 107–12.

Barker, Margaret. 2011. "Wisdom Imagery and the Mother of God." In *The Cult of the Mother of God in Byzantium: Texts and Images*, edited by Leslie Brubaker and Mary B. Cunningham, 91–108. Farnham, UK: Ashgate.

Barker, Peter. 2005. "Reconstructing Wulfstan's Cathedral." In *St Wulfstan and His World*, edited by Julia Barrow and Nicholas P. Brooks, 167–88. Aldershot, UK: Ashgate.

Barlow, Frank. 1979. *The English Church, 1066–1154*. London: Longman and Co.

Barré, Henri. 1949. "La Croyance à l'assomption corporelle en Occident de 750 à 1150 environ." *Etudes Mariales* 7:63–123.

———. 1957. "Le sermon 'Exhortatur' est-il de Saint Ildéfonse?" *Revue bénédictine* 67:10–33.

———. 1963. *Prières anciennes de l'occident à la Mère de Dieu*. Paris: P. Lethielleux.

———. 1967. "Un plaidoyer monastique pour le samedi marial." *Revue Bénédictine* 77:375–99.

Barrow, Julia. 1992. "How the Twelfth-Century Monks of Worcester Perceived Their Past." In *The Perception of the Past in Twelfth-Century Europe*, edited by Paul Magdalino, 53–74. London: Hambledon Press.

———. 1994. "English Cathedral Communities and Reform in the Late Tenth and the Eleventh Centuries." In *Anglo-Norman Durham, 1093–1193*, edited by David Rollason, Margaret Harvey, and Michael Prestwich, 25–39. Woodbridge, UK: Boydell and Brewer.

Bates, David. 2005. "1066: Does the Date Still Matter?" *Historical Research* 78:443–64.

———. 2014. "The Abbey and the Norman Conquest: An Unusual Case?" In *Bury St Edmunds and the Norman Conquest*, edited by Tom Licence, 5–21. Woodbridge, UK: Boydell and Brewer.

Baugh, Albert C. 1932. "Osbert of Clare, the Sarum Breviary, and the Middle-English *Saint Anne* in Rime Royal." *Speculum* 7:106–13.

Baun, Jane. 2004. "Discussing Mary's Humanity in Medieval Byzantium." In *The Church and Mary*, edited by R. N. Swanson, 63–72. Woodbridge, UK: Boydell and Brewer.

Bautier, Anne-Marie. 1977. "Typologie des ex-voto mentionnés dans des textes Antérieurs à 1200." In *La piété populaire au Moyen Age, Actes du 99e Congrès national des Sociétés savantes, Section de philologie et d'histoire jusqu'à 1610*, 237–82. Paris.

Bayless, Martha. 1997. *Parody in the Middle Ages: The Latin Tradition*. Ann Arbor: University of Michigan Press.

———. 2003. "The Story of the Fallen Jew and the Iconography of Jewish Unbelief." *Viator* 34:142–56.

Bayo, Juan Carlos. 2004. "Las colecciones universales de milagros de la Virgen hasta Gonzalo de Berceo." *Bulletin of Spanish Studies* 81: 849–71.

Beck, Egerton. 1924. "A Twelfth-Century Salutation of Our Lady." *Downside Review* 42:185–86.

Bedos-Rezak, Brigitte. 2000. "Medieval Identity: A Sign and a Concept," *American Historical Review*, 12: 1489-1533.

———. 2011. *When Ego Was Imago: Signs of Identity in the Middle Ages*. Leiden: Brill.

Bell, David N. 1995. *What Nuns Read: Books and Libraries in Medieval English Nunneries*. Kalamazoo, MI: Cistercian Publications.

———. 2007. "What Nuns Read: The State of the Question." In *The Culture of Medieval English Monasticism*, edited by James Clarke, 113–33. Woodbridge, UK: Boydell and Brewer. Press.

Berger, David. 2010. "The Attitude of St Bernard of Clairvaux toward the Jews." In *Persecution, Polemic, and Dialogue: Essays in Jewish-Christian Relations*, edited by David Berger, 245–60. Boston: Academic Studies Press.

Bériou, Nicole. 2000. "Les sermons latins après 1200." In *The Sermon*, edited by Beverly Mayne Kienzle, 363–447. Turnhout, Bel.: Brepols.

Berlioz, Jacques, and Marie-Anne Polo de Beaulieu. 1998. *Les Exempla médiévaux: Nouvelles perspectives*. Paris: Honoré Champion.

Bestul, Thomas H. 1977. "St Anselm and the Continuity of Anglo-Saxon Devotional Traditions." *Annuale medievale* 18:20–41.

———. 1981. "British Library Ms Arundel 60 and the Anselmian Apocrypha." *Scriptorium*, 271–75.

———. 1984. "The Collection of Private Prayers in the 'Portiforium' of Wulfstan of Worcester and the *Orationes Sive Meditationes* of Anselm of Canterbury." In *Les mutations socio-culturelles au tournant des XIe–XIIe siècles*, edited by Raymonde Foreville, 355–64. Paris: Centre national de Recherche Scientifique.

Bethell, Denis L. 1969. "English Black Monks and Episcopal Elections." *English Historical Review* 84:673–98.

Biale, David. 1999. "Counter-History and Jewish Polemics against Christianity: The *Sefer toldot yeshu* and the *Sefer zerubavel*." *Jewish Social Studies* 6:130–45.

Binns, Alison. 1989. *Dedications of Monastic Houses in England and Wales, 1066–1216*. Woodbridge, UK: Boydell and Brewer.

Bishop, Edmund. 1918a. "On the Origins of the Feast of the Conception of the Blessed Virgin Mary." In *Liturgica Historica: Papers on the Liturgy and Religious Life of the Western Church*, edited by Edmund Bishop, 238–59. Oxford: Clarendon Press.

———. 1918b. "On the Origins of the Prymer." In *Liturgica Historica: Papers on the Liturgy and Religious Life of the Western Church*, edited by Edmund Bishop, 211–37. Oxford: Clarendon Press.

Bisogni, Fabio. 2001. "Ex-voto e la scultura in cera nel tardo medioevo." In *Visions of Holiness: Art and Devotion in Renaissance Italy*, edited by Andrew Zuraw Ladis and Shelley E. Zuraw Ladis, 67–92. Athens: Georgia Museum of Art, University of Georgia.

Black, Jonathan. 2001. "The Divine Office and Private Devotion in the Latin West." In *The Liturgy of the Medieval Church*, edited by Thomas J. Heffernan and E. Ann Matter, 45-71. Kalamazoo, MI: Medieval Institute Publications.

Blair, John. 2005. *The Church in Anglo-Saxon Society*. Oxford: Oxford University Press.

Blumenkranz, Bernhard. 1948. "La *Disputatio Judei cum Christiano* de Gilbert Crispin, Abbé de Westminster." *Revue du Moyen Age Latin* 4 (3): 237–52.

———. 1954. "Juden und Jüdischen in Christlichen Wunderzählungen." *Theologische Zeitschrift* 10:417–46.

———. 1963. *Les auteurs chrétiens latins du Moyen Age sur les Juifs et le Judaisme*. Paris: Peeters.

Blurton, Heather. 2015. "The Language of the Liturgy in *Life and Miracles of William of Norwich*." *Speculum* 90: 1053-75.

Boase, T.S.R. 1962. *The York Psalter in the Library of the Hunterian Museum, Glasgow, with an Introduction and Notes*. London: Faber.

Bollo-Panadero, Maria Dolores. 2008. "Heretics and Infidels: The Cantigas de Santa Maria as Ideological Instrument of Cultural Codification." *Romance Quarterly* 55 (3): 163–74.

Bouman, Cornelius A. 1958. "The Immaculate Conception in the Liturgy." In *The Dogma of the Immaculate Conception: History and Significance*, edited by Edward Dennis O'Connor, 113–60. Notre Dame, IN: University of Notre Dame Press.

Boyarin, Adrienne Williams. 2010. *Miracles of the Virgin in Medieval England: Law and Jewishness in Marian Legends*. Woodbridge, UK: Boydell and Brewer.

Boynton, Susan. 2005. "The Customaries of Bernard and Ulrich as Liturgical Sources." In *From Dead of Night to End of Day: The Medieval Customs of Cluny*, edited by Isabelle Cochelin and Susan Boynton, 109–30. Turnhout, Bel.: Brepols.

———. 2007. "Prayer as Liturgical Performance in Eleventh- and Twelfth-Century Monastic Psalters." *Speculum* 82 (4): 896–931.

———. 2011. "The Bible and the Liturgy." In *The Practice of the Bible in the Middle Ages: Production, Reception, and Performance in Western Christianity*, edited by Susan Boynton and Diane J. Reilly, 10–33. New York: Columbia University Press.

Bradbury, Carlee A. 2013. "Dehumanizing the Jew at the Funeral of the Virgin Mary." In *Christians and Jews in Angevin England: The York Massacre of 1190, Narratives and Contexts*, edited by Sarah Rees Jones and Sethina Watson, 250–60. York: York Medieval Press.

Bradford Bedingfield, M. 2005. "Ritual and Drama in Anglo-Saxon England: the Dangers of the Diachronic Perspective." In *The Liturgy of the Late Anglo-Saxon Church*, edited by Helen Gittos and M. Bradford Bedingfield, 291–317. London: Henry Bradshaw Society.

Bradshaw, Paul F., and Maxwell E. Johnson. 2011. *The Origins of Feasts, Fasts, and Seasons in Early Christianity*. Collegeville, MN: Liturgical Press.

Brandenburg, Ton. 1995. "Saint Anne: A Holy Grandmother and Her Children." In *Sanctity and Motherhood*, edited by Anneke Mulder-Bakker, 31–65. New York: Garland.

Bremont, Claude, and Jacques Le Goff. 1982. *L'exemplum*. Turnhout, Bel.: Brepols.

Brett, Martin. 1975. "A Collection of Anglo-Norman Councils." *Journal of Ecclesiastical History* 26 26:301–8.

———. 1981. "John of Worcester and His Contemporaries." In *The Writing of History in the Middle Ages: Essays Presented to Richard William Southern*, edited by R.H.C. Davis and J. M. Wallace-Hadrill, 101–26. Oxford: Clarendon Press.

Briggs, Brian. 2004a. "Expulsio, Proscriptio, Exilium: Exile and Friendship in the Writings of Osbert of Clare." In *Exile in the Middle Ages: Selected Proceedings from the International Medieval Congress, University of Leeds, 8–11 July 2002*, edited by Laura Napran and Elisabeth Van Houts, 131–44. Turnhout, Bel.: Brepols.

———. 2004b. "The Life and Works of Osbert of Clare." PhD diss., University of St Andrews.

Brooke, Christopher N. L. 1956a. "Gregorian Reform in Action: Clerical Marriage in England, 1050–1200." *Cambridge Historical Journal* 12 (1): 1–21.

———. 1956b. "Married Men among the English Higher Clergy, 1066–1200." *Cambridge Historical Journal* 12 (2): 187–88.

———. 1975. "Archbishop Lanfranc, the English Bishops, and the Council of London of 1075." *Studia Gratiana* 12:41–59.

Brooke, Christopher N. L., and Rosalind Brooke. 1999. "The Bishops of England and Normandy in the Eleventh Century: A Contrast." In *Churches and Churchmen in Medieval Europe*, edited by Christopher N. L. Brooke, 107–16. London: Hambledon Press.

Brooks, Nicholas. 1984. *The Early History of the Church of Canterbury: Christ Church from 597 to 1066*. Leicester: Leicester University Press.

Brou, Louis. 1948. "Marie 'Destructrice de toutes les hérésies' et la belle légende du répons *Gaude Maria Virgo*." *Ephemerides liturgicae* 62:321–53.

Brubaker, Leslie, and Mary B. Cunningham. 2007. "Byzantine Veneration of the *Theotokos*: Icons, Relics, and Eighth-Century Homilies." In *From Rome to Constantinople: Studies in Honour of Averil Cameron*, edited by Hagit Amirav and R. Bas ter Haar Romeny, 235–50. Leuven: Peeters.

Brunat, Georges. 1974. *Une page d'épopée mariale: Récit de Haimon relatant les prodiges attribués à la Mère de Dieu lors de la reconstruction de l'église du monastère de Saint-Pierre-Sur-Dives*. Lisieux, Fr.

Brusa, Gionata. 2012. "Un Ufficio Inedito Per S. Anna a Vercelli." *Scrineum* 9:257–67.

Bull, Marcus. 1999. *The Miracles of Our Lady of Rocamadour: Analysis and Translation*. Woodbridge, UK: Boydell and Brewer.

Bulst, Nicholas. 1984. "La réforme monastique en Normandie: Diffusion et implantation de la réforme de Guillaume de Volpiano (Prosopographie, exploitation des nécrologues)." In *Les mutations socio-culturelles au tournant des XIe–XIIe siècles*, edited by Raymonde Foreville, 317–30. Paris: Centre national de Recherche Scientifique.

Burnett, Charles. 1997a. *The Introduction of Arabic Learning into England: The Panizzi Lectures*. London: British Library.

———. 1997b. "The Works of Petrus Alfonsi: Questions of Authenticity." *Medium Aevum* 66:42–79.

Burridge, A. W. 1936. "L'Immaculée Conception dans la théologie de l'Angleterre médiévale." *Revue d'Histoire Ecclésiastique* 32 (3): 570–97.

Burton, Janet. 1994. *Monastic and Religious Orders in Britain, 1000–1300*. Cambridge: Cambridge University Press.

Canal, J. M. 1959. "Guillermo de Malmesbury y el Pseudo-Agustín." *Ephemerides mariologicae* 9:479–89.

———. 1961. "Oficio parvo de la Virgen: Formas viejas y formas nuevas." *Ephemerides mariologicae* 11:497–525.

———. 1962. "Los sermones Marianos de Fulberto de Chartres (†1028)." *Recherches de théologie ancienne et médiévale* 29:33–51.

Carozzi, Claude. 1994. *Le voyage de l'âme dans l'au-Delà d'après la littérature latine (Ve–XIIIe siècle)*. Rome.

Carter, Peter. 1959. "An Edition of William of Malmesbury's Treatise on the Miracles of the Virgin Mary: With an Account of its Place in his Writings and in the Development of Mary Legends in the Twelfth Century." PhD diss., Merton College, Oxford.

———. 1981. "The Historical Content of William of Malmesbury's Miracles of the Virgin Mary." In *The Writing of History in the Middle Ages: Essays Presented to Richard William Southern*, edited by J. M. Wallace-Hadrill and R.H.C. Davis, 127–65. Oxford: Clarendon Press.

Chapman, David W. 2008. *Ancient Jewish and Christian Perceptions of Crucifixion*. Tübingen: Mohr Siebeck.

Charvin, Gaston, ed. 1965. *Statuts, chapitres généraux et visites de l'Ordre de Cluny*. Vol. 1. Paris: Éditions E. de Boccard.

Chazan, Robert. 1980. *Church, State, and Jew in the Middle Ages*. West Orange, NJ: Behrman House Inc.

———. 1997. *Medieval Stereotypes and Modern Antisemitism*. Berkeley: University of California Press.

———. 2004. *Fashioning Jewish Identity in Medieval Western Christendom*. Cambridge: Cambridge University Press.

———. 2010. *Reassessing Jewish Life in Medieval Europe*. Cambridge: Cambridge University Press.

Chenu, M.-D. 1976. *La théologie au douzième siècle, 3rd Edition*. Paris: Etudes de Philosophie Médiévale.

Chibnall, Marjorie. 1999. *The Debate on the Norman Conquest*. Manchester: Manchester University Press.

———. 2000. "Les Normands et les saints Anglo-Saxons." In *Les saints dans la Normandie médiévale: Colloque de Cerisy-La-Salle (26–29 Septembre 1996)*, edited by Pierre Bouet and François Neveux, 259–68. Caen, Fr.: Presses universitaires de Caen.

Ciggaar, Krijnie N. 1976. "Une description de Constantinople traduite par un pèlerin Anglais." *Revue des études byzantines* 34:211–68.

Clanchy, Michael. 1993. *From Memory to Written Record*. 2nd ed. Oxford: Blackwell.

Clark, Elizabeth. 1986. "The Uses of the Song of Songs: Origen and the Later Latin Fathers." In *Ascetic Piety and Women's Faith: Essays on Late Ancient Christianity*, edited by Elizabeth Clark, 386–427. Lewiston, NY: Edwin Mellen Press.

Clark, James G. 2007. Introduction to *The Culture of Medieval English Monasticism*, edited by James G. Clark, 1–21. Woodbridge, UK: Boydell and Brewer.

Clayton, Mary. 1986. "Aelfric and the Nativity of the Blessed Virgin Mary." *Anglia: Zeitschrift für englische philologie* 104 (3): 286–315.

———. 1987. "*Assumptio Mariae*: An Eleventh-Century Anglo-Latin Poem from Abingdon." *Analecta Bollandiana* 104:419–26.

———. 1990. *The Cult of the Virgin Mary in Anglo-Saxon England*. Cambridge: Cambridge University Press.

———. 1998. *The Apocryphal Gospels of Mary in Anglo-Saxon England*. Cambridge: Cambridge University Press.

Coates, Alan. 1999. *English Medieval Books: The Reading Abbey Collections from Foundation to Dispersal*. Oxford: Clarendon Press.

Cohen, Jeremy. 1984. *The Friars and the Jews: The Evolution of Medieval Anti-Judaism*. Ithaca: Cornell University Press.

———. 1999. *Living Letters of the Law: Ideas of the Jew in Medieval Christianity*. Berkeley: University of California Press.

———. 2002. "Christian Theology and Anti Jewish Violence in the Middle Ages: Connections and Disjunctions." In *Religious Violence between Christians and Jews: Medieval Roots, Modern Perspectives*, edited by Anna Sapir Abulafia, 44–60. New York: Palgrave Macmillan.

———. 2004. "*Synagoga Conversa*: Honorius Augustodunensis, the Song of Songs, and Christianity's *Eschatological Jew*." *Speculum* 79 (2): 309–40.

———. 2007. *Christ Killers: The Jews and the Passion from the Bible to the Big Screen*. Oxford: Oxford University Press.

Collins, Kristen, Peter Kidd, and Nancy K. Turner. 2013. *The St. Albans Psalter: Painting and Prayer in Medieval England*. Los Angeles: Getty Publications.

Constable, Giles. 1994. "The Language of Preaching in the Twelfth Century." *Viator* 25:131–52.

———. 1995. *Three Studies in Medieval Religious and Social Thought*. Cambridge: Cambridge University Press.

———. 1996. *The Reformation of the Twelfth Century*. Cambridge: Cambridge University Press.

Constas, Nikolas. 2003. *Proclus of Constantinople and the Cult of the Virgin in Late Antiquity: Homilies 1–5, Texts and Translations*. Leiden: Brill.

Corbin, Solange. 1967. "Miracula Beatae Mariae Semper Virginis." *Cahiers de civilisation médiévale* 39–40:409–33.

Corrigan, Kathleen. 1992. *Visual Polemics in the Ninth-Century Byzantine Psalters*. Cambridge: Cambridge University Press.

Cottier, Jean-François. 1996. "Le recueil apocryphe des Orationes sive meditationes de Saint Anselm: Sa formation et sa réception en Angleterre et en France au XIIe siècle." In *Anselm: Aosta, Bec, and Canterbury*, edited by David E. Luscombe and G. R. Evans. Sheffield, UK: Sheffield Academic Press.

———. 2001. *Anima Mea: Prières privées et textes de dévotion du Moyen Age Latin*. Turnhout, Bel.: Brepols.

Cousin, Patrice. 1949. "La dévotion Mariale chez les grands abbés de Cluny." In *À Cluny, Congrès Scientifique*, edited by Société des Amis de Cluny, 210–18. Dijon: Imprimerie Bernigaud et Privat.

Cullman, Oscar. 1991. "Infancy Gospels." Translated by Robert McLachian Wilson. In *New Testament Apocrypha*, edited by Wilhelm Schneemelcher, 414–69. Westminster: James Clarke and Co.

Cunningham, Mary. 1999. "Polemic and Exegesis: Anti-Judaic Invective in Byzantine Homiletics." *Sobornost* 21:46–68.

———. 2004. "The Meeting of the Old and the New: The Typology of Mary and Theotokos in Byzantine Homilies and Hymns." In *The Church and Mary*, edited by R. N. Swanson, 52–62. Woodbridge, UK: Boydell and Brewer.

———. 2008. *Wider Than Heaven: Eighth-Century Homilies on the Mother of God*. Yonkers, NY: St Vladimir's Seminary Press.

Daas, Martha Mary. 2011. *The Politics of Salvation: Gonzalo de Berceo's Reinvention of the Marian Myth*. London: Queen Mary, University of London.

Dahan, Gilbert. 1977. "Salatin, du *Miracle de Théophile* de Rutebeuf." *Le Moyen Age* 83 (3–4): 445–68.

———. 1980. "Les Juifs dans les Miracles de Gautier de Coincy." *Archives juives* 16:41–49.

———. 1982. "L'exégèse de l'histoire de Cain et Abel du XII–XIV siècle." *Recherches de Théologie ancienne et médiévale* 49:21–89, 5:5–68.

———. 1984. "Saint Anselm, les Juifs, le Judaisme." In *Les mutations socio-culturelles au tournant des XIe et XIIe siècles*, edited by Raymonde Foreville, 521–34. Paris: Editions du Centre national de la recherche scientifique.

———. 1990. *Les intellectuels chrétiens et les Juifs au Moyen Âge*. Paris: Éditions Cerf.

———. 1994. "L'usage de la *Ratio* dans la polémique contre les Juifs XIIe-XIVe siècle", in *Diálogo filosófico-religioso entre Cristianismo, Judaismo e Islamismo durante la edad media en la península ibérica*, edited by Horacio Santiago-Otero, 289-307. Bruxelles: Brepols.

———. 1995. "Un miracle de Notre Dame: La Juive narbonne convertie." In *Medieval Studies in Honour of Avrom Saltman*, edited by Bat-Sheva Albert, Yvonne Friedman, and Simon Schwarzfuchs, 97–120. Ramat-Gan, Isr.: Bar-Ilan University Press.

———. 1998. *The Christian Polemic against the Jews in the Middle Ages*. Translated by Jody Gladding. Notre Dame: University of Notre Dame Press.

Dasent, George Webbe. 1845. *Theophilus in Icelandic, Low German, and Other Tongues*. London: William Pickering.

Davis, H. Francis. 1954. "The Origins of Devotion to Our Lady's Immaculate Conception." *Dublin Review* 466:375–92.

de Gaiffier, Baudouin. 1970. "A Propos de Guy, évêque de Lescar et du culte de Sainte Anne." *Analecta Bollandiana* 88 (1–2): 74.

de Ghellinck, J. 1948. *Le mouvement théologique du XIIe siècle, 2nd Edition*. Vol. 10. Bruges: Museum Lessianum.

de la Chapelle, M. L. 1962. "Le Mystère de la pureté de Marie Chez Eadmer." *Revue d'Ascétique et de Mystique* 38:288–304.

de Vogüé, Adalbert. 1986. "Marie chez les vierges du sixième siècle: Césaire d'Arles et Grégoire le Grand." *Benedictina* 33 (1): 79–91.

Deme, Dániel. 2003. *The Christology of Anselm of Canterbury*. Aldershot, UK: Ashgate.

Denoël, Charlotte. 2011. "La bibliothèque médiévale de Saint-Martin-des-Champs à Paris." *Scriptorium* 65:67–108.

Despres, Denise L. 1994. "Cultic Anti-Judaism and Chaucer's Litel Clergeon." *Modern Philology* 91:413–27.

———. 1998. "Immaculate Flesh and the Social Body: Mary and the Jews." *Jewish History* 12 (1): 47–69.

Dewick, E. S., ed. *Facsimiles of Horae de Beata Maria Virgine*. London: Henry Bradshaw Society.

Diard, Olivier. 2003. "Histoire et chant liturgique en Normandie au XIe siècle: Les offices propres particuliers des diocèses d'Évreux et de Rouen." *Annales de Normandie* 53:195–223.

Dickinson, J. C. 1956. *The Shrine of Our Lady of Walsingham*. Cambridge: Cambridge University Press.

Dobschütz, E. 1903. "Maria Romaia. Zwei Unbekannte Texte." *Byzantinische Zeitschrift* 12:173–214.

Dobson, R. B. 1974. *The Jews of Medieval York and the Massacre of March 1190*. Vol. 45. York, UK: Borthwick Institute of Historical Research, University of York.

Dodwell, Charles Reginald. 1993. *The Pictorial Arts of the West, 800–1200*. New Haven, CT: Yale University Press.

Donahue, C. 1942. *The Testament of Mary: The Gaelic Version of the Dormitio Mariae Together with an Irish Latin Version*. New York: Fordham University Press.

Donovan, Claire. 1993. *The Winchester Bible*. London: British Library.

Douais, C., ed. 1887. *Cartulaire de l'Abbaye de Saint-Sernin de Toulouse*. Paris: Alphonse Picard.

Douglas, D. C., ed. 1932. *Feudal Documents from the Abbey of Bury St. Edmunds*. Vol. 3. Oxford: Oxford University Press.

Duffy, Eamon. 2006. *Marking the Hours: English People and Their Prayers, 1240–1570.* New Haven, CT: Yale University Press.

Dunthorne, Judith. 2012. "Anselm of Canterbury and the Development of Theological Thought, c. 1070–1141." PhD diss., University of Durham.

Dyer, Joseph. 1999. "The Psalms in Monastic Prayer." In *The Place of the Psalms in the Intellectual Culture of the Middle Ages,* edited by Nancy Van Deusen, 59–89. Albany: State University of New York Press.

Elliott, J. K. 2008. "Mary in the Apocryphal New Testament." In *The Origins of the Cult of the Virgin Mary,* edited by Chris Maunder, 57–70. London: Burns and Oates.

Elukin, Jonathan. 2009. *Living Together, Living Apart: Rethinking Jewish-Christian Relations in the Middle Ages.* Princeton NJ: Princeton University Press.

Escobar Vargas, Maria Carolina. 2011. "Image and Reality of the Magician Figure in Twelfth Century England." PhD diss., University of Reading.

Evans, G. R. 1980. "Gilbert Crispin on the Eucharist: A Postscript to Lanfranc and Berengar." *Journal of Theological Studies* 31:28–43.

———. 2004. "Anselm's Life, Works, and Immediate Influence." In *The Cambridge Companion to Anselm,* edited by Brian Davies and Brian Leftow, 5–31. Cambridge: Cambridge University Press.

———. 2007. "The Meaning of Monastic Culture: Anselm and His Contemporaries." In *The Culture of Medieval English Monasticism,* edited by James Clarke. Woodbridge, UK: Boydell and Brewer.

Fassler, Margot. 1985. "The Office of the Cantor in Early Western Monastic Rules and Customaries: A Preliminary Investigation." *Early Music History* 5:29–51.

———. 1993. *Gothic Song: Victorine Sequences and Augustinian Reform in Twelfth-Century Paris.* Cambridge: Cambridge University Press.

———. 2000a. "Mary's Nativity, Fulbert of Chartres, and the *Stirps Jesse:* Liturgical Innovation circa 1000 and its Afterlife." *Speculum* 75:389–434.

———. 2000b. "Sermons, Sacramentaries, and Early Sources for the Office in the Latin West: The Example of Advent." In *The Divine Office in the Latin Middle Ages,* edited by Margot Fassler and Rebecca A. Baltzer, 15–47. Oxford: Oxford University Press.

———. 2001. "The First Marian Feast in Constantinople and Jerusalem: Chant Texts, Readings, and Homiletic Literature." In *The Study of Medieval Chant,* edited by Peter Jeffery, 25–87. Woodbridge, UK: Boydell and Brewer.

———. 2009. *The Virgin of Chartres: Making History through Liturgy and the Arts.* New Haven, CT: Yale University Press.

———. 2013. "Mary in Seventh-Century Spain: The Mass Liturgy of Dec. 18." In *El Canto Mozárabe y su Entorno. Estudios Sobre la Música de la Liturgia Viejo Hispánica,* edited by Ismael Fernández de la Cuesta, Rosario Álvarez Mártinez, and Ana Llorens Martín, 217–36. Madrid: Sociedad Españóla de Musicología.

Ferreiro Alemparte, Jaime. 1970. "Las versiones latinas de la leyenda de San Ildefonso y su reflejo En Berceo." *Boletín de la Real Academia Española* 50:233–76.

Finucane, Ronald C. (1977) 1995. *Miracles and Pilgrims: Popular Beliefs in Medieval England.* Reprint, London: Palgrave Macmillan.

Flanigan, C. Clifford. 1991. "Medieval Latin Music-Drama." In *The Theatre of Medieval Europe: New Research in Early Drama,* ed. Eckehard Simon, 21–41. Cambridge: Cambridge University Press.

———. 2001. "The Moving Subject: Medieval Liturgical Processions in Semiotic and Cultural Perspective." In *Moving Subjects: Processional Performance in the Middle Ages and the Renaissance*, edited by Kathleen Ashley and Wim Hüskin, 35–52. Amsterdam: Rodopi.

Flanigan, C. Clifford, Kathleen Ashley, and Pamela Sheingorn. 2005. "Liturgy as Social Performance: Expanding the Definitions." In *The Liturgy of the Medieval Church*, edited by Thomas J. Heffernan and E. Ann Matter, 635–52. Kalamazoo, MI: Medieval Institute Publications.

Flint, Valerie I. J. 1972a. "The Career of Honorius Augustodunensis." *Revue Bénédictine* 82:63–86.

———. 1972b. "The Chronology of the Works of Honorius Augustodunensis." *Revue Bénédictine* 82:215–42.

———. 1974. "The Commentaries of Honorius Augustodunensis on the Song of Songs." *Revue Bénédictine* 84 (1–2): 196–211.

———. 1975. "The Elucidarius of Honorius Augustodunensis and Reform in Late Eleventh Century England." *Revue Bénédictine* 85:178–98.

———. 1977. "Place and Purpose in the Works of Honorius Augustodunensis." *Revue Bénédictine* 87:97–127.

———. 1982. "Heinricus of Augsburg and Honorius Augustodunensis: Are They the Same Person?" *Revue Bénédictine* 92:148–58.

———. 1995. *Honorius Augustodunensis of Regensburg*. Edited by Patrick L. Geary. Aldershot, UK: Varorium.

Fogle, Lauren. 2007. "The *Domus Conversorum*: The Personal Interest of Henry III." *Jewish Historical Studies* 41:1–7.

Forsyth, Ilene H. 1972. *The Throne of Wisdom: Wood Sculptures of the Madonna in Romanesque France*. Princeton, NJ: Princeton University Press.

Fournée, Jean. 1960. "L'abbaye de Fécamp et les origines du culte de l'Immaculée-Conception en Normandie." *L'abbaye bénédictine de Fécamp* 2:163–70.

———. 1981. "La place de Rouen et de la Normandie dans le développement du culte et de l'iconographie de l'Immaculée-Conception." In *Histoire Religieuse de la Normandie*, edited by Guy-Marie Oury, 123–41. Chambray: Éditions C.L.D.

———. 1984. "Du *De Conceptu Virginali* de Saint Anselm au *De Conceptione Sanctae Mariae* de son disciple Eadmer ou de la *Virgo Purissima* à la *Virgo Immaculata*." In *Les mutations socio-culturelles au tournant des XIe–XIIe siècles*, edited by Raymonde Foreville, 711–21. Paris: Centre national de Recherche Scientifique.

Fradenburg, Louise O. 1996. "Criticism, Anti-Semitism, and the Prioress' Tale." In *Chaucer: Contemporary Critical Essays*, edited by Valerie Allen and Ares Axiotis, 193–231. New York: New Casebooks.

Frank, Robert Worth. 1982. "Miracles of the Virgin, Medieval Anti-Semitism, and the Prioress' Tale." In *The Wisdom of Poetry: Essays in Early English Literature in Honor of Morton W. Bloomfield*, edited by Larry D. Benson, and Siefried Wenzel, 177–88. Kalamazoo, MI: Medieval Institute Publications.

Frassetto, Michael. 2007. "Heretics and Jews in the Early Eleventh Century: The Writings of Radulphus Glaber and Ademar of Chabannes." In *Christian Attitudes toward the Jews in the Middle Ages*, edited by Michael Frassetto, 43–59. New York: Routledge.

Freeburn, Ryan P. 2011. *Hugh of Amiens and the Twelfth-Century Renaissance*. Aldershot, UK: Ashgate.

———. 2013. "A Great Honour and a Burden: The Predicament of Matthew of Albano, Monk and Cardinal-Bishop." *Journal of Medieval History* 39 (2): 179–96.

Frere, Walter Howard, and Langton E. G. Brown. 1915. *The Hereford Breviary*. Vol. 3. London: Henry Bradshaw Society.

Friedman, Albert B. 1974–75. "The Prioress' Tale and Chaucer's Anti-Semitism." *Chaucer Review* 9:118–29.

Frizzell, Lawrence E., and J. Frank Henderson. 2005. "Jews and Judaism in the Medieval Latin Liturgy." In *The Liturgy of the Medieval Church*, edited by Thomas J. Heffernan and E. Ann Matter, 1671–92. Kalamazoo, MI: Medieval Institute Publications.

Frugoni, Chiara. 2008. "La sottomissione di Teofilo al Diavolo: A proposito di reaccomandati e vassalli." In *"Non lasciar vivere la malefica" le streghe nei trattati e nei processi (Secoli XIV–XVII)*, edited by Dinora Corsi and Matteo Duni, 129–54. Florence: Firenze University Press.

Fulton, Rachel. 1994. "The Virgin Mary and the Song of Songs in the High Middle Ages." PhD diss., Columbia University.

———. 1998. "'Quae est ista quae ascendit sicut aurora consurgens?': The Song of Songs as the *Historia* for the Office of the Assumption." *Mediaeval Studies* 60:55–122.

———. 2002. *From Judgment to Passion: Devotion to Christ and the Virgin Mary, 800–1200*. New York: Columbia University Press.

———. 2006. "Praying with Anselm at Admont: A Meditation on Practice." *Speculum* 81 (3): 700–33.

———. 2013. "Anselm and Praying with the Saints." In *Experiments in Empathy: The Middle Ages*, edited by Karl Morrison and Rudolph M. Bell, 95–112. Turnhout, Bel.: Brepols.

Funkenstein, Amos. 1971. "Basic Types of Anti-Jewish Polemics in the Later Middle Ages." *Viator* 2:373–82.

Gameson, Richard. 1999. *The Manuscripts of Early Norman England (c. 1066–1130)*. London: British Academy.

Garand, Monique-Cécile. 1979. "Une collection personnelle de Saint Odilon de Cluny et ses compléments." *Scriptorium* 33:163–80.

Garcia Rodriguez, Carmen. 1966. *El Culto de los Santos en la Espana Romana y Visigoda*. Madrid: CSIC.

Gasper, Giles. 2004. *Anselm of Canterbury and His Theological Inheritance*. Aldershot, UK: Ashgate.

Gasper, Giles, and Svein Gullbekk. 2012. "Money and Its Use in the Thought and Experience of Anselm, Archbishop of Canterbury (1093–1109)." *Journal of Medieval History* 38 (2): 155–82.

Gasquet, Francis Aidan, and Edmund Bishop. 1908. *The Bosworth Psalter*. London: George Bell and Sons.

Gazeau, Véronique. 2000. "Guillaume de Volpiano et le monachisme normand." In *La Normandie vers l'an mil*, edited by F. de Beaurepaire and J.-P. Chaline, 132–36. Rouen, Fr.: Société de l'Histoire de Normandie.

Gazeau, Véronique, and Monique Gouillet. 2008. *Guillaume de Volpiano: Un réformateur en son temps (962–1031)*. Caen, Fr.: Centre Michel de Boüard.

Geary, Patrick L. 1990. *Furta Sacra: Theft of Relics in the Central Middle Ages*. 2nd ed. Princeton, NJ: Princeton University Press.

———. 1994. *Phantoms of Remembrance: Memory and Oblivion at the End of the First Millennium*. Princeton, NJ: Princeton University Press.

———. 2006. *Women at the Beginning: Origin Myths from the Amazons to the Virgin Mary*. Princeton, NJ: Princeton University Press.

Geddes, Jane. 2005. *The St Albans Psalter: A Book for Christina of Markyate*. London: British Library.

Gibson, Margaret. 1978. *Lanfranc of Bec*. Oxford: Clarendon Press.

———. 1995. "Normans and Angevins." In *A History of Canterbury Cathedral*, edited by Patrick Collinson, Nigel Ramsay, and Margaret Sparks, 38–68. Oxford: Oxford University Press.

Gibson, Margaret, T. A. Heslop, and Richard W. Pfaff. 1992. *The Eadwine Psalter: Text, Image, and Monastic Culture in the Twelfth-Century Canterbury*. London: Modern Humanities Research.

Gittos, Helen. 2016. "Researching the History of Rites." In *Understanding Medieval Liturgy: Essays in Interpretation*, edited by Helen Gittos and Sarah Hamilton. 13–37. Woodbridge, UK: Ashgate.

———. 2013a. *Liturgy, Architecture, and Sacred Places in Anglo-Saxon England*. Oxford: Oxford University Press.

———. 2013b. "Sources for the Liturgy of Canterbury Cathedral in the Central Middle Ages." In *Medieval Art, Architecture, and Archaeology at Canterbury: British Archaeological Association Conference Proceedings*, edited by Alixe Bovey, 41–58. Leeds: Maney Publishing.

Gittos, Helen, and M. Bradford Bedingfield, eds. 2005. *The Liturgy of the Late Anglo-Saxon Church*. London: Henry Bradshaw Society.

Gittos, Helen and Sarah Hamilton, eds. 2016. *Understanding Medieval Liturgy: Essays in Interpretation*. Farnham, UK: Ashgate.

Gneuss, Helmut. 1997. "Origin and Provenance of Anglo-Saxon Manuscripts: The Case of Cotton Tiberius A.Iii." In *Of the Making of Books: Medieval Manuscripts, Their Scribes and Readers. Essays Presented to M. B. Parkes*, edited by Pamela Robinson and Rivkah Zim, 13–48. Aldershot, UK: Scolar Press.

Golb, Norman. 1984. "Les Juifs de Normandie à l'époque d'Anselme." In *Les mutations socio-culturelles au tournant des XIe–XIIe siècles*, edited by Raymonde Foreville, 149–60. Paris: Centre national de Recherche Scientifique.

———. 1998. *The Jews in Medieval Normandy*. Cambridge: Cambridge University Press.

Gold, Penny Schine. 1985. *The Lady and the Virgin: Image, Attitude, and Experience in Twelfth-Century France*. Chicago: University of Chicago Press.

Goodich, Michael. 1981. "A Note on Sainthood in the Hagiographical Prologue." *History and Theory* 20 (2): 168–74.

———. 2007. *Miracles and Wonders: The Development of the Concept of Miracle, 1150–1350*. Farnham, UK: Ashgate.

Graboïs, Aryeh. 1973. "La dynastie des 'Rois Juifs' de Narbonne (IXe–XIIIe siècles)." *Narbonne. Archéologie et histoire Moyen Age*, 49–54.

Graef, Hilda. 2009. *Mary: A History of Doctrine and Devotion*. 2nd ed. Notre Dame, IN: Ave Maria Press.

Gransden, Antonia. 1974. *Historical Writing in England: c. 550–c. 1307*. Vol. 1. London: Routledge, repr. 1996.

———. 1981. "Baldwin, Abbot of Bury St Edmunds." In *Anglo-Norman Studies*, edited by R. Allen Brown, 65–76. Woodbridge, UK: Boydell and Brewer.

———. 1989. "Traditionalism and Continuity during the Last Century of Anglo-Saxon Monasticism." *Journal of Ecclesiastical History* 40 (2): 159–207.

———. 1990. "Prologues in the Historiography of Twelfth-Century England." In *England in the Twelfth Century: Proceedings of the 1988 Harlaxton Symposium*, edited by Daniel Williams, 55–81. Woodbridge, UK: Boydell and Brewer.

———. 2004. "The Cult of St Mary at Beodericisworth and then in Bury St Edmunds Abbey to c. 1150." *Journal of Ecclesiastical History* 55 (4): 627–53.

———. 2007. *A History of the Abbey of Bury St Edmunds, 1182–1256*. Woodbridge, UK: Boydell and Brewer.

Greenland, Jonathan James. 1996. "The Iconography of the Hunterian Psalter University of Glasgow, Ms Hunter 229." PhD diss., University of Cambridge.

Grumel, V. 1931. "Le 'Miracle Habituel' de Notre-Dame de Blachernes à Constantinople." *Echos d'Orient* 30:129–46.

Guéranger, Prosper. 2000. *The Liturgical Year: Sp. Ed.* Translated by Laurence Shepherd. 15 vols. Fitzwilliam, NH: Loreto.

Guilmard, Jacques-Marie. 1994. "Une antique fête mariale au 1er Janvier dans la ville de Rome?" *Ecclesia orans* 11:25–67.

Hahn, Cynthia. 1991. "*Peregrinatio et Natio*: The Illustrated Life of Edmund, King and Martyr." *Gesta* 30:119–39.

Hall, Thomas N. 2002. "The Earliest Anglo-Latin Text of the *Trinubium Annae* (*Bhl* 505zl)." In *Via Crucis: Essays on Early Medieval Sources and Ideas in Memory of J. E. Cross*, edited by Thomas N. Hall, 104–37. Morgantown: West Virginia University Press.

Hallinger, Kassius. 1957. "Neue Fragen der reformgeschichtlichen Forschung." *Archiv für mittelrheinische Kirchengeschichte* 9 (1957): 1–32.

Hames, Harvey (Chaim). 2004. "Reason and Faith: Inter-Religious Polemic and Christian Identity in the 13th Century." In *Religious Apologetics: Philosophical Argumentation*, edited by Yossef Shwartz and Volkhard Krech, 267–84. Tübingen: Mohr Siebeck.

———. 2007. "The Limits of Conversion: Ritual Murder and the Virgin Mary in the Account of Adam of Bristol." *Journal of Medieval History* 33:43–59.

Haney, Kristine Edmondson. 1981. "The Immaculate Imagery in the Winchester Psalter." *Gesta* 20:111–18.

———. 1986. *The Winchester Psalter: An Iconographic Study*. Leicester: Leicester University Press.

Harris, Anne. 2008. "The Performative Terms of Jewish Iconoclasm and Conversion in Two Saint Nicholas Windows at Chartres Cathedral." In *Beyond the Yellow Badge: Anti-Judaism and Anti-Semitism in Medieval and Early Modern Visual Culture*, edited by Mitchell B. Merback, 119–41. Leiden: Brill.

Harris, Max. 2011. *Sacred Folly: A New History of the Feast of Fools*. Ithaca, NY: Cornell University Press.

Hawkes, Jane. 1995. "The Wirskworth Slab: An Iconography of Humilitas." *Peritia* 9:246–77.

Hayward, Paul Antony. 1998. "Translation-Narratives in Post-Conquest Hagiography and English Resistance to the Norman Conquest." In *Anglo-Norman Studies*, edited by Christopher Harper-Bill, 67–93. Woodbridge, UK: Boydell and Brewer. Press.

———. 1999. "Demystifying the Role of Sanctity in Western Christianity." In *The Cult of Saints in Late Antiquity and the Middle Ages*, edited by James Howard-Johnston and Paul Hayward, 115–42. Oxford: Oxford University Press.

———. 2004. "Gregory the Great as 'Apostle of the English' in Post-Conquest Canterbury." *Journal of Ecclesiastical History* 55:19–57.

———. 2005. "The Cult of St Albans, *Anglorum Protomartyr*, in Anglo-Saxon and Anglo-Norman England." In *More Than a Memory: The Discourse of Martyrdom and the Construction of Christian Identity in the History of Christianity*, edited by Johan Leemans, 169–99. Leuven: Peeters.

———. 2011. "The Importance of Being Ambiguous: Innuendo and Legerdemain in William of Malmesbury's Gesta Regum and Gesta Pontificum Anglorum." *Anglo-Norman Studies* 33:75–102.

Hehl, Ernst D., and Horst Fuhrmann, eds. 1987. *Die Konzilien Deutschlands und Reichsitaliens, 916–1001*, 2 Tle., Tl.1, 916–961. Hannover: Hahn.

Heisy, Daniel J. 2013. "Mary and Mysticism in Bede's Homilies." *American Benedictine Review* 63 (1): 3–16.

Henry, Avril. 1990. *The Eton Roundels*. Aldershot, UK: Ashgate.

Heslop, T. A. 1978. "The Romanesque Seal of Worcester Cathedral." In *Medieval Art and Architecture at Worcester Cathedral*, edited by Antonia Gransden, 71–79. Leeds: British Archaeological Association.

———. 1980. "English Seals from the Mid-Ninth Century to 1100." *Journal of the British Archaeological Association* 133:1–16.

———. 1981. "The Virgin Mary's Regalia and Twelfth-Century English Seals." In *The Vanishing Past: Studies of Medieval Art, Liturgy, and Metrology Presented to Christopher Hohler*, edited by Alan Borg and Andrew Martindale, 53–62. Oxford: British Archaeological Reports International Series.

———. 1984. "Seals." In *Catalogue English Romanesque Art, 1066–1200, at the Hayward Gallery*, edited by George Zarnecki, 298–319. London: Weidenfeld and Nicholson.

———. 1995. "The Canterbury Calendars and the Norman Conquest." In *Canterbury and the Norman Conquest: Churches, Saints, and Scholars, 1066–1109*, edited by Richard Eales and Richard Sharpe, 53–85. London: Hambledon Press.

———. 2001. "Worcester Cathedral Chapterhouse and the Harmony of the Testaments." In *New Offerings, Ancient Treasures: Studies in Medieval Art for George Henderson*, edited by Paul Binski, 280–98. Stroud, UK: History Press.

———. 2005. "The English Origins of the Coronation of the Virgin." *Burlington Magazine* 147:790–97.

———. 2007. "Manuscript Illumination at Worcester c. 1055–1065: The Origins of the Pembroke Lectionary and the Caligula Troper." In *The Cambridge Illuminations: The Conference Papers*, edited by Stella Panayotova, 65–75. London: Harvery Miller Publishers.

Hiley, David. 1986. "Thurstan of Caen and Plainchant at Glastonbury: Musicological Reflections on the Norman Conquest." *Proceedings of the British Academy* 72:57–90.

———. 1993. "Changes in English Chant Repertories in the Eleventh Century as Reflected in the Winchester Sequences." *Anglo-Norman Studies* 16:137–54.

———. 1994. "Chant Composition at Canterbury after the Norman Conquest for Max Lütolf on His Sixtieth Birthday—in Memory of an Excursion." In *Max Lütolf Zum 60. Geburtstag Festschrift*, edited by Bernhard Hangartner and Urs Fischer, 31–46. Basel: Wiese Verlag.

Hillaby, Joseph. 1995. "The London Jewry: William to John." *Jewish Historical Studies* 33:1–44.

———. 2003. "Jewish Colonisation in the Twelfth Century." In *Jews in Medieval Britain: Historical, Literary, and Archaeological Perspectives*, edited by Patricia Skinner, 15–40. Woodbridge, UK: Boydell and Brewer.

Holopainen, Toivo J. 1996. *Dialectic and Theology in the Eleventh Century*. Leiden: Brill.

———. 2004. "Logic and Theology in the Eleventh Century: Anselm and Lanfranc's Heritage." In *Anselm and Abelard: Investigations and Juxtapositions*, edited by Giles Gasper and Helmut Kohlenberger, 1–16. Toronto: Pontifical Institute of Mediaeval Studies.

———. 2012. "'Lanfranc of Bec' and Berengar of Tours." *Anglo-Norman Studies* 34:105–21.

Horowitz, Elliott. 2006. *Reckless Rites: Purim and the Legacy of Jewish Violence*. Princeton, NJ: Princeton University Press.

Hoyland, Robert G., and Sarah Waidler. 2014. "Adomnán's *De Locis Sanctis* and the Seventh-Century near East." *English Historical Review* 139 (539): 787–807.

Huber, Jane Elizabeth. 2013. "Unfolding Song: The Matins Celebration for the Marian Feast of the Assumption. Early Origins to Medieval Example." PhD diss., Union Theological Seminary.

Hüe, Denis. 1991. "La fête normande." In *Provinces, Régions, Terroirs au Moyen Age de la Réalité à l'imaginaire*, edited by Bernard Guidot, 39–56. Strasbourg: Presses Universitaires de Nancy.

Huglo, Michel. 1993. "Remarks on the Alleluia and Responsory Series in the Winchester Troper." In *Music in the Medieval English Liturgy: Plainsong and Medieval Music Society Centennial Essays*, edited by Susan Rankin and David Hiley, 47–58. Oxford: Clarendon Press.

Huguet, Paul. 1859. *Notice historique sur l'ancien Prieuré Saint-Martin-des-Champs et sur le Conservatoire Impérial des arts et Métiers*. Neuilly, Fr.: Typographie de Giraudet.

Hunter, David G. 2007. *Marriage, Celibacy, and Heresy in Ancient Christianity: The Jovinianist Controversy*. Oxford: Oxford University Press.

Huntington, Joanna. 2003. "Virginity in the Construction of Edward the Confessor as a Saint." In *Medieval Virginities*, edited by Sarah Salih and Ruth Evans, 119–39. Cardiff: University of Wales Press.

Hyamson, Albert M. 1928. *A History of the Jews in England*. London: Methuen and Co.

Ihnat, Kati. 2012. "Getting the Punchline: Deciphering Anti-Jewish Humour in Anglo-Norman England." *Journal of Medieval History* 38 (4): 408–23.

———. 2014. "Early Evidence for the Cult of Anne in Twelfth-Century England." *Traditio* 69:1–44.

———. 2015. "'Our Sister Is Little and Has No Breasts': Mary and the Jews in the Sermons of Honorius Augustodunensis." In *The Jewish-Christian Encounter in Medieval Preaching*, edited by Jonathan Adams and Jussi Hanska, 119–38. New York: Routledge.

———. Forthcoming a. "Between Politics and Ethics: William of Malmesbury's Marian Miracles and the Jews." In *Discovering William of Malmesbury*, edited by Emily Dolmans, Rodney M. Thomson, and Emily Winkler. Woodbridge, UK: Boydell and Brewer.

———. Forthcoming b. "The Earliest Office of Mary in the West: Innovation in the Old Hispanic Liturgy."

———. Forthcoming c. "Liturgy against Apostasy: Marian Commemoration and the Jews in Visigothic Iberia."

Iogna-Prat, Dominique. 1993. "Politische Aspekte der Marienverehrung in Cluny um das Jahr 1000." In *Maria in der Welt: Marienverehrung im Kontext der Sozialgeschichte 10.–18. Jahrhundert*, edited by Claudia Opitz, Hedwig Röckelein, Gabriela Signori, and Guy P. Marchal, 243–51. Zurich: Chronos.

———. 1996. "Le culte de la Vierge sous le règne de Charles le Chauve." In *Marie: Le Culte de la Vierge dans la Société Médiévale*, edited by Dominique Iogna-Prat, Éric Palazzo, and Daniel Russo, 65–98. Paris: Beauchesne.

———. 2002. *Order and Exclusion: Cluny and Christendom Face Heresy, Judaism, and Islam (1100–1150)*. Translated by Graham Robert Edwards. Ithaca, NY: Cornell University Press.

Jackson, Peter, and Michael Lapidge. 1996. "The Contents of the Cotton-Corpus Legendary." In *Holy Men and Holy Women: Old English Prose Saints' Lives and Their Contexts*, edited by Paul E. Szarmach, 131–46. Albany: State University of New York Press.

Jeffery, Peter. 1995. "Rome and Jerusalem: From Oral Tradition to Written Repertory in Two Ancient Liturgical Centers." In *Essays on Medieval Music: In Honor of David G. Hughes*, edited by Graeme Boone, 207–47. Cambridge, MA: Harvard University Press.

Jennings, J. C. 1962. "The Writings of Prior Dominic of Evesham." *English Historical Review* 77:298–304.

Jestice, Phyllis G. 2007. "A Great Jewish Conspiracy? Worsening Jewish-Christian Relations and the Destruction of the Holy Sepulchre." In *Christian Attitudes toward the Jews in the Middle Ages*, edited by Michael Frassetto, 25–42. New York: Routledge.

Jones, Sarah Rees, and Sethina Watson, eds. 2013. *Christians and Jews in Angevin England: The York Massacre of 1190, Narratives and Contexts*. York: York Medieval Press.

Jonsson, Ritva. 2005. "Unica in the Cotton Caligula Troper." In *Music in the Medieval English Liturgy: Plainsong and Medieval Music Society Centennial Essays*, edited by Susan Rankin and David Hiley, 11–45. Oxford: Clarendon Press.

Jordan, William Chester. 1992. "Marian Devotion and the Talmud Trial of 1240." In *Religionsgespräche Im Mittelalter*, edited by Bernard Lewis and Friedrich Niewöhner, 61–76. Wiesbaden: Otto Harrassowitz.

Jugie, Martin. 1901–2. "Saint André de Crête." *Echos d'Orient* 5:378–87.

———. 1923. "La première fête mariale en Orient et en Occident, l'Avent primitif." *Échos d'Orient* 22:129–52.

———. 1944. *La mort et l'Assomption de la Sainte Vierge: Étude historico-doctrinale*. Vol. 114. Vatican City: Biblioteca Apostolica Vaticana.

———. 1952. *L'Immaculée-Conception dans l'écriture sainte et dans la tradition orientale*. Rome: Academia Mariana.

Karras, Ruth Mazo. 1996. *Common Women: Prostitution and Sexuality in Medieval England*. Oxford: Oxford University Press.

Kauffmann, C. M. 2001. "British Library, Lansdowne Ms 383: The Shaftesbury Psalter?" In *New Offerings, Ancient Treasures: Studies in Medieval Art for George Henderson*, edited by Paul Binski and William Noel, 256–79. Thrupp, UK: Sutton Publishing.

———. 2003. *Biblical Imagery in Medieval England, 700–1550*. London: Harvey Miller Publishers.

Ker, N. R. 1969. *Medieval Manuscripts in British Libraries*. Oxford: Clarendon Press.

Kienzle, Beverly Mayne. 1997. "Exegesis on Luke 10:38 around 1100: Worcester Ms F. 94, F. 1r–2r." *Medieval Sermon Studies* 40:22–28.

———. 2000. *The Sermon*. Turnhout, Bel.: Brepols, 2000.

Kishpaugh, Mary Jerome. 1941. "The Feast of the Presentation of the Virgin Mary in the Temple: An Historical and Literary Study." PhD diss., Catholic University of America.

Kjellman, Hilding. 1977. *La deuxième collection anglo-normande des miracles de la Sainte Vierge*. Geneva: Slatkine Reprints.

Klauser, Theodor. 1972. "Rom und der Kult der Gottesmutter Maria." *Jahrbuch für Antike und Christentum* 15:120–35.

Klein, Holger A. 1998. "The So-Called Byzantine Diptych in the Winchester Psalter, British Library, Ms Cotton Nero C. Iv." *Gesta* 37 (1): 26–43.

Kleinschmidt, P. Beda. 1930. *Die heilige Anna: Ihre Verehrung in Geschichte, Kunst und Volkstum*. Düsseldorf: L. Schwann.

Klukas, Arnold William. 1984. "The Architectural Implications of the *Decreta Lanfranci*." In *Anglo-Norman Studies*, edited by R. Allen Brown, 136–71. Woodbridge, UK: Boydell and Brewer.

Knowles, David. 1943. "The Cultural Influence of English Medieval Monasticism." *Cambridge Historical Review* 7 7:146–59.

———. 1966. *The Monastic Order in England*. Cambridge: Cambridge University Press.

Knowles, David, Christopher N. L. Brooke, and Vera C. M. London. 2001. *The Heads of Religious Houses: England and Wales, 940–1216*. 2nd ed. Cambridge: Cambridge University Press.

Knowles, David, and R. Neville Hadcock. 1971. *Medieval Religious Houses: England and Wales*. 2nd ed. London: Longman and Co.

Koopmans, Rachel. 2011. *Wonderful to Relate: Miracle Stories and Miracle Collecting in High Medieval England*. Philadelphia: University of Pennsylvania Press.

Kriss-Rettenbeck, Lenz. 1972. *Ex-voto. Zeichen, Bild und Abbild im Christlichen Votivbrauchtum*. Zurich: Atlantis.

Kurth, Betty. 1945. "The Iconography of the Wirksworth Slab." *Burlington Magazine* 86:114–21.

Labande, Edmond-René. 1984. "Guibert de Nogent, disciple et témoin de Saint Anselm au Bec." In *Les mutations socio-culturelles au tournant des XIe–XIIe siècles*, edited by Raymonde Foreville, 229-236. Paris: Centre national de Recherche Scientifique.

Lagueux, Robert. 2004. "Glossing Christmas: Liturgy, Music, Exegesis, and Drama in High Medieval Laon." PhD diss., Yale University.

———. 2009. "Sermons, Exegesis, and Performance: The Laon *Ordo Prophetarum* and the Meaning of Advent." *Comparative Drama* 43 (2): 197–220.

Lamy, Marielle. 2000. *L'Immaculée-Conception: Étapes et enjeux d'une controverse au moyen-âge (XIIe–XVe siècles)*. Paris: Institut d'Études Augustiniennes.

Langmuir, Gavin. 1990a. *History, Religion, and Anti-Semitism*. Berkeley: University of California Press.

———. 1990b. *Toward a Definition of Anti-Semitism*. Berkeley: University of California Press.

———. 1990c. "Thomas of Monmouth: Detector of Ritual Murder." In *Toward a Definition of Anti-Semitism*, 209–36. Berkeley: University of California Press.

———. 1992. "The Faith of Christians and Hostility to Jews." In *Christianity and Judaism*, edited by Dianna Wood. 77–92. *Studies in Church History* 29. Oxford: Blackwell Publishers.

Lapidge, Michael. 1991. *Anglo-Saxon Litanies of the Saints*. Woodbridge, UK: Boydell and Brewer.

Lawrence, Anne. 1982. "Manuscripts of Early Anglo-Norman Canterbury." In *Medieval Art and Architecture at Canterbury before 1220*, edited by Nicola Coldstream and Peter Draper, 101–11. Leeds: British Archaeological Association.

Lazar, Moshe. 1972. "Servant of Two Masters: The Pre-Faustian Theme of Despair and Revolt." *MLN* 87:31–50.

Leclercq, Henri. 1921. "Anne." *Dictionnaire d'archéologie chrétienne et de liturgie*, edited by Fernand Cabrol and Henri Leclercq 1 (2): cols. 2162–74. Paris: Librarie Letouzey (1921–53).

———. 1932. "Marie (Je Vous Salue)." In *Dictionnarie d'archéologie chrétienne et de liturgie*, edited by Fernand Cabrol and Henri Leclercq, 10(2) cols. 2043–62. Paris: Librairie Letouzey (1921–53).

Leclercq, Jean. 1952. "Dévotion et théologie mariales dans le monachisme bénédictin." In *Maria: Études sur la Sainte Vierge*, edited by D'Hubert Du Manoir, 549–78. Paris: Beauchesne.

———. 1954. "Saint Bernard et la dévotion médiévale envers Marie." *Revue d'ascétique et mystique* 30:361–75.

———. 1960. "Formes anciennes de l'office marial." *Ephemerides liturgicae* 74:89–102.

———. 1961. *The Love of Learning and the Desire for God*. New York: Fordham University Press.

Leftow, Brian. 1995. "Anselm on the Necessity of the Incarnation." *Religious Studies* 31:167–85.

———. 1997. "Anselm on the Cost of Salvation." *Medieval Philosophy and Theology* 6:73–92.

Lenker, Ursula. 2005. "The Ministries of the Canons: Liturgical Rubrics to Vernacular Gospels and their Functions in a European Context." In *The Liturgy of the Late Anglo-Saxon Church*, edited by Helen Gittos and M. Bradford Bedingfield, 185-212. Woodbridge: Boydell and Brewer.

Limor, Ora. 2005. "Mary and the Jews: Three Witness Stories." *Alpayim: A Multidisciplinary Publication for Contemporary Thought and Literature* 28:129–51.

———. 2006. "Mary and the Jews: Story, Controversy, and Testimony." *Historein* 6:55–71.

Limor, Ora, and Guy Stroumsa, eds. 1996. *Contra Iudaeos: Ancient and Medieval Polemics between Christians and Jews*. Tübingen: Mohr Siebeck.

Linder, Amnon. 1987. *The Jews in Roman Imperial Legislation*. Detroit: Wayne State Press.

Lipman, Vivian D. 1984. "Jews and Castles in Medieval England." *Transactions of the Jewish Historical Society of England* 28:1–19.

Lipton, Sara. 1999. *Images of Intolerance: The Representation of Jews and Judaism in the Bible Moralisée*. Berkeley: University of California Press.

———. 2005. "'The Sweet Lean of His Head': Writing about Looking at the Crucifix in the High Middle Ages." *Speculum* 80:1172–208.

———. 2008. "Where Are the Jewish Women? On the Non-Iconography of the Jewess in the Cantigas de Santa Maria." *Jewish History* 22:139–77.

———. 2014. *Dark Mirror: The Medieval Origins of Anti-Jewish Iconography*. New York: Metropolitan Books.

Little, Lester K. 1969. "The Function of the Jews in the Commercial Revolution." In *Poverta e Ricchezza Nella Spiritualita dei secoli XII e XIII*, 271–87. Todi, Ita.

———. 1983. *Religious Poverty and the Profit Economy in Medieval Europe*. Ithaca, NY: Cornell University Press.

———. 1993. *Benedictine Maledictions: Liturgical Cursing in Romanesque France*. Ithaca, NY: Cornell University Press.

MacGregor, Alistair. 2008. "Candlemas: A Festival of Roman Origin." In *Origins of the Cult of the Virgin Mary*, edited by Chris Maunder, 137–53. London: Burns and Oates.

MacLachlan, Elizabeth Parker. 1986. *The Scriptorium of Bury St. Edmunds in the Twelfth Century*. London: Garland Publishing.

Magennis, Hugh. 1996. "St Mary of Egypt and Aelfric: Unlikely Bedfellows in Cotton Julius E. Vii?" In *The Legend of Mary of Egypt in Medieval Insular Hagiography*, edited by Erich Poppe and Bianca Ross, 99–112. Dublin: Four Courts Press.

Maître, Claire. 1996. "Du culte marial à la célébration des vierges: A propos de la psalmodie de matines." In *Marie: Le culte de la Vierge dans la société médiévale*, edited by Dominique Iogna-Prat, Éric Palazzo, and Daniel Russo, 45–64. Paris: Beauchesne.

Mansi, J. D. 1759–98. *Sacrorum Conciliorum Noua et Amplissima Collectio*. Florence: Expensis Antonii Zatta Veneti.

Marcus, Ivan G. 1996. "Images of the Jews in the *Exempla* of Caesarius of Heisterbach." In *From Witness to Witchcraft: Jews and Judaism in Medieval Christian Thought*, edited by Jeremy Cohen, 247–56. Wiesbaden: Harrassowitz.

Marenbon, John. 1988. *Early Medieval Philosophy (450–1150)*. 2nd ed. London: Routledge.

Marino Malone, Carolyn. 2005. "Interprétation des pratiques liturgiques à Saint-Bénigne de Dijon d'après ses coutumiers d'inspiration clunisienne." In *From Dead of Night to End of Day: The Medieval Customs of Cluny*, edited by Susan Boynton and Isabelle Cochelin, 221–50. Turnhout, Bel.: Brepols.

Markus, Robert A. 1995. "The Jew as a Hermeneutic Device: The Inner Life of a Gregorian Topos." In *Gregory the Great: A Symposium*, edited by John C. Cavadini, 1–15. South Bend, IN: Notre Dame University Press.

Martimort, A.-G. 1992. *Les lectures liturgiques et leurs livres.* Typologie des Sources du Moyen Age Occidental. Vol. 64. Turnhout, Bel.: Brepols.

Martínez Díez, Gonzalo, and Félix Rodríguez, eds. 1992. *La Colección Canónica Hispana.* Vol. 5. Madrid: CSIC.

Mason, Emma. 1996. *Westminster Abbey and Its People.* Woodbridge, UK: Boydell and Brewer.

Matter, E. Ann. 1990. *The Voice of My Beloved: The Song of Songs in Western Medieval Christianity.* Philadelphia: University of Pennsylvania Press.

Mayr-Harting, Henry. 2004. "The Idea of the Assumption in the West, 800–1200." In *The Church and Mary,* edited by R. N. Swanson, 86–111. Woodbridge, UK: Boydell and Brewer.

McCord Adams, Marilyn. 2004. "Anselm on Faith and Reason." In *The Cambridge Companion to Anselm,* edited by Brian Leftow and Brian Davies, 32–60. Cambridge: Cambridge University Press.

McCulloch, John M. 1997. "Jewish Ritual Murder: William of Norwich, Thomas of Monmouth, and the Early Dissemination of the Myth." *Speculum* 72:698–740.

McKinnon, James. 2000. *The Advent Project: The Later Seventh-Century Creation of the Roman Mass Proper.* Berkeley: University of California Press.

McNamer, Sarah. 2010. *Affective Meditation and the Invention of Medieval Compassion.* Philadelphia: University of Pennsylvania Press.

Meersseman, G. G. 1960. *Der Hymnos Akathistos im Abendland.* Vol. 2. Freiburg: Universitätsverlag Freiburg Schweiz.

Mesler, Katelyn, and Kati Ihnat. Forthcoming. "From Christian Devotion to Jewish Sorcery: The Curious History of Wax Figurines in the Middle Ages." In *Authority and Knowledge in the Long Thirteenth Century,* edited by Ruth Mazo Karras, Elisheva Baumgarten, and Katelyn Mesler. Philadelphia: University of Pennsylvania Press.

Mews, Constant J., ed. 2001. *Listen, Daughter: The Speculum Virginum and the Formation of Religious Women in the Middle Ages.* New York: Palgrave.

Milburn, R.L.P. 1993. "The Historical Background of the Doctrine of the Assumption." In *Women in Early Christianity,* edited by David M. Scholer, 55–86. New York: Garland Publishing.

Mimouni, Simon C. 1996. "De l'Ascension du Christ à l'Assomption de la Vierge. Les *Transitus Mariae*: Représentations anciennes et médiévales." In *Marie: Le culte de la Vierge dans la société médiévale,* edited by Dominique Iogna-Prat, Éric Palazzo, and Daniel Russo, 471–509. Paris: Beauchesne.

Monroe, Elizabeth. 2007. "'Fair and Friendly, Sweet and Beautiful': Hopes for Conversion in Synagoga's Song of Songs Imagery." In *Beyond the Yellow Badge: Anti-Judaism and Antisemitism in Medieval and Early Modern Visual Culture,* edited by Michael J. Merback, 33–62. Leiden: Brill.

Montclose, Jean de. 1971. *Lanfranc et Bérenger: La controverse eucharistique du XIe siècle.* Leuven: Spicilegium Sacrum Lovaniense.

Moore, R. I. 2007. *The Formation of a Persecuting Society: Authority and Deviance in Western Europe, 950–1250.* 2nd ed. Malden, MA: Wiley.

Morgan, Nigel. 1999. "Texts and Images of Marian Devotion in English Twelfth-Century Monasticism, and Their Influence on the Secular Church." In *Monasteries and Society in Medieval Britain: Proceedings of the 1994 Harlaxton Symposium,* edited by Benjamin Thompson, 117–36. Stamford, UK: Paul Watkins.

———. 2012. *English Monastic Litanies of the Saints after 1100*. Vol. 1. Cambridge, UK: Boydell and Brewer.

———. 2013. *English Monastic Litanies of the Saints after 1100*. Vol. 2. Woodbridge, UK: Boydell and Brewer.

Morton, Vera, and Jocelyn Wogan-Browne. 2003. *Guidance for Women in 12th Century Convents*. Woodbridge, UK: Boydell and Brewer.

Muessig, Carolyn. 2002. "Audience and Preacher: Ad Status Sermons and Social Classification." In *Preacher, Sermon, and Audience in the Middle Ages*, edited by Carolyn Muessig, 255–78. Leiden: Brill.

Mundill, Robin R. 1998. *England's Jewish Solution: Experiment and Expulsion, 1262–1290*. Cambridge: Cambridge University Press.

———. 2010. *The King's Jews: Money, Massacre, and Exodus in Medieval England*. London: Continuum.

Mussafia, Adolfo. 1887–91. *Studien zu den Mittelalterlichen Marienlegenden*. 4 vols. Vienna: Oesterreichische Akademie der Wissenschaften.

Nelson, Benjamin N., and Joshua Starr. 1939–44. "The Divine Surety and the Jewish Moneylender." *Annuaire de l'Institut de Philologie et d'Histoire Orientales et Slaves* 7:289–338.

Newman, Barbara. 1995. "Flaws in the Golden Bowl: Gender and Spiritual Formation in the Twelfth Century." In *From Virile Woman to Womanchrist: Studies in Medieval Religion and Literature*, edited by Barbara Newman, 19–45. Philadelphia: University of Pennsylvania Press.

Niblaeus, Erik. 2010. "German Influence on Religious Practice in Scandinavia, c. 1050–1150." PhD diss., University of London.

Nirenberg, David. 1996. *Communities of Violence: Persecution of Minorities in the Middle Ages*. Princeton, NJ: Princeton University Press.

———. 2013. *Anti-Judaism: The Western Tradition*. New York: W. W. Norton.

Nixon, Virginia. 2004. *Mary's Mother: Saint Anne in Late Medieval Europe*. University Park: Pennsylvania University Press.

Norris, Richard A., ed. 2003. *The Song of Songs Interpreted by Early Christian and Medieval Commentators*. Grand Rapids, MI: William B. Eerdmans Publishing.

Novikoff, Alex. 2011. "Anselm, Dialogue, and the Rise of Scholastic Disputation." *Speculum* 86:387–418.

———. 2013. *The Medieval Culture of Disputation: Pedagogy, Practice, and Performance*. Philadelphia: University of Pennsylvania Press.

Ortenberg, Veronica. 1992. *The English Church and the Continent in the Tenth and Eleventh Centuries: Cultural, Spiritual, and Artistic Exchanges*. Oxford: Clarendon Press.

Pächt, Otto, Charles Reginald Dodwell, and Francis Wormald. 1960. *The St Albans Psalter*. London: Warburg Institute.

Palazzo, Éric. 1990. "Le rôle de *Libelli* dans la pratique liturgique du haut moyen âge: Histoire et typologie." *Revue Mabillon, Nouvelle Série* 1:9–36.

———. 1996. "Marie et l'élaboration d'un espace ecclésial au haut moyen âge." In *Marie: Le culte de la Vierge dans la société médiévale*, edited by Dominique Iogna-Prat, Éric Palazzo, and Daniel Russo, 313–25. Paris: Beauchesne.

———. 1998. "Foi et croyance au moyen âge: Les mèdiations liturgiques." *Annales* 53 (6): 1131–54.

Palazzo, Éric, and Ann-Katrin Andrews Johansson. 1996. "Jalons liturgiques pour une histoire du culte de la Vierge dans l'occident latin (Ve–XIe siècle)." In *Marie: Le culte de la Vierge dans la société médiévale*, edited by Dominique Iogna-Prat, Éric Palazzo, and Daniel Russo, 15–43. Paris: Beauchesne.

Parish, Helen. 2010. *Clerical Celibacy in the West: c. 1100–1700*. Aldershot, UK: Ashgate.

Parkes, Henry. 2014. "St Edmund between Liturgy and Hagiography." In *Bury St Edmunds and the Norman Conquest*, edited by Tom Licence, 131–59. Woodbridge, UK: Boydell and Brewer.

Patton, Pamela A. 2014. "The Little Jewish Boy: Afterlife of a Byzantine Legend in Thirteenth-Century Spain." In *Byzantine Images and Their Afterlives*, edited by Lynn Jones, 61–80. Farnham, UK: Ashgate.

Paz, Tovar. 1994. *"Tractatus, Sermones atque Homiliae": El cultivo del género literario del discurso homilético en la Hispania tardoantigua y visigoda*. Cáceres, Sp.: Universidad de Extremadura.

Pelikan, Jaroslav. 1996. *Mary through the Centuries*. New Haven, CT: Yale University Press.

Pentcheva, Bissera. 2011. "The Miraculous Icon: Medium, Fantasy, and Presence." In *The Cult of the Mother of God in Byzantium*, edited by Leslie Brubaker and Mary B. Cunningham, 263–77. Aldershot, UK: Ashgate.

Pfaff, Richard W. 1980. "The *Abbreviatio Amalarii* of William of Malmesbury." *Recherches de théologie ancienne et médiévale* 47:77–113.

———. 1992a. "The Calendar." In *The Eadwine Psalter: Text, Image, and Monastic Culture in Twelfth-Century Canterbury*, edited by Margaret Gibson, T. A. Heslop, and Richard W. Pfaff, 62–87. London: Modern Humanities Research Association.

———. 1992b. "Lanfranc's Supposed Purge of the Anglo-Saxon Calendar." In *Warriors and Churchmen in the High Middle Ages: Essays Presented to Karl Leyser*, edited by Timothy Reuter, 95–108. London: Hambledon Press.

———. 2009. *The Liturgy in Medieval England: A History*. Cambridge: Cambridge University Press.

Pfisterer, Andreas. 2002. *Cantilena Romana: Untersuchungen zur Überlieferung des Gregorianischen Chorals*. Paderborn, Ger.: Ferdinand Schöningh.

Philippart, Guy. 1996. "Le récit miraculaire marial dans l'occident médiéval." In *Marie: Le culte de la Vierge dans la société médiévale*, edited by Dominique Iogna-Prat, Éric Palazzo, and Daniel Russo, 563–90. Paris: Beauchesne.

Pigeon, E. A. 1876. *Histoire de la cathédrale de Coutances*. Coutances, Fr.: Impremerie de E. Salettes fils.

Plenzat, Karl. 1926. *Die Theophiluslegende in den Dichtungen des Mittelalters*. Berlin: E. Ebering.

Poleg, Eyal. 2011. "'A Ladder Set up on Earth': The Bible in Medieval Sermons." In *The Practice of the Bible in the Middle Ages*, edited by Susan Boynton and Diane J. Reilly, 205–27. New York: Columbia University Press.

———. 2013. *Approaching the Bible in Medieval England*. Manchester: Manchester University Press.

Pollins, Harold. 1982. *Economic History of the Jews in England*. Madison, NJ: Fairleigh Dickinson University Press.

Poncelet, Albert. 1904. "Catalogus codicum hagiographicum latinorum bibliothecae publicae Rotomagensis." *Analecta Bollandiana* 23:129–75.

———. 1902. "Index Miraculorum B.V. Mariae Quae Saec. VI–XV Latine Conscripta Sunt." *Analecta Bollandiana* 21:242–360.

Power, Kim E. 2001. "From Ecclesiology to Mariology: Patristic Traces and Innovation in the *Speculum Virginum*." In *Listen, Daughter: The Speculum Virginum and the Formation of Religious Women in the Middle Ages*, edited by Constant J. Mews, 85–110. New York: Palgrave.

Quadrio, Giuseppe. 1951. *Il Trattato "De Assumptione Beatae Mariae Virginis" dello Pseudo-Agostino e il suo Influsso Nella Teologia Assunzionistica Latina*. Analecta Gregoriana 52. Rome: Apud Aedes Universitatis Gregorianae.

Reames, Sherry. 2004. "Origins and Affiliations of the Pre-Sarum Office for Anne in the Stowe Breviary." In *Music and Medieval Manuscripts: Palaeography and Performance*, edited by John Haines and Randall Rosenfeld, 349–68. Aldershot, UK: Ashgate.

Reilly, Diane J. 2001. "Picturing the Monastic Drama: Romanesque Illustrations of the Song of Songs." *Word and Image* 17:389–400.

———. 2011. "Lectern Bibles and Liturgical Reform in the Central Middle Ages." In *The Practice of the Bible in the Middle Ages*, edited by Susan Boynton and Diane J. Reilly, 105–25. New York: Columbia University Press.

———. 2012. "Cistercian Art." In *The Cambridge Companion to the Cistercian Order*, edited by Mette Birkedal Bruun, 125–39. Cambridge: Cambridge University Press.

———. Forthcoming. *The Cistercian Reform and the Art of the Book in Twelfth-Century France*.

Remensnyder, Amy. 1999. "Review of *Maria zwischen Kathedrale, Kloster und Welt: Hagiographische und historiographische Annaeherungen an eine hochmittelalterliche Wunderpredigt*." *Speculum* 74: 1123–25.

———. 2014. *La Conquistadora: The Virgin Mary at War and Peace in the Old and New Worlds*. Oxford: Oxford University Press.

Renna, Thomas. 2007. "The Jews in the Golden Legend." In *Christian Attitudes Towards Jews in the Middle Ages: A Casebook*, edited by Michael Frassetto, 137–50. New York: Routledge.

Resnick, Irven M. 1996. "Anselm of Canterbury and Odo of Tournai on the Miraculous Birth of the God-Man." *Mediaeval Studies* 58:67–86.

Reynolds, Brian K. 2012. *Gateway to Heaven: Marian Doctrine and Devotion, Image and Typology in the Patristic and Medieval Periods*. 2 vols. New York: New City Press.

Ridyard, Susan. 1987. "*Condigna Veneratio*: Post-Conquest Attitudes to the Saints of the Anglo-Saxons." *Anglo-Norman Studies* 9:179–206.

Riley-Smith, Jonathan. 2003. *The First Crusade and the Idea of Crusading*. London: Continuum.

Robinson, J. Armitage. 1911. *Gilbert Crispin, Abbot of Westminster: A Study of the Abbey under Norman Rule*. Cambridge: Cambridge University Press.

Roper, Sally Elizabeth. 1993. *Medieval English Benedictine Liturgy: Studies in the Formation, Structure, and Content of the Monastic Votive Office, c. 950–1540*. New York: Garland Publishing, Inc.

Roschini, Gabriele. 1953. *Il Dottore Mariano: Studio sulla dottrina Mariana di S. Bernardo di Chiaravalle*. Rome: Edizione Cattoliche.

Rosenwein, Barbara. 1971. "Feudal War and Monastic Peace: Cluniac Liturgy as Ritual Aggression." *Viator* 2:129–57.

Roth, Cecil. 1951. *The Jews of Medieval Oxford*. Oxford: Clarendon Press.

Rubenstein, Jay. 1999. "Liturgy against History: The Competing Visions of Lanfranc and Eadmer." *Speculum* 74:271–301.

———. 2002. *Guibert of Nogent: Portrait of a Medieval Mind*. New York: Routledge.

Rubin, Miri. 1991. *Corpus Christi: The Eucharist in Late Medieval Culture*. Cambridge: Cambridge University Press.

———. 1992. "Desecration of the Host: The Birth of an Accusation." In *Christianity and Judaism*, edited by Diana Wood, 169-85. *Studies in Church History* 29. Oxford: Blackwell Publishers.

———. 2004. *Gentile Tales: The Narrative Assault on Late Medieval Jews*. Philadelphia: University of Pennsylvania Press.

———. 2009a. *Emotion and Devotion: The Meaning of Mary in Medieval Religious Cultures*. Budapest: Central European University Press.

———. 2009b. "Gestures of Pain, Implications of Guilt: Mary and the Jews." Supplement, *Past and Present* 4:80–95.

———. 2009c. *Mother of God: A History of the Virgin Mary*. London: Allen Books.

Rucquoi, A. 1997. "Ildéfonse de Tolède et son traité sur la virginité de Marie." *Etudes Mariales* 57:105–25.

Rutledge, Elisabeth. 2012. "The Medieval Jews of Norwich and Their Legacy." In *Art, Faith, and Place in East Anglia*, edited by T. A. Heslop, Elizabeth Mellings, and Margit Thøfner, 117-29. Woodbridge, UK: Boydell and Brewer.

Sansterre, Jean-Marie. 1999. "L'image blessée, l'image souffrante: Quelques récits de miracles entre Orient et Occident (VIe–XIIe siècle)." In *Les images dans les sociétés médiévales: pour une histoire comparée*, edited by Jean-Marie Sansterre and Jean-Claude Schmitt, 113–30. Brussels: Bulletin de l'Institut historique belge de Rome.

———. 2006. "*Omnes qui coram hac imagine genua flexerint*: La vénération de saints et de la Vierge d'après les textes écrits en Angleterre du milieu du XIe siècle aux premières décennies du XIIIe siècle." *Cahiers de civilisation médiévale* 49:257–94.

———. 2011a. "Percevoir ou imaginer un espace urbain et suburbain extraordinaire aux XIe–XIIe siècles: Constantinople d'après quelques textes occidentaux." *Revue Belge de Philologie et d'Histoire / Belgisch Tijdschrift voor Filologie en Geschiedenis* 89:701–9.

———. 2011b. "Sacralité et pouvoir thaumaturgique des statues mariales (Xe siècle–première moitié du XIIIe siècle)." *Revue Mabillon, Nouvelle Série* 22:53–77.

———. 2013. "La imagen activada por su prototipo celestial: Milagros occidentales anteriores a mediados del siglo XIII." *Codex Aquilarensis* 29:77–98.

———. 2015. "Vivantes ou comme vivantes: L'animation miraculeuse d'images de la Vierge entre moyen âge et époque Moderne." In *Les images miraculeuses au premier âge moderne, entre dévotion locale et culte universel*, edited by Ralph Dekoninck and Silvia Mostaccio. Special edition of *Revue de l'histoire des religions* 232:155–82.

Schäffer, Peter. 2007. *Jesus in the Talmud*. Princeton, NJ: Princeton University Press.

———. 2011. *Toledot Yeshu ("The Life Story of Jesus") Revisited*. Edited by Michael Meerson and Yaacov Deutsch. Tübingen: Mohr Siebeck.

Schatzmiller, Joseph. 1985. "Politics and the Myth of Origins." In *Les Juifs au regard de l'histoire. Mélanges en l'honneur de Bernhard Blumenkranz*, edited by Gilbert Dahan, 49–61. Paris: Picard.

Scheck, Helen. 2008. *Reform and Resistance: Formations of Female Subjectivity in Early Medieval Ecclesiastical Culture*. Albany: State University of New York Press.

Scheil, Andrew P. 2004. *The Footsteps of Israel: Understanding Jews in Anglo-Saxon England*. Ann Arbor: University of Michigan Press.

Schmitt, Jean-Claude. 2006. "L'exception corporelle: À propos de l'Assomption de Marie." In *The Mind's Eye: Art and Theological Argument in the Middle Ages*, edited by Jeffrey F. Hamburger and Anne-Marie Bouché, 151–85. Princeton, NJ: Princeton University Press.

Schreckenberg, Heinz. 1988. *Die Christlichen Adversus-Judaeos-Texte (11.–13. Jh.): Mit einer Ikonographie des Judenthemas bis zum 4. Laterankonzil*. Frankfurt am Main: P. Lang.

Scott, John, ed. 1981. *The Early History of Glastonbury: An Edition, Translation, and Study of William of Malmesbury's De Antiquitate Glastonie Ecclesie*. Woodbridge, UK: Boydell and Brewer.

Sepet, Marius. 1867–68. "Les prophètes du Christ." *Bibliothèque de l'École de Chartes, Revue d'Érudition* 3–4.

Shachar, Uri. 2015. "Inspecting the pious body: Christological morphology and the ritual-crucifixion allegation," *Journal of Medieval History* 41:21-40.

Sharpe, Richard, James P. Carley, and Rodney M. Thomson. 1996. *English Benedictine Libraries: The Shorter Catalogues*. Vol. 4. London: British Library.

Shaw, Philip. 2006. "The Dating of William of Malmesbury's *Miracles of the Virgin*." *Leeds Studies in English* 37:391–405.

Shea, Jennifer. 2004. "The Influence of the Cult of the Virgin Mary on Christian Perceptions of Jews, with Particular Reference to the Role of Marian Miracle Stories in England and France, c. 1050–c. 1300." PhD diss., University of Cambridge.

———. 2007. "Adgar's Gracial and Christian Images of Jews in Twelfth-Century Vernacular Literature." *Journal of Medieval History* 33:181–96.

Sheingorn, Pamela. 2003. "The Wise Mother Image of St Anne Teaching the Virgin Mary." In *Gendering the Master Narrative*, edited by Mary Erler, 105–34. Ithaca, NY: Cornell University Press.

Sheingorn, Pamela, and Kathleen Ashley. 1990. Introduction to *Interpreting Cultural Symbols: Saint Anne in Late Medieval Society*, edited by Pamela Sheingorn and Kathleen Ashley, 1–43. Athens: University of Georgia Press.

Shepard, Dorothy M. 2007. *Introducing the Lambeth Bible: A Study of Texts and Imagery*. Turnhout, Bel.: Brepols.

Shepardson, Christine. 2008. *Anti-Judaism and Christian Orthodoxy: Ephrem's Hymns in Fourth-Century Syria*. Washington, DC: Catholic University of America Press.

Shoemaker, Stephen J. 1999. "'Let Us Go and Burn Her Body' The Image of the Jews in the Early Dormition Traditions." *Church History* 68:775–823.

———. 2002. *Ancient Traditions of the Virgin Mary's Dormition and Assumption*. Oxford: Oxford University Press.

———. 2008a. "Marian Liturgies and Devotion in Early Christianity." In *Mary: The Complete Resource*, edited by Sarah Jane Boss, 130–45. Oxford: Oxford University Press.

———. 2008b. "The Cult of the Virgin in the Fourth Century: A Fresh Look at Some Old and New Sources." In *The Origins of the Cult of the Virgin Mary*, edited by Chris Maunder, 71–87. London: Burns and Oates.

Shuve, Karl. Forthcoming. *The Song of Songs and the Fashioning of Identity in Early Latin Christianity.* Oxford: Oxford University Press.

Sigal, Pierre-André. 1977. "Histoire et hagiographie: Les miracula aux XIe et XIIe siècles." *Actes des congrès de la société des historiens médiévistes de l'enseignement supérieur public* 8:237–57.

———. 1983. "L'ex-voto au moyen âge dans les régions du Nord-Ouest de la Méditerranée (XIIe–XVe siècles)." *Provence historique* 33:13–31.

———. 1985. *L'homme et le miracle dans la France médiévale (XIe–XIIe siècle).* Paris: Cerf-Histoire.

Signer, Michael, and John H. Van Engen, eds. 2001. *Jews and Christians in Twelfth-Century Europe.* Notre Dame, IN: University of Notre Dame Press.

Signori, Gabriela. 1995. *Maria zwischen Kathedrale, Kloster und Welt. Hagiographische und historiographische Annahrungen an eine hochmittelalterliche Wunderpredigt.* Sigmaringen, Ger. Jan Thorbeke.

———. 1996. "La bienheureuse polysémie, miracles et pèlerinages à la Vierge: Pouvoir thaumaturgique et modèles pastoraux (Xe–XIIe siècles)." In *Marie: Le culte de la Vierge dans la société médiévale*, edited by Dominique Iogna-Prat, Éric Palazzo, and Daniel Russo, 591–617. Paris: Beauchesne.

Skubiszewski, Piotr. 1988. "Une vision monastique de l'église au XIIe siècle." *Cahiers de Civilisation Médiévale* 31:361–76.

Slocum, Kay. 2012. "Goscelin of Saint-Bertin and the Translation Ceremony for Saints Ethelburg, Hildelith and Wulfhild." In *Barking Abbey and Medieval Literary Culture: Authorship and Authority in a Female Community*, edited by Donna Alfano Bussell and Jennifer Brown. Rochester, NY: York Medieval Press, 73–93.

Smid, Harm Reinder. 1965. *Protevangelium Jacobi: A Commentary.* Assen, Nld.: Van Gorcum and Co.

Snijders, Tjamke. 2010. "Celebrating with Dignity: The Purpose of Benedictine Matins Readings." In *Understanding Monastic Practices of Oral Communication, Tenth to Thirteenth Centuries*, edited by Steven Vanderputten, 115–36. Turnhout, Bel.: Brepols.

Sønnesyn, Sigbjørn Olsen. 2012. *William of Malmesbury and the Ethics of History.* Woodbridge, UK: Boydell and Brewer.

Southern, Richard W. 1954. "St. Anselm and Gilbert Crispin, Abbot of Westminster." *Medieval and Renaissance Studies* 3:78–115.

———. 1958. "The English Origins of the 'Miracles of the Virgin.'" *Medieval and Renaissance Studies* 4:176–216.

———. 1966. *Saint Anselm and His Biographer: A Study of Monastic Life and Thought.* Cambridge: Cambridge University Press.

———. 1970. "The Place of England in the Twelfth-Century Renaissance." In *Medieval Humanism and Other Studies*, edited by Richard W. Southern, 158–80. Oxford: Basil Blackwell.

———. 1990. *Saint Anselm: A Portrait in a Landscape.* Cambridge: Cambridge University Press.

Southern, Richard W., and F. S. Schmitt. 1969. *Memorials of St Anselm*. Oxford: Oxford University Press.

Stacey, Robert. 1988. "1240–60: A Watershed in Anglo-Jewish Relations?" *Historical Research* 61:135–50.

———. 1992. "The Conversion of Jews to Christianity in Thirteenth-Century England." *Speculum* 67:263–83.

———. 1995. "Jewish Lending and the Medieval English Economy." In *A Commercialising Economy: England 1086 to c. 1300*, edited by Richard H. Britnell and Bruce M. S. Campbell, 78–101. Manchester: Manchester University Press.

———. 1998. "From Ritual Crucifixion to Host Desecration: Jews and the Body of Christ." *Jewish History* 12:11–28.

———. 2013. "King Henry III and the Jews." In *Jews in Medieval Christendom: Slay Them Not*, edited by Kristine T. Utterback and Merrall L. Price, 117–27. Koninklijke, NL: Brill.

Staunton, Michael. 2004. "Exile in the Lives of Anselm and Thomas Becket." In *Exile in the Middle Ages: Selected Proceedings from the International Medieval Congress, University of Leeds, 8–11 July 2002*, edited by Laura Napran and Elisabeth Van Houts, 159–80. Turnhout, Bel.: Brepols.

Steiner, Ruth. 1993. "Marian Antiphons at Cluny and Lewes." In *Music in the Medieval English Liturgy*, edited by Susan Rankin and David Hiley, 175–204. Oxford: Clarendon Press.

Stenton, Frank. 1943. *Anglo-Saxon England*. Oxford: Oxford University Press.

Stirnemann, Patricia. 2013. *Une Renaissance: L'art entre Flandres et Champagne*. Paris: Musée de Cluny.

Stock, Brian. 1983. *The Implications of Literacy: Written Language and Models of Interpretation*, Princeton NJ: Princeton University Press.

Stone, Carole. 1999. "Anti-Semitism in the Miracle Tales of the Virgin." *Medieval Encounters* 5:364–74.

Stow, Kenneth. 2006. *Jewish Dogs: An Image and Its Interpreters, Continuity in the Catholic-Jewish Encounter*. Stanford CA: Stanford University Press.

Susser, Bernard. 1993. *The Jews of South-West England: The Rise and Decline of Their Medieval and Modern Communities*. Exeter: University of Exeter Press.

Symes, Carol. 2016. "Liturgical Texts and Performance Practices." In *Understanding Medieval Liturgy: Essays in Interpretation*, edited by Helen Gittos and Sarah Hamilton, 239–67. Farnham: Ashgate.

Symons, Thomas, ed. 1953. *Regularis Concordia: The Monastic Agreement*. London: Thomas Nelson and Sons.

Teviotdale, Elizabeth C. 1992. "Some Thoughts on the Place of Origin of the Cotton Troper." In *Cantus Planus*, edited by David Hiley, 407–12. Pécs: Hungarian Academy of Sciences.

Texier, Pascal. 1998. "Orient, Occident: Les avatars du pacte diabolique du clerc Théophile." In *Anthropologies Juridiques. Mélanges Pierre Braun*, edited by Jacqueline Hoareau-Dodinau and Pascal Texier, 777–98. Limoges, Fr.: University of Limoges.

Thomas, Hugh. 2005. *The English and the Normans: Ethnic Hostility, Assimilation, and Identity, 1066–1220*. Oxford: Oxford University Press.

Thompson, Sally. 1991. *Women Religious: The Founding of English Nunneries after the Norman Conquest*. Oxford: Clarendon Press.

Thomson, Rodney M. 1971. "Early Romanesque Book Illustration in England; the Dates of the Pierpont Morgan 'Vitae Sancti Edmundi' and the Bury Bible." *Viator* 2:211–25.

———. 1972. "The Library of Bury St Edmunds in the Eleventh and Twelfth Centuries." *Speculum* 47:617–45.

———. 1982. *Manuscripts from St Albans Abbey, 1066–1235*. Vol. 1. Woodbridge, UK: Boydell and Brewer.

———. 1983. "England and the Twelfth-Century Renaissance." *Past and Present* 101:3–21.

———. 2003a. "Satire, Irony, and Humour in William of Malmesbury." In *Rhetoric and Renewal in the Latin West, 1100–1540: Essays in Honour of John O Ward*, edited by Constant J. Mews, Cary J. Nederman, and Rodney M. Thomson, 115–27. Turnhout, Bel.: Brepols.

———. 2003b. *William of Malmesbury*. 2nd ed. Woodbridge, UK: Boydell and Brewer.

———. 2010. "The Bury Bible: Further Thoughts." In *Tributes to Nigel Morgan: Contexts of Medieval Art, Images, Objects, and Ideas*, edited by Julian M. Luxford and M. A. Michael, 175–84. London: Harvey Miller Publishers.

———. 2015. "William of Malmesbury's Diatribe against the Normans." In *The Long Twelfth-Century View of the Anglo-Saxon Past*, edited by David Woodman and Martin Brett, 113–21. Farnham, UK: Ashgate.

Thomson, Rodney M., and Michael Gullick. 2001. *A Descriptive Catalogue of the Medieval Manuscripts in Worcester Cathedral Library*. Woodbridge, UK: Boydell and Brewer.

Thorpe, Benjamin. 1843–44. *The Homilies of the Anglo-Saxon Church: The First Part, Containing the Sermones Catholici, or Homilies of Aelfri*. 2 vols. London: Aelfric Society.

Thurston, Herbert. 1904. "The Legend of Abbot Elsi." *Month*, 2–15.

Tinti, Francesca. 2015. "Benedictine Reform and Pastoral Care in Late Anglo-Saxon England." *Early Medieval Europe* 23: 229–51.

Tolan, John. 1993. *Petrus Alfonsi and His Medieval Readers*. Gainesville: University Press of Florida.

———. 1996. "La epístola a los peripatéticos de Francia." In *Estudios Sobre Pedro Alfonso de Huesca*, edited by Ma. Jesús Lacarra, 381–402. Huesca, Sp.: Instituto de Estudios Altoaragoneses.

———. 2015. "The First Imposition of a Badge on European Jews: The English Royal Mandate of 1218." In *The Character of Christian-Muslim Encounter: Essays in Honour of David Thomas*, edited by Douglas Pratt, Jon Hoover, John Davies, and John Chesworth, 145–66. Leiden: Brill.

Toubert, Hélène. 1996. "La Vierge et les sages-Femmes: Un jeu iconographique entre les évangiles apocryphes et le drame liturgique." In *Marie: Le culte de la Vierge dans la société médiévale*, edited by Dominique Iogna-Prat, Éric Palazzo, and Daniel Russo, 327–60. Paris: Beauchesne.

Townsend, David. 1993. "Anglo-Latin Hagiography and the Norman Transition." *Exemplaria* 3:385–434.

Trachtenberg, Joshua. 1943. *The Devil and the Jews: The Medieval Conception of the Jew and Its Relation to Modern Antisemitism.* New Haven, CT: Yale University Press.

Uhlig Crown, Carol. 1975. "The Winchester Psalter: Iconographic Sources and Themes of the Virgin Mary, Kingship, and Law." PhD diss., Washington University.

Utterback, Kristine T., and Merral Llewelyn Price, eds. 2013. *Jews in Medieval Christendom: "Slay Them Not."* Leiden: Brill.

Utz, Richard. 2005. "Remembering Ritual Murder: The Anti-Semitic Blood Accusation Narrative in Medieval and Contemporary Cultural Memory." In *Genre and Ritual: The Cultural Heritage of Medieval Rituals*, edited by Eyólf Østrem, Mette Birkedal Bruum, Nils Holger Petersen, and Jens Fleischer, 145–62. Copenhagen: Museum Tusculanum Press.

Vacandard, E. 1897. "Les origines de la fête de la Conception dans le diocèse de Rouen et en Angleterre." *Revue de questions historiques* 61:169–72.

van Dijk, Stephanus Josef Petrus. 1954. "The Origins of the Latin Feast of the Conception of the Blessed Virgin Mary." *Dublin Review* 228:251–67, 428–42.

Vanderputten, Steven. 2012. "Abbatial Obedience, Liturgical Reform, and the Threat of Monastic Autonomy at the Turn of the Twelfth Century." *Catholic Historical Review* 98:241–70.

Van Engen, John H. 1983. *Rupert of Deutz.* Berkeley: University of California Press.

Vanderputten, Steven. 2013. *Monastic Reform as Process: Realities and Representations in Medieval Flanders, 900–1100.* Ithaca, NY: Cornell University Press.

Vaughn, Sally N. 1981a. *The Abbey of Bec and the Anglo-Norman State.* Woodbridge, UK: Boydell and Brewer.

———, ed. 1981b. *Vita Lanfranci.* Woodbridge, UK: Boydell and Brewer.

———. 1993. "Lanfranc, Anselm, and the School of Bec: In Search of the Students of Bec." In *The Culture of Christendom: Essays in Medieval History in Commemoration of Denis L. T. Bethell*, edited by Marc Anthony Meyer, 155–82. London: Hambledon Press.

———. 1994. "Anselm in Italy, 1097–1100." *Anglo-Norman Studies* 16:245–70.

———. 2012. *Archbishop Anselm, 1093–1109: Bec Missionary, Canterbury Primate, Patriarch of Another World.* Farnham, UK: Ashgate.

Verdier, Philippe. 1980. *Le Couronnement de la Vierge: Les origines et les premiers développements d'un thème iconographique.* Montreal: Institut d'études médiévales Albert-le-Grand.

Vincent, Nicholas. 1994–96. "Two Papal Letters on the Wearing of the Jewish Badge, 1221 and 1239." *Jewish Historical Studies* 34:209–24.

———. 2004. "King Henry III and the Blessed Virgin Mary." In *The Church and Mary*, edited by R. N. Swanson. 126–46. *Studies in Church History* 39. Woodbridge, UK: Boydell and Brewer.

Visser, Sandra, and Thomas Williams. 2009. *Anselm.* Oxford: Oxford University Press.

Waddell, Chrysogonus. 1991. "The Reform of the Liturgy from a Renaissance Perspective." In *Renaissance and Renewal in the Twelfth Century*, edited by Robert L. Benson, Giles Constable, and Carol D. Lanham, 88–109. 2nd ed. Cambridge, MA: Harvard University Press.

———. 1999. "La Vierge Marie dans la liturgie cistercienne au XIIe siècle." In *La Vierge dans la tradition cistercienne*, edited by Jean Longère, 123–36. Paris: Médiaspaul.

Waldman, Thomas. Forthcoming. "Hugues 'd'Amiens' et la Vierge Marie." In *Autour de Lanfranc: Réformes et Réformateurs dans l'Europe de l'Ouest (XIe–XIIe siècle)*, edited by Julia Barrow, Fabrice Delivre, and Véronique Gazeau. Caen, Fr.: Presses universitaires de Caen.

Walker Bynum, Caroline. 1987. *Holy Feast and Holy Fast: The Religious Significance of Food to Medieval Women*. Berkeley: University of California Press.

———. 2011. *Christian Materiality: An Essay on Religion in Late Medieval Europe*. New York: Zone Books.

Ward, Benedicta. 1982. *Miracles and the Medieval Mind*. Philadelphia: University of Pennsylvania Press.

Ward, H.L.D. 1883. *Catalogue of Romances in the Department of Manuscripts of the British Museum*. London: British Museum.

Warner, Marina. 1976. *Alone of All Her Sex: The Myth and the Cult of the Virgin Mary*. London: Vintage Books.

Webber, Teresa. 1997. "The Patristic Content of English Book Collections in the Eleventh Century: Towards a Continental Perspective." In *Of the Making of Books: Medieval Manuscripts, Their Scribes and Readers; Essays Presented to M. B. Parkes*, edited by Pamela Robinson, Rivkah Zim, and M. B. Parkes, 191–205. Aldershot: Scolar Press.

———. 1998. "The Provision of Books for Bury St Edmunds Abbey in the Eleventh and Twelfth Centuries." In *Bury St Edmunds: Medieval Art, Architecture, Archaeology, and Economy*, edited by Antonia Gransden, 186–93. Leeds: British Archaeological Association.

———. 2010. "Reading in the Refectory: Monastic Practice in England, c. 1000–c. 1300." In *London University Annual John Coffin Memorial Palaeography Lecture*, 1–49. Unpublished.

———. 2013. "Monastic Space and the Use of Books in the Anglo-Norman Period." In *Anglo-Norman Studies*, edited by David Bates, 221–40. Woodbridge, UK: Boydell and Brewer.

———. 2014a. "Books and Their Use across the Conquest." In *Bury St Edmunds and the Norman Conquest*, edited by Tom Licence, 160–89. Woodbridge, UK: Boydell and Brewer.

———. 2014b. "Talking Books: Reading Aloud in the Middle Ages." In *Reuter Lecture at the University of Southhampton*, May 27.

———. 2015. "Bede's *Historia Ecclesiastica* as a Source of Lections in Pre- and Post-Conquest England." In *The Long Twelfth-Century View of the Anglo-Saxon Past*, edited by Martin Brett and David Woodman, 47–76. Aldershot, UK: Ashgate.

Weber, Annette. 2002. "The Hanged Judas of Freiburg Cathedral: Sources and Interpretations." In *Imagining the Self, Imagining the Other: Visual Representation and Jewish-Christian Dynamics in the Middle Ages and Early Modern Period*, edited by Eva Frojmovic, 165–88. Leiden: Brill.

Wei, Ian. 2012. *Intellectual Culture in Medieval Paris*. Cambridge: Cambridge University Press.

Whitelock, Dorothy, Martin Brett, and Christopher N. L. Brooke, eds. 1981. *Councils and Synods with Other Documents Relating to the English Church, 871–1204*. Oxford: Clarendon Press.

Williams, A. Lukyn. 1935. *Adversus Judaeos: A Bird's-Eye View of Christian Apologiae until the Renaissance*. Cambridge: Cambridge University Press.

Wilmart, André. 1924. "La tradition des prières de Saint Anselme." *Revue Bénédictine* 36:52–71.

———. 1925–26. "Les compositions d'Osbert de Clare en l'honneur de Saint Anne." *Annales de Bretagne* 27:1–33.

———. 1928. "Sur les fêtes de la Conception et de Sainte Anne: Chants en l'honneur de Sainte Anne dans un manuscrit français du XIe siècle." *Ephemerides liturgicae* 42:258–68.

———. 1930. "Les propres corrections de Saint Anselme dans sa grande prière à la Vierge Marie." *Recherches de théologie ancienne et médiévale*, 189–204.

———. 1932. *Auteurs spirituels et textes dévots du moyen âge latin*. Paris: Bloud et Gay.

Wilson, Christopher. 2012. "The Dissemination of Visions of the Otherworld in England and Northern France, c. 1150–c. 1321." PhD diss., Exeter University.

Winterbottom, Michael. 2010. "William of Malmesbury and the Normans." *Journal of Medieval Latin* 20:70–77.

Witzling, Mara R. 1984. "The Winchester Psalter: A Re-Ordering of Its Prefatory Miniatures according to the Scriptural Sequence." *Gesta* 23 (1): 17–25.

Wolter, Eugen. 1879. *Der Judenknabe: 5 Griechische, 14 Lateinische und 8 Französische Texte*. Halle, Ger.: Max Niemeyer.

Woods, David. 2002. "Arculf's Luggage: The Sources for Adomnán's De Locis Sanctis." *Ériu* 52:25–52.

Wormald, Francis. 1946. *English Benedictine Kalendars after A.D. 1100*. Vol. 2. London: Henry Bradshaw Society.

———. 1952. "Some Illustrated Manuscripts of the Lives of the Saints." *Bulletin of the John Rylands Library* 35:248–66.

———. 1973. *The Winchester Psalter*. London: Harvey Miller and Medcalf.

Yardley, Anne Bagnall. 2006. *Performing Piety: Musical Culture in Medieval English Nunneries*. New York: Palgrave Macmillan.

Yarrow, Simon. 2006. *Saints and Their Communities: Miracle Stories in Twelfth-Century England*. Oxford: Clarendon Press.

Younge, George. 2013. "An Old English Compiler and His Audience: London, British Library Ms Cotton Vespasian D. Xiv, Fols. 4–169." In *English Manuscript Studies, 1100–1700: English Manuscripts before 1400*, edited by A.S.G. Edwards and Orietta Da Rold, 1-26. vol. 17. London: British Library.

Yuval, Israel. 2006. *Two Nations in Your Womb: Perceptions of Jews and Christians in Late Antiquity and the Middle Ages*. Translated by Barbara Harshav and Jonathan Chipman. Berkeley: University of California Press.

Zamberlan, Nereo. n.d. "L'omelia Nativitatis gloriosae e il commento In Matthaei Evangelium di Pascasio Radberto nell'ufficio «Gaude mater Ecclesia» del Ms. lat. 18168 della Bibliothèque nationale de France." http://www.molite.it/Archivio/Gaude%20 mater%20ecclesia_articolo.pdf (accessed February 25, 2016).

Zarnecki, George. 1951. *English Romanesque Scuplture*. London: Alec Tiranti.

———. 1984. *English Romanesque Art, 1066-1200, Exhibition Hayward Gallery*. London: Weidenfeld and Nicholson.

Zieman, Katherin. 2008. *Singing the New Song: Literacy and Liturgy in Late Medieval England*. Philadelphia: University of Pennsylvania Press.

Ziolkowski, Jan. 2001. "Put in No-Man's-Land: Guibert of Nogent's Accusations against a Judaizing and Jew-Supporting Christian." In *Jews and Christians in Twelfth-Century Europe*, edited by John H. Van Engen and Michael Signer, 110–22. Notre Dame, IN: University of Notre Dame Press.

Zitter, Emmy Stark. 1991. "Anti-Semitism in Chaucer's 'Prioress' Tale.'" *Chaucer Review* 25:277–84.

Index

||||||||||||

Where the content of an endnote is indexed, the page reference is to the text page on which the note superscript is found.

Martin-des-Champs, 26–28, 130; spread of, 22–26
Constantinople, 51, 102, 116n100, 117, 129, 145, 151n83, 157, 158, 168, 171, 172
Contra Celsus (Origen), 51
Contra Judaeos, Arianos et Paganos (Quodvultdeus), 51, 55
conversion: in miracle stories, 149, 176–79 (*see also* miracle stories: Jewish boy and Jacob of London); in Sigillum, 92–94, 135; of Synagoga, 92–98
Coronation of the Virgin. *See* iconography
Cosmas Vestitor, 78
Council: of Clermont-Ferrand, 33, 117, 178: of Erfurt, 156; of Lateran I, 8; of London, 25–26, 122–23; of Winchester, 18
Coutances, 102, 160
Coventry, 160
Crusades: and persecution of Jews, 11, 12, 167, 178; call to (First Crusade), 11, 12, 33, 167, 168, 178; and Hugh of Die, 167–68, 169; in miracle stories, 168

Damian, Peter, 7, 33, 38, 78, 112, 119
Daniel, 27
De armatura castitatis (Osbert of Clare), 29
De ecclesiasticis officiis (Amalarius of Metz), 74
De gloria martyrum (Gregory of Tours), 102, 129, 158
De Inventione (Cicero), 74
De locis sanctis (Adomnán of Iona), 157, 158
De virginali conceptu et originali peccato (Anselm of Canterbury), 61, 62, 128
Dialogue against the Jews (Peter Alfonsi), 91
Dicta Anselmi (Alexander of Canterbury), 103, 104, 108
Disciplina clericalis (Peter Alfonsi), 134, 147
Dol, 116
Dominic of Evesham, 102, 105, 106, 108, 115, 118, 124, 127, 134, 145, 146, 150–52, 154, 157, 184
Domus conversorum, 189
Dormans, 102
Dunstan, 104, 113–14, 126, 127
Durham, 19n26, 44n230
Eadmer: life of and general introduction to, 20; and the Conception feast, 20, 21, 22, 23, 123; and the *De excellentia*, 45–46, 47, 153, 166, 180; and the doctrine of the Immaculate Conception, 60, 64, 65–70, 71,

72, 73, 74, 75, 77, 79, 84, 85, 98, 99; and the *Historia Novorum,* 177–78
Eadwine Psalter, 96, 98
East Anglia, 24
Easter ritual (colaphus), 173–76
Ecclesia, 85, 94, 96–98
ecclesiastical reform: and Anselm, 8, 83; and clerical celibacy/virginity, 6–10, 28–30, 83–84, 86–87, 133; "Gregorian," 4, 6–9, 100; at Görze, 32; and Honorius, 83–87, 132–36; and the liturgy, 8, 18–20, 111, 125; and pastoral care, 4, 8, 58, 83–84, 107, 132–36; in tenth-century England, 4, 6–7, 17–18, 114
Edmund, St., 39, 103, 105, 127, 128
Edricus, 116
Elizabeth of Schönau, 73, 80, 128, 189
Elizabeth, St., 110
Elucidarius, 83
Ely, 23, 26, 27, 109
Ember Wednesday, 39, 51
Ernulf, 178
ethics: and commerce, 170–73; and Mary as example, 74–76, 107–8, 171–73; in miracle stories, 108
Eucharist, 153–54; debates about, 14, 153–54; and host desecration, 14, 162, 166; and Jewish boy, 148–49, 153–54; miracles about, 129, 148–49, 153–54, 166, 186; and William of Malmesbury, 153
Eulalia, 111, 126
Evagrius Scholasticus, 148, 149
Evesham, 4, 19, 23, 30, 84, 102, 104, 108, 112, 152
exegesis, 60, 84, 156
Exeter, 4, 20, 27, 77, 117, 118
Exhortatur nos (sermon), 55
Eynsham, 19n26, 44n230, 131
Ezechiel, 156, 157

feast: Anglo-Saxon heritage of, 18–21; of Anne (*see* Anne: feast of); of Annunciation, 18, 24, 32, 39, 83, 115, 124, 129, 130, 132, 135; of Assumption, 13, 18, 19, 30, 60, 73, 74, 76, 77, 78, 80, 83, 84, 87, 88, 90, 94, 99, 128, 132, 135, 144, 163; Byzantine Marian roots of, 18; Conception (*see* Conception feast); of Nativity (of Mary), 18, 20, 27, 28, 32, 64, 65, 72, 74, 83, 86, 122, 124, 125, 128, 129, 131, 132, 135, 144; octave of, 20, 28, 124; Old Hispanic, 24, 55, 103, 123,

Index of Manuscripts

||||||||||||||||||||||||||||||||||||||||||||||||

LIST OF MANUSCRIPTS OF MIRACLE COLLECTIONS

Cambridge
Corpus Christi College Library, MS 42

Chicago
University Library, MS 147

Copenhagen
Thott, MS 26.8
Thott, MS 128.2

London
Lambeth Palace Library, MS 214
British Library, Add. MS 15723
British Library, Add. MS 35112
British Library, Arundel MS 346
British Library, Cotton MS Cleopatra C. x
British Library, Royal MS 6 B. xiv
British Library, Egerton MS 2947

Oxford
Balliol College Library, MS 240
Bodleian Library, Laud Miscellania MS 410
Bodleian Library, Canon. Liturg. MS 325

Paris
BnF, MS lat. 2672
BnF, MS lat. 2873
BnF, MS lat. 12169
BnF, MS lat. 14463
BnF, MS lat. 18168
BnF, MS lat. 12606
BnF, MS lat. 2769
BnF, MS lat. 3809A

Rome
Vatican Library, Reg. lat. MS 543

LIST OF MIRACLE STORIES

"Anselm's collection" (i.e., "HM," found in many manuscripts, e.g., Elise Dexter, *Miracula Sanctae Virginis Mariae.* Madison: University of Wisconsin Studies in the Social Sciences and History, 1927)
1. Ildefonsus
2. Drowned sacristan
3. Cleric of Chartres
4. Five Gaudes
5. Charitable Almsman
6. Ebbo the Thief
7. Monk at St. Peter's Cologne
8. Pilgrim to St. James
9. Priest of one mass
10. Two Brothers at Rome
11. Rustic removing landmarks
12. Prior of St. Saviour's, Pavia
13. Jerome of Pavia
14. Stained corporal
15. Fire
16. Cleric of Pisa
17. Murieldis
18. Jewish boy

"TS" (found in many manuscripts, e.g,. Elise Dexter, *Miracula Sanctae Virginis Mariae.* Madison: University of Wisconsin Studies in the Social Sciences and History, 1927; added incrementally to HM)
Three Knights
Eulalia
Aelfsige (Elsinus)
Mead
Toledo
Foot cut off
Musa
Mater misericordiae (monk-thief of Cluny)
Lydda
Gethsemane
Virgin's image insulted
Devil in three shapes
Sollempnem memoriam (Saturday sermon)
Leofric
Milk: Monk laid out as dead (verse)
Sudden death (verse)

Dominic's Collection (cf. Dominic of Evesham, "El Libro De Miraculis Sanctae Mariae de Domingo de Evesham (m.c. 1140)," ed. J. M. Canal. *Studium Legionense,* 39 (1998): 247-283)
1. Jewish boy
2. Theophilus
3. Childbirth at Sea
4. Julian the Apostate
5. Chartres saved